STARS FOR FREEDOM

EMILIE RAYMOND

Stars for

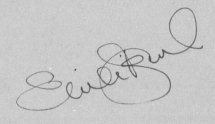

Freedom

HOLLYWOOD, BLACK CELEBRITIES, AND THE CIVIL RIGHTS MOVEMENT

A Capell Family Book
A V Ethel Willis White Book

UNIVERSITY OF WASHINGTON PRESS
Seattle and London

Publication of *Stars for Freedom* was made possible in part by grants from the
V Ethel Willis White Endowment, which supports the publication of books on
African American history and culture, and the Capell Family Endowed Book
Fund, which supports the publication of books that deepen the understanding
of social justice through historical, cultural, and environmental studies.

UNIVERSITY OF WASHINGTON PRESS
www.washington.edu/uwpress

LIBRARY OF CONGRESS CATALOGING-IN-PUBLICATION DATA
Raymond, Emilie, 1973–
    Stars for freedom : Hollywood, Black celebrities, and the civil rights movement /
Emilie Raymond.
        pages   cm
    Includes bibliographical references and index.
    ISBN 978-0-295-99480-2 (hardcover : alk. paper)
    1. African American political activists—History—20th century.   2. African American
entertainers—Political activity—History—20th century.   3. Politics and culture—United
States—History—20th century.   4. African Americans—Civil rights—History—20th
century.   5. United States—Race relations—History—20th century.   I. Title.
    E185.615.R36 2015
    323.1196'073—dc23   2014046332

The paper used in this publication is acid-free and meets the minimum requirements
of American National Standard for Information Sciences—Permanence of Paper for
Printed Library Materials, ANSI Z39.48–1984.∞

For my parents

CONTENTS

PREFACE

SPEAKING AT THE EVENT ON THE FIFTIETH ANNIVERSARY OF THE March on Washington, the actor Jamie Foxx recognized the singer, actor, and activist Harry Belafonte for his commitment to the civil rights movement. "He marched," said Foxx, "and he bailed Martin Luther King, Jr., out of jail so he could march." Urging a new wave of celebrity civil rights activism, Foxx beckoned to such contemporaries as the actors Will Smith and Kerry Washington and the musicians Jay Z, Alicia Keys, and Kanye West to "pick it up now, so when we're eighty-seven years old, talking to other young folks, we can say it was me."[1] Such a call is not a fantastical goal; it is rooted in past alliances. A strong celebrity contingent participated in the 1963 March on Washington, including Belafonte; the actors Ossie Davis, Ruby Dee, and Sidney Poitier; the comedian Dick Gregory; and the consummate entertainer Sammy Davis, Jr. And this was only one of these celebrities' many civil rights activities. This group—whom I refer to as the Leading Six—would prove to be the movement's most outspoken, effective, and consistent celebrity activists, seemingly unafraid of the potential consequences to their careers. The Leading Six received help from a small interracial coalition in Hollywood that included such stars as Theodore Bikel, Marlon Brando, Diahann Carroll, Dorothy Dandridge, Charlton Heston, Lena Horne, Eartha Kitt, Burt Lancaster, Paul Newman, and Frank Sinatra, among others. These "Stars for Freedom," as King would call them, contributed to the civil rights movement by developing its financial infrastructure and mobilizing constituents in its support.[2] While small in numbers, these stars changed the racial climate in Hollywood and helped establish a blueprint for celebrity politics that has only become more significant in contemporary political culture.

That Hollywood celebrities were engaged in the civil rights movement is generally well-known, but few historians have appreciated the degree to which they were involved or the effect they had. In *Just My Soul Responding*, Brian Ward focuses on R&B artists' involvement in the movement and describes the commitment of Hollywood actors and personalities, while in *Freedom Sounds*, Ingrid Monson highlights the activism of jazz singers and musicians.[3] Both Ward and Monson note that fear of economic or physical reprisals led many celebrities and artists to avoid overt and consistent activism. This book aims to show how the Stars for Freedom, responding to the constraining political and racial environment of Hollywood, contributed to the success of the civil rights movement. It also aligns with those scholars who have emphasized the role of Northerners in civil rights histories.

The Stars for Freedom, as residents of Los Angeles, Chicago, and New York—far removed from the Deep South—do not fulfill the standard trope of Southern, workaday activists that is emphasized in traditional narratives. Such works highlight dramatic confrontations in the South between nonviolent demonstrators and Southern authorities, such as the Freedom Rides and the Selma campaign, and massive demonstrations such as the March on Washington, in the effort to stop Jim Crow segregation and win voting rights for African Americans. Celebrities assisted at these events, using their gifts as "dramatists." However, as the historians Thomas Sugrue and Martha Biondi have pointed out, a Northern network of financial, legal, and spiritual support was just as crucial to the success of the movement, and the Stars for Freedom played a major role in shaping this network.[4] Additionally, their efforts in desegregating Northern entertainment venues, promoting better cultural images of African Americans, opening up economic opportunities for them in the film industry, and agitating for open housing in California adds to the growing body of literature about national discriminatory patterns.[5] Fighting such widespread racism required a broad civil rights agenda and many different types of activists. The Stars for Freedom did not define the civil rights movement so much as fill an important niche as well-connected spokespersons and fund-raisers. None of them saw their participation as being more important than that of the everyday activists who devoted their lives to the cause. Poitier points out that celebrities "weren't leading the charge. We weren't at the forefront, getting our heads cracked open."[6] Nevertheless, due to their visibility and influence, they fulfilled important functions that few others could.

The Stars for Freedom served first and foremost as patrons of the movement, raising or contributing from their own pockets hundreds of thousands of dollars. They spearheaded and participated in a creative array of benefit programs—from film screenings and concerts to comedic acts and house parties—that generated substantial profits for a number of civil rights organizations. The philosophy behind a benefit was simple: stars drew crowds to a performance, entertaining the spectators while generating profit and publicity for the civil rights organizations sponsoring the program. Further funds could be raised through VIP parties, in which, for an additional fee, program attendees could mingle with the stars before or after the show. Stars also raised money through direct mail campaigns, signing their names to "Dear Friend" letters that appealed directly to the recipients. Finally, stars frequently wrote sizable personal checks to their favorite civil rights organizations. Sammy Davis, Jr., conventionally and mistakenly regarded as an "Uncle Tom," raised the most of any star, establishing his role as the "benefactor" of the movement. This money was crucial in sustaining the civil rights movement. The costs associated with lawsuits and demonstrations, as well as maintaining administrative offices, were enormous, and most civil rights organizations struggled to balance their accounts and pay their administrative staffs. For activists in the Deep South, an infusion of cash could literally mean the difference between life and death.

Stars also played a significant strategic role in the civil rights movement. Several meetings took place in stars' homes, most frequently in the New York apartment of Belafonte, who had a close relationship with King and was the chief "strategist" of the Leading Six. Celebrities deliberated with activists about where, when, and how demonstrations should proceed, and discussed how they, as stars, could participate. Most commonly, their role was to raise a substantial sum of money before an event, both underwriting an otherwise improbable march, demonstration, or campaign and helping to stage it. Sometimes celebrities used their clout to pull strings with the politically powerful, as both Sammy Davis, Jr., and Belafonte did with John and Robert Kennedy, or to bring together disparate individuals within the movement. Ossie Davis and Ruby Dee acted as important intermediaries between mainstream organizations and the radicals Malcolm X and the Black Panthers, serving as important "facilitators" in the movement. Stars could also play a valuable role in attracting the sympathies and financial contributions of white Americans. King considered white support crucial to the success of the movement, and in instances in which he felt that sentiments might be tenuous, he counted on stars who had already been successful in winning over white audiences for assistance.

Celebrities also drew publicity to issues and events. By virtue of their star stature, celebrities could attract the media to stories that they might not have found interesting otherwise. For example, Gregory drew attention to school desegregation efforts and voter registration campaigns by purposefully getting arrested and going to jail. Such activities made him a virtual "field secretary" for the movement. Not only could stars attract attention, but it was generally favorable, a factor that should not be overlooked. Civil rights organizations continually struggled to publicize their messages and all too often found themselves at the mercy of the media, being pummeled by negative and inaccurate journalism, particularly in the South. The media gave stars a wide berth. They could directly attack racism using language that would have created ire if delivered by a workaday activist. One leading activist said of Gregory, "We usually asked him to come in when things were getting too much out of control, because he could say the same things that everybody else was saying, but it kind of lessened the tension in terms of his performance and his political jokes."[7]

Celebrities also affected the civil rights movement by providing moral support to activists who worked for the cause. Full-scale activism could be psychologically difficult to sustain, as demonstrators dealt with indifference at one extreme and violent hostility on the other. A celebrity's support showed not only that a famous and successful person agreed with them but also cared about them. Stars also provided entertainment during rallies and marches. These song, dance, and comedic routines kept demonstrators focused and optimistic. They also had the added benefit of easing tension among crowds that had the potential to grow restless. The civil rights movement counted a disciplined, nonviolent crowd as one of its strongest weapons, and stars helped foster such an atmosphere. Of course, "morale" is difficult to quantify, but it was important enough to the activist Stokely Carmichael that he stated that the value of support from figures such as Poitier "was beyond measure," especially because they were "the kind of folk you respected greatly but never really imagined you'd ever get a chance to meet."[8] As the most successful Hollywood actor of the Leading Six, Poitier served as the movement's "icon" and was a resolute and elegant spokesman.

Hollywood restrictions had impeded civil rights activism among the previous generation of black actors. Before World War II, the six major studios that monopolized the film industry had promoted a "star system" that demeaned African Americans. The studios portrayed white stars as glamorous and captivating personalities in fan magazines and gossip columns (indeed, extensions of their onscreen characters) out of the belief that audiences idolized the actors more than the films. Corporations and politicians, recognizing that white stars could mobilize public desires for consumer products or ideological causes, recruited film stars for their advertising and political campaigns, particularly during World War II.[9] However, black actors did not have an equal place in the star system. The film historian Donald Bogle identifies the five typical characters played by African Americans: the loyal Tom, the foolish coon, the tragic mulatto, the asexual (and often obese) mammy, and the brutal buck.[10] Often relegated to menial roles, such as maids, porters, butlers, and the like, black actors often served as comic relief by using improper dialects and engaging in exaggerated mannerisms and outright foolishness. Their roles reflected the second-class position of blacks in Hollywood. Their pay was substantially less than that of their white costars, and the studios employed no black crew members, producers, or directors.[11] When the publicists for *Gone with the Wind* (1939) ignored the actor Hattie McDaniel's protests of their promoting her as a real-life maid playing a mammy, they were simply following industry norms.[12] African American actors struggled to build public images that they could be proud of, while advertisers and political figures did not value the public personas they projected.[13]

In fact, civil rights organizations often considered black actors to be impediments. In 1942, the National Association for the Advancement of Colored People (NAACP) executive secretary Walter White began pressuring Hollywood studios to improve their portrayal of African Americans, but did so at the expense of such familiar character actors as Hattie McDaniel, Clarence Muse, Bill Robinson, Louise Beavers, and Lincoln Perry (known by his stage name Stepin Fetchit). White rarely included these actors when meeting with the studio chiefs and went so far as to blame them for the dismal state of affairs in Hollywood, declaring, "One of the most important elements in [achieving] progress will be the behavior of Negro actors themselves in playing their roles with sincerity and dignity instead of mugging and playing the clown before the camera."[14]

In White's view, the willingness of these performers to play stereotypes compromised the civil rights cause, and the black press tended to follow his lead. White began promoting the sophisticated nightclub performer Lena Horne as the "proper" model of an African American screen persona.[15] In an unsuccessful attempt to force White out of the film debate, preserve their livelihoods, and forge better roles for themselves, McDaniel, Muse, and other "old guard" actors formed the Hollywood Fair Play Committee.[16] Such squabbling did little to promote constructive change in Hollywood. The studios became wary of hiring African Americans at all, which further reduced their opportunities to use the cult of celebrity for civil rights gains.

Although changes in the film industry after World War II (especially the breakdown of the studio system and the advent of television) would give rise to improved roles and more alluring public images for black actors, epitomized by Dandridge and Poitier, many of the old stereotypes and attitudes remained. Thus, this book will open with the story of the making of the film *Porgy and Bess* (1959), which illustrates the complexities of black celebrity and the need to apply movement pressure to Hollywood. The next five chapters are devoted to individuals and events that particularly exemplify the influence of the Stars for Freedom on the civil rights movement and the guidance provided by the Leading Six: Sammy Davis, Jr.'s fund-raising efforts; Harry Belafonte's strategic work with Martin Luther King, Jr., and the Student Nonviolent Coordinating Committee; the Arts Group that brought a celebrity delegation to the March on Washington; Dick Gregory's grassroots work; and the Stars engaged in the Selma campaign and its aftermath. The final chapter discusses celebrity activism and ongoing developments in the film and television industries during the Black Power era. The book ends with the story of the making of the film *Buck and the Preacher* (1972), which illustrates how Hollywood was important in the pursuit of the economic opportunities and cultural goals of the broader civil rights agenda. To start with *Porgy and Bess* and end with *Buck and the Preacher*, both of which starred Poitier, highlights the new opportunities and ongoing challenges in Hollywood.

The Stars for Freedom proved serious in their intent and effective in their execution, undermining the generally negative way that scholars have portrayed the effects of celebrity culture on American society. Their assumption is that celebrities, and the entertainment industry from which they hail, have "trivialized America" in a sad effort to "amuse ourselves to death."[17] However, the sociologists Robert D. Benford and Scott A. Hunt show how social movements often rely on dramatic strategies such as scripting, staging, and performing to succeed. The historians Steven J. Ross, Donald T. Critchlow, and Kathryn Cramer Brownell demonstrate the contributions that stars have made to the national political debate on conservative and liberal issues alike. As the sociologist Chris Rojek asserts, "Celebrity culture is the expression of social form."[18] In other words, celebrities can become symbols of meaning shaping the broader political discourse—a possibility fulfilled by celebrities in the civil rights movement.

Celebrities' careers rely on public opinion, and their involvement in the civil rights movement of the 1950s and 60s, which was neither a politically nor a publicly popular cause, should not be underestimated. The Stars for Freedom helped provide mainstream legitimacy to the movement, and in doing so opened new channels of star activism for other controversial issues, such as the Vietnam War, gun rights, and global warming. Without the involvement of the Stars for Freedom, the civil rights movement would have had been far more isolated, insolvent, and persecuted, and the struggle to achieve its political, economic, and cultural goals would have been far more protracted.

ACKNOWLEDGMENTS

SUPPORT FOR THIS PROJECT CAME FROM A TREMENDOUS NETWORK of institutions, colleagues, and friends.

The College of Arts and Sciences and the Faculty Research Council at Virginia Commonwealth University (VCU) provided research funding, as did the American Philosophical Society. That VCU also granted me leave time proved extremely helpful. Robert Holsworth and Catherine Ingrassia were two early champions of my work at crucial times.

Many archivists at research institutions across the country helped me track down important documents, and I am truly in debt to Barbara Hall, formerly with the Margaret Herrick Library at the Academy of Motion Picture Arts and Sciences.

Readers for journals and on conference panels provided insightful feedback that helped me develop this project in even its roughest stages. Thank you to Greg Schneider, Lary May, Randal Maurice Jelks, Aram Goudsouzian, and the late Richard Iton.

That numerous civil rights veterans gave their valuable time to talk with me was simply humbling, and I am thankful to have engaged in these consultations.

I am grateful to have colleagues who are genuinely enthusiastic about my work, and I particularly want to thank my VCU colleagues Lisa Abrams, Ryan Smith, Norreece Jones, Brooke Newman, Gregory Smithers, Carolyn Eastman, John Herman, Ted Tunnell, Joe Bendersky, Karen Rader, Tim Thurber, Antonio Espinoza, and John Kneebone; Katie Brownell Cramer and Donald T. Critchlow, two scholars also engaged in the conflation of Hollywood and politics; Joshua Farrington, a young scholar kind enough to share documents with me; and Robert M. Collins, whose position as my graduate school advisor has evolved into a lifetime role.

My editor Ranjit Arab has been a superb champion of this project from the beginning and has offered thoughtful feedback and given great attention to detail through every draft.

I am lucky to have so many terrific people in my life, who are supportive in various ways. My parents Gary and Judi Raymond have given me strength and assurance. My husband Craig Dober is a terrific sounding board on myriad issues and a wonderful partner. My young daughter Rebecca's schedule required me to be remarkably productive at odd hours of the day, and she inspired me to keep plugging away. And finally, my friends Kim Baker, Laura Cavender, Kathleen Gacek, Jill Gasper, Kristin Swenson—you are my heroes!

STARS FOR FREEDOM

Cleaning Up
Catfish Row

BLACK CELEBRITY AND THE
MAKING OF *PORGY AND BESS*

Only Sidney was beautiful enough to pull off being a sex symbol
who crawled around on the floor . . . he just reeked of nobility
and dignity, even amid all that art-directed Negro squalor.
—Diahann Carroll, on Sidney Poitier
as Porgy in *Porgy and Bess*

IN 1957, THE POWERFUL HOLLYWOOD PRODUCER SAMUEL GOLDWYN
announced that he was making a cinematic production of the folk opera
Porgy and Bess, the story of two lovers in the African American neighborhood of Catfish Row in Charleston, South Carolina, in 1912. Goldwyn's
plans for this racially loaded project met with concern among African
American actors, the black press, and social commentators, most of
whom felt the film should not be made. Leveraging his power in the film
industry, Goldwyn strong-armed Sidney Poitier into the lead role and
thus filled in the rest of the cast, with Dorothy Dandridge as Bess, Sammy
Davis, Jr., as Sportin Life, and Pearl Bailey as Maria. Despite these actors'
general lack of influence in Hollywood, in an effort to improve the representation of the black characters, they used their rising celebrity clout to

significantly alter the film's content, including its dialect, imagery, costumes, and character interpretations. This marked the first time African American actors had a significant say in a major film release. *Porgy and Bess* premiered July 24, 1959, to great fanfare and lingering frustration. Endorsed by one reporter as "the Emancipation Proclamation of the Negro artist," it was bemoaned as "the white man's vision of Negro life" by another. As Poitier put it, "You just can't win with that movie."[1]

*   *   *

If the 1930s were the nadir of black interests in the film industry, the 1940s brought about an important shift. World War II, coupled with the breakdown of the studio system, put African Americans in a better position to control their film careers and public personas; but persistent racism and the Cold War political culture continued to constrain African Americans in Hollywood.

In the estimation of some, the National Association for the Advancement of Colored People's (NAACP) campaign in Hollywood, led by Walter White, had resulted in fewer roles for black actors, but White's argument for portraying "a truer picture of the Negro as a normal member of society" resonated when the Office of War Information (OWI) also put pressure on the studios. The OWI considered victory in the war to be dependent on a united home front, and thus encouraged racial cooperation and understanding in wartime visual images.[2] Several war pictures included nonstereotypical black supporting characters: a foot soldier (Kenneth Spencer) in *Bataan* (1943); a noncommandant (Rex Ingram) in *Sahara* (1943); and a stoker (Canada Lee) in *Lifeboat* (1944).[3] Even more important was the documentary film *The Negro Soldier* (1944). Overseen by the Hollywood director Frank Capra and the African American writer Carlton Moss, it was originally commissioned by the US Army to motivate black troops but soon received widespread release. Shown to capacity audiences and demanded by church and civic groups across the country, the film proved a watershed for the postwar "message movies": films that featured liberal racial themes and better parts for black actors.[4] The rise of the "message movie" also came from structural changes in the film industry.

In 1944, the California Court of Appeal ruled that actors were not bound to perform services beyond seven years from the start of their contracts, a decision that became state law.[5] The "seven-year rule" allowed actors more discretion in choosing their own roles, which was particularly important to black actors, as they could reject the demeaning roles the studios had typically demanded of them. This does not mean that black actors were immediately offered parts. Good black roles were few and far between. In fact, as actors increasingly became free agents, they needed to sell their ideas to the studios using their public images as leverage. To do so, they worked with independent publicists and agents, who had quickly become an industry standard.[6] While the new circumstances certainly served black actors better than the old studio system, they were not without complications. Veteran black actors, such as Lincoln Perry (better known as Stepin Fetchit) and Hattie McDaniel, who had come to emblemize demeaning stereotypes, had difficulty finding work.[7] Also at question was how to establish a better public image when so few films addressed racial themes. Furthermore, the publicists, like the studio chiefs, were all white, and did not always understand their clients' needs. Nevertheless, the "seven-year rule" intersected with other destabilizing forces in the film industry that affected black actors.

The "Paramount decision" gave rise to the independent filmmakers behind the "message movie" trend. In a lawsuit brought by the Justice Department against eight movie studios, the government claimed that the studios' production, distribution, and exhibition practices had allowed them to control the film industry, thus violating antitrust laws. The Supreme Court ruled in spring 1948 for the studios' immediate divestiture of their theater chains. The "Paramount decision," coupled with a postwar attendance drop, brought about a financial crisis. Studio profits declined from $120 million in 1946 to $31 million in 1950.[8] Because of this precarious state of affairs, independent producers gained prominence in Hollywood. Often working on shoestring budgets, these filmmakers more willingly took risks with their film subjects. They addressed themes, such as racial and religious prejudice, that the major studios deemed too controversial.[9] The success of the 1949 films *Home of the Brave*, *Pinky*, *Lost Boundaries*, and *Intruder in the Dust* proved the financial viability of "the social problem" film. As *Variety* reported, "Film's leading b[ox] o[ffice] star for 1949 wasn't a personality, but a subject matter. And a subject—racial prejudice—that until very recently was tabu."[10]

"Message movies" presented welcome opportunities for a new generation of black actors, a number of whom were already involved in the

American Negro Theater (ANT) in New York. Formed in Harlem in 1940 by the writer Abram Hill and the actor Frederick O'Neal, ANT's primary goal was to destroy black stereotypes.[11] The American Negro Theater allowed for a common sensibility among its members, including those involved in the training program for beginning actors. Poitier, Harry Belafonte, Ossie Davis, and Ruby Dee all studied there and became fast friends. Although from various backgrounds and experiences, they embraced the arts as a tool for social justice.

Poitier was born February 20, 1927, to Bahaman tomato farmers Reginald and Evelyn Poitier during a selling trip in Miami. He grew up on tiny Cat Island, where his family lived relatively well but was always close to poverty. Poitier considered himself lucky to have spent his childhood in the West Indies. Living in a country with a black majority population meant that many individuals of social authority, such as doctors, nurses, lawyers, and policemen, were black, too. Belafonte experienced the same social climate when he lived in Jamaica for four years as a young teenager. "I firmly believe," Poitier says, "that we both had the opportunity to arrive at the formation of a sense of ourselves without having it fucked with racism as it existed in the United States."[12] Poitier saw his first movie after the family moved to Nassau when Poitier was eleven. Awestruck by what he saw on screen, Poitier was determined to go to Hollywood. Four years later, he immigrated to Miami to live with his older brother. But he soon fled the South, embittered by the virulent racism there. He made his way to New York City and worked as a dishwasher. Barely literate, Poitier struggled to survive, even sleeping on a roof under thick newspapers for a couple of months. Young, scared, and terribly shy, Poitier also suffered from extreme lack of confidence, and he flailed about, moving from job to job, with little sense of direction.

It was not until Poitier got involved with ANT that he found his stride. Curious, Poitier went in for an audition, but his thick West Indian accent and poor reading skills resulted in automatic rejection. Deeply hurt but also inspired, Poitier began an intense self-education process. For hours each evening, he read aloud from newspapers and magazines and mimicked the radio announcers from news programs. By the time Poitier returned to ANT, he was fully literate and had cultivated the measured, slightly exotic speech for which he became known, but he still knew next to nothing about the acting profession.[13] His first job at ANT was as a janitor. As he became familiar with the theater, he eventually won speaking roles and played to good reviews. Poitier was the first of his class to win a Broadway role, which led to his first film in 1949.

The dramatic thriller *No Way Out* set the tone that guided his career. Poitier played Luther Brooks, a doctor at an urban county hospital who is confronted with a series of ethical questions when he attends to a racist patient who dies under his care. The role was revolutionary not only in that Poitier played a polished professional but in that he confronted racism with confident conviction. One biographer calls Poitier's performance a blend of "an appealing dignity and barely controlled anger."[14] His scathing delivery of the last line of the movie—"Don't worry, white boy, you're going to live"—illustrates that attitude. He brought this same persona to subsequent films and starred in a number of other independent productions throughout the decade. Both Davis and Dee appeared in the film in small roles, as well.

Davis and Dee, having met when performing the lead roles of the Broadway play *Jeb*, formed a deep lifetime partnership. Raised in Georgia, Davis felt he had been inculcated with a terror of whites from an early age. The Ku Klux Klan consistently threatened his father for "taking jobs," the police temporarily jailed and harassed Davis when he was only six years-old, and his all-black school, in an effort to keep its students safe, emphasized deference to whites, a lesson Davis believed left him "crippled forever." He coped by daydreaming, escaping into stories and films (even as he slowly became aware of the negative images of African Americans presented by Hollywood), and by leaving the South to attend Howard University. While there, Davis became fascinated by his developing passions in both "white" literature and music, such as Keats and Tchaikovsky, and in "Negro" literature, and by his propensity toward both humor and intellectual life. He attended the opera singer Marian Anderson's famed concert at the Lincoln Memorial in 1939 after the Daughters of the American Revolution refused to grant her permission to sing for an integrated audience at Constitution Hall. The experience "married in my mind forever the performing arts as a weapon in the struggle for freedom."[15]

Dee was born Ruby Ann Wallace in 1922 and raised in Harlem. As a child, she joined pickets against Blumstein's Department Store for refusing to employ African Americans as anything but maintenance workers, and she saw myriad examples of racial tension and violence on the streets of Harlem. These experiences gave her a sense of "what the Negro has got to do" to survive. Dee's intelligence and oratorical gifts won her admission to the prestigious Hunter College High School, and she went on to graduate from Hunter College. Naturally drawn to acting, she was put off by the profession in high school when the drama club director refused to consider her for a part other than a maid. She began a career as a translator before she learned of ANT and played in *On Strivers Row*. "This event," Dee claimed, "was the beginning of one of the most significant times of my life . . . along the journey to myself as a human being and as a performer."[16]

Dee continued to work as a translator, acting in one ANT production per year. Meanwhile Davis had moved to Harlem and performed in four plays with the Rose McClendon Players, another all-black production company, while also trying to write his own material. Dee took a war job as a translator while Davis enlisted in the US Army and worked as a surgical technician in the 25th Station Hospital, the first black one of its kind in Liberia. The two finally met in 1945, and their work on *Jeb* led to parts in *Anna Lucasta*, a huge Broadway hit and originally an ANT production. The publicity surrounding the play led to their being cast in independent films, including *No Way Out* with Poitier, who, along with Belafonte, became like "little brothers" to the couple. They realized that their new prominence as artists put them in the position of being "new pioneers" who "were being watched, measured, compared, aware that everything we did reflected credit or discredit on the black community." Making *No Way Out* affected them as powerfully as it had Poitier. As Dee explained, "I was conscious of the film's political and social themes. I was also vividly aware of the discrepancy between the fictional world of the film and the reality of racist discrimination on the lot, and in the film industry."[17] When they returned to New York, where they married in 1948, they considered themselves not "celebrity heroes" but "foot soldiers in a larger racial movement," a sentiment shared by Belafonte.

Belafonte was born March 1, 1927, to Melvine and Harold George Belafonte, Sr., in Harlem, where he spent much of his youth. By the time he was seven years old, his father had effectively abandoned the family. Without a husband to help her supervise Belafonte and his brother while she worked long hours, Melvine sent her sons to live in Jamaica with relatives from 1935 until 1939. "It was a terribly unhappy period for us," Belafonte remembers, and he was downright angry when he returned to New York.[18] He constantly fought with other kids and persistently challenged his teachers, believing some of them to be "anti-Negro." He dropped out of high school within a year of his return and joined the navy, where he was placed in an all-black unit. A medical condition prohibited Belafonte from overseas duty, and he spent most of his time in the brig for resisting discipline. Only partially literate when he entered the military, he left as a voracious reader engaged in African American history.[19]

It was only after being discharged from the navy that Belafonte became interested in performing. When he became involved in ANT, he also took advantage of the GI Bill and enrolled in the drama workshop at the New School for Social Research. Even though Belafonte loved acting, he found it easier to land singing gigs than stage roles. His first job was singing popular tunes at the Broadway nightclub the Royal Roost, which led to a national tour and a deal with Capitol Records. However, Belafonte was displeased with his career choices, feeling they smacked of inauthenticity.[20] He abandoned the popular jazz scene and discovered a new passion for folk music, appreciating its tradition, simplicity, and honesty. He considered the genre an avenue for tapping into different cultures, including his own West Indian and Caribbean heritages. He made frequent trips to the Library of Congress to unearth long lost songs. The theatrical producer Jack Rollins helped Belafonte revise the words and music to suit his own taste. They agreed Belafonte should only perform folk songs identified with no other singer, and he wrote some originals, such as "Mark Twain" and "Diamond Joe," to round out his repertoire.[21] Belafonte soon signed Rollins as his manager and consulted with him to design a whole new image.

Belafonte awed audiences with his innovative approach. The folk artists most familiar to Americans at the time included Burl Ives, the Weavers, Woodie Guthrie, Josh White, and Lead Belly. These performers, while gifted and passionate about their craft, did not possess Belafonte's dramatic flair and sexual energy. He burst on stage in an open-neck silk shirt, tight black pants, and a wide sash to belt out his first number. Roaming about the stage, he used his hands for dramatic expression rather than for strumming a guitar. As one observer describes it, "He expressed strong emotions, overwhelmed the audience and even got them to participate."[22] Belafonte played to packed clubs all across the country, signed a recording contract with RCA in 1952, and scored his first big hit in 1953 with the calypso song "Matilda." His success as a musician would open doors in Hollywood.

As the number of independent producers increased, so did new depictions of African American life, especially as the B picture units of the major studios seemed to follow the lead of the independents. This gave Poitier, Belafonte, and other black actors opportunities that their predecessors never had. For example, the recently formed Eagle Lion Films worked with United Artists to make *The Jackie Robinson Story* in 1950, starring Robinson as himself and Dee as his wife Rae. Universal Pictures made the B picture *Red Ball Express* in 1952. Poitier costarred in this film about one of the few integrated army units during World War II, as well as in another B picture, *Go, Man, Go!*, in 1954. Released by United Artists, it told the story of the white owner of the Harlem Globetrotters and the team's players. All of these films portrayed racial discrimination, interracial friendships, and the heroic status of the African American characters.[23] MGM's *Bright Road*, a B picture starring Belafonte and Dorothy Dandridge, was an anomaly in that the plot was not race-driven. It showed a schoolteacher, played by Dandridge, who mentors a troubled student, and a school principal, played by Belafonte. *Bright Road* was a turning point in both actors' careers, as it was Belafonte's first film role and Dandridge's first opportunity to play a role other than "the exotic."[24]

The film *Carmen Jones*, which also costarred Belafonte and Dandridge, brought together various trends to mark a turning point in the nature of black celebrity. The longtime Hollywood director Otto Preminger had recently renegotiated his contract with Twentieth Century Fox and was free to pursue whatever projects he wanted.[25] He set his sights on Oscar Hammerstein's Broadway revue, which featured skits loosely based on the Bizet opera *Carmen* but with new music written for a black cast and set in the World War II South. It told the story of Carmen (Dandridge) who seduces a soldier named Joe (Belafonte) only to jilt him for a prizefighter; overcome with rage, Joe strangles her. Preminger did not intend to make a racial statement. He had embraced the project out of "instinct" and hoped that his personal enthusiasm for the story and the characters would translate onto the screen.[26] He nevertheless recognized the significance of making a film with black actors in starring roles, and with potentially inflammatory material. The songs include black dialect, and Carmen's overt sexuality propels the plot. Preminger sent the script to Walter White at the NAACP for his feedback. According to Preminger, "While White indicated that he principally is opposed to an all-Negro show as such, because their fight is for integration as opposed to segregation in any form, he likes this particular script very much and has no objection to any part of it."[27]

Moreover, *Carmen Jones* provided a substantial number of compelling roles at a time when parts for black actors were in decline. Although the quality of African American roles had increased, the quantity had fallen from 300 to about 145.[28] It was both Belafonte's and Dandridge's first leading role in a major Hollywood film, and the first film role of any kind for Diahann Carroll and Brock Peters. Of his casting, Peters said, "Film to a black performer back then seemed a long way away—the very thought of Hollywood was so remote and so unattainable for black youngsters."[29] Also sensing the film's importance, Dandridge was determined to win the leading role. In her first audition, Preminger had believed her too self-contained, too sophisticated. But Dandridge wowed him at a second meeting by dressing as Carmen and oozing sexuality. Once she got the part, however, friends cautioned her about playing a role that could reinforce negative preconceptions, and she decided to turn it down. "I had the fear that I might displease the Negro community," she explained. Preminger used the idea of the film turning her into Hollywood's first dark-skinned leading lady to convince her to reconsider.[30]

The promotion and success of *Carmen Jones* greatly enhanced the status of African Americans in 1950s Hollywood. Preminger, who had become romantically involved with Dandridge by this point, personally handled her publicity. He gave her the same sort of star buildup that the studios had once reserved exclusively for their white contract players. He booked her to sing, dressed as Carmen, on live television, and he arranged for the acclaimed Gjon Mili to photograph her for two major magazines. One was for *Ebony*'s "The Five Most Beautiful Negro Women in the World." Founded by John H. Johnson after World War II to promote a more holistic view of African Americans, *Ebony* and its sister magazine *Jet* served as important outlets for African American beauty and glamour.[31] Preminger landed a major coup when *Life*, with its first African American on the cover, also featured Dandridge as Carmen and portrayed her as a captivating leading lady.[32] She is gorgeously photographed and described as a "beauty" playing a "fiery" character, "a hot blooded temptress." Photographs of costars Pearl Bailey, Olga James, and Belafonte are included in the essay, enhancing their stature as well.[33]

Some observers criticized the "sensationalistic" focus on Dandridge's body in the promotion of the film, as well as *Jet* and *Ebony*'s complicity in making her a "sex goddess."[34] In Hollywood at the time, however, such imagery was considered a bankable ideal—the most obvious example being Marilyn Monroe—and necessary to selling Dandridge as a leading lady. The film opened to rave reviews and huge crowds, the world premiers giving Dandridge multiple opportunities to dazzle the public with her beauty and style. She became a source of adulation everywhere she went, and "emerged as America's first bona fide black movie star." *Carmen Jones* grossed $3 million and earned Dandridge an Academy Award nomination for best actress in a leading role, the first African American to be honored in this category (she lost to Grace Kelly in *Country Girl*).[35] *Carmen Jones* showed the bankability and glamorous appeal of African Americans in the film industry, thus paving the way for *Porgy and Bess*. It also reflects the Cold War environment in Hollywood, as Twentieth Century Fox required Belafonte to denounce communism before it would sign him.

Their shared theater training had drawn Belafonte, Davis, Dee, and Poitier toward cultural politics, as did their friendship with the artist and activist Paul Robeson. A renowned singer and actor, Robeson had a towering physique and a powerful voice that led to roles in such films as *The Emperor Jones* (1933) and *Show Boat* (1936). Although the roles were not demeaning, the characters were somewhat stereotypical, and Robeson ultimately focused on stage work and concert tours in which he performed African American folk songs and spirituals. In the 1940s, he became the first black actor to portray Shakespeare's *Othello* on Broadway. Robeson's artistic principles impressed his young protégés, and due to his influence Belafonte embraced his own folk music career. Meanwhile, Robeson had come to support the Communist Party, in large part due to its position as one of the few interracial organizations willing to denounce American racism. Inspired by the intellectual fervor of Robeson's activities, Belafonte, Davis, Dee, and Poitier became involved in various artistic initiatives in Harlem sponsored by the Communist Party in the late 1940s and early 1950s. For example, Dee starred in a benefit performance of *Anna Lucasta* sponsored by a Theater vs. Intolerance Committee on behalf of Georgia lynching victims in 1946.[36] Likewise, the friends all performed in Community for the Negro in the Arts (CAN) productions, the only black theater in New York City after the collapse of ANT in 1949. Indeed, Davis and Dee considered themselves "fellow travelers." This was before they began working in Hollywood, however, and soon, Poitier says, Robeson urged them not to appear "too radical" in an effort to protect them from the kind of persecution he had experienced.[37] By the time of their first films, Robeson's career had been destroyed after the House of Un-American Activities Committee (HUAC) had targeted him in a larger effort to root out communism in American life.

In 1947, HUAC had launched an investigation of the motion picture industry. The "Hollywood Ten," a group of screenwriters and directors who refused to testify, were cited for contempt of Congress and blacklisted. To avoid more HUAC investigations or outright censorship by the government, fifty top Hollywood executives met at the Waldorf Astoria Hotel in New York and pledged to deny work in the motion picture industry to suspected subversives. This pact became known as the "Waldorf declaration" and led to the studio blacklist. Anyone connected, no matter how loosely, with communist or communist-front organizations, past or present, could find themselves on the blacklist, often as a result of being identified as communists or communist sympathizers in anticommunist publications such as *Counterattack*. Many actors found it prudent to deny such affiliations. In 1948, the Screen Actors Guild overwhelmingly voted for a resolution requiring officers, directors, and committee members to sign individual affidavits swearing that they did not belong to the Communist Party, and, by 1953, all new members were required to make the same pledge.[38] Given the Communist Party's professed commitment to racial equality, any organization addressing racial injustice proved vulnerable to red-baiting and individual artists connected to it were deemed threatening. Robeson experienced the worst of the fallout, in part because he increasingly championed the Soviet Union.

After traveling to Moscow in 1949, Robeson declared it unthinkable for "American Negroes to go to war on behalf of those who have oppressed us . . . against a country [the Soviet Union] which in one generation has raised our people to the full dignity of mankind."[39] This statement led HUAC to hold hearings in the summer of 1949 to determine if communists had infiltrated minority groups. As these hearings got underway, it became clear that the best way for African Americans to convince HUAC of their loyalty to the United States was to denounce Robeson. When the actor Canada Lee refused to testify, he was blacklisted. A cross section of prominent African Americans and whites questioned Robeson's authority as a spokesperson for African Americans and asserted the loyalty of blacks to the United States, especially in times of war. The baseball player Jackie Robinson, under great external pressure, was the most high-profile African American to take the stand. He warned that racial inequalities in America needed to be addressed before more blacks turned to communism. Nevertheless, he called Robeson's statement "silly" and testified that most African Americans despised communism. In the wake of these hearings, Robeson's reputation was so tarnished that he was unable to secure stage contracts or concert engagements, and music stores refused to carry his recordings. When he tried to perform overseas, the US State Department confiscated his passport. Robeson's annual income plummeted from $104,000 to a mere $2,000, and when progressive groups offered to hold benefits for him, hostile mobs shouted Robeson off stage. Also in these hearings, CAN was identified as a Communist-front organization.[40]

These developments devastated Belafonte, Davis, Dee, and Poitier, given their close friendship with Robeson, and also put them in a vulnerable position. In fact, Counterattack had labeled all four of them as "unpatriotic" at various points between 1950 and 1957, and they came under pressure to sign various loyalty oaths.[41] Poitier managed to avoid ever doing so, largely, he says, because the filmmakers who cast him wanted to work with him specifically and did not worry about an oath. During the making of Blackboard Jungle in 1955, a lawyer for MGM demanded Poitier sign an anticommunist pledge, but when he refused, the director Richard Brooks continued filming, cavalierly saying "fuck 'em." They proceeded without further interference.[42] When Poitier ran into a similar situation with the NBC legal department during the filming of "A Man Is Ten Feet Tall" for Philco Television Playhouse, the scriptwriter negotiated a compromise with NBC that precluded Poitier from signing the oath.[43] Davis and Dee boldly spoke out against the blacklist, even when called into court. They decided that catering to an audience of minorities and the working class would "at least give us enough money to pay our rent and buy food for our children" and allow them to survive, with or without Hollywood and Broadway.[44] Belafonte did not make such a successful principled stand, however, and acquiesced to the studio's demands for starring in Carmen Jones. He told Counterattack that he hated communism, denied his presence at certain radical functions, and claimed that he thought CAN was a cultural organization unattached to the Communist Party, even saying that he "now intends to become actively anti-Communist." This was a "painful time" for Belafonte; his friends on the Left felt betrayed, and his shame of having made false statements and in not having stood by his principles haunted him henceforth.[45]

The culture of celebrity was fraught with opportunities and challenges alike. Hollywood actors now had more freedom in shaping their public personas, but to achieve stardom those personas had to be managed within certain constraints. For Poitier, Belafonte, Davis, Dee, and Dandridge, their ascent into stardom developed just as the civil rights movement gained momentum, making the stakes surrounding cultural politics and social activism even higher. These circumstances shaped the making of and response to *Porgy and Bess* at the end of the decade.

*   *   *

When Goldwyn announced his intention to make *Porgy and Bess*, he hoped to capitalize on the success of *Carmen Jones*; however, the material for *Porgy and Bess* was much more controversial and already had a turbulent history. The original source was the 1925 best-selling novel *Porgy* by the white author DuBose Heyward. It tells the story of a legless beggar who lives in the fictitious Charleston slum Catfish Row and unsuccessfully attempts to rescue Bess from her brutish boyfriend Crown and the drug-pusher Sportin Life. Influenced by the primitivism movement, Heyward pursues "folk exotic" themes in the novel. The characters' Gullah dialect, superstitious religious beliefs, propensity toward song and dance, and pathological behavior emphasize Catfish Row's estrangement from white society.[46] The novel would be the basis for the Broadway play *Porgy* in 1927 and the folk opera *Porgy and Bess* composed by George and Ira Gershwin in 1935, which included such instant classics as "Summertime" and "It Ain't Necessarily So." *Porgy and Bess* enjoyed considerable success in the 1940s and a triumphant international tour in the 1950s. However, when the producers attempted a similar American tour, the NAACP denounced its "libelous" depiction of African Americans, and Southern theater owners attempted to bar blacks from the audience, leading to the show's cancellation.[47]

The same controversies regarding black stereotypes and segregated theaters had the potential to reemerge, but they were not imposing enough problems to dissuade Goldwyn. He had a tremendous track record with such hits as *Wuthering Heights* (1939), *The Best Years of Our Lives* (1946), and *Guys and Dolls* (1955). All total, twenty-seven of his films had won Academy Awards in various categories. Goldwyn was a Hollywood legend as much for his malapropisms as for his films. As he liked to say,

"I am willing to admit that I may not always be right, but I am never wrong." Thus, he confidently proceeded with *Porgy and Bess*, hiring N. Richard Nash to write the screenplay. He instructed Nash to use both the novel and the play as sources but to also anticipate using the songs from the opera. Goldwyn took responsibility for the cast.[48] However, only one high-profile performer was actively pursuing a part—the nightclub performer Sammy Davis, Jr.

Davis was born December 8, 1925, to the performers Elvera Sanchez and Sam Davis, Sr. As a small child he performed with his father in a troupe organized by the song-and-dance man Will Mastin, and they later formed the Will Mastin Trio. They traveled the United States and Canada for opening act bookings, during which Davis met the rising singing sensation Frank Sinatra. Captivated by Sinatra's style, Davis became a "fan," determined to match his idol's success and effortless persona. When Davis joined the army in 1943, he realized that his father and Mastin had managed to shield him from racial indignities when they were on the road. He faced palpable racism for the first time in his life, peaking with a series of confrontations and physicals altercations during Davis's preparations for an intercamp talent show. A group of white soldiers dragged him to a remote part of the camp, wrote "I'm a nigger" on his chest and "I'm a coon" on his forehead, and forced him to tap dance for thirty minutes. When he went forward with his show a few days later, he realized that the "haters" energized and strengthened him. He concluded, "My talent was the weapon, the power, the way for me to fight. It was the only way I might hope to affect a man's thinking."[49]

At war's end, Davis grew determined to become a star, and he developed a public persona of the daring and deferential that facilitated this goal. He established his own office in Hollywood, the first black entertainer to do so. With no successful model to emulate, Davis forged his own path. He hired white agents to pitch ideas to the studios and appointed both white and black publicists to manage press relations with mainstream publications and the black press.[50] Davis operated largely by instinct when managing his persona, much as he did with his live performances. He struck a balance of audacious and acquiescent behavior that appealed to black and white audiences alike. A gifted mimic, Davis impersonated white stars, such as Humphrey Bogart, James Cagney, and Edward G. Robinson, something no other black performer dared. Sam Sr. worried that these routines would endanger their lives, but they delighted audiences. Even though Davis openly mocked white stars, he did so in a way that was more reverential than disparaging. Likewise, although Davis avoided vaudevillian humor due to the "Tomming" it required, he still addressed racial matters with self-deprecating humor.

Davis's amiable persona endeared him to the mainstream in a revolutionary way, but he also proved his willingness to participate in the broader effort, similar to such performers as Josephine Baker, to desegregate Northern cultural spaces like nightclubs and hotels.[51] A sensational showing at Ciro's nightclub in Beverly Hills in 1952 catapulted Davis into stardom. He signed at the Copacabana club in New York for $5,000 per week and, within a few years, was offered a staggering $25,000 per week at the Sands Hotel in Vegas. He was the first black performer signed by the Copacabana, and he insisted on integrated audiences in Las Vegas, where in the recent past, he had been barred from the casino hotels. He then conquered Broadway with the 1956 show *Mr. Wonderful*. Not only did the success of the production prove that an African American could carry a Broadway musical, but Davis ensured that the cast and crew were a "revolutionary" 50 percent black.[52]

Davis hoped that Hollywood stardom would follow, but he found the industry exceedingly difficult. After his smashing debut at Ciro's, Davis appeared on Eddie Cantor's television variety show. However, when Cantor embraced Davis at the end of his performance, the episode generated so much hate mail that the show's advertising sponsors threatened to pull the plug. It was only because of Cantor's personal intervention that Davis was allowed to return for two more episodes (and even more hugging). Meanwhile, Davis longed to do dramatic roles but had been rebuffed by the studios so many times that he told his agent to temporarily "forget pictures 'cause it's been like we've got the Ku Klux Klan running the motion picture department here."[53] During this period he mostly appeared on television variety shows. He received an offer to play the male lead opposite Eartha Kitt in the independent film *Anna Lucasta*, but the project had not come to fruition by the time Goldwyn announced his plans for *Porgy and Bess*. Recognizing the potential benefit to his career, Davis enthusiastically pursued the role of Sportin Life, "pull[ing] out," he admitted, "every stop to win the part."[54] Goldwyn's first order of business, however, was to find a male lead to play Porgy.

Goldwyn's difficulty casting the lead role reflected the newfound ability of African Americans to control their public images. Without a "name" for the lead, the producer could not expect to fill the remaining roles with prestigious talent. This reticence stemmed from the controversies associated with the 1952 production and from statements issued by high-profile African Americans objecting to the film. The most outspoken opponent was Belafonte, who, as soon as he heard that Goldwyn was considering him for Porgy, announced he would not take the part. Soon thereafter, an ad appeared in the *Hollywood Reporter* under the aegis of the "Council for the Improvement of Negro Theater Arts" urging black actors to refuse to work on the production.[55] "I love the music of George and Ira Gershwin," Belafonte admitted, but "it's the mediocre, vicious book (by Dubose Heyward) I despise." He elaborated, "I'm not opposed to showing Negroes living in poverty or even the use of dialect because it reflects folklore. But the leading character is a prostitute addicted to narcotics. Another lead peddles dope. The next guy is a big black African full of lust and sex. And the community itself—the only way they know now to relax and have fun at the end of the day is to shoot craps."[56]

Indeed, at this point in his career, Belafonte had become highly critical of the film industry and even of his own films. He lambasted their "stinking" quality, calling *Bright Road* a "nice, bland Lassie-like thing" and *Carmen Jones* "bootleg Bizet." He lamented that he had been "catapulted out of drama school in to a series of compromises like these pictures."[57] It is possible that Belafonte was more disappointed in the political compromises he had made than in the films themselves, but by 1959 his stature in the film industry had changed. The stunning success of his 1956 album *Calypso*, which included the popular track "Day-O," kicked off a "calypso craze" in the United States. Calypso night clubs opened up in cities across the country, where patrons gamely learned the faddish Chalypso dance, and audiences flocked to see Belafonte on his national concert tour.[58] He broke attendance records at nearly every venue he played. Twentieth Century Fox capitalized on this interest by casting Belafonte in *Island in the Sun,* a 1957 film about the politics of race and the complexities of interracial romance on the fictional Caribbean island of Santa Marta. But Belafonte was no more impressed by this effort. "Wonder of wonders—I get to best James Mason," he groused sarcastically about his costar's character.[59] Furthermore, none of the interracial couples were allowed to kiss onscreen. Belafonte started Harbel Productions, an independent film company, to address some of the problems he perceived of the film industry.

Harbel Productions was just getting off the ground when Goldwyn announced his plans for *Porgy and Bess*. Belafonte was making *The World, the Flesh, and the Devil* for MGM and was in the process of securing financial backing for future projects, including *Odds Against Tomorrow*. Belafonte's primary goal with these films was to eliminate demeaning caricatures of blacks, but he also hoped to offer a more complex and everyday view of African American life. Even though Belafonte was close friends with Poitier, he thought the types of roles Poitier played were growing stale. "He always plays the role of the good and patient fellow who finally wins the understanding of his white brothers." Belafonte promised that his films would "bridge the gap between the current crop of dramas of interracial conflict, and simple, straightforward dramas of comprehension—written around the everyday problems of Negroes as people."[60] In other words, Belafonte intended to make films in which blacks would be seen in a variety of roles and the driving conflict was not necessarily race specific. A big-budget film version of *Porgy and Bess* seemed to fly in the face of everything he hoped to accomplish.

In light of Belafonte's critiques, Goldwyn attempted to cultivate racial goodwill. He announced that the film version would portray the people of Catfish Row as triumphant over racism.[61] He also pledged all profits from the film to charity, and contributed $1,000 to a local fund-raising drive for the NAACP. Even though critics denounced Goldwyn's contribution as a shameless ploy to buy his way into the good graces of African Americans, his overtures largely succeeded. The NAACP did not take a position against, much less boycott, the film. In fact, the West Coast chapter outright endorsed the production, saying it had "complete confidence" in Goldwyn to portray African Americans fairly.[62]

Perhaps it was the disappointing results of the NAACP's most recent Hollywood campaign that led to the organization's obliging position toward *Porgy and Bess*. In 1951, Walter White had learned that CBS intended to bring the radio show *Amos 'n' Andy* to network television. Although wildly popular, *Amos 'n' Andy* generated considerable controversy, as white actors voiced the black working class characters and sometimes used demeaning stereotypes. White proposed a resolution condemning the program and calling for local NAACP branches to pressure CBS's affiliate stations and the show's sponsor, Blatz Beer. A prominent rift in the membership ensued. Whereas middle-class blacks believed that the show held back the race by featuring its worst elements and supported the boycott, working-class blacks opposed the NAACP's position, finding the show harmless, entertaining, and an accurate representation of some aspects of black life. Moreover, the show employed more black actors than any other series on television. Some branches refused to support the resolution, and members of the black press flatly denounced it. *Amos 'n' Andy* ran for two successful seasons and was even nominated for an Emmy Award for best comedy series. Still, the controversy associated with the NAACP protest led CBS to abandon the series. This was not necessarily a successful conclusion. No other network television series would cast a black actor in a central role until 1965.[63] Few actors would consider the aftermath of the *Amos 'n' Andy* protest a victory, and resentment toward the national office lingered.

White died in 1955 and was succeeded as NAACP executive secretary by Roy Wilkins. Even though Wilkins had endorsed the *Amos 'n' Andy* protest, he was reluctant to plunge into a similar brouhaha over *Porgy and Bess*. An attempted boycott would have again exposed disagreement between local chapters and the national leadership. Wilkins explained, "Among Negro Americans there is a division of opinion as to the value of this play." The basis for these differences seemed to again fall along class lines, as Wilkins admitted that those who opposed *Porgy and Bess* feared "that the public may regard Catfish Row as a typical picture of Negro American life rather than as a period piece depicting merely a segment." And there was still the issue of jobs, which were so sparse for black actors. Furthermore, the NAACP could ill-afford another unsuccessful boycott attempt. The official position of the NAACP on *Porgy and Bess*, then, was to take no position.[64]

Meanwhile, Davis was still the only big name vying for a role. Contrary to Belafonte, he did not consider the overall depiction of Catfish Row as negative. "The picture isn't all crap shooting and dope addicts," he explained. "This community . . . has a cross-section of intellectuals and dummies, of evil and good as any community does."[65] Goldwyn was open to casting him but not yet convinced that Davis had the acting chops for film. To persuade the producer, one of Davis's agents brought Goldwyn to his act at the Moulin Rouge nightclub in Los Angeles. At one point, Davis stopped the show to announce, "Ladies and gentlemen, you can't see them. I can't either. But Samuel Goldwyn and his wife are up there. Mr. Goldwyn, I'll do the role of Sportin' Life for nothing."[66] Davis also asked friends such as Sinatra, George Burns, and Jack Benny to use their influence with Goldwyn. Finally, the producer knocked on Davis's dressing room door and pronounced, "Mr. Davis, you are Sportin' Life. The part is yours. Now will you get all these guys off my back?"[67] Davis enthusiastically began incorporating some of Sportin Life's material into his nightclub routine.[68] However, signing on Davis made little difference in persuading the rest of the cast—perhaps because Davis's pursuit of the part reflected his more deferential side.

The three leading women being considered for the film—Dorothy Dandridge, Pearl Bailey, and Diahann Carroll—all had qualms. Bailey was particularly concerned about the dialect the role would require. Even though she acknowledged the dialect's historical roots, she argued that "dese" and "dose" "tasted like mud in 1958."[69] Likewise, Carroll remembers that when she was first approached to play the part of Clara, she decided to turn it down. She explains, "I thought it was negative, that all of the characters were primarily a negative influence."[70] Dandridge was conflicted. She believed *Porgy and Bess* to be "an accurate picture of the harsh, terrorized lives of Negroes forced to live in ghettoes," and she also recognized that the film offered dramatic and complex roles. She reflected thoughtfully, "Porgy is a half-man, as it were; he is a stumped, legless figure who withal is human, real, warm, capable of love—and of murder. Normally this would be a prize role for any Negro male lead." However, she believed that if the material was not handled properly, the film would be a disaster. She remained undecided.[71] Despite their reservations, all of these women would agree to play in the film, and their acquiescence hinged largely on Goldwyn successfully recruiting Poitier for the lead role. Even though it was still early in Poitier's career, his reputation for refusing roles he considered demeaning meant that his acceptance would give the film a seal of approval and allow it to proceed.

Poitier was determined to maintain the dignified and independent persona he had established as Dr. Luther Brooks even when it was financially risky to do so. Although *No Way Out* can be considered Poitier's "big break," it by no means made him rich or all that famous. He was paid only $750 per week for a total of $3,000 for the picture. Subsequent film projects paid equally as dismally. In 1955, Poitier received his largest salary to date—$15,000—for *Edge of the City*.[72] These depressed salaries resulted from working on low-budget independent films with limited runs in the South. The studios also habitually gave Poitier a lesser billing, even when he had the leading role, and paid him less than his white costars. Poitier was looking for a project that would elevate him from a supporting actor to a bona fide leading man, with the salary and billing to back it. One of his agents believed *Porgy and Bess* was just the jolt his career needed, but Poitier worried it would damage his reputation.

As soon as Poitier learned he was being considered for Porgy, he refused the part, but it was already too late. Within a week of Goldwyn's initial announcement of the making of *Porgy and Bess*, Poitier's West Coast agent, Lillian Schary Small, had enthusiastically written the producer and suggested Poitier, "the greatest Negro actor in the whole world," for Porgy.[73] Poitier, who was in Saint Thomas at the time, had already told his East Coast agent, Martin Baum, that he did not want to be involved in the production, but Small was unaware of his feelings. Goldwyn pressured her to bring him on board. Cognizant that her reputation in Hollywood could be ruined if she did not deliver, Small wrote Goldwyn and confirmed a deal with Poitier, even though five months had passed since her original recommendation, and at this point, she knew Poitier's feelings.[74] Because of Small's promise, Goldwyn considered Poitier locked into the role. Small then pleaded with Poitier to reconsider, arguing that Goldwyn was a liberal and humane man. "I believe it would be impossible [for him] to do anything in bad taste," she explained, "and aside from all his convictions, he is much too smart a businessman to attempt to make a motion picture which might depict the Negro in any bad light." She reassured Poitier that he would not have to shoot craps and, in a seemingly desperate move, enclosed an article from the black newspaper the *Kansas City Call* and a statement by President Dwight D. Eisenhower, both of which endorsed *Porgy and Bess*.[75]

By this time, a number of prominent individuals, both black and white, were weighing in on whether or not Poitier should star in *Porgy and Bess*. According to the popular *New York Post* columnist Leonard Lyons, the esteemed African American diplomat Ralph Bunche had voiced his approval, saying, "I'm all for it. *Porgy and Bess* is a classic and ought to be presented on film. I'm sure Mr. Goldwyn will be faithful to it."[76] Even though Bunche had said nothing about Poitier specifically, Lyons apparently believed that if Poitier knew Bunche's opinion on the material, the actor might reconsider. On the other hand, Poitier's close friends Lena Horne and Belafonte said he should abide by his original decision. Then, Poitier remembers, "All kinds of other people . . . began calling me and saying, 'What is this about Sam Goldwyn? Why don't you do *Porgy and Bess*? We think it's one of the best operas ever written and it's won this kind of award and that kind of award.'" Poitier knew that Goldwyn was friends with Lyons and suspected that the producer was also behind the deluge of phone calls.[77] Goldwyn soon tried to ratchet up the pressure even more.

Baum convinced his client to meet Goldwyn at his home in Beverly Hills to discuss *Porgy and Bess*. Even though Poitier was "suspicious," he agreed to the meeting, which Baum and Small also attended, because he believed it would be "good politics" and a chance for him to explain his feelings about the material. The two men went round and round for about ten minutes until Goldwyn surprised Poitier by ending the meeting and merely asking him to think about the role. In the meantime, the independent producer Stanley Kramer offered Poitier the lead in *The Defiant Ones*, an interracial drama about two convicts who escape a chain gain. But there was a catch. Kramer explained that he feared Goldwyn might, in light of Small's promise, bring action against the proceeding of *The Defiant Ones*. They could not go ahead until Poitier got a release. Of course, Goldwyn refused. Poitier realized he had been manipulated into a crisis situation. "I refuse to believe that Goldwyn didn't know about the Kramer project and know that I would flip for it." He continued, "I'm also sure that my agents knew I would flip for it."[78] If he continued to refuse *Porgy and Bess*, he ran the very real risk of not only forgoing *The Defiant Ones* but being blackballed and never working in Hollywood again, such was Goldwyn's power. Poitier believed Kramer's film offered a special opportunity "to represent for me and other black actors a step up in the quality of parts available to us, and at the same time afford the black community in general a rare look at a movie character exemplifying the dignity of our people." Thus, Poitier decided to survive by starring in *Porgy and Bess*, even if he had to "give up some blood to do so."

In the meantime, Dandridge faced similar pressures. Her sympathy for the material had not yet outweighed her concerns about it. Learning of her ambivalence, Belafonte tried to discourage her. "Harry telephoned me from New York," she remembered. "'Don't do it, it isn't right,' he urged. 'I'm out of it.'" She consulted Goldwyn about his plans for the production and about how she would be able to interpret Bess. It was during these conversations that she learned of Goldwyn's correspondence with various civil rights organizations and his determination to move forward with the picture. When a still-unsigned Poitier called her about playing Bess, she told him she had decided—unofficially—to do it. "[Goldwyn's] going to do this picture with or without me. He will do it with or without you," she explained. "Now the way I'm thinking, if I can bring some dignity to the role, maybe that's what it needs." Dandridge also received a number of letters from fans. "Why must you play a prostitute?" one asked. In fact, Bess was Dandridge's best offer since *Carmen Jones*. At age thirty-five, she feared she was past her prime, and she needed a prominent leading part to dispel that perception.[79]

With his leads in place, Goldwyn at first exercised the upper hand in a way reminiscent of the studio chiefs in Old Hollywood. At the same meeting at which Goldwyn and Poitier came to terms, the producer told him, "I think we should sit down and prepare a joint statement for the press. But don't you worry about it—your agents and my press people will work something up and show it to you before it goes out." Soon thereafter, Poitier found himself at a joint press conference with Goldwyn, reading a prepared statement. Poitier felt that he had been "screwed again," because the press release "was all to Goldwyn's advantage."[80] Indeed, Poitier told the media that he had been torn "by a dual kind of emotion" and that he had given the role "a great deal of thought in the succeeding weeks" after turning it down. He explained that Goldwyn and the director he had hired, Rouben Mamoulian, had convinced him that they would handle the film with integrity. The statement concluded with Poitier claiming that Goldwyn was "almost as sensitive as I am" on matters of race.[81]

Despite his hard-nosed tactics, Goldwyn sweetened the deal for the actors in ways that reflected their rising statures. Goldwyn assured the cast that if there was anything in the script or in the way the director handled the material to which they objected, their complaints would be taken seriously and with consideration. Furthermore, the contracts for the four leads were more generous than what was standard for African American actors. Goldwyn paid Poitier, Dandridge, Bailey, and Davis $75,000 each, which was unprecedented for all except Dandridge, who had received an equal salary for *The Decks Ran Red* (1958).[82] Poitier also received an expense account of $200 per week. Bailey negotiated for the right to select her own hairdresser, an important issue for African American actresses, who previously had been allowed only white hairdressers who were inexperienced at, and often downright hostile about, styling their hair.[83] Furthermore, the production value of the picture promised to be much more lush than the other films on which they had worked, which brought an overall level of prestige to the project.

Still, Poitier was concerned about Belafonte's reaction. They were good friends at this point, and had a relationship that Poitier "felt was worth protecting and respecting." Even though Poitier explained the details of the situation to Belafonte, "I didn't convince him that I had to do *Porgy and Bess* so that I could do the other picture," he says. "He didn't buy it—he would have preferred me just to walk away from the whole thing." Belafonte said that had the situation been reversed, he hoped that he would have had the strength to turn down Goldwyn. Poitier admitted that Belafonte's unwillingness to accept his decision "bothered me for a long time."[84] Likewise, Poitier's decision to trade *Porgy* for *The Defiant Ones* reverberated with Belafonte for decades. In 1996, he complained to the *New Yorker*, "A host of people in the black community said no. The one who broke the chain was Sidney, who agreed to do it." Without acknowledging Goldwyn's machinations, Belafonte explained, "Sidney was always more pliable, more accommodating."[85] Belafonte's grudge may stem from the fact that Poitier would go on to enjoy a long and successful film career, while Harbel Productions fell apart and Belafonte did not star in a single major motion picture during the 1960s. Whatever the reasons, these types of disagreements—in which Belafonte insinuated both privately and publicly that Poitier was not "pure" enough as an artist, activist, or African American—would be a running theme of their friendship. But whereas Belafonte had a singing career to fall back on, Poitier could not, as he says, "sing for beans."[86]

Davis's difficulties with pitching ideas to the studios, Poitier's dealings with Goldwyn, and Belafonte's problems with Harbel Productions show that even though by the end of the 1950s most actors worked as free agents, the ability to choose their own roles and make their own films did not come without complications and compromises. Managing one's public image could be a difficult task, especially for black actors dealing with the white power structure in Hollywood. Goldwyn's determination to cast Poitier does, however, allude to Poitier's stature, a position that the actor would successfully exploit.

* * *

Once shooting began, the cast used its influence to affect the film in a fashion that was unprecedented for black actors in Hollywood. In light of the ongoing racial controversies and the rising statures of the stars, the studio acted prudently to incorporate their demands.

Having grown frustrated with his original choice for director, Gold-wyn fired Mamoulian and replaced him with Otto Preminger, a move that touched off another round of racial controversy. Most observers initially sympathized with Mamoulian, viewing him as another victim of Gold-wyn's bullying ways as the two fought over innumerable details. The cast was surprised by Mamoulian's firing, and the Screen Directors Guild issued a statement defending him.[87] Then the actor Leigh Whipper, a member of the cast and president of the Negro Actors Guild of America (NAG), issued his own statement in which he defended Mamoulian and attacked Preminger. Whipper claimed, "I have first hand information concerning the new director which brands him, to me, as a man who has no respect for my people," in effect calling Preminger a racist.[88] Whipper then renounced his part in the film, which was actually quite minor. After Whipper's press conference, the focus shifted from defending Mamoulian to supporting Preminger.

In an interesting development, the cast used its clout to protect Prem-inger from the racial controversy. Pearl Bailey and Brock Peters, both of whom had previously worked with the director on *Carmen Jones*, issued statements defending him, in conjunction with Davis and Loren Miller, chairman of the NAACP's West Coast Legal Committee. Even if they had sympathy for Mamoulian, they believed it was unfair to attack Prem-inger. As Bailey said, "My thinking might have been different if these statements about racial matters hadn't gotten ugly," and she denied Preminger's alleged racism. Davis argued that the director had done a "superb job" with *Carmen Jones*.[89] Likewise, Noble Sissle, a member of NAG, wrote to Goldwyn bemoaning Whipper's "shocking" accusation: "No one of the Guild had the slightest idea of what his personal griev-ances are about." It soon became apparent that Mamoulian had engi-neered the attack.[90] In the meantime, both the Screen Actors Guild and the Screen Directors Guild sided with Goldwyn. Mamoulian was forced to back off. Preminger stepped in as director, and although he had a repu-tation as a loud-mouthed bully, he was known to be a progressive on racial matters. Poitier says, "It was soon established that he *was* indeed a liberal when it came to racial questions, but he was also a tyrant whose monster within surfaced frequently on his bad days."[91]

Preminger lived up to his reputation as a tyrant on the set, but the cast asserted itself again. At first, the only cast member to escape Prem-inger's wrath was Bailey, likely because of their previous working relationship. One by one, three other actors managed to win him over as well. Davis and Preminger became friendly and caroused together. "We'd hit the nightclubs most nights," Davis remembered. "All he ever wanted to talk about was broads. As I could always muster up half a dozen good-looking ladies with a couple of phone calls, I found I couldn't get rid of Otto even if I'd wanted to." Poitier's handling of Preminger showcased the "controlled anger" for which he was known. After the director threw one particularly fierce fit, Poitier walked off the set and refused to return until Preminger apologized and promised not to behave that way again.[92] The director did, and he and Poitier became "very good friends." Poitier's approach impressed his colleagues. Carroll remembered, "I had never seen . . . any black man deal with the white world with his kind of self-assurance and strength."[93] Likewise, when Preminger yelled at Ivan Dixon, the actor retaliated: "Don't you ever yell at me again. Ever!" Preminger backed off.

However, when the director continued to browbeat the rest of the cast, especially Dandridge (whose romantic involvement with Preminger had ended by this point), the cast banded together. They met privately and decided to call a meeting with Preminger. According to Nichelle Nichols, they "ate him alive. He knew he had a mutiny on his hands." Having deliberately called the meeting for when Dandridge (who always seemed to fall apart around Preminger) had two days off, they demanded better treatment of the cast as a whole and of Dandridge specifically. Nichols felt the meeting was relatively successful in that Preminger "was more respectful of us," but he was only "a little more respectful" of Dandridge.[94] Still, the cast's willingness to challenge Preminger signaled a shifting confidence among African Americans in Hollywood.

Perhaps anticipating the cast's assertiveness, Goldwyn, Preminger, and Nash (the screenwriter) all maintained that they were advancing the interests of African Americans with *Porgy and Bess* and made decisions about the material with that argument in mind. As early as February 1958 (six months before shooting was scheduled to begin), Nash had written Goldwyn explaining his efforts to avoid "gag" and "dialogue type of word-humor," meaning humor that could be labeled as stereotypical and thus be "severely criticized on the grounds of good taste."[95] Likewise, immediately after he had been named the new director, Preminger wired Goldwyn with suggestions regarding Sportin Life's character. Believing that the role had been conceived of as vaudevillian, Preminger worried that such an interpretation would result in Davis "mugging" for the camera in stereotypical fashion. Therefore, Preminger proposed modifying Sportin Life's scenes to be less stylized, so Davis would "come across as a legitimate actor" and not a vaudevillian.[96] This directly opposed the vision of Mamoulian, who had advocated trying to achieve "a poetical stylization."[97] Preminger's efforts suggest his desire to maintain his reputation as a prestigious director and to serve the actors in the production well. Goldwyn accepted both Nash's and Preminger's suggestions.

In a similar spirit, the studio was relatively accommodating to the requests of the cast, beginning with their concerns about stereotypical images in the script. Despite Nash's seemingly genuine intention to write a screenplay "in good taste," he also tried to be true to Heyward's original material in both the novel and the play.[98] Therefore, the cast found many elements in the script objectionable. At the start, Bailey bristled at the references to "watermelon" in the screenplay. Originally, the script called for a crowd to chant, "Crown cockeyed drunk, he can't tell dice from a watermelon! Crown cockeyed drunk . . ." and so on during a crap game. Later, in a description of the street during the parade, the script effusively detailed the wagonloads of food, including fish, live chickens, produce, "and the one special wagonload of watermelons, atop which are a few small boys jumping gleefully up and down on the brilliant green fruit, play King-of-the-Hill on the greenest hill that ever was!"[99] After Bailey protested, the gambling chant was revised and the description of the wagonload of watermelons scratched out. However, the final version of the screenplay contained a number of elements that the cast still found offensive. By comparing the final version of the script in Goldwyn's archival papers to the film version, it is possible to see the dramatic changes the cast made to *Porgy and Bess*.

First, the cast modified the dialect. According to one observer, on the first day on the set with Preminger, the cast was nervous about the dialect; they didn't know what Preminger would demand or expect them to say. Poitier set the tone when he spoke his lines in another extremist fashion: Old English. When he "got positively Shakespearean," the rest of the cast followed suit, until Poitier got on his feet and asked Preminger if they could discuss the script.[100] "With Sidney leading the way," Davis remembered, "we sat down and worked out a dialogue system which would be authentic but not offensive to the Negro. We have a Southern accent, not a Negro dialect."[101] Instead of saying "dese," "dose," and "dat," as the script originally read, the actors said "these," "those," and "that." Not all of the cast agreed with the revisions made by the film's stars, but Bailey was prepared to use her position as a leading character to enforce them. During one rehearsal, a minor actor who had performed in the Broadway version of *Porgy and Bess* used the line "Ain't I done told you?" Bailey told him that that he should use the new version. When the actor refused, Bailey threatened to demand a casting change if he did not comply. "I was plenty serious about that dialect business," she told one newspaper. "We're still rehearsing, and I wanted it stopped before we started shooting." It was "insane to use it if it's not insisted on. . . . I don't care if it's Negro or Italian or Greek or French, it's in bad taste."[102] Preminger agreed with the revisions, he himself not caring for the original dialect.

Out of concern about behavior that smacked of "Uncle Tom" or made African Americans appear "dumb," the cast made changes that altered the relationship between the residents of Catfish Row and Charleston's "white folks."[103] The screenplay sometimes shows hostility towards whites. For example, one of Porgy's first lines reads, "Luck been riding high with Porgy today. I got a pocket full of the white folk money, and it's goin' to any man what got the guts to shoot if off me." However, the references to whites more often expressed fear of them. When it is suggested he take an ill Bess to "de white folks' hospital," Porgy refuses. Likewise, a child named Scipio spies the police approaching from a row house rooftop. When he shouts, "Dey's a white man comin'! White man!" everyone scatters and hides. After the cast revised the screenplay, all references to "white folks" were excised. Porgy simply says he has a "handful of money." The characters say "policemen" instead of white folks and simply call the hospital a "hospital." Scipio hollers that the "patrol wagon's coming" and no longer makes hysterical reference to an approaching white man. These changes minimized the friction between black and white Charleston and deemphasized the inferior social status of the black residents of Catfish Row.[104]

Most significantly, in removing the "Uncle Tom," the cast made it so that the black characters treated the white characters with far less deference. In the screenplay, the black characters always call the white characters "Boss," a word that not only indicated the characters' social inferiority but also showed that they "knew their place" and were unwilling to challenge the social norms. "Boss" was replaced with "Sir," a word that shows respect but not inferiority. One of the most dramatic changes was a scene between Bailey's character, Maria, and the police, who are investigating Crown's murder. As described in the screenplay, the detectives enter the cook shop and she is "very, very courteous" when answering their questions. She feigns ignorance, saying, "Me?—I don' know nothin', Boss! I is the know-nothin'est woman on Catfish Row! (with a big friendly laugh) I is lovable, Boss—but I is dumb!" In the film, Maria continues to be uncooperative but masks her intentions with far less deference and more humor. When she sees the police approaching her door, she covers the bloody fish she is carving with a sheet. When the police see blood on the floor, they think she is hiding a dead body until she pulls the sheet back, clearly having fun with the authorities. Maria then says sweetly, "Who me? I don't know nothin'. I'm the know-nothinist woman on Catfish Row. I'm lovable, but I'm dumb." Even though the line is similar to the one scripted, the removal of the dialect and the word "Boss," along with the addition of the fish gag and Bailey's delivery, give the scene a different tone. It is no longer an awkward exchange between white authorities and a nervous black woman but a humorous scene in which a confident Maria shows she will not be intimidated. Since she is wielding a meat cleaver, it is the police who seem nervous.[105]

In other scenes, references that were originally meant to be humorous but in reality were demeaning were removed. In both cases, the laughs were originally written at the expense of the characters' intellect. At one point, Clara asks her husband Jake not to take his boat out on the water because there is a chance of storms. Pointing to their baby, Jake answers, "How do you tink dat boy goin' get a college education if I don't work hard and make money? (with a laugh) Right Porgy?" With the dialect and the laughter directive, the message is that the baby has neither the intellect nor the resources to attend college. In the film, however, Jake asks seriously, "How do you think this boy's gonna get a college education if I don't work hard and make money?" Without the exaggerated dialect and the laughter directive, the message is that the residents of Catfish Row can aspire to social mobility. In another scene, a lawyer takes advantage of Porgy by persuading him to buy Bess a "divorce" from Crown, even though the two were never actually married. It is then revealed that the lawyer has similarly taken advantage of other black Charleston couples. This entire scene is removed from the film, likely because the cast felt it made blacks appear gullible and unintelligent.[106]

Also excised are all references to buzzards. Meant to foreshadow tragedy or doom, both the novel and the play include images of buzzards hovering over Catfish Row and putting fear into Porgy. Nash included some of this imagery in the screenplay in an effort to use the birds as "an omen" or "punctuation of" misfortune.[107] In the first draft of the script, Porgy superstitiously tells two white lawyers, "Look out! Dat's a buzzard! Boss, dat bird mean trouble. Once de buzzard fold his wings and light over yo' home, all yo' happiness done dead." Then Porgy gratuitously breaks out in a song about a buzzard. When Mamoulian was still the director, he asked that some of these references be removed for aesthetic reasons, feeling that their constant presence was "like painting the lily." By the final version of the screenplay, the song about the buzzard had been cut, but Porgy's warning remained. Plus, a new reference had been added in which a buzzard circled Catfish Row after everyone left for a picnic. After the cast revised the screenplay, however, the buzzard imagery was removed completely, likely out of concern that Porgy's fear of buzzards gave an impression of backwardness that they did not want associated with African Americans. Between the changes made to the dialogue and the content of the script, the actors significantly altered Nash's screenplay.[108]

Bailey also pushed for significant changes in the costuming. She protested the cast being barefoot. "The poorest section of any town is not doing that bad!" she complained. The cast received shoes. She also objected to the women donning bandana scarves, the traditional headdress of the stereotypical mammy. Surprisingly, that is not the reason Bailey gave for refusing to wear one. Instead, she argued, "There is no place in the world where females dress identically—they don't like each other that much."[109] The reaction of the costume designer, Irene Sharaff, to this request spoke volumes. She characterized Bailey as having "created havoc" with her demand, saying with condescension that "a discussion somewhat like an international conference" ensued. Even though Sharaff considered Bailey's concerns "ridiculous," Preminger, again, accommodated the actress's request.[110] Bailey never wore a kerchief; Dandridge wore one in only one scene; and the rest of the female cast members wore them intermittently. This change allowed the lead actresses to develop their own identities and to distance themselves from some of the stereotypical images of black women in film.

Dandridge, Bailey, Poitier, and Davis all reinterpreted their characters in ways much different from their characterizations in the script. When

Mamoulian was still at the helm, Dandridge met with him to discuss her character. He assured her that "her Bess" could be a new interpretation.[111] The script describes Bess as a "liquor-guzzlin' slut."[112] Dandridge's goal was to make Bess more "ladylike." She worked with a trainer to learn to move more gracefully. Dandridge's delicate and refined Bess is weak-willed but not crass. Likewise, Baileys' interpretation of Maria is a decided improvement over the stereotypical figure for which the screenplay calls. Described as a "massive" and domineering figure, Maria was written to represent the overdone mammy. At one point, the script distastefully calls for Maria to do "an improvisational shuffle which becomes a comic dance."[113] Bailey's Maria is very different from this swashbuckling caricature. She is the conscience of the neighborhood, attractive and insightful.

Davis's reinterpretation of Sportin Life also brought more gravitas to the role. Audiences were used to Cab Calloway, a Broadway actor, playing the mischievous character. His vaudevillian and comedic stylings had captivated audiences in 1952, but since Preminger had discouraged such an interpretation, Davis had the opportunity to reinvent Sportin Life. Believing that the character represented temptation, as opposed to simply evil, Davis tried to bring more nuance to the role. He explained, "People had to hate him, yet he had to be lovable as well." He added a number of "special touches" in an attempt to make Sportin Life captivating without relying on comic farce. He never simply walked on or off the set. Instead, he "would leap on or suddenly appear from nowhere, giving that shazzam quality of the appearance of sudden evil." Davis also invented a particular walk in which he moved gracefully and slinkily across the set, at once both sophisticated and slimy. The long brown cigarette his character smoked attracted extra attention when he dramatically struck his match against the wall and lit it. Even though Davis checked with Preminger when devising his new moves, the actor found that "he never gave me the thumbs-down on an idea."[114] Davis's inspirations made for a character that represented neither the threatening black man nor the silly self-deprecating comedian. These complexities, along with Davis's existing star power, allowed Sportin Life to emerge as a major character in the movie, even though he had very few lines and only two musical numbers.

All told, the cast of *Porgy and Bess* exercised a considerable amount of control over the content of the finished picture in a way that was unthinkable in Hollywood only a few years earlier. According to one black Hollywood veteran, their power was unprecedented. Clarence Muse, who had performed in one hundred films between 1930 and 1959, came out of retirement to play Honey Man in *Porgy and Bess*. He marveled at the influence the members of the cast possessed, telling one newspaper that "in his fifty years of show business, the filming of 'Porgy' was the first time that Negro performers had been given the velvet treatment." Claiming that they "were given the free run of the set" and that "all of their wishes were catered to," Muse was especially impressed that the cast had collectively revised the dialogue.[115] Although few members of the cast felt that they had any real power in Hollywood, Muse's perspective shows that the influence of African American actors had improved substantially.

The cast's efforts, coupled with the studio's inclinations, resulted in the elevation of the social status of the story's characters. The Catfish Row of earlier treatments was clearly a ghetto, and its inhabitants had little hope for a better future. The Catfish Row of the film is a working-class community that struggles but is upwardly mobile. With the dialect and Uncle Tomming removed, there appear to be few cultural differences between blacks and whites and no barriers to the black characters' futures. The set's buildings, with the exception of Porgy's shack, all seem more "shabby chic" than truly shabby. And since the female characters look fashionable, they do not seem truly down-and-out. Porgy, too, gains some social status. His neighbors traditionally had viewed him with pity and found his goat a foul-smelling annoyance. In the film, Porgy enjoys the respect of his neighbors, and the goat, their affection. Indeed, the heroes of Catfish Row are more apparent. Even though Sportin Life, Crown, and Bess are still main characters, the neighborhood clearly disapproves of them. It is the community, with Porgy at the forefront, that is the hero. Porgy eliminates Crown, and his neighbors encourage him to pursue Bess after Sportin Life whisks her away to New York. The happy tone at the end of the film suggests that he will be successful in his mission. He appears nothing like the pitiful Porgy audiences once knew. Overall, the heroic theme overshadows the pathological behavior of Crown, Sportin Life, and Bess.

Nevertheless, the making of *Porgy and Bess* illustrates more of the constraints of African Americans in Hollywood than opportunities. Indeed, with the exception of the cast, no African Americans worked on the production crew. The set was practically segregated; everyone who appeared *in* the film was black, everyone who worked *on* the film was white. Therefore, even though the cast could make suggestions and even outright demands, it was ultimately a white person, indeed a white man, who had the final word. The cast exercised as much influence as it could have in this constrained environment, and they modernized *Porgy and Bess* as much as a period piece could be updated. Nevertheless, the overall effort to make *Porgy and Bess* acceptable to the 1950s audiences also opened up the film to a new kind of criticism.

*   *   *

Porgy and Bess premiered July 24, 1959, to great fanfare and big box office returns, enhancing the cast's star power. Soon, however, ticket sales dropped off, and audience response grew mixed. The criticism the film received revealed the ironies of maintaining black celebrity in Hollywood during the civil rights era.

That Goldwyn promoted *Porgy and Bess* to the same degree as his other pictures strengthened the celebrity stature of the cast. In addition to an almost two-year publicity build in the black press, Goldwyn arranged for a twelve-page spread in *Life* magazine one month before the film's release.[116] The article describes the film's plotline and music, but the emphasis is on the actors, who are featured in large, color photographs. Taken during filming, the photos capture the film's highlights, including Crown's attempts to seduce Bess, his fight with Porgy that ends in his death, and Sportin Life's provocative song "Ain't Misbehavin'." Catfish Row is identified as the setting, but the driving themes of the piece are the love story and the struggle between good and evil. Little attention is paid to race or to the controversies associated with the film. The actors are not identified as "Negro actors," and the picture is not characterized as a "Negro picture," as was often the case.[117] It is a visually compelling piece that features the actors as dramatically gifted stars. Likewise, Goldwyn arranged for the production of one million copies of a hard-cover souvenir book with lavish color stills from the film and biographies of the principal actors.[118]

The actors' images as charismatic and alluring celebrities were enhanced by the film's premiere. At the world opening at the palatial Warner Cinerama Theater in New York, a huge, interracial group of fans surrounded the entrance to see the stars, as well as Samuel Goldwyn, Otto Preminger, and their wives. Dandridge electrified the crowds in a white satin evening gown and shawl. Fans clamored for her autograph or to simply touch her.[119] The glamour of the film's leading ladies won special attention in the press. Goldwyn's wife Frances made a point of praising "Negro beauty." She proclaimed that Dandridge's popularity was "very healthy. It makes our concept of beauty more interesting."[120] Another article highlighted the "wild shopping spree" Carroll enjoyed after cashing her earnings. "I used to go without lunch to have a taxi-ride home," she admitted. "I've always been extravagant, but I didn't have the money."[121] These types of articles reflected a general sentiment in the black press that, whereas *Porgy and Bess* had once been a parochial vehicle, the film "offers more glamour, improved speaking parts with dialect deleted and goes further as a spectacular than any of the several stage versions."[122]

The production quality of the film enhanced this perception. Photographed in Technicolor, the film stretched across the wide screen in a projection process known as Todd-AO, giving it a huge and "glittering" feel. The use of filters gave the film a "remarkable lushness," according to one critic.[123] Furthermore, the esteemed André Previn composed the Gershwin score and served as the conductor of a seventy-two piece orchestra. The sound, heard in the theaters on a six-track stereophonic system, had the same richness of quality as the photography. Meanwhile, Goldwyn nominated Poitier, Davis, and Bailey for Academy Award consideration, and tickets sold rapidly. At the Warner Brothers Theater in Los Angeles, the movie set a record at that venue by making $37,000 in its first week. The Toronto returns were even more impressive. The film made $45,000 during its first week at the Tivoli, and the theater was almost completely sold out for the next two weeks. Within six weeks, the film had already grossed nearly $2 million.[124] Such developments led members of the black press to optimistically speculate on the future of African Americans in Hollywood.

Izzy Rowe, the theatrical columnist for the *Pittsburgh Courier*, proclaimed that *Porgy and Bess* "opened a whole new world for Negro thespians"; likewise, in giving the film its endorsement, the *California Eagle* predicted "this year might well be the beginning of a new era for the Negro actor in Hollywood." An article in the *Daily Defender* went even further:

The overwhelming acceptance of the Goldwyn film at the box office has opened new vistas for Negro stars. Its tremendous gross is proof of new drawing power on the silver screen. Since the opening of *Porgy*, its top stars,

Dorothy Dandridge, Sidney Poitier, Sammy Davis, Jr., and Pearl Bailey have made great strides in the film world. In fact, *Porgy* has done for the Negro in Hollywood and throughout the entertainment world, an undeniable good. Contrary to the belief of some "do-gooders," the Samuel Goldwyn screen version of Gershwin's world renowned opus could well be the Emancipation Proclamation of the Negro Artist in quest of equality in Hollywood.

This enthusiasm was driven by more than employment numbers; it was also the fact that a picture with racial themes had received the lavish attention of a typical studio release. The *Daily Defender* even juxtaposed the film with those made by Harbel Productions. "Certainly . . . *Odds Against Tomorrow* and *The World, the Flesh, and the Devil* were major productions that rate Harry at the top," the newspaper opined. "However, for mass participation in a spectacular . . . Goldwyn shot the works." That the stars of the film received top billing, and enjoyed the fame and fortune that status entailed, particularly impressed the black press.[125]

As more of the viewing public saw the film, however, *Porgy and Bess* suffered from a variety of critiques that hampered ticket sales and undermined the power of black celebrity. Some critics focused on the artistic problems, especially the decision to dub most of the singing and the static quality of the directing. In their minds, the frozen action resulted in a "stodgy bore" and "a ponderous failure."[126] Echoing Belafonte's earlier critiques, a number of African Americans bemoaned the images of southern blacks presented in the film. The playwright Lorraine Hansberry complained about the images of "wicked women and weak men" that Bess and Porgy portrayed. Scores of readers wrote to the *Los Angeles Tribune* to complain about the paper's endorsement of the film. One reader castigated the "stereotypical" portrayal of the characters, worrying that such images would be used to justify contemporary racism. He feared that the film would convince white Americans "that the Negro cannot safely be given the vote—he is too childlike, too ignorant, too superstitious, too vicious, and too degenerate."[127] The most searing complaint, however, focused on the efforts to "clean up" Catfish Row.

In the effort to portray African Americans in a more dignified manner, a seemingly necessary precondition to making the film, the filmmakers then faced the accusation of having made life on Catfish Row unrealistic. That the film had diluted, and even deleted, such common practices and features of ghetto living as playing craps, speaking in dialect, being poor, and having a generally pessimistic view of the future generated other complaints. Even before the film's release, *Daily Defender* columnist Hazel A. Washington commented on Poitier's objections to the "vulgarity" of crap shooting. "We do not want the rest of us to be stamped as using such low grade language," she admitted, but she believed that for the film to be realistic, vile behavior was a "necessary factor."[128] Likewise, the *Time* magazine film critic objected to the new dialogue and the improvements in the lead characters. He characterized their "precise, cultivated accents" as "wrong" and complained that "Poitier's Porgy is not the dirty, ragtag beggar of the Heyward script, but a well-scrubbed young romantic hero who is never seen taking a penny from anybody." Furthermore, Dandridge "makes something of a nice Nellie out of bad Bess."[129] The optimistic ending irked Robert Hatch at the *Nation*, who complained, "When Porgy at the end gets into his goat cart and takes off for New York in pursuit of Bess, the gesture seems grotesquely ignorant and not at all poetic."[130] The overall effect, these critics complained, underplayed the social conditions that produced ghettoes such as Catfish Row in the first place.

Dandridge made a similar point in her autobiography, even though she kept silent about the changes at the time of filming and was herself responsible for the improvement of Bess's character. Due to "outside pressure there was an attempt to clean up Catfish Row! An actual attempt to make life on Catfish Row look not so bad," she said. "Everyone connected with the movie embarked on a program to take the terror, fright, and oppression out of ghetto living." Ultimately, it was a mistake, she explained, because the changes "wrecked it both as an entertainment vehicle and as a vehicle of instruction."[131] Dandridge's conflicting desire for improved onscreen images of African Americans and a realistic film that more clearly damns white racism illustrates an ongoing conflict for many black celebrities. And, indeed, to many observers, the most offensively unrealistic aspect of *Porgy and Bess* was the minimization of white forces in the film.

Some of the most substantial changes to the film minimized the friction between blacks and whites. Therefore, the characters' condition seemed more a matter of choice than oppression. One *Los Angeles Tribune* reader wrote that Catfish Row existed in isolation and that therefore none of the racism its residents would have encountered was evident.

James Baldwin complained that the Catfish Row of the film was "a charming place" but nothing like the real Catfish Rows in America. He argued that the film reflected the viewpoints of whites as opposed to the lifestyle of African Americans, because it "assuages their guilt about Negroes and it attacks none of their fantasies."[132] Diahann Carroll would make a similar criticism, reflecting, "It is a depiction of a group of people that are of no threat at all to the white community . . . they're lost children, as I've heard many white people say." One historian believes that the "beautiful" stars undermined the film even further: "Diahann Carroll, Sammy Davis, Jr., and they're having a good time in *Porgy and Bess*," notes Darlene Clark Hine. "And there are [sic] no visible evidence of white oppression here."[133] As Poitier noted, one "couldn't win" with this material in 1959, as "cleaning up" Catfish Row escaped the stereotypes but underplayed the social context at a time when racial issues had come to the forefront of the national agenda.

There was, however, consistent critical praise for the actors' excellent performances. Especially outstanding were Bailey, Peters, and Davis. Bailey's Maria was one of the few lighthearted characters in the film, and the actress played her as generous, good natured, and capable of occasional, biting sarcasm. As Crown, Peters was handsome, virile, and brutal, oozing with crude and powerful magnetism. Davis's Sportin Life won the most attention and praise. His efforts to play the role for slime instead of laughs enhanced Davis's reputation as an actor. There was even talk of an Oscar for his "gracefully slinky" performance, but he was not nominated.[134] Even though Poitier never felt good about the movie, he delivered a fine performance. Dandridge did not come across as powerfully as her costars. Nevertheless, the performances were overwhelmingly praised, even if the production as a whole was not. Most critics were sorry to see the actors' talents "wasted" in the film.

The Gershwin estate refuses to make the film available to audiences today. Some observers believe this dormancy is for the best. One journalist calls it "the last of the old Mammy musicals produced by the Hollywood studios" and says that it should stay locked away.[135] Others disagree. Brock Peters argues, "It represented a special assemblage of talent, and students of film are unfairly being deprived of seeing it. It is a work of art, and I am proud to have been a part of it." One film scholar bemoans its place in film history, saying it is "one of the most misunderstood, underrated, and unfairly treated works in the history of American film."[136]

Indeed, the varying artistic and racial interpretations are part of what make this film an important historical work, as does its significance to the careers of the cast. Until its release, audiences will have to be satisfied with the Broadway version, which continues to be performed to the present day.

* * *

By the end of the 1950s, Poitier, Dandridge, and Davis had achieved stardom, but it had come at the cost of somewhat dissatisfying black audiences. Dandridge felt uncomfortable with her "sex goddess" image. Even if it did resemble such white luminaries as Marilyn Monroe and Grace Kelly, she resisted the characterization, feeling "trapped" in an image so foreign to her real personality. Another danger for black stars was appealing to white audiences without staying connected to the black market through such means as concert touring.[137] The bourgeoning civil rights movement provided such opportunities to "cross back," although the Cold War environment made it a risky endeavor. Black celebrities needed the civil rights movement almost as much as it needed them. It would potentially allow them to apply civil rights gains to the film industry, and thus improve their positions there, while also asserting racial solidarity. And the fact that these stars had already assimilated and found success in the white world, amid its frustrations, made them sought-after spokespersons for the movement.

Sammy Davis, Jr.

DARING, DEFERENTIAL, AND "MONEY"

> You know my biggest problem these days? Finding kosher pigs' feet.
> —Sammy Davis, Jr., 1964

IN JANUARY 1961, SAMMY DAVIS, JR., AND THE LEGENDARY RAT Pack headlined a "Tribute to Martin Luther King, Jr." that raised $22,000 in a single night for the Southern Christian Leadership Conference (SCLC), providing one-quarter of the organization's proposed operating budget that year. An extraordinary occasion, the tribute marked Davis's ascendance as the dominant celebrity fund-raiser of the civil rights movement and showed the substantial role he played in establishing a liberal, interracial coalition of civil rights supporters. Davis's path to stardom reflected the interplay between the film and television industries in Hollywood, and television particularly shaped his public image. Davis displayed a novel combination of both daring and deference, epitomized by his formation of the Rat Pack with Frank Sinatra, Dean Martin, Peter Lawford, and Joey Bishop. The apparent friendship of these stars allowed them to showcase the possibilities of integration to nightclub, television, and film audiences, yet Davis admitted that his role as a "mascot" to Sinatra was unflattering. Despite the fundamental drawbacks to this image, the behavior that made Davis controversial also allowed him to become the premiere benefactor of civil rights fund-raising.

Davis integrated into the white show business world in a completely revolutionary way, not only for the number of "firsts" he accomplished and the types of characters he played but also in the way he immersed himself in white Hollywood's social scene. His personal lifestyle became important to the growing complexity of his public image.

When the cash-strapped Davis first arrived in Los Angeles, he encountered a partially segregated city. Although public spaces such as theaters and beaches had been integrated since the 1920s, restrictive covenants in the real estate industry had shaped residential patterns into "colored" and "white" sections of town. Successful actors such as Louise Beavers and Hattie McDaniel and a handful of other wealthy blacks had moved into the West Adams enclave and successfully challenged racial covenants there in 1945, but most African Americans lived along Central Avenue, and Davis refused to reside in the "colored section."[1] Having grown up in Harlem, Davis says, "I was never again going to live in a ghetto. Not even if the wall around it were made of solid gold," he explained. When no one in the Hollywood Hills would rent to him, he took a room at the Sunset Colonial Hotel, on the very edge of the star-studded neighborhood. A few years later, when he could afford more spacious quarters, a white business associate rented a Hollywood Hills home for him in his own name to outwit the real estate agents. Davis became the first black resident of the neighborhood and experienced the indignities that came along with this role. On his first Christmas in his new home, a vandal painted "Merry Christmas Nigger!" across the garage door.[2] Nevertheless, living in the Hollywood Hills made it easier for Davis to party and socialize with the white Hollywood establishment.

Davis grew close with Jeff Chandler, a handsome actor who became a major star in the 1950s after being nominated for an Academy Award for his role as Conchise in *Broken Arrow* (1950), as well as Tony Curtis and Janet Leigh. He also became close friends with Jerry Lewis, who provided invaluable professional support. Davis even did impressions of Lewis's high-pitched voice and slapstick antics in his own routines. Lewis introduced Davis to other show business stalwarts, such as the comedian Jack Benny, and offered him advice on everything from his stage attire to his contracts.[3] Likewise, Chandler pulled some strings with Universal Pictures, and the studio hired Davis to sing the title song for *Six Bridges to Cross* (1955), a finished film starring Curtis.[4]

The performer's guidance Davis most sought and whose praise he most craved was that of the singer and actor Frank Sinatra. Davis and Sinatra had become acquainted in 1941, just as Sinatra was leaving the Tommy Dorsey band for a solo career during which he became the chart-topping "idol of the bobby soxers." Said Davis, "He just walked over, matter-of-factly, to Will, my dad, and me, and stuck out his hand and introduced himself." Davis explained, "That might sound like nothing much, but the average top vocalist in those days wouldn't give the time of day to a Negro supporting act." Over the next several years, Davis commented, "every contact I had with Frank, he went out of his way to do something for me, to help me up."[5] Tina Sinatra explains that her dad "thrilled to Sammy's talent and loved helping him." He critiqued Davis's performances and suggested ways to improve them, helped him get bookings, and bolstered his ego when Davis was feeling down about his career or about racist treatment. Tina believed that "their friendship was intertwined with my father's ingrained hatred of bigotry."[6] It was through Sinatra that Davis was further drawn into the swinging Hollywood scene, a lifestyle that would soon inform both of their professional images.

The depth of Davis's friendships became apparent after a severe car accident in 1954. On a return trip from Las Vegas to Los Angeles, Davis's car crashed into the back of another driver's Chrysler, pushing the engine of his Cadillac into the seat. If not for his small frame, Davis may have been crushed. His injuries were extensive: his left eye pulled from the socket, a broken nose, and a crushed kneecap. Davis feared he could never perform (or dance) again, but his friends rallied around him. Chandler even offered to give Davis one of his eyes, but Davis wore a glass eye instead.[7] When he was finally released from the hospital, Sinatra invited him to convalesce at his Palm Springs home.[8] Davis made a celebrated stage comeback only a few months later, his dance moves seemingly even more refined. The accident also inspired Davis's religious conversion.

In 1954, Davis announced his conversion to Judaism, a decision that had transpired through conversations with a rabbi during his recovery.[9] Davis began wearing the Star of David and attending temple to the skepticism of both friends and critics. When he told Lewis—himself Jewish—about his decision, the comedian replied with his typical sarcasm, "You don't have enough problems already?" More cynical skeptics viewed

Davis's sudden interest in Judaism as just another of his absurd attempts to fit into white Hollywood, perhaps under the assumption that Hollywood was invented by Jews. One of Davis's biographers does not believe his interest in the Jewish faith was very deep or meaningful, writing, "Actually, it was just Sammy being Sammy—shrewd, opportunistic, heart-touched, and childlike."[10] Davis's understanding of Judaism may possibly have been shallow; however, he professed that his conversion actually deepened his identification with and respect for his racial heritage, and his commitment to Judaism endured until his death.[11] Nevertheless, this commitment, which became more apparent in later years, did not shield him from accusations in the 1950s that he was striving to be white.

Davis's persistence and determination to integrate into white Hollywood met with the most success on television in the early 1950s. In fact, at the industry's inception, a number of hopeful observers, including *Ebony* magazine, believed it would be an "impartial space" for African Americans, where they could counteract the negative stereotypes from the film industry. Live theatrical performances, a staple of early TV, allowed for a wider range of black roles. The *Philco Television Playhouse*, for example, pushed racial boundaries in its production of "A Man Is Ten Feet Tall" with Sidney Poitier in 1955. African Americans also appeared on game shows, sporting contests, religious programs, and local shows made by individual affiliates.[12] These opportunities, along with variety and musical shows, allowed African Americans to be themselves, and thus more impressive than the images that had typically been promulgated by the film studios. Such influential hosts as Steve Allen and Ed Sullivan insisted on booking black talent and treating them respectfully. Sullivan went so far as to lead an industry "blast" at Georgia governor Herman Talmadge in 1952 when the segregationist bemoaned the intermixing of white and black performers on variety shows.[13] However, the experimental nature of early TV gave way to more filmed programming made in Hollywood studios and contracted by the networks.[14] Fiction programs featuring blacks typically revived the old stereotypes. *The Beulah Show* (ABC 1950–52) featured a maid in the title role who drew criticism for perpetuating the "mammy"; *The Jack Benny Program*'s (CBS 1950–64; NBC 1964–65) "Rochester," the lazy "coon"; and *The Little Rascals*' (syndicated on CBS in 1955) "Buckwheat," a "pickinanny." A spate of jungle documentaries and programs, such as *Sheena, Queen of the Jungle*

(1955–56), portrayed blacks as primitives. And of course, *Amos 'n' Andy* generated the most controversy.[15] Black performers most likely found bookings on variety shows as the decade progressed, and these shows constituted Davis's primary means of developing a relationship with a national audience at this time.

Between 1952 and 1960, Davis appeared on television at least forty-nine times, where he simultaneously pushed racial boundaries and presented white audiences with images to which they were accustomed. He most frequently made guest appearances on Eddie Cantor's *Colgate Comedy Hour* (NBC 1950–55; eight episodes) and on *The Steve Allen Plymouth Show* (NBC 1956–60; ABC 1961; seven episodes), for which he provided musical and comedic entertainment, but Davis found bookings on over twenty different programs during the 1950s. He engaged in his jocular and still-shocking impressions of white performers, but he also did impersonations that incorporated vaudevillian humor. He occasionally mimicked "Kingish" from *Amos 'n' Andy*, and in one *Colgate Comedy Hour* appearance, he interrupted his own song to lampoon black dialect: "Honey child, I'd climb the highest mountain if I could find a pair of shoes that was easier on my feet. 'Cause I know when I got to the other side of that mountain, honey baby, honey lamb, kidney stew, I'd find big, fat, dilapidated you." In a bit on the *Steve Allen Show*, Allen plays a magician and Davis his assistant while the director Orson Welles orchestrates the trick. At one point Welles tells Davis to kneel on the floor. Not missing a beat, Davis tells Allen, "That'll be $2," jokingly referencing a shoeshine.[16] Although such moments were amusing and only a small part of Davis's routines, they harkened back to the "clownish coon."

Furthermore, although Davis mixed comfortably with whites (which was controversial in and of itself), he also came across as gracious, humble, and deferential. For example, in a 1955 interview on Edward R. Murrow's *Person to Person* (CBS 1953–61) program, Davis emphasized his wholesome act and lifestyle. He told Murrow that nightclub audiences "are sick of dirty, smutty material" and promised that his routine would be a "clean" show that entire families could attend. During the tour of his home, as was customary on the show, Davis said his biggest satisfaction was being able to buy a house in Hollywood where he and his grandmother could live. When his grandmother made an appearance, he sweetly kissed her on the cheek.[17] When guest starring on the *What's My Line?* (CBS 1950–67) game show soon thereafter, Davis again mentioned his grandmother, telling the contestants that he regularly watched the program with her. For all of these appearances he was impeccably dressed, used modulated speech, and addressed everyone as "sir" or "ma'am," even when they addressed him as "Sammy."[18] Clearly, his goal was to soften up a national viewing audience, but his methods gave the impression that he was asking for acceptance more than demanding it on his own terms, again harkening to stereotypical images such as the "loyal Tom." Indeed, Davis's determination to integrate into show business struck some observers not as an attempt to break down racial barriers but rather as a desperate personal quest, similar to his conversion to Judaism, to be white.

Also fueling this notion was Davis's string of affairs with white women. His biggest priority was his career—not establishing a stable home life with a wife. He viewed sex as a pleasurable pursuit and a symbol of success. When his conquests included white women, all the better for an ego constantly in fear of being rejected for his race. The women he became serious about during the 1950s tended to be white actresses, each more blonde and illustrious than the last. The one exception was the striking performer Eartha Kitt. Impressed by her sophistication and confidence, Davis asked Kitt to marry him. She, however, considered Davis immature and with low self-esteem—not someone she could marry. The rest of his serious courtships were with white women, including his first love, Helen Gallagher, a nightclub dancer and aspiring actress Davis dated for several months before he met Kitt. After Kitt broke things off, he became involved with the rising singer and actress known as the "pretty, perky Peggy King." This relationship also fell apart. Davis felt it prudent to keep all of his relationships with white women secret for fear that the public and the studio chiefs in Hollywood would disapprove and his career would suffer. Still, his penchant was not lost on anyone.

Davis received extensive and generally adulatory coverage by the black press. Two of the most influential writers for the nationally circulated *Pittsburgh Courier*, Evelyn Cunningham and George Pitts, professed their "love" for Davis and continuously endorsed him as America's greatest entertainer.[19] However, he tended to ruminate on negative remarks and became acutely defensive in his reaction to them. He responded directly to journalists, complained to the white press about the black press, and wrote extensively about his frustrations with "my own people" in his biography *Yes, I Can*, published in 1965. In the book he repeatedly recounts articles that harangued him, such as one that chastised him for not patronizing the black part of town after a show in San Francisco and for hosting all-white parties when he performed in Las Vegas. "Is Sammy ashamed he's a Negro?" the title pointedly asked. Davis also caviled about jokes made at his expense. As one went: "Sammy Davis was sitting in Danny's Hideaway in New York when a guy looks at him and calls out 'Nigger, nigger, nigger!' Sammy Davis jumps up and yells: 'Where, where, where?'"[20] Although Davis's defensiveness could be unappealing, it also seemingly inspired his first forays into the civil rights movement. When Robert Sylvester of the *Daily News* wrote that he had once admired Davis but no longer felt that affection, Davis took action.

In 1955, Davis decided he needed to "completely remake my image" as someone who took pride in his heritage. One strategy was meeting with columnists individually. Davis hoped to at least ensure accuracy in their reporting but also to make enough of a personal connection with them that they would not feel comfortable flinging accusations or questioning his loyalty to his race. One of Davis's associates, Cliff Cochrane, also suggested that he appear more charitable. "We should hit it from another direction, too. You should start appearing at every benefit for every important cause," he advised. "The new image needs that kind of dimension." Indeed, Davis began a slew of benefit performances for charitable causes, such as children's hospitals and civil rights groups, doing as many as ten benefits a week at one point.[21]

Davis could not "completely remake" his image, however, because he was unwilling to cease the behavior that had caused the controversies in the first place. In 1957, he began an illicit romance with the movie star Kim Novak. When gossip columnists heard of the affair, Davis faced unprecedented criticism in the black press, including this damning charge: "Sammy Davis, Jr., once a pride to all Negroes, has become a never-ending source of embarrassment." Citing his "amorous trips gaily from one bedroom to another" and "leering" photos on magazine covers, the paper accused him of "dragging us through the mud along with him." It concluded, "Mr. Davis has never been particularly race conscious but his current scandal [with Novak] displays him as inexcusably *unconscious* of his responsibility as a Negro. Look in the mirror, Sammy. You're still one of us."[22] An even graver threat came from Harry Cohn, the president of Columbia Pictures, where Novak was under contract. Cohn feared a public scandal, and his goons not only persuaded Davis to end the relationship but likely pressured him to marry an African American dancer named Loray White. She agreed to marry Davis with the understanding that it was not a "real" union. They filed for divorce within nine months, and Davis resumed dating white women, including Joan Stuart, an entertainer who looked much like Novak, and May Britt, whom he soon married. Indeed, Davis came to the realization that his reputation as a risk taker was a defining element of his public image and that such a persona could be used constructively.

In fact, Davis became even more of a fixture in the swinging Hollywood scene when he befriended the prominent actor Humphrey Bogart. Bogart was as known for his abhorrence of Hollywood phoniness as for his love of cigarettes and liquor. He and his wife Lauren Bacall kept close company with such like-minded friends as David Niven and his wife Hjordis, John Huston, Angie Dickinson, Sinatra, Judy Garland and her husband Sid Luft, and others. After one particularly debauched weekend in Las Vegas, the teetotaling Bacall took one look at the morning wreckage and proclaimed, "You all look like a god damn rat pack." The name stuck. She and Bogart hosted get-togethers at their home or met with the others at Romanoff's night club in Beverly Hills. Always in pursuit of "witty conversation, conviviality, clowning and generous after-hours libation," it was not unusual for the group to travel together in search of a new locale for their roistering.[23] No African American had run with them until Sinatra and Bogart drew in Davis in 1956. "Frank took me up to the Bogarts' and those were beautiful evenings," Davis remembers. "Bogart could have been colorblind. He got to know a man before he decided if he liked him or not."[24] Bogart's death in 1957 did not spell the demise of the Rat Pack. By 1960, it would be revived and reconfigured under the tutelage of Sinatra, Dean Martin, and Davis. As Davis's reputation as a swinging "cat" expanded, so did his involvement in civil rights activities.

Cold War and industrial realities shaped Davis's deferential persona, and thus his willingness to take on civil rights would set him apart from most African Americans on TV in the mid-to late-1950s. Television, according to one scholar of the medium, simply "would not tolerate militant Afro-American reformers."[25] The specter of Paul Robeson's collapsed career continued to loom, as did that of Hazel Scott. She had been the first black woman to have her own television show in 1950, but the series was canceled after her outspokenness on racial issues brought her before the House of Un-American Activities Committee.[26] When the short-lived drama *Harlem Detective* (WOR-TV 1953–54), the first series to show an interracial pair of detectives, was canceled in 1954, Sidney Poitier and Ossie Davis blamed the political climate for the show's demise. The black lead, William Marshall, had been accused by *Counterattack* of involvement in "Communist-inspired" activities affiliated with civil rights.[27] It is no wonder that other African American TV performers kept their civil rights activities to a minimum. Louis Armstrong, Nat King Cole, and Pearl Bailey all maintained affable personas similar to Davis's, and although they often promoted black interests in the entertainment industry, they rarely worked with civil rights organizations and leaders in an overt fashion. Davis even engaged in a public spat with Armstrong in which he accused the jazz musician of "hypocrisy" for chastising President Dwight D. Eisenhower over the Little Rock crisis while continuing to play before segregated audiences. "I'm just so damned mad," Davis told the press.[28] That Davis would make a public alliance with the movement was not only unusual but further contributed to the "daring" aspect of his public image.

Additional factors certainly played a part in Davis's expanding civil rights activities. Davis was not one to turn down any invitation to perform. Sinatra joked, "He goes to the refrigerator for a snack, opens the door, and when that light hits him, he does forty-five minutes of his act."[29] Furthermore, Davis desired to be perceived as a generous benefactor. He had begun cultivating that image early in his career. For example, on the closing night of his first booking at the Copacabana club in New York, he handed out gold watches engraved with the words "Thanks, Sammy, Jr." to all of the wait captains and key staff attendants.[30] Of course, Davis's friendships with Sinatra, Belafonte, and Poitier influenced him a great deal. Sinatra had earned praise for giving his time and talent to promote racial tolerance as early as 1945. He spoke at a number of high schools in his home state of New Jersey in an effort to end a student-led strike against racial integration. That same year, Sinatra also starred in *The House I Live In*, a short film that promoted tolerance. The film won an honorary Academy Award and a special Golden Globe award in 1946. Standing up against racism was something Sinatra often encouraged Davis to do, as did Belafonte and Poitier. After Davis, Belafonte, and Poitier participated in a civil rights march together in 1957, Belafonte coaxed Davis to lend his talent to even more civil rights events.[31]

Davis proved himself a consistent supporter of the civil rights movement, but his biographers have undervalued his contribution. This is largely a result of focusing too much on the "agreeable" aspects of Davis's public image and underestimating the riskiness of his behavior. According to Wil Haygood, Davis's most recent biographer, his civil rights efforts were largely self-serving and a result of peer pressure from Belafonte. However, Davis continued his activism even after abandoning his short-lived efforts to "prove" his pride in his race. And while Belafonte did encourage his friend's activism, Davis donated his talent to numerous civil rights events without Belafonte's knowledge or intervention. Gerald Early, another Davis scholar, is more forgiving, but he ultimately attributes Davis's charitable ways to guilt.[32] Such emotions are difficult to measure, but even if an element of guilt was at play, it is unlikely that it outweighed the risk Davis knew he was taking—and, at this point, even embracing.

* * *

In the mid to late-1950s, Davis, along with Ossie Davis, Ruby Dee, Poitier, and Belafonte, emerged as one of the most politically active celebrities of the era. He used his public image as an agreeable risk-taker to raise money for civil rights actions and organizations; encourage membership in these organizations; recruit fellow celebrities for fund-raisers and other supportive activities; and broaden the base of liberal support for the movement as a whole. These activities often proved crucial to the organizations they benefited, boosting their coffers and expanding public awareness at opportune times. Although Davis's commitment to the movement exceeded that of most celebrities, his involvement reflected a growing strategy among civil rights organizations to recruit star support. The first to do so was the National Association for the Advancement of Colored People (NAACP).

Fresh off its victory in the 1954 *Brown v. Board of Education* decision, the NAACP was the nation's strongest civil rights organization, but its survival was in jeopardy. The Montgomery Bus Boycott, led by Martin Luther King, Jr., in 1955 and 1956, resulted in a host of restrictions against the NAACP. Segregationist Alabama attorney general John Patterson blamed the organization for bringing public transportation in Montgomery to a standstill. Midway through the boycott, Patterson obtained a court order against the NAACP on the basis that it was financing the "illegal" action. Patterson's request banned most of the NAACP's activities within the state, including fund-raising, dues collection, and the solicitation of new members. When the NAACP resisted a corollary order to surrender its membership and contribution lists to Patterson, the judge issued a $100,000 contempt-of-court fine. During what would become an eight-year legal battle, the Alabama NAACP disbanded. By 1957, the NAACP was entangled in twenty-five separate lawsuits challenging its right to operate in the South.[33] At its annual report meeting in January 1958, the association revealed that in 1957 its membership had decreased by almost forty-eight thousand persons (or 14 percent) as a direct result of "stepped-up legal attacks on Southern units" by Southern governments. With fewer members and more court cases, the association ran a deficit of $52,784 for 1957. This situation lent to a sense of rivalry between the NAACP and King's newly formed Southern Christian Leadership Conference.[34] Whatever fissures existed between the two organizations, they nevertheless presented a united front to the public and cosponsored a number of important events that drew celebrities, including Davis, into the movement.

The Madison Square Garden rally marked the first of such events. The rally was organized by a newly formed group called In Friendship that brought together representatives of various labor and civil rights organizations, including the NAACP. Chaired by the longtime labor leader and activist A. Philip Randolph, In Friendship was originally founded to provide financial help to blacks in the South who had been victims of segregationist violence or economic reprisals due to their involvement in the civil rights movement. As the Montgomery Bus Boycott dragged on and the campaign against the NAACP intensified, In Friendship reached out to King and to the NAACP as well. Randolph envisioned an event "to arouse public opinion to what is happening in the South today." He felt that "encouragement must be given to Negroes in Alabama, Mississippi, and South Carolina victimized by 'the squeeze'" and was worried that "the drive on the high level to alienate the NAACP from the people and discredit the organization may gain headway." Randolph suggested a mass parade down Fifth Avenue and a huge rally in Madison Square Garden in New York as a way to bring attention to the plight of Southern activists and to allow the NAACP to regain its status. In Friendship established a special committee to publicize the affair.[35]

The role of show business personalities in the Madison Square Garden rally was relatively minimal. The promotional materials for the event mentioned that "stars of stage, screen, radio, and television" would provide "special music and entertainment," but no stars were identified. Instead, civil rights activists and political leaders were highlighted as the main draw. These individuals included Autherine Lucy, the first black student to attend the University of Alabama (she was expelled on her third day of classes); King (who came from the Montgomery Bus Boycott to attend the event); the president of the Regional Council of Negro Leadership in Mississippi, Dr. T. R. M. Howard; and Gus Courts, a victim of a racially motivated murder attempt. At the end of one flyer was this proud announcement: "For the first time together with Eleanor Roosevelt, A. Philip Randolph, Roy Wilkins, Congressman Adam C. Powell (D-NY), and Rev. James Robinson."[36] The stars seemed to be merely providing the dessert to what would be a serious meal of political speechmaking and religious oratories.

Even if the celebrities did not receive much advance promotion, they entertained the crowd for about one-third of the three-and-half-hour affair. They sang and danced and told jokes between speeches, breaking up the program and alternating light-hearted and serious subjects. Those in attendance included Davis, Belafonte, Poitier, Pearl Bailey, and Tallulah Bankhead. The irrepressible Bankhead was the only star identified by name on the event program, and it is not clear why organizers focused on her so singularly. It is possible that she was the only star from whom the organizers had received a commitment. More likely, however, is that Bankhead's unusual position as both a prominent Broadway performer and the daughter of a powerful Democratic Southern family made her particularly valuable to program organizers. Indeed, she "stole the show" when she kissed Rosa Parks and Lucy, and proclaimed to the crowd in her distinct drawl, "I'm a Bankhead and there have been generations of Bankheads in Alabama, but I'm not proud of what's happening there today."[37] For his part, Davis not only did bits from his usual nightclub routine but also brought much of the cast from *Mr. Wonderful* to perform with him.

As one of the first occasions on which celebrities lent their talents to the cause of civil rights, the Madison Square Garden rally was a learning experience for social activists trying to use these entertainers' artistic gifts. Eighteen thousand supporters attended the event, and In Friendship raised $7,000.[38] The entertainers certainly contributed to the positive atmosphere and the results. However, organizers of the rally ran up against what would be a continuous dilemma: dealing with the complexities of show business, including the regulations of performers unions. Even if an artist was willing to perform for free, union regulations may not have allowed him to do so. When In Friendship sent out mass invitations asking entertainers to participate in the rally, an "appalled" American Guild of Variety Artists brought action to restrict the number of performers involved in the event. The influential radio talk show host Barry Gray then condemned the NAACP, both on his radio program and in his newspaper column in the *New York Post*, for its "benefit practices which take free from the performer the only thing he has to sell, namely his talent."[39] The NAACP defended it actions, arguing that the rally was not a benefit show per se but a testimonial occasion to which no admission was charged.[40] Nevertheless, this would not be the last time that union statutes hampered NAACP attempts to amass celebrity support.

Despite the controversy over union contracts, neither In Friendship nor the NAACP shied away from inviting celebrities to participate in future events, and African American performers played a more prominent role in the 1957 Prayer Pilgrimage for Freedom to Washington, DC, the next major civil rights demonstration to follow the Madison Square Garden rally. Again organized by In Friendship, King, Wilkins, and Randolph agreed that the purpose of the event would be to support the Eisenhower administration's proposed voting rights bill. In contrast to the program for the Madison Square Garden rally, which mostly included civil rights activists and political leaders, the speakers for the Prayer Pilgrimage generally consisted of preachers, such as Mordecai Johnson, William Holmes Borders, and Fred Shuttlesworth, or celebrities, including Ruby Dee, Belafonte, Poitier, and Sammy Davis, Jr., who departed from New York City on a special freedom train to attend the ceremonies.[41] The gathering at the Lincoln Memorial attracted thirty thousand supporters and turned into a high-spirited affair that lasted nearly three hours and ended with King leading the crowd in a chant demanding the ballot.

Historians disagree on the overall effectiveness of the Prayer Pilgrimage, but at the very least it did establish a concrete relationship between the civil rights movement and its small cadre of celebrity support. Belafonte and Dee had once been somewhat wary of King. Dee and her husband Ossie Davis had first learned of the reverend during the Montgomery Bus Boycott. Although they were impressed with the results of the campaign, they feared that King's philosophy of nonviolence was "dangerous nonsense."[42] Belafonte had been similarly suspicious due to his long-standing hostility to authority and general uneasiness around preachers.[43] However, once they met and worked with him, Davis, Dee, and Belafonte were convinced that King could be a powerful force in the movement. King, in turn, realized how useful celebrities, and Sammy Davis, Jr., in particular, could be in achieving his goals. According to Belafonte, it was during the Prayer Pilgrimage that King realized that of all of the African American celebrities on the program, Davis had the easiest rapport with whites and thus had the biggest fund-raising potential. Thereafter, King frequently encouraged Belafonte to bring Davis on board for various events.

It was the NAACP, however, that reaped the immediate gains of Davis's newfound activism, largely because the organization already had an established fund-raising mechanism in place. Between 1945 and 1954, the NAACP developed a Freedom Fund to raise the necessary capital to initiate lawsuits on questions of labor discrimination and school segregation.[44] In developing the fund, the NAACP turned to several prominent African Americans to give it additional glamour and exposure. One of the organization's most fruitful partnerships was with Jackie Robinson, who had retired from baseball and expanded his political activities. Robinson chaired the NAACP's Freedom Fund Drive in 1957 and served on the organization's board until 1967. The drive included such programs as membership campaigns and fund-raising banquets, and Robinson worked extensively with both. The NAACP also established a public relations department under the direction of Henry Lee Moon to enhance its image in the face of the Southern campaign to discredit the organization. Moon drew upon the success of the Freedom Fund to organize a speakers bureau, conduct an advertising campaign in major newspapers, and publish pamphlets and brochures about the organization's goals, philosophy, challenges, and methods.[45] When the NAACP began collaborating with Davis, it was part of the organization's overall effort to develop its Freedom Fund and enhance its image through celebrity partnerships.

Immediately after the Prayer Pilgrimage, the NAACP recruited Davis to lead a drive selling "Life Memberships" for the organization. Having already bought a membership himself, Davis was featured in a promotional pamphlet designed for general audiences. It read, "Join the Stars— Sammy Davis—Take Out a $500 Life Membership and play a stellar role in the Fight for Freedom."[46] Davis also signed off on a "dear friend" letter designed to appeal to his fellow artists. Referring to the Southern campaign to outlaw the NAACP, Davis conveyed that the organization was "fighting for its own life" and was "facing a crisis." Telling the recipients, "We artists have set an inspiring example of tearing down race barriers in our own field," he then argued, "We must put our time, our money, our whole-hearted efforts on the line with our conscience." He appealed to his artistic colleagues to take out their own Life Memberships and to consider giving benefit performances.[47] The NAACP was thrilled with the results of the campaign. One staff person told Davis that the news of his "membership and great interest in the NAACP has spread like wildfire!" Indeed, the national office was bombarded with requests for Davis to make appearances at local branches.[48] The excitement surrounding Davis's Life Membership drive generated ideas for even grander fund-raising ventures.

Davis's popularity with its membership inspired the NAACP to attempt a week-long benefit concert series in the autumn of 1957 that would include Davis, as well as six other renowned performers. Originally conceived to be held at the Apollo Theater in Harlem with a rotating bill of artists, this would be the biggest fund-raising effort as of yet for the NAACP. It differed from both the Madison Square Garden rally and the Prayer Pilgrimage in that not only would entertainers be the main draw, but they would explicitly be raising money. Having learned about some of the difficult procedural criteria of the performers' unions during the earlier rally, the NAACP received the permission of the Theatre Authority for the show. A branch of Actors' Equity, a union for stage performers, the Theatre Authority was founded to protect artists involved in charitable causes. Having its seal of approval allowed the NAACP to request the participation of any performer it chose and shielded it from the kind of criticism it had received after the rally for "taking advantage" of artists.[49]

Even with this hurdle cleared, the NAACP still faced a number of setbacks when planning the Apollo Theatre benefit—particularly due to the challenge of finding artists who were willing to perform free of charge. The NAACP was unable to recruit enough performers to stage the kind of show it envisioned. It is likely because of this dearth of volunteer entertainers that the benefit was postponed until the spring of 1958. Even with an additional six months to plan, however, the only major star the NAACP could confirm was Davis, and its only other lead was the jazz musician "Count" Basie, who, rumor had it, would appear in one show. When the NAACP contacted Basie's manager, however, the organization learned that he expected to be paid $12,500 for his performance. Somewhat desperately, the NAACP appealed to Robinson, asking him to intervene with Basie on its behalf. The athlete reported, however, that he "couldn't do anything about Count Basie."[50] At this point, the NAACP found it necessary to revise its plans for the benefit.

The NAACP finally announced its plan for the Apollo Theatre benefit in April 1958. The event would take place over the course of a week, as it was originally conceived, but instead of seven different headliners alternating their performances, only one artist would perform night after night and for free each time: Davis. The NAACP would pay the costs of the show, and the Apollo Theatre would donate the proceeds from the ticket sales to the NAACP. Although the NAACP would pay for Davis's expenses, he would not receive a salary for his performances. At that point, filming for *Porgy and Bess* had begun, but Davis was granted an "extension" to reporting for rehearsals due to the engagement.[51] Appearing on the bill with him would be the singer Fran Warren, the comedian Redd Foxx, and the dance teams of Coles & Atkins and Hortense Allen, as well as Davis's twenty-six piece band.[52] None of these artists, however, planned on donating their salaries to the NAACP. Therefore, what the organization had originally hoped to be a group fund-raising effort by a bevy of black artists devolved into a series of solo philanthropic performances by Davis alone.

The NAACP grossed $18,071 for the shows, but had considerable costs to cover, too. Those included the bill for Davis's expenses and his staff salaries, as well as the payment to his band, which totaled $10,172; the fees for the other performers on the bill, which totaled $3,300; a $900 sum paid to the Theatre Authority, and $73 in miscellaneous expenses. Therefore, the accounting indicated that the NAACP would make about $3,600 from the benefit. Frank Schiffman, the owner of the Apollo Theatre, donated an additional $1,400, making the total profits from the benefit about $5,000.[53] The NAACP considered this a respectable sum for its first big benefit, especially in light of the problems the organization had experienced during its planning.

However, the organizers soon became agitated when faced with what they considered unreasonable demands. Local 802 of the Associated Musicians of Greater New York billed the theatre an additional $1,140 in overtime expenses for the band for what Schiffman and the NAACP considered "technicalities of the union contract."[54] Then, Davis's secretary sent the NAACP a bill for over $2,000 from the Waldorf-Astoria Hotel, where Davis had stayed during the week of the benefit. Because of union regulations, Schiffman was forced to pay the overtime costs. The NAACP flatly refused, however, to pay Davis's hotel bill. Given that the organization had already paid $5,000 toward his expenses, the bill simply seemed excessive. Plus, paying it would have reduced the net income from the event to about $1,700. The NAACP protested: "none of us," including the star, "who gave so unstintingly of himself on our behalf," would "be willing to accept this as the net return to the NAACP from Sammy Davis' week at the Apollo."[55] All told, the NAACP made $3,859 from the Apollo Theatre benefit.

Although Schiffman and the NAACP were disappointed with the financial returns, they were generally pleased with the benefit and saw it as a good test run for future events. Schiffman indicated that he wanted to "tackle a project similar to this in the not too-distant-future," and believed they could "learn from the totally unexpected demands which were made upon us."[56] There certainly did not seem to be any hard feelings between the NAACP and Davis. At the last of his concerts that week, Wilkins presented Davis with a certificate of merit "in recognition of his great talent."[57] A week later, when the NAACP realized that its proceeds would be short of what had been calculated, sentiments had not changed. Wilkins's assistant, John Morsell, told Davis, "Although there had been some suggestion before the week started that the net return financially might be a good deal larger than it was, I do not believe that anyone here was in any sense disappointed." He continued, "Our return was far from negligible, and I think it is unquestionably true that you sowed more good will for the Association in what you said and did than could have been purchased for many times that amount."[58] As a relatively controversial organization, the NAACP needed any "good will" it could get.

While the concert series is not mentioned in civil rights histories or biographies of Davis, it was important. The NAACP was the first civil rights organization to intentionally cultivate celebrity activism for the purpose of fund-raising and public relations, and other civil rights groups would soon launch similar letter-writing campaigns and benefit shows. Equally important, the benefit undermines the prevailing belief that Davis was a half-hearted supporter of the civil rights movement. Some observers have portrayed him as a belated and disinterested activist whose involvement was driven by peer pressure. Haygood has been particularly harsh on this account, characterizing Davis's relationship to the movement as merely "glimpsing—unlike Poitier and Belafonte, who seemed spiritually invested in it." He claims that Belafonte "browbeat" Davis into social activism and mocks his participation in the Prayer Pilgrimage as "a peculiar sight" in which Davis snapped "photographs in a tireless effort to fit in." Haygood contemptuously concludes, "Forevermore, [Davis] would be considered a latecomer to the movement."[59] This perspective is ill-informed and unfair. Davis devoted a week of his time to do the Apollo benefit when no other performer would, and he did so in 1958, well before the civil rights movement had gained traction. For this, he received a "public salute" by the *Chicago Daily Defender* as "the top of the stars" willing to aid benefit causes.[60]

*　*　*

By 1960, Davis's performing career and lifestyle had become inextricably intertwined, both charged with racial and political themes. Davis continued to work with the civil rights movement and made new forays into electoral politics. In the meantime, the Rat Pack, revived under Sinatra's leadership, took the nation by storm. Davis's involvement in the Rat Pack solidified his image with the public as someone who was both a "cool cat" and an effective activist, a captivating combination matched by few celebrities during this time period, but one loaded with personal and political hazards.

Reflecting his rising status in Hollywood, Davis successfully pushed for several guest-starring appearances in dramatic roles on television westerns that carried subtle civil rights messages. In a 1959 episode of *Zane Grey Theater* (CBS 1956–61), the narrator asserts that the all-black 10th Cavalry unit "was one of the most respected units" on the American frontier, but Davis's character Corporal Smith struggles with the contradictions of defending a country that discriminates. His unit receives a mission that involves fooling a group of Apache warriors. "Never figured they'd suspect us. Too important," says his commanding officer, alluding to their lower status in the army. When an Apache tells Smith, "You are fools to fight for a land that does not want you," Smith is unconvinced that the warrior has his best interest in mind. Nevertheless, the point about American racism is clear.[61] Likewise, when Davis played a cowboy named Willie Shay in a 1961 episode of *Lawman* (ABC 1958–62), a cohort of white cattlemen kill his cherished steer Blue Boss. A devastated Shay is not mollified that the perpetrator is arrested on the charge of destruction of property. "Blue Boss wasn't property to me. . . . He was my partner. Look, and don't tell me nothin' about property. I know somethin' about that," he says, referencing the legal classification for slavery.[62] Only two other black actors made guest appearances on TV's most popular genre: Rex Ingram in *Black Saddle* in 1959, and Frank Silvera in *Johnny Ringo* in 1960. The presence of African Americans on television had actually declined since the 1950s. Therefore, while Davis's television appearances merely made commentary on historic racism, they pushed television culture and contributed to his daring image.

Davis also began campaigning for Democratic candidates at this time, although he was not particularly partisan or inherently loyal to any one party. One scholar characterizes the entertainers' politics as "personal and psychological," meaning Davis's devotion to a candidate had less to do with his support for specific policy ideas than with his personal connections to the individual.[63] The first important politician to take an interest in Davis was Vice President Richard Nixon, who made a point of meeting with the performer in 1954 before he was a major star. Davis was surprised and pleased to learn that Nixon and his wife Pat had made arrangements to attend a performance at the Copacabana club. The couple visited him backstage after the show, and they all hit it off, making enduring impressions on one another.[64] But it was the Democratic Party that Davis was working for during this period, perhaps due to the influence of Sinatra, whose family had long been supportive of the Democrats, or of Jule Styne, the producer of *Mr. Wonderful*, with whom Davis grew close in 1956, the year his politicking blossomed. Davis hobnobbed with Senator John F. Kennedy and his wife, Jacqueline, at one New York City party, and attended another for the Democratic presidential candidate Adlai Stevenson. He performed a number, posed for pictures, and signed autographs, adding some glamour to the Stevenson party in a fashion he would replicate at any number of political events.[65] Two years later, Davis and Judy Garland led a victory rally for governor-elect Edmund G. "Pat" Brown in Los Angeles.[66] It wasn't until Kennedy ran for president in 1960, however, that Davis became a committed campaigner for a candidate seeking office.

In an unusual conflation between show business and electoral politics, Davis's role as a Kennedy campaigner originated at the Sands Hotel in Las Vegas. He, along with Martin, Joey Bishop, and Peter Lawford, had gathered there in the fall of 1959 at the behest of Sinatra, who had a 9 percent ownership stake in the hotel. Sinatra had cast them in his new film *Ocean's Eleven*, and made arrangements for the five men to perform twenty shows in the Sands' Copacabana Room in the evenings after shooting scenes during the day.[67] Loose, spontaneous, and silly, the highly entertaining nightclub act was so popular that the film virtually became an afterthought. People from all over the country flocked to Las Vegas to catch a show and to mingle with the stars in the casino. The act was so popular that they continued well beyond the original twenty-show stand and performed until 1963. The Rat Pack was reborn. Whereas during the Bogart years, their existence had largely been a private joke among themselves, during the filming of *Ocean's Eleven*, the Rat Pack became an enduring cultural icon, with Sinatra, Martin, and Davis as its principle figures.

Their shows so charmed audiences because of their appealing combination of 1950s traditionalism and 1960s progressivism. Sinatra had made his distaste for rock-and-roll quite apparent, and the group's 1940s-era ballads went over well with their middle-aged audiences. Indeed, the Rat Pack itself was middle-aged, with Davis the youngest at thirty-four and Sinatra in his mid-forties. Although Davis was still incredibly spry, the group's performances did not include the physically controversial moves of other artists, such as Elvis's hip swivels or Little Richard's shrieks. Therefore, the Rat Pack's routine was old-fashioned enough to draw suburban couples from across America who preferred the nightclub atmosphere of reserved seating, linen tablecloths, late suppers, and chilled champagne to rowdy concert halls filled with screaming teenagers. Despite its traditional charm, the Rat Pack was not stodgy or stuffy. Since the men were such close friends, their performances had a relaxed and easy feel atypical of most stage shows. They could interrupt and insult one another without fear of offense, and their shared sense of humor gave the impression that they were carrying on as usual rather than presenting a rehearsed production. The color of Davis's skin made the apparent closeness of the Rat Pack revolutionary. Although black and white entertainers had certainly performed together onstage before the Sands performances took place, never before in America had they interacted with one another so intimately and informally.[68] Nor had a group of integrated entertainers so willingly joked about racial matters in front of audiences primarily consisting of white patrons, audiences that did not entirely share the group's liberal approach.

The Rat Pack's direct racial and ethnic humor cut in a variety of ways and left out no one. With two Italians, one white Jew, one black Jew, and a WASP, the group had copious material. On some occasions, the jokes could be self-deprecating. For example, in order to distinguish himself from Martin, Sinatra introduced himself as "the other Italian." Midway through the show, Sinatra marched across stage while banging a bass drum that read "Eat at Puccini's" across its side in a shameless act of Italian-American promotion. In another bit, Martin asked Bishop, "Did you ever see a Jew jitsu?" Bishop, who was playing a waiter, told the two Italians to cool it "because I got my own group—the Matzia."[69] In a similarly self-effacing fashion, Davis joked, "I represent the NAACP at these meetings, as well as B'nai B'rith." When the laughter died down, he continued, "I'm glad a few of my people showed up tonight."[70]

As willing as they were to make fun of themselves, the group ribbed one another even more enthusiastically, often interrupting each other's solo routines to do so. This teasing almost invariably rested on ethnic humor. During one of his vocal numbers, Martin sang about "Jewsicles" until Davis stormed on stage, demanding that he "be fair." How would Martin like it "if I sang about WASPsicles?" he asked. Martin raised his hands in defense and told Davis to "hold it." When Davis retorted, "I'm not gonna hold it, Whitey!" Sinatra, who was trying to play peacemaker, dissolved in laughter at the epithet. To be sure, Davis often turned the tables on his race-baiting cronies. During one show, he interrupted Sinatra's solo with a stage whisper to Martin, "He sings pretty good for a white guy." And his cohorts capitalized on their white identity to garner laughs. To kick off one show, Martin tore back a sheet from their standard prop—the rolling bar cart. When the sheet landed on Davis's head, Martin suggested gleefully: "Let's start the meeting," presumably referring to a gathering of the Ku Klux Klan. Davis's tiny size made it even easier to taunt him, and his pals found ways to combine racial humor with physical comedy. During one of his more crass introductions, Martin coaxed the "little colored bloke" to sing a number. In another infamous bit, Martin, whose height reached almost six feet, hoisted Davis in his arms and presented him to the audience. "I'd like to thank the NAACP for this wonderful trophy," Martin chortled while Davis shrieked. He finally demanded to be set down.[71]

As irreverent as the Rat Pack often was about racial matters, it could also take a firm stance on both race and politics. When the Vegas moguls carped about Davis spending time in the casinos, Sinatra made it clear that Davis was in his inner circle and would go anywhere he wanted. Such grumblings grew stronger after Kennedy, now a Democratic presidential contender, attended a show in February 1960. Attracted to the glamour and sensuality of the Vegas nightlife, Kennedy considered the Rat Pack like-minded companions. Equally as smitten, Sinatra encouraged his friends to campaign for the candidate. Lawford, who was married to Kennedy's sister Patricia, was already active in the campaign. As Kennedy's popularity increased, Southern Democrats connected to the candidate openly deplored Sinatra's and Davis's friendship, worried about the possible negative effect it would have on the campaign, especially the connection with the "Brother-in-Lawford." Again, Sinatra brushed them off and stood firm in his association with Davis.[72]

Whenever Davis performed outside of Las Vegas, campaign officials gave him a list of rallies and cocktail parties to attend at which he mingled with guests and usually performed, and he attended functions in a total of twenty cities for Senator Kennedy. Davis was thrilled with being able to "add to the excitement that was building around the figure of JFK." He then compared notes with the rest of the Rat Pack, who participated in similar events all over the country.[73] When they all attended the Democratic National Convention together in Los Angeles in July 1960, Davis remembered thinking, "My presence on that stage brought me the extra satisfaction of knowing that through television and the thousands of newspapers focused on the moment, millions of people from Los Angeles to Moscow who'd been exposed to the race riots in Little Rock were also seeing democracy proving its definition." In the next moment, however, the Mississippi delegation attempted to boo him off the stage.[74]

Davis continued to be a lightning rod for controversy, becoming engaged to the Swedish actress May Britt that summer. Brit was tall, with long blonde hair, and she and Davis were a study in contrasts in both appearance and lifestyle. In a classic case of opposites attracting, the two fell madly in love. News of their impending wedding provoked a passionate public response. *Life* magazine gave the couple positive coverage and bemoaned that Nazi protesters had assembled outside a London restaurant where they had been dining to protest their engagement.[75] When four Nazi picketers attempted to stage a similar demonstration in Los Angeles, a larger crowd assembled to disperse them. "Mob Routs Nazis at Davis Show" proclaimed the *Los Angeles Mirror*.[76] Furthermore, Davis was pleased to learn that the *Pittsburgh Courier*'s Evelyn Cunningham endorsed their union in her column.[77] Despite these signs of acceptance, the negative backlash far outweighed the positive. Davis and Britt received a deluge of hate mail, some critics promising violent reprisals. After learning about a series of bomb threats at the theatre at which he was headlining, Davis hired extra security and even began taking a loaded gun on stage with him. He also began carrying an umbrella with a retractable knife tip when he was offstage.[78]

In the meantime, complaints about Davis's role in the Kennedy campaign intensified. A newspaper clipping arrived in the mail that portrayed a caricature of Davis in a two-panel cartoon. In the first panel was a drawing of Davis as a butler, grinning and serving a platter of fried chicken and watermelon to Kennedy. In the second panel, he was sitting at the table eating the food with him. The caption read, "Will it still be the *White* House?" Adding to the tension was the political commentary questioning Sinatra's agreement to be Davis's best man in his wedding ceremony. Newspaper columnists weighed in with such remarks as "Public opinion experts say that when Frank Sinatra appears at pal Sammy Davis, Jr.'s interracial marriage it will cost Kennedy as many votes, maybe more, as the crooner has been able to swing via his successful JFK rallies."[79] Davis received hate mail about the issue as well. One letter read, "Dear Nigger Bastard, I see Frank Sinatra is going to be the best man at your abortion. Well, it's good to know the kind of people supporting Kennedy before it's too late."[80] This type of commentary led Davis to postpone his wedding until after the election.

Davis's upcoming wedding was not the only source of controversy; his association with the Rat Pack also generated criticism, as some observers felt that he appeared to be a mascot to, as opposed to an equal within, the group. Increasingly, Davis's assistants, other comedians, and the public thought that he too frequently allowed himself to be the butt of racial jokes and believed that he too easily laughed off the barbs. This tendency led the comedian Jack Carter to quip, "Sammy cares about his people." Long pause. "And black people, too."[81] Tina Sinatra defended the dynamic between Davis and her father. She argued, "It was always clear to me that Sammy's ethnic humor—however incorrect by today's standards—was meant to poke fun at bigotry, not endorse it. In real life, Dad was offended by racial jokes and epithets, and wouldn't stand for anyone using them in his presence."[82] Nevertheless, Davis's admiration for Sinatra was so wholly obvious that it exacerbated a sense of his inferiority within the group. Thus, one scholar argues that Davis served as "the circumscribed black man in the Rat Pack, a status which allowed Sinatra and Martin to playfully highlight his color while piously denigrating racism."[83] In an even more cynical view, the film historian Donald Bogle says, "In an era in which token niggers were popping up in offices throughout America, he became the 'showcase nigger' for white stars."[84]

Davis's closest confidants were also uneasy about his relationship with the Rat Pack leader. Even though Britt was friendly with Sinatra, she complained about her husband's genuflection to the star. When Davis tried explaining to her that he would always be "the kid" to Sinatra, she retorted that she did not feel comfortable seeing her spouse treated like a kid. He admitted, "I knew that by 'kid' she really meant 'lackey.' And I knew too that I sometimes gave that impression when I was with him. But that was my doing, not his."[85] Indeed, Davis confessed, "I was his little mascot. But I didn't look upon myself as his little mascot, not when this man was fighting for my motion picture salary, not when he was fighting to get me billings."[86] Davis's personal secretary Shirley Rhodes claims that Belafonte and Poitier also resented their relationship. "Harry, Sidney, and Sammy were very close, but they took umbrage at Frank putting his arms around Sammy. They felt Sammy had defected to Frank," she remarked.[87]

Whatever the controversies, the animosities, or the exasperation about Davis and the Rat Pack, there is no denying their enormous popularity with the American public. Even those who did not have the resources to see the Sands performances could witness the antics of the Rat Pack, albeit in tamer fashion. *The Frank Sinatra Timex Show* (ABC), a series of four television episodes hosted by Sinatra and on which the rest of the Rat Pack made guest appearances, aired between the autumn of 1959 and the spring of 1960. Similar to the Vegas routine, the *Timex Show* involves copious vocal and dance numbers punctuated by dry, witty banter. The men are entirely sober, and they only moderately indulge in their characteristic ethnic humor. But the shows still had the same overall feel, especially in one episode in which Davis and Bishop appeared. One of the funniest bits involves Davis doing his trademark impersonations, but every time he opens his mouth, Bishop does the impression from offstage before Davis can speak. Then Sinatra walks onstage moving his lips to Bishop's voice. Bishop asks, "What are you doing, Frank? I'm doing the impression; what are you walking out and taking a bow for?" Davis laughs but then tells them to leave the stage. "There'll be no more kibitzing," he pronounces in Yiddish slang. He then proceeds with his routine, ending in an imitation of Kingfish from *Amos 'n' Andy*. Davis loudly declares, "If all the women in Texas look like your mama, Sapphire, the Lone Ranger is gonna be alone for a lo-ong time!"[88]

Even more reminiscent of the group's live performances was the film that brought them all to Vegas in the first place: *Ocean's Eleven*. Released in August 1960, the film possessed all of the elements of the Sands shows. The fundamental nature of the characters and the plot reflect the traditional/progressive dynamic of the Rat Pack's appeal. The eleven main characters all flew in the 82nd Airborne during World War II and were highly decorated soldiers, reflecting traditional values. Yet they are an integrated outfit—Davis's character even goes so far as to bemoan racism in the South; they enjoy a swinger lifestyle, replete with a steady stream of liquor and fawning women; and they rob all seven of the casinos in Las Vegas with little discussion of the immorality of their theft. The plot revolves around this heist, but the film still follows the basic performance structure of the Sands shows: Sinatra is the leader, both Davis and Martin sing musical numbers, there is constant drinking and smoking, and the comrades engage in playful banter, including their customary ethnic humor. At one point, all of the men darken their faces with grease paint to resemble trash collectors, everyone except Davis. "I knew this color would come in handy one day," he chuckles. When Lawford cracks, "Hey . . . how do you get this stuff off," Davis responds with a passive-aggressive laughing growl. The characters also use the same lingo customary of the Sands shows with such slang as "Clyde" (loser), "hey-hey" (sex), "Charley" (chum), and a constant barrage of "Baby"s. Also typical of the live performances were cameo appearances by celebrity friends. Comedian Red Skelton and actress Shirley MacLaine both make memorable turns in the film.[89]

By the end of 1960, the American public was well acquainted with the Rat Pack, and it swooned in its approval of the group. Sinatra was the biggest star in America, and the Rat Pack was on its way to becoming Hollywood's most powerful syndicate of talent. One commentator remembers that the group had become a myth in their own time. "And even if only a fraction of it were true, what a myth!" she gushes. Another observer succinctly summed up their appeal: "The Rat Pack is the Mount

Rushmore of men having fun."[90] If a group this popular and influential could be convinced to devote its time and talent to the civil rights movement, the payoff could be boundless. Belafonte put aside any discomfort he may have had about Davis and his gang to help organize just such an event.

*   *   *

Davis and the Rat Pack pioneered a new type of celebrity activism for the civil rights movement by performing in high-profile benefit shows to interracial audiences. These performances generated record-breaking profits and drew additional celebrities to the cause. The Rat Pack's participation evolved out of Davis's involvement with the NAACP and the Urban League, but soon came to include the Southern Christian Leadership Conference (SCLC) as well.

In August 1960, the Chicago Urban League staged a musical gala at Comiskey Park to benefit its civil rights programs. Originally conceived to be a "jazz festival," the program changed markedly after Davis agreed to be on the bill. He had been involved with the Urban League since at least January 1960, when a service club had honored him at a charity ball for the Los Angeles chapter.[91] He then agreed to serve as chairman of the Chicago Urban League Financial Council, a position that led him to perform at the jazz festival. The jazz artists, who included Dizzy Gillespie and the Cannonball Adderly Quintet, ended up functioning as warm-up material for Davis and his "guests": Sinatra and Lawford, as well as the television actors Peter Brown from *Lawman* and Edd "Kookie" Byrnes from *77 Sunset Strip* (ABC 1958–64).[92] Their participation boosted sales so unexpectedly that Urban League officials installed more speakers twice, opened two additional seating sections, and, at the last minute, placed seats and sound horns on the field itself to accommodate the ever-growing crowd. All told, approximately fifteen thousand people attended the concert, and the Chicago Urban League raised $250,000. It is not clear if this figure represents gross or net profits. Nevertheless, the funds generated by Davis and his "guests" far outweighed their costs, because they all performed free of charge. Davis's efforts won him an Urban League Citation of Merit.[93]

This festival demonstrated how profitable a "crossover" event could be. Whereas the Apollo Theatre benefit primarily showcased black performers at a historically black venue, the Urban League festival offered an integrated show at a baseball stadium that had long accommodated both white and black fans. That the profits from the festival far outweighed those of the Apollo benefit not only demonstrated the popularity of the Rat Pack but showed that the time was ripe for movement organizers to build an interracial coalition. The enormous success of the Urban League festival did not go unnoticed by King or his advisors, who hoped that the SCLC could undergo its own transformation from a tiny, regional organization with little financial support outside of the black church to a large, national organization with a solid and broadly-based financial structure.

In mid-1960, this goal seemed rather far-fetched. The SCLC's budget that year was a mere $60,000; it employed only three people in its administrative office; no permanent fund-raising apparatus existed; and it was in danger of being overshadowed by the sit-ins that had begun earlier that spring and inspired the popular new Student Nonviolent Coordinating Committee (SNCC). Despite the fact that King was relatively well-known, the Reverend Wyatt Tee Walker, a colleague at SCLC, said that rallies generated only about $1,000 or $1,500 at that time. The SCLC, says one historian, was still "a blueprint for an organization."[94] In order to graduate from the minor leagues to become a real political player, the SCLC needed to raise more capital, expand its staff, and gain a higher national profile. Widening its base of support to include Northern and white Americans would help achieve these goals.

Belafonte, who was working in close collaboration with King and the SCLC at that point, explains why the organization reached out to Davis in its expansion. "America watched Sammy Davis, Jr. People tuned into Sammy. If you told people, 'Sammy Davis, Jr., will be at this or that benefit,' you got more people coming," he said.[95] And if Davis brought his Rat Pack cronies to a particular event with him, then the audiences grew even bigger. Within a few weeks of the Urban League Festival, King asked Davis to stage a similar event for the SCLC. Davis recalls that King visited him at his home in Los Angeles to impress upon him the dire straits in which the organization found itself. "We're hurting for money. We can hardly function," he told Davis. "$100,000 would pay our debts and give us some breathing room."[96] Davis agreed to produce the show and again recruited his friends to help. He approached Sinatra, Martin, Lawford, and Bishop in the Sands Hotel steam room, a favorite setting for off-hours relaxation and hijinks. The four men agreed to be in the show. They called it "Tribute to Martin Luther King, Jr."

When the SCLC received confirmation that the Rat Pack would perform, the organization made the most of their participation. Unlike the Urban League, who could reveal Davis's "mystery guests" only at the last minute, the SCLC was able to advertise the group's involvement well ahead of time. Davis presided over a high-profile press conference announcing the affair, in which he promoted the performers and the cause to a prestigious audience. Among those present was New York governor Nelson Rockefeller.[97] The SCLC established the Committee to Aid the Southern Freedom Struggle as the organizational structure for the benefit. Starting with the stationary printed expressly for all correspondence related to the event, the committee used every opportunity to highlight their collaboration with the Rat Pack. "Frank Sinatra/Dean Martin/Sammy Davis, Jr./Joey Bishop/Peter Lawford in a tribute to Martin Luther King, Jr.," the letterhead boldly read. The SCLC promoted the Rat Pack's involvement not just because of their popularity but also because of what the interracial group represented. Belafonte, along with the poet Maya Angelou, cochaired the committee. He told the press that the gang's support of King had "vast significance. It shows a broader, more outspoken liberal front in America," he argued. "Frank Sinatra has millions of followers who cannot help but be impressed and influenced."[98]

The committee's efforts to secure sponsors for the King Tribute further illustrate its attempt to broaden the SCLC's reach. Starting with only twelve patrons, four of whom were on the committee, Belafonte and Angelou worked to expand their sponsorship list in the weeks leading up to the event. In early December, they sent scores of telegrams and letters to labor leaders, as well as to "political and cultural figures" known to be sympathetic to civil rights.[99] By mid-January the list of sponsors had grown to sixty-seven. Of these individuals, seventeen were artists or somehow involved in show business, seventeen were labor leaders, fifteen held political office, and seven were religious authorities. In terms of their racial background, fifty of the sponsors were white, and fourteen were black (the racial identity of three sponsors is unclear). The most well-known sponsors included Steve Allen, composer Leonard Bernstein, American Federation of Labor and Congress of Industrial Organizations president George Meany, and former First Lady Eleanor Roosevelt.[100] Belafonte explained that the committee "felt that it was important to get prominent personalities in America to identify themselves with Dr. King and his objectives and to support the demonstrations."[101] As the number of sponsoring personalities grew, the committee showcased their names in the left-hand margins of the stationary. By publishing the names of the diverse group of leaders, the committee hoped to use their fame and authority to draw even more supporters into the fold and to build the liberal coalition of blacks and whites King believed necessary to the success of the movement.

The choice of Carnegie Hall as the venue for the King Tribute also indicates a new fund-raising direction for the SCLC. Located near Central Park in New York City and considered the most prestigious concert stage in the United States, Carnegie Hall was a long way from the Southern churches at which the SCLC had done the bulk of its fund-raising thus far. Moreover, several SCLC events had been mass gatherings where money may have been collected but admission was not charged. Tickets for the tribute were offered at anywhere between $3 for balcony seats to $100 for a "Patron's Box" near the stage. "Special Labor Boxes" were also available for $200. Those sitting in box seats would have the privilege of attending a private reception after the show and meeting the guest of honor himself. In 1960, a typical concert ticket cost about $5, so the committee was deliberately trying to appeal to a crowd that could afford to pay well beyond that, presumably an upper-middle-class, white audience. King aide Stanley Levison admitted that the event was "very much out of our usual class in terms of prices," but reasoned, "We have to start sometime looking for real money."[102] A benefit concert by the hottest group in show business at the most renowned concert hall in America was the optimal kickoff to the SCLC's goals of financial solvency and popular appeal.

The SCLC's collaboration with the Rat Pack came with a certain amount of complication, as well. In typical political fashion, after Sinatra agreed to do the tribute, he expected King to endorse Kennedy. Just days after the singer's participation had been confirmed, Sinatra pressured King, through Davis, to attend a Kennedy rally on the West Coast. King had already taken a "nonpartisan position" on the presidential election, and Levison urged him to maintain that stance. King and his advisors feared that appearing partisan would damage the credibility of the civil rights leader. "You can't be as persuasive to apathetic Negroes," Levison said, "if they feel you are appealing to them as a partisan person who may be seeking to build up voters for his own future candidacy." He believed that a celebrity's decision to endorse a candidate came with little personal consequence but that the same was not true for King. "Frank, Sammy, and the others are not intellectual leaders nor moral leaders so their decision can be more easily arrived at without the singular weight that attaches to a decision or stand by you," Levison commented in a long letter to King about the matter. The advisor believed Davis would understand, but he predicted that Sinatra would subject King "to heavy pressure."[103] Sinatra was known for demanding strict loyalty from his friends and associates, and even permanently excluding anyone who violated this code of virtual subservience. When King failed to endorse Kennedy, Sinatra told Davis to convey to King that he should not count on his help for the tribute.[104]

Martin Luther King, Sr., known as "Daddy King," also pressured his son to endorse Kennedy after a series of dramatic and emotional events. On October 19 (within just a few days of Levison's letter), King was jailed for his participation in a student sit-in in Georgia. After he was sentenced to hard labor, a pall fell over the movement for fear of what would happen to him in prison. Levison, Belafonte, and other aides close to King called lawyers, union leaders, politicians, entertainers, and anyone else they knew who might be able to use their position to secure King's release, including Nixon and Kennedy. Whereas Nixon, who had a respectable civil rights record compared to Kennedy, decided he should stay out of the situation, Kennedy's advisors searched for a way for him to quietly use his influence. Kennedy called King's wife Coretta to express his concern and to offer his support. His brother Robert Kennedy persuaded the judge in the case to reconsider the sentence. After nine days in jail, King was released. His elated father told him to abandon his neutrality and to repay his debt to Kennedy. Belafonte repeatedly called King and urged him to do no such thing. At one point, Daddy King picked up the phone and talked to Belafonte himself. "You can't have a man do what Kennedy did and not pay your debt," he explained. When Belafonte countered that King "shouldn't play the game like a politician, on a lesser level," an exasperated Daddy King hung up on him.[105]

King never endorsed Kennedy, and Sinatra never made good on his threat to bail out of the concert. Perhaps the circumstances of Kennedy's victory kept Sinatra in the fold. Even though King refused to abandon his neutrality, his father had no such compunctions. Daddy King broke ranks with the traditionally Republican black Southern leadership to endorse Kennedy and effusively expressed his gratitude to the candidate in public statements. After the news about Kennedy's expression of sympathy to Coretta King rippled through Southern churches the Sunday before election day (for the facts about Robert's string-pulling had not yet been revealed), black voters turned out in much higher numbers for the Democrat than earlier polls had indicated. Given the tiny margins of the electoral results—only two-tenths of one percent separated the two candidates—one historian calls the Kennedy phone calls for King "a necessary cause of Democratic victory."[106] Sinatra certainly could not ignore this, however, it is more likely his loyalty to Davis that prevented him from bowing out of the tribute. Although much has been made about Davis's adulation for Sinatra, the elder's allegiance to his young colleague was just as strong. Forsaking the concert would have contradicted the nature of their friendship, especially since Davis had delayed his wedding out of consideration for Sinatra's involvement in the presidential campaign.

Now that the election was over, however, the wedding could proceed. Davis and Britt wed on November 13, just five days after Americans had cast their ballots. The press surrounded Davis's house, where the small ceremony took place. Inside were Sinatra and Lawford, both gathered under the chupah. In Davis's view, both Sinatra and Lawford were putting their reputations in jeopardy by attending his wedding. "With all [Frank's] independence, still he knows where [fame] comes from, and how quickly a career can go down the drain on the whim of the public," he said. "It was not a minor thing for Frank to be my best man, nor for Peter and Pat, the President's sister and brother-in-law, to be in the wedding party.[107] One scholar calls Davis and Britt's union "the most famous interracial marriage in American social history."[108] Indeed, the social relevance of their marriage is well-illustrated by their role, or lack thereof, in Kennedy's inauguration.

At the same time that Davis was organizing the performers for the King Tribute, Sinatra was busily planning for the inauguration gala he was producing for Kennedy. Arrangements for both events were progressing splendidly. Advance reports showed that the committee had sold $35,000 in tickets to the tribute, indicating that the SCLC would come out at least $10,000 in the black. An optimistic Levison predicted, "a good profit is assured."[109] Indeed, King was thrilled with Davis's efforts. "When

I solicited your help for our struggle almost two months ago," he told the entertainer, "I did not expect so creative and fulsome a response. All of us are inspired by your wonderful support. . . . I hope I can convey our appreciation to you with the warmth which we feel it."[110] Sinatra was planning an equally star-studded event. A bevy of artists, including Belafonte, Jimmy Durante, Nat King Cole, Leonard Bernstein, Aidan Quinn, Poitier, Bette Davis, and Frederick Oliver were all to attend the gala and perform. Naturally, Sinatra asked Davis and the rest of the Rat Pack to take part in the festivities. Only three days before the inauguration, however, Kennedy's secretary called Davis in New York and told him not to attend. Although both Robert Kennedy and Lawford had protested the decision, several other advisors convinced Kennedy that Davis's presence with his new white wife would put him off on the wrong foot with Southern Democrats. Sinatra, according to his daughter Tina, was "appalled."[111] Davis was incensed—and deeply wounded. He called Britt to break the shameful news. "It hurt like a motherfucker," he stated.[112] Davis remained close with Robert Kennedy, but his friendship with the president was forever damaged, and the two men barely spoke again.

One week later, Davis was back in New York, presiding over the King Tribute. He and the comedian Nipsey Russell emceed a longer, heftier, and more frenzied version of the Sands show. For almost five hours, the sell-out audience witnessed what one journalist described as "high-octane, frequently inspired, sometimes zany, but thoroughly exciting entertainment."[113] The first half of the show featured a host of entertainers, including Mahalia Jackson, the Count Basie Orchestra, Tony Bennett, Carmen McRae, and the mimic George Kirby, all of whom had been convinced by Davis to perform gratis. Other stars, such as Poitier, spoke passionately on behalf of the cause. Davis and Russell kept the audience in stitches between the performances until the Rat Pack took over in the second half of the show with their usual songs, dances, jokes, and pranks. As one journalist put it, "In a wild and frantic series of skits, Sinatra, Martin, and Davis almost wrecked staid Carnegie Hall and the packed house loved it."[114] The sell-out crowd lent to the kinetic energy within the theatre, especially because there were more ticket holders than seats available. Extra chairs were placed on the stage at the last minute, and people crowded along the sides and the rear of the hall.[115] This fed into the fervor onstage, in a show Davis considered "one of the most magnificent things I've ever done."[116]

In a single evening, the King Tribute raised one-quarter of what King told Davis he believed the organization needed for the year. Once all of the expenses were paid, the SCLC netted $22,000 from the event, setting a record for money raised at Carnegie Hall.[117] The concert would end up providing the SCLC with twelve percent of its budget that year, as opposed to twenty-five percent, because the benefit allowed the organization to expand its fund-raising operation and budget. Having so many stars pay homage to King gave the civil rights leader an element of stardom himself. One historian says that the benefit "established King as the possessor of a celebrity drawing power that ambitious politicians could not ignore."[118] Furthermore, due to the infusion of funds, the SCLC could afford to hire three new workers. Both of these developments resulted in an improved financial situation, as the newly hired Walker focused particularly on the professionalization of fund-raising. Walker encouraged King to capitalize on his celebrity stature by taking on more speaking engagements as a way to promote the SCLC, systematically solicit cash donations, and develop mailing lists. The SCLC's income reached almost $200,000 by August of that year, twice what King had told Davis his organization needed. This turn of events transformed the SCLC from an organization-in-waiting to a strong political force. Walker described the months following the concert as a time of "laying permanent foundations, re-structuring the organization, building a team and charting the course we should travel."[119] The Rat Pack's Tribute to Martin Luther King, Jr., played an important role in that evolution.

By no means was the tribute the only factor behind the SCLC's growth. As will be apparent in chapter three, Belafonte and Poitier were involved in other fund-raising projects that significantly affected the SCLC. Furthermore, the sit-ins and Freedom Rides sustained primarily by SNCC brought more attention to the movement and had the spillover effect of facilitating fund-raising efforts for the SCLC.[120] Nevertheless, the tribute should be considered a crucial event in the organization's development. The concert added money to the organization's coffers, brought publicity, and furthered the alliance between black civil rights activists and a white liberal constituency that up until that time had been fairly weak. King certainly appreciated the tribute and understood what Davis could bring to the movement. He told the entertainer, "I'm gonna call on you again." The Rat Pack would, indeed, go on to do several more benefits for the SCLC, including one at Westchester Auditorium in White Plains, New

York, a few months later that raised almost as much money as the Carnegie Hall event.

Davis's determination to play in elite white clubs, his appeal to both black and white audiences, and his identification with the Rat Pack had allowed him to integrate into show business as a bona fide star, but also prompted disgruntled critics to bemoan his behavior. His marriage to Britt only inflamed them. But the controversies also illustrate Davis's significance in the developing civil rights movement. To be considered a national movement, civil rights had to capture the attention of the white mainstream, and the Rat Pack's fund-raisers for the SCLC helped do that. Not only was the Carnegie Hall event primarily a white-oriented affair, but its biggest single contributor was Julie Podell, the owner of the Copacabana club that had once refused to grant Davis admittance. Podell bought the highest-priced full-page ad available for the concert program, in addition to three boxes for the event at eight hundred dollars apiece. If Davis had won over Podell, who else could he bring into the cause? As one scholar notes, Davis was "not simply mixing with two races" but operated "as a link to bringing two races together."[121] For a movement with the primary goal of integration, this quality was invaluable.

* * *

Although civil rights organizations had been holding benefit concerts since the 1930s, such events increasingly became the fund-raising method of choice for reasons illustrated by the Tribute to Martin Luther King, Jr. Not only did they raise money, they also helped build a national constituency for the civil rights movement. One historian asserts, "Many of these events offered a dramatic forum in which Northern audiences could hear directly from Southern activists about day-to-day life on the front lines of the movement."[122] When the mainstream press did not always give events in the South extensive or accurate coverage, these concerts could be an important source of news. Furthermore, the personal testimonies given there served to connect audiences with the everyday realities associated with trying to bring down segregation in the South. Through these shows, performers and paying customers alike could feel a sense of "ownership and participation" with the workaday activists. But celebrity involvement with and the increased ticket prices of benefit concerts also brought an air of glamour to the movement that had been virtually nonexistent before such high-profile entertainers as Davis, Poitier, Belafonte, Sinatra, Lawford, and Martin became involved. Coupled with the Kennedy campaign and inauguration, these benefits helped further celebrity politics as glamorous, attractive, and a vital subject of conversation at both the grassroots and national levels.[123]

Three months after the King Tribute, Davis guest-starred at the Detroit NAACP's annual Fight for Freedom dinner. Attended by thirteen hundred guests, the event raised a record $60,000 for the association.[124] In 1962, Davis proclaimed his willingness to help the NAACP "any time, any place"—and he would live up to that promise. Between his fundraising efforts and out-of-pocket donations, it is estimated that he generated $750,000 for civil rights organizations in the 1960s (equivalent to about $5.6 million in 2014), leading one scholar to proclaim that Davis "was probably the best fund-raiser of the civil rights movement outside of King himself."[125] Particularly significant is that Davis did his initial work for the NAACP when the organization was under siege and for the SCLC when it was floundering and trying to find its direction. Furthermore, he achieved a balance between career success and civil rights activism that had eluded many performers to become the movement's chief celebrity fund-raiser. In the meantime, Belafonte moved to take advantage of the stronger link between the White House and Hollywood to become the movement's foremost celebrity strategist.

Harry Belafonte and the Northern Liberal Network

Work all night on a drink of rum/
Daylight come and me wan' go home,
                    —from "Day-O" by Harry Belafonte, 1956

We took a trip on the Greyhound bus/
Freedom's coming and it won't be long.
                    —from "Civil rights" version of "Day-O,"
                    first sung on the Freedom Rides, 1961

HARRY BELAFONTE, LIKE SAMMY DAVIS, JR., PARTICIPATED IN numerous rallies and marches for civil rights and headlined benefit concerts and membership drives for various organizations. But Belafonte's primary contribution to the movement was how he opened his New York City apartment to the cause. His luxurious home served as an informal Northern headquarters for the promotion of the movement in the North and for the support of direct action in the South. As Belafonte explains, "We always had meetings at my home in New York, because it was in that environment that [King] met what we call the New York delegation."[1] It was there that key New York–based Southern Christian Leadership Conference (SCLC) supporters, such as the attorneys Stanley Levison and Clarence Jones, met with Belafonte and Martin Luther King, Jr., to plan fund-raising activities and to develop strategy for the organization. A hotbed of civil rights activity, the apartment evolved into a networking arena that fostered relationships, provided neutral ground, and offered respite to any number of activists. Although scholars such as Martha Biondi and Thomas Sugrue have written about a Northern network, Belafonte has received scant attention for fostering this network in his own home. It was not a definitive Stars for Freedom headquarters. The major civil rights organizations had their own offices, and other important celebrity supporters, such as Charlton Heston, Theodore Bikel, and Dick Gregory came to the movement independently. Furthermore, Belafonte's film career fizzled. Nevertheless, he maintained a presence in Hollywood through his television work and personal friendships, and his apartment remained a crucial site for developing Northern liberal support among celebrities for the civil rights movement.

*   *   *

While the rest of the Leading Six certainly struggled to negotiate their identities within the confines of the culture of celebrity, Belafonte in particular seemed to internalize this process. He had held long-conflicting feelings about his performing career. His transition from a pop vocalist to a folk singer and songwriter and his struggles as a film producer reflected his desire for achieving cultural authenticity, but his commercial success led him to question his methods. He went so far as to blame his husky voice—a symptom of chronic laryngitis—on "subconscious feelings of guilt about my success."[2] He also felt despondent about the possibility of change in America. He said, "I was a wounded beast like so many others looking for vengeance and I was not just bent on having anger because they had . . . ripped off [Paul] Robeson. I was looking for where to go with it and do what must be done."[3] While Belafonte admired Robeson for his suffering, he could not bring himself to become a martyr, too. His own ambition and the realization that he could not be a constructive agent of change without money or a platform took him down a different path. In fact, he told one journalist that part of the reason he remained in show business was to make enough money to further his social goals and "do something good."[4] His apartment became the launchpad for this strategy.

The process of buying his apartment was a social struggle in itself.

Belafonte and his wife Marguerite had separated in late 1954, shortly after the birth of their second daughter, and he had attempted to find an apartment in Manhattan—to no avail. No one in the city had been willing to rent to a black man. After striking gold with *Calypso* in 1956, Belafonte tried again. At this point, he had divorced Marguerite and was married to Julie Robinson, a white dancer with the Katherine Dunham Company. They had a son, Belafonte's third child, and wanted something spacious as well as fashionable. Belafonte again hit a roadblock, however, when landlords on the exclusive Upper East Side refused to rent to him, in spite of the spate of negative publicity over their apparent racism. Belafonte targeted the Upper West Side with a more covert approach. He registered with two partners under a corporate name to buy a luxurious apartment building at 300 West End Avenue, only two blocks from Central Park. He took the fifth floor for his family and then sold co-ops to other wealthy African Americans, including Lena Horne, thus integrating the Upper West Side.[5]

The Belafontes decorated their apartment in a style reminiscent of his music: contemporary folk with an Afro-Caribbean motif and leftist accents. Hanging on the walls were paintings by artists known for their modern approach to folk subjects. Marc Chagall's Jewish peasants and Diego Rivera's Mexican workers inspired Belafonte and paralleled the social realism he attempted to bring to his music. Belafonte's appreciation for indigenous art also led him to acquire hand-crafted pieces during his travels. Wooden statues from Haiti populated the apartment. Numerous books about African American history and culture, as well as photographs of Robeson and King, rounded out his collection. The apartment's decor served as a reminder of Belafonte's artistic ideal: using art to inspire, educate, and prompt social action. He believed in the "use of art and the power of art for social and human development and thinking." "So," he says, "art to me was always quite political in its application. That was its principal purpose. And that, yes, entertainment was also a part of art."[6] King convinced Belafonte that the tactic of nonviolent direct action was another promising means of furthering his social goals.

The two men met in 1956 as King began to receive national attention for his role in the Montgomery Bus Boycott, with the press heralding him as "Alabama's modern Moses." In an effort to capitalize on this publicity, King traveled to New York to raise money for the boycott. Before returning to Alabama, he invited Belafonte to a private meeting in Harlem. The entertainer was skeptical. The media's emphasis on King's religious martyrdom did little to quell Belafonte's suspicion of preachers. And he harbored resentment against traditional black leaders—with whom he associated King—for failing Robeson. Nevertheless, Belafonte's curiosity drew him to the meeting, and he walked away impressed. King managed "to show me," he said, "that there was a larger humanity than anything my anger could imagine," and that one could channel energy toward nonviolence. "That was the most profound thing that happened to me."[7] After this epiphanic meeting, Belafonte performed in several benefits during the mid- to late 1950s, the biggest of which was a concert in December 1956 to raise money for the Montgomery Bus Boycott, and he appeared at the same mass rallies in which Sammy Davis, Jr., took part in 1956 and 1957, namely the Madison Square Garden rally and the Prayer Pilgrimage for Freedom.

In 1958 Belafonte evolved from a participant to a leader of civil rights events when he cochaired the Youth March for Integrated Schools. Conceived of by A. Philip Randolph, the march was to take place in Washington, DC, for the purpose of demonstrating support for *Brown v. Board of Education* and opposition to those who were obstructing its implementation, such as Arkansas governor Orval Faubus. What was novel about this march was that planners intended to involve students—from the fourth grade through college—in the event.[8] Another untested strategy was recruiting celebrities to cochair and lead the march, a decision made when King became incapacitated after being stabbed by a psychotic admirer a few weeks earlier.[9] Although Randolph and Bayard Rustin did much of the legwork in planning the details, both Jackie Robinson and Belafonte were involved in the planning committees. Furthermore, they led the students in a parade down Constitution Avenue until Belafonte broke ranks with a small delegation to deliver a statement about integration at the White House. Robinson and Belafonte then delivered remarks to a crowd of 9,500 at the Lincoln Memorial. Even though the two men, as well as a handful of other celebrities, had been involved in demonstrations before this event, it is only with the Youth March that stars such as Belafonte and Robinson became so highly involved in the planning and execution of such a large affair.

Robinson's and Belafonte's leadership generated additional interest in the event, but their involvement was not an unqualified success. At least one participant did not welcome Belafonte's presence on the stage at all. She told Randolph that she planned to chaperone her daughter and her classmates at the march, but that she had "misgivings" about the unconventional cochair. "It is my feeling that the choice of Harry Belafonte to read the youth pledge at the Washington rally is unwise from a purely tactical point of view in that it could conceivably give our enemies a chance to raise the extraneous issues of intermarriage and communism," she explained.[10] Moreover, Belafonte's celebrity status did not win him admission to the White House grounds when he attempted to reach out to President Dwight D. Eisenhower, although he used the rebuff as another talking point with the press. He predicted a "strong feeling of indignation among the students and the people of the world" when they learned of the unwelcome reception.[11] Also disappointing was the minimal press coverage the march received. Although Robinson and Belafonte generated some headlines, activists who had led a group from Harlem to Washington, DC, told Randolph of their frustration "that so few onlookers from the 'outside world' seemed to be present."[12] These problems, however, did not detract from "the power of that crowd," Belafonte remembers. "For the first time I felt: We are omnipotent. We will not be stopped."[13]

Only a few months later, Belafonte and Robinson again worked with young people when they teamed up with Poitier to promote Airlift Africa. This program was founded to assist African students who had received scholarships to American colleges but could not afford to travel to their respective campuses. The three celebrities pledged personal donations and solicited further funds through a letter campaign to raise the $39,000 necessary to underwrite expenses for the eighty-one students.[14] Robinson largely served as the point man, while Belafonte honed his fund-raising skills. In this case, he was not being asked to perform for or speak to the public. Instead, he tapped his contacts through personal letters, thus cultivating his fund-raising network. As the 1960s progressed, Belafonte increasingly employed such methods to raise money for the civil rights movement, often with Poitier's assistance.

Indeed, Belafonte and Poitier grew very close during the 1950s, but their friendship did not insulate them from professional enmity, much of which was fueled by Belafonte. On personal matters, Belafonte could be a sensitive confidant. For example, after Poitier's marriage to his first wife Juanita fell apart, Poitier credited Belafonte with helping him cope with the painful experience.[15] On professional matters, however, Belafonte often lashed out at his friend, as he did during the *Porgy and Bess* controversy, frequently insinuating that Poitier too willingly took on projects that did not meet Belafonte's personal standards for the appropriate portrayal of African Americans. The likely source of this resentment was Belafonte's short-lived film career, a career that had once seemed so boundless. In 1958, Belafonte had stated his intention of doing one movie per year with Harbel Productions. He coproduced *The World, The Flesh, and The Devil* with MGM in 1959, and only six months later, United Artists released Belafonte's first film, in which he served as both the star and fully independent producer. Titled *Odds Against Tomorrow*, the film was to be the first of six that Belafonte made with United Artists. He announced plans to do a black Western and a film about Russian poet Alexander Pushkin. Belafonte also bought the film rights to the 1959 novel *To Sir, with Love* as a vehicle for Poitier and himself.[16] However, *Odds Against Tomorrow* ended up being Belafonte's last film for the next thirteen years. In the meantime, Poitier's career took off; in that same period, he made twenty-two films, becoming one of Hollywood's most successful actors.

It is not entirely clear what killed Belafonte's film career during the 1960s. By his own telling, the studios were too timid, and he walked away from Hollywood. They refused to consider his ideas, rejecting "out of hand" the scripts he submitted to producers. What they did allow, they modified. MGM infuriated Belafonte when the studio changed the script for *World* and effectively "neutered" the interracial romance in the plot.[17] Conversely, he rejected the films offered him, including, he claims, *Lilies of the Field*, for which Poitier won an Academy Award, and *To Sir, with Love*. The studios' unwillingness to take on some of his projects (the black Western, for example) certainly rings true. Sammy Davis, Jr., encountered the same resistance. That Belafonte was offered and turned down two roles that helped define Poitier's career is less plausible and may be an example of his distorting the past to best his rival and prove his own artistic integrity. His claim that he refused to star in *To Sir, with Love* is especially questionable since he at one point owned the rights to it. Furthermore, Belafonte's track record did not ingratiate him with the studios. *World* and *Odds Against Tomorrow* did only moderately well at the box office. He admits, "It made no money" and "I knew . . . the bottom line, is the bottom line." Ultimately, he concluded, "there's no point in trying to change this monster."[18] The demise of Belafonte's film career appears to be a replication of his experience as a pop performer—the two sides gave up on each other. Nevertheless, Belafonte perceived himself as a performer who sacrificed popularity for principles and thus explained the disappointing results of his experience in Hollywood.

This perception blinded Belafonte to the compromises he himself had made. He stubbornly refused to acknowledge that he, too, chose commercialism over authenticity on more than one occasion. For example, for all his railing against the making of *Porgy and Bess*, he opportunistically arranged for his duet recording of the opera with Lena Horne to be released in conjunction with the premier of the movie.[19] He was similarly contradictory in his attitude toward his calypso music. On one hand, he admitted that he "modified the dialect . . . [and] put it into a rhythm that was more closely identified with the American scene," but on the other, he pompously complained that it made him "good and mad when songwriters sitting in New York offices grab hold of a facet of another people's culture like calypso and prostitute it and dilute it."[20] Not only did Belafonte essentially do the same thing, but he also "sexed up" folk music with his custom-made form-fitting attire: tight black pants and shirt unbuttoned to his navel. His stage show was a glamorous production replete with choreographed dance moves, colorized lighting, and an orchestra. Nevertheless, Belafonte never viewed himself as part of the establishment.

In fact, he chafed under the approval of the establishment, even as he became one of the decade's most popular entertainers. He downplayed the nickname "Calypso King," protesting that he sang in many other genres as well. And he despised the title "the first Negro matinee idol." This resentment stemmed in part from Belafonte's knowledge that his mocha skin and good looks did not threaten white audiences. As one of his friends commented in the late 1950s, "Although he is brown-skinned and unmistakably Negro, he is acceptable in terms of white standards of beauty. Brown up Tab Hunter and you could hardly tell him from Harry Belafonte."[21] Also irritating him was the implication of his mass-market appeal. That a leftist, bohemian outsider could be one of America's biggest stars in a decade that was considered conservative, bourgeois, and conformist indicated that either Belafonte was not as radical or America was not as close-minded as he had thought, at least not on an individual basis. Both possibilities caused him discomfort. Reluctant mainstream star that he may have been, Belafonte's anger gave way to a fierce commitment to the civil rights movement, and he possessed an unusual combination of drive and resources that he marshaled toward its success.

*   *   *

In 1960, Belafonte began to use his celebrity status more aggressively, as he evolved from a civil rights supporter into a political strategist by working closely with several civil rights leaders and the Kennedy administration. His apartment served as a meeting place for any number of political operatives who discussed tactics and plotted strategy with Belafonte to further their objectives. In the process, Belafonte became a go-between for the Kennedy brothers, Martin Luther King, Jr., and the Student Nonviolent Coordinating Committee (SNCC), promoting them individually and working to align their causes.

In February 1960, Belafonte helped form the Committee to Defend Martin Luther King, J. (CMDLK) to help King fight felony tax evasion charges brought by the state of Alabama. The politically motivated indictment came after a protracted audit regarding SCLC expenses in which King agreed to pay $1,667 in back taxes only to be charged with perjury—a felony—for agreeing to pay them and implicitly admitting to false tax returns.[22] Belafonte worked with Bayard Rustin, A. Philip Randolph, Stanley Levinson, and others to raise the funds to meet King's legal fees in fighting the charges. King insisted that the CMDLK also establish a separate cache of funds—named the Revolving Bail Fund—to bail out jailed protesters.[23] Prepared to raise $200,000, the committee worked feverishly over the next three months, meeting as a group on a weekly basis and in separate subcommittees even more frequently. Belafonte's apartment, in addition to an office on the Upper West Side, became a favorite meeting spot.

Belafonte took on multiple responsibilities for the CDMLK, placing an advertisement in the *New York Times* and recruiting celebrities to sign off on it.[24] Cowritten with Rustin, the piece was titled "Heed Their Rising Voices" to play off of one of the newspaper's own editorials from the previous week. The long ad explained that Southern authorities were doing everything in their power to ensure that African Americans *not* be heard. Poignantly describing conditions in the South and King's inspirational leadership, it characterized the charges against him as an effort to "remove" King "physically as the leader to whom the students and millions of others look for guidance and support, and thereby to intimidate *all* leaders who may rise in the South." In addition to the ministers and civil rights activists who agreed to support the CDMLK, Belafonte recruited as many film and television actors, including Stella Adler, Marlon Brando, Diahann Carroll, Nat King Cole, Dorothy Dandridge, Ossie Davis, Sammy Davis, Jr., Ruby Dee, Anthony Franciosa, Eartha Kitt, Hope Lange, Poitier, and Shelley Winters, among others. A large coupon positioned near the supporters' names provided readers with directions for making contributions.[25] Appearing March 29, 1960, on a full page in the *Times*, the advertisement brought national attention to King's legal plight and marked the first indication of drawing both black and white celebrities into a larger liberal network. Within three weeks, the CDMLK had raised almost $5,000 from the advertisement alone.[26]

In the meantime, Belafonte also took on the chairmanship of the CDMLK's "Cultural Division." Regarded as the most important of the CDMLK's five committees—which included Church, Student, Labor and Legal Advisory Divisions—Belafonte was "empowered to conduct its activities with a degree of autonomy." Indeed, the steering committee allowed his division to "set up its own office, print special stationery, and plan its operations without routine checking with the staff or board." It is not clear why the Cultural Division was deemed the most significant. Although its activities were sure to raise money and attention, the Church and Labor Divisions raised just as much cash, if not more, than the Cultural Division. Furthermore, the Legal Advisory Division served the very purpose of the CDMLK's founding. Perhaps it was granted this VIP status because of Belafonte's celebrity stature. Whatever the case, Belafonte took advantage of the privilege by initiating a creative array of programs, especially after he convinced Poitier to serve as cochair.

The two friends made good use of their show business contacts and backgrounds. They undertook a letter-writing campaign, reaching out to actors, writers, directors, and producers they believed would be responsive to their cause. Belafonte wrote an initial contact letter, explaining to recipients the charges against King and asking them to sign a pledge of support for him. In two weeks, he and Poitier had secured the names of thirty-eight sponsors, some in time to include in the *New York Times* ad. Poitier then wrote a follow-up letter to those who had not yet responded. The two used these same mailing lists to ask for monetary donations and to recruit participants for the cultural events they were planning. Belafonte reported to the rest of the CDMLK that on May 17, the Saturday before King's trial, his committee would oversee a wreath-laying ceremony at the Statue of Liberty followed by a fund-raising rally that afternoon. Both events were to include "substantial numbers" of "prominent artists."[27]

The letter-writing campaign and programming ideas gained momentum in the following weeks. That Belafonte and Poitier were able to obtain thirty-eight sponsors was a victory in itself and gave them the confidence to add a benefit concert to the events on May 17. Nevertheless, this progress did not come without its share of headaches. For example, some stars sent money to the CDMLK but asked that their support not be publicized. The television talk show host Steve Allen, who donated $200, was one such individual. Other celebrities, such as the director George Stevens, pledged their support but never appear to have donated any money to the committee. Even more troubling was that Belafonte was unable to secure firm commitments from many of the stars who had agreed to participate in the benefit. The Cultural Division was forced to "proceed on publicity" with only "the limited number of performers now definitely committed." Belafonte also could not guarantee a location for the event. He wanted to rent the 369th Regiment Armory, but for some inexplicable reason, the armory refused. The venue was not secured until New York governor Nelson Rockefeller intervened on the CDMLK's behalf.[28] A libel lawsuit brought by the state of Alabama against the *New York Times* and the ministers named in the ad also complicated matters and raised questions within SCLC as to whether Belafonte and Rustin had overstepped their bounds. The situation looked dismal: one promising method of raising money was curtailed just as another expensive lawsuit was added to the group's agenda.[29] Nevertheless, with the May 17 activities and the trial less than a month away, the CDMLK pressed forward.

In fact, Belafonte and Poitier could not have asked for a better outcome. Their various cultural ventures captured the attention of the national press, which, as the Youth March made evident, was not a given. Both the Hearst newsreel series "News of the Day" and the *New York Times* publicized at least some of the Cultural Division's events.[30] This interest was perhaps a result of the large turnout but more likely it was because of Belafonte's and Poitier's prominent role in the day's activities. They led a morning ferry excursion to the ceremony at the Statue of Liberty. Belafonte's rendition of the "Star Spangled Banner" opened the proceedings, after which a host of women from New York's five boroughs placed wreaths and heaped flowers at the base of the statue. A number of ministers, activists, and artists also offered prayer, testimony, and song deploring the practice of segregation.[31] They returned to downtown Manhattan for a noon rally in the Garment District. A crowd of over fifteen thousand greeted the brigade with a long ovation. After quieting the crowd, Belafonte and Poitier pointed out that they were not only artists but also parents. Belafonte said that as a father, he would not "be able to sleep at night if he did not take part in the fight against segregation," and Poitier said that he was fighting for his daughters for "the freedom that was not forthcoming to me as a child."[32]

Later that night, the two friends greeted an equally large and enthusiastic crowd at Harlem's 369th Armory for the benefit show. Poitier emceed along with Dorothy Dandridge, who flew in from Los Angeles. Comedians, singers, dancers, and musicians warmed up the audience for the evening's headliner: Belafonte and his singers. Belafonte's performance was the climax of what observers applauded as "rare entertainment for Harlem and rewarding for the cause of civil rights."[33] In fact, the show was pronounced the largest indoor gathering the armory had ever staged. That Belafonte and Poitier were able to produce three very different and successful events on the same day is testament to their organizational skills and show business know-how.

The immediate upshot was the financial profit generated by the benefit. The Cultural Division reported a hefty $10,000 net income from the show. Even more promising were the potential long-term advantages of Belafonte and Poitier's organizing efforts. An optimistic Levison told King, "Harry Belafonte has stirred the cultural forces as never before and they should become a new and increasing source of strength."[34] Belafonte's proven knack for producing large and profitable affairs would make it easier for him to organize more benefits—such as the Tribute to Martin Luther King, Jr.—in the future. The mailing list that Belafonte and Poitier put together provided the SCLC with a catalogue of go-to sponsors and financial supporters. This would be important in emergency situations when funds were low. Belafonte and Poitier's work also indicated a changing political climate in Hollywood. As one historian notes, the stars' "readiness to back King not only pointed to a freer political atmosphere but also testified to the failure of segregationists' attempts to portray the civil rights movement as communist-inspired."[35] Indeed, since the studios had scrapped the blacklist in 1960, artists were growing more comfortable reentering the political arena, and Belafonte worked to direct their attention to King and the cause of civil rights. "It was my task to make sure that I had a strong celebrity core, that I had a lot of artists to bring validation to the table," Belafonte said. "Dr. King understood the great value of that." The SCLC operative Reverend Wyatt Tee Walker says that Belafonte and Poitier were "key" to bringing more artists to the organization.[36]

The positive results of the Cultural Division's work mirrored the larger success of the CDMLK. The organization was able to raise over $85,000 in three months, and this financial support allowed King to retain an able and effective legal team. In fact, Alabama's suit against him did not result in the prolonged legal struggle they had anticipated. The trial lasted one week, and three hours and forty-five minutes after going into deliberation, the all-white jury shocked the courtroom by pronouncing King "not guilty." It was King's first victory in an Alabama courtroom, one that almost defied explanation and meant that the CDMLK had, in another surprising turn of events, extra cash on hand. After paying King's legal fees and its own operating expenses, the committee distributed the remaining funds to other legal defense projects, including one for the libel suit against the Alabama ministers, and disbanded.[37] The fundraising methods that Belafonte and the rest of the committee had spearheaded were soon incorporated into the SCLC's regular program, as was the revolving bail fund.[38]

Belafonte's experience with the CDMLK led him to become more involved in the politics of the civil rights movement. During a follow-up meeting in which the executive committee met at his apartment, the singer argued that they should help establish a new national membership organization. According to the longtime activist Daisy Bates, who was also present at the meeting, Belafonte said, "The NAACP is not doing the job that needed to be done."[39] His attitude reflected the general perception of the New York delegation that the National Association for the Advancement of Colored People was a "gradualist" organization out of touch with the increasingly militant masses. Whereas the NAACP still stressed taking legal action to challenge segregation, Belafonte wanted to spearhead an organization that could draw a large membership and coordinate the type of protests King had led. Rustin agreed with Belafonte's recommendation, and they set up a committee to explore the possibility. This never came to fruition, because it presently became clear that the sit-in movement would give rise to SNCC, with which Belafonte soon became involved. Nevertheless, Bates, herself a NAACP member, relayed news of Belafonte's machinations to Roy Wilkins, and the NAACP leader would be suspicious of the singer henceforth. Belafonte's reputation as a strategist did lead to more constructive relationships, however, namely with members of the Kennedy circle during the 1960 presidential primaries.

The Kennedy team heavily recruited Belafonte, and over the course of the campaign Belafonte distinguished himself from the typical celebrity supporter by his attempts to influence the candidate on civil rights. Belafonte at first refused to even meet with Kennedy, in part because he had already committed to supporting Adlai Stevenson. The singer was not impressed by Kennedy's civil rights record in the US Senate or his seeming lack of friendships with blacks. Belafonte also admitted to harboring a bigoted perception of the candidate: "So he was kind of like this Irish Catholic guy that was the classic stereotype for us of what Irish Catholics were, which were always drunk racists. So caught up in their religious dogma that nothing else breathed in the world."[40] However, Belafonte relented when Jackie Robinson, still one of the most admired black celebrities, indicated that he was considering giving his endorsement to Richard Nixon. Robinson had started as a Hubert Humphrey supporter, but as the Minnesota Democrat's campaign fizzled, the athlete announced that he favored Nixon as a second choice. Robinson, who already had a friendly rapport with Nixon, also noted that the candidate had a decidedly better record on civil rights issues.[41] A dismayed Kennedy camp pushed hard to meet with Belafonte, who, still not willing to endorse Kennedy, used the occasion to talk black celebrity politics.

When Kennedy arrived at Belafonte's apartment, the two men settled in for what became a three-hour discussion. Kennedy first asked if the singer could explain why the baseball player would ever consider endorsing Nixon. Belafonte gingerly reminded Kennedy that he was not well known by African Americans, who naturally tended to support the candidates with whom they were familiar and who had a substantial record on civil rights. Nevertheless, Belafonte admitted that he too had been surprised by Robinson's stance, which he saw as resulting from a fit of "anger with the Democratic Party for some slight that had been put upon him."[42] This comment reflects Belafonte's disappointment more than his true understanding of the baseball player's motives. Since Robinson's political choices did not comport with his own, the singer characteristically dismissed them as personal and petty. In reality, the Reverend Gardner Taylor, another one of King's top aides, had asked Robinson to support Nixon. With King intent on staying neutral, Taylor told Robinson that "we needed black people on both sides of the contest, in both parties, to insure that progress would be made." Robinson agreed with Taylor's logic, and since the baseball player was already friendly with Nixon, he was open to the idea.[43] Unfortunately for Robinson, many other observers reacted like Belafonte, and were first baffled, then derisive.

To Kennedy's next question, Belafonte offered more discerning advice. The candidate asked him if, in the event he secured the nomination, Belafonte would be willing to organize black stars for his candidacy, in an effort to offset Robinson's defection. Belafonte surprised Kennedy when he argued against finding "the pulse of Black America" through a celebrity. With an insight atypical of many superstars, Belafonte told Kennedy that trying to tap into the black mood through a celebrity would "mislead" him, because stars "pretend a life that is not anywhere near as complicated in its social conflict and the kind of choices we make as does the rest of the tribe." Belafonte suggested that Kennedy look to movement leaders for direction instead and identified King in particular. "The time you've spent with me would be better spent talking to him and listening to what he has to say because he is the future of our people," Belafonte said. Taken aback by how little Kennedy actually knew about King, Belafonte suggested he learn about King's agenda and "get his favor."[44] Likewise, in a phone call immediately after the meeting, Belafonte told King, "Make every effort to get to know John Kennedy." Kennedy and King met soon thereafter for a rendezvous arranged by Harris Wofford, an aide to Kennedy who was interested in civil rights.[45] This meeting would sow the seeds for the delicate alliance that would soon develop between the two men.

After Kennedy won the nomination, Belafonte finally agreed to endorse him and tried to push a civil rights agenda within the campaign. When he was invited to the National Conference on Constitutional Rights that Kennedy hosted that October, one Kennedy aide recalled, "Belafonte was very vigorous in his demand that this business about civil rights . . . [had] to be taken seriously and he wanted some action."[46] Belafonte performed and glad-handed across the country at a number of fund-raisers for Kennedy and other candidates running on the Democratic ticket. Unlike most celebrity supporters, Belafonte also made a campaign commercial. In the one-minute spot, Belafonte listened to Kennedy profess his commitment to equality of opportunity in all areas of American life, particularly jobs and housing. Satisfied, Belafonte turned to the camera and said, "I'm voting for the Senator. How about you?"[47] Proud of his effort, Belafonte believed the ad would win over undecided black voters. Instead, the campaign pulled the commercial from the airwaves after Southern Democrats complained. Given no explanation by Kennedy, Belafonte admitted that the decision was "not the kind of courage that I had hoped and expected," but he nevertheless "stayed the course."[48] Belafonte got the impression that Kennedy was somewhat disappointed in him as well when word leaked that Belafonte had led the charge against a King endorsement in the wake of his release from jail. In Belafonte's mind, that a number of people in King's inner circle had taken to the hustings for Kennedy should have been enough. He also believed, somewhat pompously, that a public letter in which King thanked Kennedy for calling his wife Coretta was "tantamount to an endorsement, and they should be thankful that our wisdom was such that led to this." The singer concluded that his position "carried some consequence" in that Kennedy now seemed to view him with an "eye of caution."[49] The feeling was mutual.

Kennedy's victory and inauguration seemed to dissipate these mutual grudges. "We put things together in a very, very wonderful way for what was, I think, the greatest inaugural presence of artists and celebration ever in this country," Belafonte said. Although he believed Kennedy had treated Sammy Davis, Jr., rudely by revoking his invitation to the inauguration, he also thought Davis had brought it on himself for being a "loose cannon" and "stirring controversy" with his personal behavior. "Typically, he'd managed with his marriage to May to make as much news as possible."[50] For himself, Belafonte felt that the inauguration set the tone for a "rhythm of favorable encounters" with the administration. In fact, King considered Robert Kennedy, John's brother and the new attorney general of the United States, the movement's "number one target." He admonished, "You find his soul, find his moral center, and win him to our course." Thus charged, Belafonte made it a point to grow closer to Robert Kennedy. "Each time an invitation was extended where there was someplace he would be . . . I would make it my business to be there," he said.

When he was asked in March 1961 to serve on the advisory council of the newly formed Peace Corps, Belafonte leapt at the chance. The appointment placed him in a better position to reach out to Robert and to keep both the Kennedy and King camps personally informed of one another's aims and concerns. Indeed, Belafonte's position within the administration showed its advantages almost immediately with the Freedom Rides.

* * *

The Freedom Rides began in Washington, DC, on May 14, 1961. A joint project between members of the Congress of Racial Equality (CORE), the Fellowship of Reconciliation, and the SNCC, the Freedom Rides were initiated by thirteen black and white riders who wanted to test the Supreme Court ban on racial discrimination in interstate travel. The riders planned to travel through Virginia, the Carolinas, Georgia, Alabama, Mississippi, and Louisiana to reach New Orleans. They were not breaking any laws and thus could have reached New Orleans with little notice, but quite the opposite happened. The sight of blacks and whites sitting side by side on the buses and integrating waiting rooms provoked an intense reaction in the Deep South, propelling the civil rights movement to new heights and leading Belafonte to take on an active advisory role in the SNCC.

Before the Freedom Rides, Belafonte had been encouraging of the sit-in movement but had not been involved in SNCC, the organization that grew out of the demonstrations. John Lewis, one of the leaders of the Nashville sit-ins, remembered how heartening it was when the demonstrators received telegrams of support from Belafonte and other prominent individuals such as Eleanor Roosevelt and Ralph Bunche during their thirty-day term in jail. "Without these people, I don't know what would have happened," Lewis said.[51] The students, who had been arrested for breaking segregation laws by sitting at department store lunch counters, had been given the choice between a fifty dollar fine and thirty days in the county workhouse. They chose to enter the workhouse, arguing that if they paid the fines, they would be contributing to the sustenance of a corrupt system. When newspapers across the country published pictures of the students performing manual labor in their prison garb, individuals from all walks of life—including Belafonte—wanted the students to know they had support "on the outside."[52] Despite his affinity for the students, Belafonte was too consumed with his work for the CDMLK to offer anything more than verbal encouragement for their efforts.

In fact, Jackie Robinson had been the celebrity to do the most for the students during the sit-ins. The jailed students agreed that one of them should post bond to cultivate outside help, and the individual they targeted first was Robinson. The students had considered turning to Roy Wilkins or King, but deemed both of them too "political," unlike Robinson, whom they saw as a hero. The baseball player sat down with student representatives over deli sandwiches and soft drinks, and out of this meeting came the idea for the Student Emergency Fund. Robinson made telephone calls and sent letters to his friends and associates, asking each of them to donate money, send supplies, and contact ten more people. Within a matter of days, Robinson and his allies had raised over $20,000 for the Student Emergency Fund and had amassed scores of books, cigarettes, and candy to send to the jailed students. Robinson went on to organize a benefit concert to further boost the fund and to publicize the students' letters from jail to raise awareness about their cause.[53] This indicates that perhaps Kennedy had not been off base in his efforts to tap into the black psyche through Robinson. Nevertheless, by the spring of 1961, political circumstances had changed, and Robinson's endorsement of Nixon caused him to lose credibility with some African Americans and precluded him from having the same insider status that Belafonte had with his Peace Corps appointment.

Belafonte used his position to defend the actions of the Freedom Riders to the Kennedy administration. Although the activists had traveled relatively safely through the Upper South, enraged throngs repeatedly attacked them in Alabama, attracting the attention of the national media. Since the Riders were not breaking any laws, they argued that the federal government should protect them, but the Kennedys tried unsuccessfully to halt the Rides. Robert worried about the legal implications of federal intervention, while the president stewed about the international implications prior to his upcoming summit with Soviet premier Nikita Khruschev in Vienna. Robert finally sent the national guard into Montgomery to prevent rioting, but the fate of the Freedom Rides remained in question. During the disorder, Belafonte happened to be at a Peace Corps Advisory Council meeting. At this—his first meeting at the White House—Belafonte was somewhat humbled by his surroundings. Kennedy aide Harris Wofford observed that an angry Belafonte became subdued after the president entered the room. At the meeting's end, Belafonte finally, "in very low key, in his quiet hoarse voice, said 'Mr. President, I know how much you're doing in civil rights. And I know all these other things are going on. But perhaps you could say something a little more about the Freedom Riders.'"[54] An annoyed Kennedy left the meeting, but perhaps Belafonte's conciliatory tone inspired the Kennedys to ask him to serve as an intermediary between the White House and SNCC only a few days later.

The administration had made little headway with SNCC in developing an alternative to the Freedom Rides. Robert Kennedy had concluded that since voting was "the area in which we had the greatest authority," then "this was where the most good could be accomplished."[55] He summoned a group of SNCC representatives to a meeting to discuss a voter registration project, but the students were hostile, in part due to Kennedy's condescending behavior toward them and to their inherent suspicions of the power structure. Just days earlier, Kennedy had made a deal with the governors of Alabama and Mississippi that as long as they prevented mob violence, the federal government would not interfere to prevent local police from arresting the Freedom Riders. After a contentious discussion, the students agreed to take the idea under consideration and even to consider calling off the Freedom Rides.[56] However, the next day, Sammy Davis, Jr., organized a rally at the Los Angeles Sports Arena that gave new life to the Freedom Ride movement. As the rally's headliner, King told an audience of twenty thousand that the Freedom Rides should continue. The cheering crowd voiced its approval, while Davis, and the comedian Dick Gregory, who was somewhat new to the movement, passed a giant cardboard donation box through the audience and offered autographs for donations. The rally raised $30,000, and thousands of disappointed supporters had to be turned away once the arena reached capacity.[57]

Unnerved by this avowed enthusiasm for the Freedom Rides, Kennedy hastily summoned Belafonte to a meeting at his Hickory Hill home in Virginia that same day. Would Belafonte, Kennedy implored, use his influence with the students to encourage political action? Belafonte agreed, feeling somewhat awkward, as he had crashed a dinner party celebrating Kennedy's tenth wedding anniversary. After several of these types of tête-à-têtes—"in the middle of a game of touch football, and in the middle of some lunch, and in the middle of a cocktail party"—Belafonte began to sense a feeling of "closeness" between himself and the attorney general.[58] Indeed, a sense of trust would develop between them, in part because Belafonte was able to deliver results.

Within ten days, Belafonte convinced a cohort of SNCC's most active leaders to champion voter registration. Still in Washington, he met with a group of students led by the sit-in veterans Charles Jones and Tim Jenkins. Already somewhat open to the idea of promoting voter registration, the students debated with Belafonte the merits and drawbacks of taking it on. Although they generally agreed on the necessity of the issue, they told Belafonte that they were reluctant to abandon direct action and to rely on the Kennedy administration for the funds necessary to carry out the project. Belafonte recommended that they form a "political vanguard" within the Freedom Rider movement, thus obviating the feeling that they were "abandoning" their principles. Indeed, since a number of Freedom Riders were still in jail, direct action remained at the forefront of their agenda. As for the matter of funding, Belafonte offered $40,000 of his own money (equivalent to almost $320,000 in the present day) to help launch the voter registration campaign. Although Stokley Carmichael, a SNCC activist who became increasingly prominent in the organization, was not present at this meeting, he remembers that "folks were just overwhelmed" by the extremely "generous" offer.[59] Persuaded by Belafonte's reasoning and impressed with his willingness to place a personal stake in the project, the group endorsed voter registration as their next campaign. Known as "the Belafonte committee," the cadre of activists then prevailed upon the rest of the organization to win their support as well.[60]

A number of SNCC activists resisted the Belafonte committee. John Lewis, for example, said, "I didn't take that trip to meet with Belafonte, but I heard all about it. And I didn't like it." Lewis felt that the organization's success thus far had depended on public demonstrations and therefore such action needed to be pushed further.[61] Others were not convinced that SNCC had the resources to carry out the type of project the Belafonte committee envisioned, either in terms of money or personnel. Indeed, Charles Jones proposed expanding the organization to include over one hundred thousand students. Considering that only about two hundred SNCC activists had participated in the Freedom Rides, this seemed far-fetched. In the meantime, the Kennedy administration had quietly promoted the development of the Voter Education Project (VEP), a tax-exempt organization responsible for distributing private moneys to organizations engaged in voter registration, including SNCC if it so chose, to be managed by the Council of Federated Organizations (COFO).[62] Ultimately, the students agreed to take on a voter registration project but decided to create two separate programs. One would be devoted to direct action and under the leadership of the dynamic Diane Nash, a principle leader from the Nashville movement. The other would focus on voter registration and operate under Charles Jones.[63] Thus, the Belafonte committee became its own wing within SNCC.

Belafonte's interference with SNCC significantly shaped the development of the organization, starting with his own connection to it. In Carmichael's estimation, the summer of 1961 "marked the beginning of Brother Belafonte's long relationship—as adviser, benefactor, and big brother—to the young freedom-fighting organization."[64] The singer became a member of the SNCC executive committee and was closely intertwined with the group thereafter. As he says, "I sort of suspected I was signing on to be SNCC's major angel for years to come."[65] Even more significant was the effect of voter registration on the organization. That SNCC moved in this direction without becoming a supplicant to the Kennedy administration is due in part to Belafonte's political sophistication. Although he fostered the organization's cooperation with the administration, he also helped the students remain financially independent and encouraged them to maintain their commitment to direct action. In fact, voter registration would soon evolve into its own form of direct action.

Soon after SNCC established its first voter registration school in McComb, Mississippi, Belafonte was needed in a new capacity—that of emergency contact. Robert Moses had opened the school in August 1961 and was beginning the painstaking process of enlisting volunteers to register. He also attempted to expand into nearby Amite and Walhall Counties with demonstrations and sit-ins, which prompted violent reprisals. Herbert Lee, a local fifty-two year-old African American who attended the school, was shot and killed for his participation. During one protest, local whites ferociously attacked Moses and two other SNCC workers until police intervened and arrested all 122 demonstrators. Only Charles Jones managed to escape. Knowing that he was SNCC's only link to the outside world but also terrified for his life, Jones ducked into a nearby butcher shop and called Belafonte to ask for bail money. He then called John Doar of the Justice Department and requested protection.[66] Doar arrived shortly thereafter but offered no better advice than for Jones to draw the shades to the shop and continue hiding. The $5,000 promised by Belafonte arrived a few days later. This incident indicated that Belafonte could be counted on in a pinch but also that very few people involved in voter registration had fully understood what the organization would be up against. Moses and his colleagues returned to Atlanta for an emergency staff meeting to discuss if and how they should continue what was already proving to be an expensive and dangerous project.[67]

Despite the new challenges posed by voter registration, student activism had breathed new life into the civil rights movement by generating more publicity for the cause and capturing the attention of sympathizers nationwide, including a handful of celebrities. The actor Charlton Heston, famed for his religious roles in *The Ten Commandments* (1956) and *Ben-Hur* (1959), was one such individual. When Heston learned about events such as the Montgomery Bus Boycott and Southern practices such as segregation, he found himself lamenting the underlying racism but realized that simply carping about the problem was rather unsatisfying. His longtime friend Dr. Jolly West was involved in a desegregation campaign in Oklahoma City with a colleague, Dr. Chester M. Pierce, and the local NAACP Youth Council. Heston invited West and Pierce to his home in Beverly Hills to discuss the possibility of his involvement. According to Heston's son, Fraser, the gist of these meetings was that "tyranny triumphs when good men do nothing," and Heston, who possessed a strong sense of civic duty, felt it was his responsibility to *something*.[68] Heston made arrangements to join West and Pierce for a demonstration against segregated lunch counters at the city's downtown department stores. Upon arriving in Oklahoma City in late May 1961, Heston helped paint placards in preparation for the event. His sandwich board read, "All Men Are Created Equal— Jefferson" on the front, and "Racial Discrimination Is Un-American" on the back, and he wore it over his shoulders during the march.

Heston's presence did not draw widespread press coverage so much as mobilize supporters. The indefatigable Clara Luper, the principle organizer of the Oklahoma City movement, recalled the electrifying effect Heston had on the campaign. For three long years, Luper had led students into downtown stores every day after school and on Saturdays. Although her brigade rarely encountered violence or was placed under arrest, the activists faced palpable white hostility on a daily basis. In 1958, the Youth Council had achieved early victory at two downtown drug stores. However, the bulk of the downtown establishments, including John A. Brown's department store, remained segregated in the spring of 1961.

Luper and the students had grown weary of the long campaign, but news of Heston's involvement injected them with new energy. Word of his arrival "had spread like wild fire and large crowds had assembled on Main Street to get a quick glimpse of the star." She attests that "the crowd was caught up in the unbelievable realities of the moment," and when the celebrity trio met Luper and the students, "wild applause went up in the air. Oklahomans sounded like they do when the Big Red football scores against Texas or Nebraska." Heston responded in kind, shaking hands with fans and chatting with bystanders along the way. Luper found the scene so inspiring that she gushed, "Every step that Heston, West, and Pierce took was adding tons of Freedom vitamins to our tired bodies that had been protesting for three years."[69]

Although Heston told the activists he was ashamed that he had not participated in such demonstrations earlier, he optimistically predicted, "I suspect the next time I come to Oklahoma City, there won't be anything to demonstrate. The sentiments of the city are clearly in favor of desegregation." This prognostication proved correct. Soon after Heston departed, the widow of John A. Brown finally agreed to meet with Luper. After an hour-long discussion, Brown promised to eliminate segregation at her store. By July 1961, 171 restaurants had desegregated as well, a remarkable breakthrough. It is not clear how much credit Heston should receive for this success. After all, he never met with Brown personally, and perhaps she had already decided to desegregate her store before he came to town. Furthermore, Luper and the students had laid the groundwork. At the very least, however, the excitement and publicity associated with Heston's visit appear to have hastened the desegregation of Oklahoma City and perhaps even marked the turning point there. The campaign was certainly significant to Heston's public persona. His roles in biblical epics had established his image as force of righteous independence. His participation in the Oklahoma City march furthered that reputation, as would his subsequent political activities. He claimed that he "rode the tiger" of political affairs henceforth and that the march established his lifelong commitment to civil rights.[70]

Heston's work in Oklahoma also marked a milestone in the relationship between Hollywood stars and the civil rights movement. He was not the first major white star to speak out on behalf of civil rights, but he was the first to participate in a direct-action campaign. Thus far, the few white stars who had supported civil rights had done so with financial contributions or by performing in benefits. Heston's taking to the streets in a local demonstration, albeit in the Upper South, was a risky act. Although the demonstrators were not breaking any laws, and the local police had historically treated them fairly, the potential for arrest was an ever-present reality. Furthermore, unlike at a benefit show, a friendly crowd was not a guarantee. Despite Heston's overwhelming welcome at the demonstration, one heckler shouted, "Go back to Hollywood, you Jew!" (apparently confusing Heston's movie roles with his real life). Another group of detractors carried signs: "Is Beverly Hills integrated?" These mild confrontations were less dramatic than an admittedly anxious Heston had expected. As he told the crowd, "I was very pleased with the march. I'm used to taking part in marches and chariot races only when they're fixed," referring to his exodus through the Red Sea as Moses and to his famed chariot race in *Ben-Hur*. Also at risk was his film career. Heston was an internationally known superstar, and *Ben-Hur* had played to packed theaters for over two years. Even so, studio heads urged him not to go to Oklahoma City for fear that he might "alienate moviegoers." Heston brushed them off.[71] Aspiring stars could not necessarily afford to be so cavalier, but as a Screen Actors Guild officer (and later president), Heston would prove to be an influential link to the Hollywood community.

In the summer of 1961, the actor and singer Theodore Bikel also emerged as a spokesperson for civil rights. Born in Austria, Bikel and his family had fled the Nazi-occupied state during World War II, after which Bikel attended the Royal Academy of Dramatic Art in London. He made his film debut in 1951 in *The African Queen* and went on to build a solid film and stage career throughout the 1950s in such productions as *The Defiant Ones* with Sidney Poitier, and Broadway's *The Sound of Music*, in which Bikel originated the role of Captain von Trapp. During this same period, he also released several albums of Jewish folk songs. His success on this front led Bikel to cofound the Newport Folk Festival with Pete Seeger, an iconic folk singer whose leftist political associations had brought him under the scrutiny of House Un-American Activities Committee, and George Wein, a jazz producer and promoter, in 1959. Bikel's own experiences with racism and his associations with leftist political causes led him to the bourgeoning civil rights movement. He told African Americans that he could not "fully understand your lot, but I can understand persecution because I've been dealing with it all my life."[72]

Bikel came to believe that the most important assistance celebrities brought to the civil rights movement were their cultural standing and "eloquence and audibility." The benefits of fame and the essential qualities of a performer, he believed, allowed him to contribute in a way that perhaps others could not. Committed and passionate celebrities "beat the drum better," he asserted, because performers can attract attention and often state the needs and goals of the movement better than those who are not used to articulating such things. Furthermore, stars often boosted the morale of activists, he claimed, "because it helped them to know they were not alone. And . . . sometimes support could come from unexpected quarters."[73] The longtime SNCC activist Bob Zellner also says that Bikel had a "wonderful" gallows humor that they could "live on" during intense moments.[74]

Bikel first used his celebrity status to organize and headline benefit shows. Working in conjunction with CORE in 1961, Bikel coproduced and appeared in a telethon to aid the Freedom Riders that raised nearly $30,000 for the organization.[75] His partnership with CORE led Bikel to become more acquainted with SNCC, with which he felt a particular compatibility. "Although they were younger than my generation," Bikel admits, "I felt close to them because of my involvement with folk music which had always been the province of the young." He soon went to Greenwood, Mississippi, to organize a folk festival there with his friends and fellow singers Pete Seeger and Bob Dylan in what was Dylan's first trip South. Still an up-and-comer at that point, Dylan was so strapped for cash that Bikel paid his travel fare. Through these types of events, Bikel hoped that he could facilitate the movement's efforts to tap into a broader constituency. He played an important role in furthering the relationship between SNCC and the intellectual and Jewish Left, including labor unions, in New York.[76]

Bikel, impressed with the expansion of SNCC's program into voter registration, also volunteered for direct-action campaigns. "The integration of public facilities . . . was something all the organizations fought for," he explained, "but the voter registration drive was one of SNCC's primary objectives, and that appealed to my view that the black community needed a tactical first step in order to be drawn into the political process."[77] Bikel traveled the dangerous roads of rural Mississippi in an effort to mobilize the locals there. His function lied primarily in talking with Jewish Southerners, because "I had some standing with them." Nevertheless, he admits that he had just as difficult time changing minds in the Deep South as the workaday activists.[78] Whereas Bikel focused on mobilizing Jewish supporters to the cause, the comedian Dick Gregory, in Zellner's words, "practically became a SNCC field secretary" with his emphasis on local direct action.[79]

Gregory grew up "not poor, just broke" in segregated Saint Louis with a single mom and five siblings, but by 1962 was one of America's best-known comics. From a young age, the scrappy youngster learned the "power of a joke," using humor to disarm detractors and to stand up for himself. A high school and college track star, Gregory emerged a natural leader who addressed racist conditions with tenacity and wit. He brought those same qualities to his stand-up routine. His big break came in 1961 at the Playboy Club in Chicago. What was meant to be a one-night stand became a three-year contract when Gregory successfully played to an audience of white Southern executives in town on business. Part of his routine went as follows:

> Last time I was down South I walked into this restaurant, and the white waitress came up to me and said: "We don't serve colored people here."
>
> I said: "That's alright, I don't eat colored people. Bring me a whole fried chicken."
>
> About that time these three cousins come in, you know the ones I mean, Klu, Kluck, and Klan, and they say: "Boy, we're givin' you fair warnin'. Anything you do to that chicken, we're gonna do to you." About then the waitress brought me my chicken. "Remember, boy, anything you do to that chicken, we're gonna do to you." So I put down my knife and fork, and I picked up that chicken, and I kissed it.[80]

Gregory soon had regular gigs at top comedy clubs across the country and was a frequent guest on *The Jack Paar Tonight Show*.

Gregory had an unusual ability to poke fun at African American life without sinking to the "colored humor" of vaudeville, and to shrewdly lampoon racism so that white audiences laughed at themselves. His comedy had roots in the "chitlin circuit," in which Nipsey Russell, Slappy White, George Kirby, Redd Foxx, and Moms Mabley also honed their crafts. Gregory's transition into white clubs was made easier by his avoidance of the "blue humor" often characteristic of the circuit, as well the increasing popularity of such white satirists as Arch Lustberg and Mort Sahl, who drew on political absurdities for material.[81] One critic observed,

"Gregory's delivery is the slow windup and then the fast breaking punch line, coupled with the technique of taking long-accepted concepts and twisting them so that they explode over his pale-faced audience like a bomb."[82] In one bit, Gregory told his upscale audience how much he loved baseball: "It's the only sport in the world where a Negro can shake a stick at a white man and it ain't start no riot." When he elicited laughs, he pointedly said, "Thank you very much but don't clap for me. Just take me to lunch when it's not brotherhood week."[83] In an appearance on Paar's show, Gregory received the most applause from his all-white audience when he told them, "You're a good audience tonight and treat me nice because with President Kennedy's new housing bill I might be your neighbor now."[84] Indeed, although Gregory frequently cracked jokes about the South (often involving the Ku Klux Klan), he did not make a scapegoat out of the region and often reminded listeners of deep racial tensions in the North. Arguing that very few whites actually knew any black people, he felt he was "enlightening people" about the wrongs endured by African Americans, as well as their aspirations. It was on the nightclub circuit that Gregory became friends with Sammy Davis, Jr., which led to their emceeing the Freedom Riders rally in Los Angeles. In the fall of 1962, Gregory took a trip to Mississippi that changed his life's direction.

Gregory credits Medgar Evers, NAACP field secretary for Mississippi, with convincing him to go to Greenwood, center of the voter registration in the state. He admits, "A fear came over me. . . . It's one thing to be bold in New York or Chicago—it's a whole other matter to be bold in Mississippi." Impressed by the "black success stories" of local preachers, teachers, and business owners, Gregory was also deeply disturbed by the poverty and corrupt power structure of the South. He engaged in food relief efforts and began speaking at civil rights rallies.[85] After police unleashed dogs on the activists and local whites torched the main office, he joined in demonstrations for the first time in Greenwood in early April 1963.[86] The CORE activist David Dennis believes Gregory experienced "a conversion" during a series of marches to the local courthouse. The comedian was disappointed by his first march when the group of fifty returned to headquarters rather than being arrested. Gregory, who had brazenly taunted the police as simpletons unable to pass voter literacy tests themselves, volunteered to lead another group the next day. Dennis recalls that Gregory seemed to perceive himself as "the one to lead them to 'the promised land.'" However, Gregory "couldn't believe" how he was manhandled at the second march and how others were dragged into police vehicles. "He really changed" after that, Dennis says, and became committed to non-violent direct action, realizing that his fame could raise awareness.[87] The Greenwood police refused to arrest Gregory, even as he continued to disparage them as "dirty dogs," but the major news outlets, such as the *New York Times* and *Newsweek,* still publicized his involvement in the Greenwood marches.[88] Gregory's activities in Mississippi foreshadowed a greater leadership role at the local level, and he publicly expressed his willingness to die for the cause, although his frequent TV appearances indicated that his focus remained on promoting his comedic career.

In the meantime, even though Belafonte's film career had stalled, his television special "Tonight with Belafonte" indicated a potential breakthrough for the medium. Produced in 1959 for *The Revlon Revue,* an hour-long variety show that featured a different star each week, Belafonte brought his social realist approach to the small screen. The show also featured the blues singer Odetta, the Belafonte Folk Singers, and the blues musicians Sonny Terry and Brownie McGhee, and Belafonte employed stark sets and simple musical accompaniment for his folk numbers. His emphasis on chain gangs and rural churches represented African American interests in a fashion atypical of 1950s television. While the show certainly had its light and lively moments, with various "nonsense songs" and energetic dancing, for example, the overall message about racial persecution was obvious.[89] While the networks proved increasingly willing to commission documentary programming on race relations and other serious matters (mostly foreign policy), it had not yet embraced such material for primetime entertainment.[90] When the highly rated program received an Emmy, it appeared that Belafonte might have broken through that barrier. He signed a contract with Revlon to do five more episodes. However, when Southern affiliates complained about the next installment's mixed cast, and Belafonte refused to change the format, he and Revlon parted ways.[91] Although Belafonte continued to make guest appearances on game and variety shows, he would not produce another special (in which he controlled the programming and cast the performers) until 1966.

Not to let Hollywood off the hook, after the formation of SNCC, Belafonte earmarked his television appearance fees to go directly to the organization, a practice that other stars, such as Marlon Brando, would take up in the future. The combination of Heston's work in Oklahoma City, Bikel and Gregory's newfound outspokenness, and Belafonte's multifaceted efforts indicated that the cause of civil rights was catching on among the Hollywood set. By no means, however, could such activism have been called a trend, or trendy, in the autumn of 1961. Only a handful of celebrities were engaged in the movement at that time, and despite the actions of such high-profile stars as Sinatra and Heston, few white stars had come out in its support.

Belafonte was easily the celebrity most intricately engaged in the politics of the civil rights movement, and, in fact, it was rare for any activist to be so heavily involved in both the SCLC and SNCC. Only a few individuals, including John Lewis, Ella Baker, James Bevel, and Diane Nash, vested substantial time in both organizations. Belafonte continued to work as an intermediary between the Kennedy administration and both organizations, and he remained closely connected to the executive committees of both organizations. Thus, his activities generally encompassed larger goals than simply the event with which he was involved. For example, he planned a benefit performance for the SCLC in Atlanta in June 1962 with the added goal of assisting King in his efforts to desegregate the city. Belafonte and his mixed-race troupe registered without incident at their hotel and performed before an integrated audience.[92] Likewise, when Belafonte headlined a concert for SNCC in February 1963, it was with the intention of establishing a permanent fund-raising mechanism for the organization. According to SNCC executive director James Forman, this "marked the beginning of a support base among many black artists and writers together with liberal and progressive whites."[93] Such support was desperately needed. In 1962, SNCC had raised only $50,000. Belafonte's concert helped SNCC increase its income to $307,000 in 1963, of which over 10 percent came from similar fund-raising events. As its finances became more secure, SNCC could afford to expand voter registration into more than a dozen Mississippi counties, and into four more states, as well as to pay twelve office workers and sixty field secretaries.[94]

Belafonte also shared the trappings of his wealthy lifestyle. Belafonte's apartment, valuable as a meeting place, also provided activists with a respite from their harried schedules and relief from the violence of the Deep South. On the occasions that King traveled to New York, he had an open invitation to stay at Belafonte's apartment, and the same was true for SNCC activists, who grew accustomed to crashing at Belafonte's comfortable quarters. King, an aficionado of such luxuries as silk pajamas, first-class hotel suites, and fine dining, reveled in his frequent visits. The two men and their wives enjoyed relaxing over a bottle of Harvey's Bristol Cream sherry that Julie kept on hand exclusively for King. The Belafontes teased the reverend about how much he savored the liquor, and he joked that he was monitoring the contents of the bottle to make sure they weren't drinking any of "his" sherry.[95] For SNCC activists, most of whom scraped by on a paltry salary of ten dollars per week, Belafonte's generosity was even more consequential. During their visits, the singer invited them backstage at his concerts and presented them with a variety of gifts, including his cast-offs. "We used to get his clothes," one SNCC worker remembered wistfully, "Oh God, he had such rich clothes." Indeed, the luxuries to which Belafonte had grown accustomed served as sources of rare indulgence for the civil rights workers.

Belafonte's connection to both the SCLC and SNCC became especially important as tensions emerged between the two groups. Initially, relations between them had thrived. King's example had motivated the students, and they had appreciated his public support for the sit-ins and the Freedom Rides, although he had participated in neither. And Belafonte had helped organize SCLC-backed concerts that paid tribute to the students. At one such event, the SCLC had awarded $500 scholarships to ten student Riders.[96] In 1962, however, relations between the two groups steadily eroded, in part due to finances. SNCC activists increasingly felt that SCLC was hijacking their sources of funding. The commonalities between the organizations, in addition to the SCLC's habit of telling the press that SNCC operated as its adjunct, often led donors to send checks that were intended for the students to the SCLC.[97] Also detrimental was the unsatisfactory development of the Albany [Georgia] Movement, during which SNCC worked with local NAACP leaders to challenge segregation across the city. By enforcing "public order" rather than segregation laws, and by not using weapons when rounding up protesters, the Albany police were able to incarcerate protesters without attracting much attention, and SNCC had no funds for their release. The organization reluctantly requested King's assistance. He joined the students in jail, but they soon felt he was trying to take over "their" campaign. When King agreed to a compromise with Albany's white officials, the SNCC students were so resentful that they privately told King they endorsed the settlement but publicly criticized him in *Time* magazine for taking it. That the students increasingly saw themselves as the vanguards of the movement and King merely as its figurehead undermined their partnership.[98]

As the grumbling against King and the SCLC continued, Belafonte felt compelled to step in. In March 1962, he held a fund-raiser for SNCC at his apartment to which he invited key SNCC activists, as well as King, to be his guests of honor. SNCC leaders Robert Moses, Charles Jones, Charles Sherrod, Tim Jenkins, and Charles McDew all attended. Desperate for the funds necessary to reinvigorate both voter registration and the Albany Movement, the students obliged Belafonte to a long discussion during which he gently chastened them for their attitude toward King. When they complained that King was too cautious, detached, and distracted by his own fame, Belafonte defended the leader. He reminded them of King's sacrifices and argued that the reverend was not as bourgeois as they thought. Snickering about Coretta's stylish pearls and pillbox hats and King's expensive taste in pajamas and vacations, they were not convinced. They did concede his point, however, that few other individuals would have tolerated their effrontery. Appeasing their benefactor, they temporarily forwent their grievances, a posture facilitated by King's conduct later that evening. He mingled easily with the guests, delivering a speech only at Belafonte's request and then in devotion to the students. He talked about how much he had learned from their sacrifices and introduced each of them, turning over the floor so they could share with the guests the nature of their work. King concluded by urging the crowd to support SNCC, never mentioning his own organization.[99]

Although the tensions between SNCC and King never fully dissipated, Belafonte's party did help prevent open warfare during the ongoing Albany Movement. Reinvigorated by local activism and King's return in the summer of 1962, the campaign finally attracted the national spotlight when King was again arrested and jailed. The federal government pressured Albany officials to desegregate, indicating that victory was at hand. The city did cease enforcement of segregation, but only because it shut down public facilities such as libraries and parks rather than bow to federal pressure. The campaign was perceived as a limited success at best, and a failure at worst.

* * *

In the immediate aftermath of the Albany Movement, the civil rights movement plateaued. While SNCC and the SCLC regrouped, the Kennedy administration successfully siphoned the national urgency from the cause. King would seek to reinvigorate the movement in Birmingham, Alabama, in the spring of 1963 with "Project C" (Project Confrontation). Belafonte served as a key operative in this plan from the outset. As the drama of Project C unfolded, Dick Gregory and Theodore Bikel became more deeply involved as well, marking Birmingham as the direct-action campaign with the most celebrity involvement to date.

Before the Birmingham movement got underway, King reflected on the events of 1962 with mixed feelings. Most heartening was the SCLC's strong financial position. A December benefit concert featuring Sammy Davis, Jr., and Peter Lawford in White Plains, New York, had concluded a successful year of fund-raising for the organization. The show netted $12,000, adding to the already unprecedented profits generated by other charitable performances, mass mailings, and King's speaking engagements that year. The Albany Movement had proved the necessity of reserving adequate money for bail bonds, and the momentum behind the organization's various fund-raising endeavors indicated that targeting Birmingham, which SCLC operatives concluded would cost as much as $1 million, was now a reasonable goal.[100] King's attitude toward the president, however, had soured due to the administration's claims that it could do little to protect the activists and locals involved in the very voter projects it had encouraged. In the meantime, riotous mobs descended upon the University of Mississippi to prevent James Meredith from desegregating the school. Kennedy eventually dispatched federal authorities to impose order, and Robert made a deal with the Mississippi governor to secure Meredith's entrance to Ole Miss. The Kennedy administration had once again handled what King considered a moral issue by striking a bargain with a white racist politician, and he and other civil rights leaders felt like "pawns." King felt that the administration believed that because it had enacted "positive deeds," it could now coast on civil rights. This, when voter registration had stalled and desegregation was proceeding at a snail's pace.[101]

Kennedy did little to quell black America's suspicions, and he may have even exacerbated them by his treatment of Sammy and May Britt Davis at a White House function in February 1963. In an effort to smooth relations between Kennedy and African Americans, the presidential aide Lewis Martin had proposed that the president host a large reception for leading black Americans in conjunction with Abraham Lincoln's birthday. Martin believed that the symbolism of Kennedy's hosting a predominately African American group at the White House would counteract feelings that the president had been too cautious on civil rights and that, as had been reported, he was ill at ease in the company of blacks. Kennedy agreed to the reception, but the emboldened Lewis violated social protocol when he invited the Davises (since they had been barred from the inauguration). The aide went so far as to surreptitiously reinsert Davis's name after White House officials had scratched him from the list. One staffer remembers that Kennedy was "absolutely feathered" when he spotted the couple at the reception. Fearful of the publicity, the president desperately tried to enlist the First Lady in shuffling them away from photographers. When she refused, his aides did the job instead. Presidential advisers were taken aback. "It was as though the whole thing was a flop," one said of Kennedy's attitude. Even though the details of Kennedy's reaction were not known at the time, the black press picked up on the slight. Said *Jet* magazine, "To Sammy and May Britt Davis—no pics of you, but everybody knew you were there. Great show and you all have so much charm and dignity."[102] Indeed, Kennedy's behavior at the event validated black American's general wariness toward him. King hoped that the Birmingham campaign would force Kennedy to take the moral stand that he had thus far dodged.

Project Confrontation officially commenced at Belafonte's apartment on March 31, 1963, after a year's worth of planning and several delays. The Reverend Fred Shuttlesworth, a member of the SCLC's executive committee and longtime resident of Birmingham, had convinced King to come to Alabama's largest city. Birmingham's segregation laws were some of the most rigidly enforced in the South, giving the city a reputation for oppressive backwardness. Most of Birmingham's black residents and any of their white allies had been cowed into silence. Shuttlesworth had once spearheaded a lawsuit against the city and a boycott against the downtown stores, actions that had resulted in little more than his arrest and attempts against his life. His activities, nevertheless, gave King a firm foundation from which to work. King reasoned that while "a campaign in Birmingham would surely be the toughest of our civil rights careers," the SCLC's relatively secure financial position and Shuttlesworth's presence gave them a reasonable chance of success there. This triumph, they hoped, would "break the back of segregation all over the nation." Thus decided, King and his advisors delayed the campaign twice so that it would not conflict with, and thus become a political issue in, Birmingham's mayoral elections that spring. In the interim, Belafonte persuaded King to take the unconventional route of launching the campaign from his New York City apartment.

Belafonte and Stanley Levison suggested this tactic as a way to effectively galvanize King's Northern supporters. Too often, they observed, King appealed for help in the midst of a crisis. Perpetually operating on an emergency basis not only limited their ability to solicit funds but also made them appear disorganized. Since the plans for the Birmingham campaign were well-ordered, Belafonte and Levison urged that they make the most of these circumstances. By reaching out to trusted insiders in advance, they could give their supporters a sense of being "in the know" and thus line up funding ahead of time. King agreed, and Belafonte's secretary extended confidential invitations to some seventy prestigious civil rights supporters. Not everyone in King's circle was impressed by this plan. The Reverend Wyatt Tee Walker, SCLC executive director and chief tactician of Project C, stayed in Birmingham. He viewed the meeting as a "stroking session" for a bunch of stars who wanted to "feel as if they were on the ground" but could hardly appreciate the complexities of the campaign. Furthermore, by divulging their plans to this group of "VIPs," Walker worried that they risked the chance of compromising Project C.[103] The potential payoff, however, convinced the rest of the SCLC's high command to support Belafonte's proposal. King, Shuttlesworth, Ralph Abernathy, and other key SCLC operatives journeyed to New York for the secretive planning session.

The buzz of anticipation in Belafonte's apartment on March 31, 1963, escalated until he called the meeting to order at 9:30 PM. Of the seventy-five guests, few were privy to the reason for their summation. Belafonte's secretary, Gloria Cantor, had revealed little when she had extended the invitations via telephone. "Dr. King and Rev. Shuttlesworth are meeting with some of their friends at Harry's apartment," she had said. "They hope that you will be able to attend." When pressed for more details, she had mysteriously beckoned, "Come along, and you'll find out." Ruby Dee, Ossie Davis, Sidney Poitier, Aidan Quinn, and Frederic March were among the stars who had found the invitation too intriguing to pass up.[104] To a jammed house, Belafonte dramatically revealed the purpose of the meeting: to "do the unprecedented and announce an impending protest campaign well in advance of its scheduled occurrence." King soberly informed his supporters of the basic details of Project C. A much more emotional Shuttlesworth then rose to explain the dangers and intensity of the campaign. He shocked the crowd into silence, saying, "You have to be prepared to die before you can begin to live."[105] When Belafonte broke the quietude and appealed for their support, the guests clamored to fulfill what Belafonte stated as their biggest known need: "tremendous sums of money for bail bonds." They also abided by their vows of secrecy and leaked no news about what had taken place at what proved to be a hugely successful meeting.

Although the two men had worked closely in the past, King was especially impressed with Belafonte's commitment and adeptness during Project C. Not only had Belafonte's precursory meeting been a big financial success, but the artist did not rest there. The same night, Belafonte organized a committee to raise even more money. Since they did not know how many activists would be jailed and what Birmingham authorities would set for bond, no amount of money would be too small to reserve. King attested, "For the next three weeks, Belafonte, who never does anything without being totally involved, gave unlimited hours to organizing people and money." Belafonte wheedled his wealthy friends and associates for cash and encouraged his contemporaries to participate in fundraising rallies being planned by the SCLC's regional offices. And this was just the beginning. "Throughout the subsequent campaign, he talked with me or my aides two or three times a day," King remembered. "It would be hard to overestimate the role this sensitive artist played in the success of the Birmingham campaign."[106]

Belafonte's outreach efforts indicated that celebrities could be a significant component of Project C, a prospect that King cultivated as "a wonderful new dimension for the movement."[107] In fact, King counted on celebrity support before it was fully warranted in an effort to rouse Birmingham locals, an approach that largely backfired. When King returned to Birmingham in early April to launch the direct action phase of Project C, the resistance of local blacks to his plans alarmed him.[108] He painted pictures of peaceful picketing and marches, surprising his aides with visions of such notables as Jackie Robinson, Belafonte, and Sammy Davis, Jr., coming to town. That King had indicated that there would be a visit from Davis was ironic, as it had been a long-standing joke between them that Davis would go anywhere King called him—in the North.[109] More problematic, King announced to the press that the singer Ray Charles would help lead demonstrations. Apparently the arrival of the blind bluesman Al Hibbler in Birmingham had led King to conclude that Charles would be willing to participate in the campaign as well. In what became a public relations imbroglio, however, Charles's booking agent vehemently denied the idea. "They'll be lucky if they can get him to come down there and sing for them. He certainly isn't going to get mixed up in politics," claimed the booker. "Charles is blind. How would he lead any protest march?"[110]

The incident led Bill Berry of the Chicago Urban League to write a long editorial for the *Chicago Daily Defender* urging more stars to participate in Southern demonstrations. He questioned why none, other than Dick Gregory, had been willing to go to jail and asserted, "Direct participation by Negro stars is the answer to many of the racial problems in this country." Although Berry acknowledged the stars' work as spokespersons and fund-raisers, he demanded more. "Where are you?" he called, naming Belafonte, Davis, Horne, Poitier, and a number of jazz artists. Berry posed the question "Could it be that they are too good for jail?" Most civil rights supporters, celebrity or otherwise, were not willing to be incarcerated. One historian estimates that King could count on only 5 percent of locals to do so.[111] To expect many stars to risk arrest seemed implausible. Nat King Cole took Berry's editorial head-on, calling it "idiotic" that celebrities should do the jobs of "ministers, lawyers and other vocally trained professional civil rights fighters." He argued that entertainers were "not trained in such fighting" and that the entertainment they provided often "set the stage" for the integration carried out by civil rights organizations. In the case of Birmingham, Cole said, "Nobody ever asked me." He would have, nevertheless, declined an invitation. "It would do my people no good and finish me in the only life I know," he argued.[112] In Belafonte's case, it was better for him not to be in jail, as he was able to raise money on several occasions to keep the campaign going. Still, Gregory and Bikel did agree to demonstrate.

News of the comedian's participation in Project C did exactly what King hoped it would: it roused the locals and attracted national publicity. On Thursday, May 2, King announced at a nightly rally that Gregory would arrive that Sunday, eliciting cheers from the crowd. The following day, King issued a press release about Gregory's impending arrival. An anxious President Kennedy called the comedian and said, "Dick, do me a favor and don't go down to Birmingham. I feel that Dr. King is wrong." The president had just dispatched Burke Marshall to mediate a settlement in Birmingham, and he urged Gregory to let Marshall settle in to begin the negotiation process. "Your going will just create problems," he warned. Unabashed, Gregory told Kennedy that he had promised King he would arrive in Birmingham by Monday, May 6, and that he intended to fulfill his pledge.[113] Bikel's participation did not generate the same publicity, but it demonstrated his commitment to the nonviolent direction that had attracted him to CORE and SNCC.

Gregory took on an authoritative stance in Birmingham, fulfilling the conversion that had begun in Greenwood. When Gregory and Bikel arrived, the city had already turned violent. On Friday, May 3, Police Chief Theophilus "Bull" Connor had ordered his men to turn fire hoses and to sic dogs on the demonstrators, most of whom were schoolchildren. This finally attracted national media attention. The sickening images had prompted Kennedy to send Marshall to Birmingham, hoping that a negotiated settlement between the SCLC and Birmingham's business community would prompt King to cancel the demonstrations. With momentum finally on his side, however, King declined. As marchers gathered, Gregory made a point of talking to them individually and urging them not to breach the code of nonviolence essential to the action. He also took responsibility for the first wave of marchers, nineteen young boys and girls. When the police tried to halt them, he refused. "Dick Gregory says they will not disperse," announced the captain over the bullhorn. They were soon taken into custody.[114] Approximately one thousand marchers went to jail that day, and King's aides estimated that they could recruit six thousand more. As SCLC worked toward a settlement, however, the incarcerated activists faced intolerable conditions in the city jail.

Gregory and Bikel both experienced beatings during their five-day stays, although they faced different circumstances in the segregated jail. The guards left the white demonstrators to the inmates. As Bikel tells it, the guards informed the other white prisoners that "we were a bunch of nigger lovers. And these thieves and rapists suddenly felt superior. They also surmised that no one would stop them if they roughed us up. Sure enough, they did just that." Gregory was temporarily placed in solitary confinement but soon found himself in a crowded cell. His efforts to protect the children brought him to blows with the guards. Gregory used the beating to gain greater publicity for the movement. After his release, he held a press conference and accused the police of brutality. "You leave the world when you go into the Birmingham jail," he said. He recounted being "whipped by five policemen using billy clubs, hammers, and sawed-off pool sticks." His report led the Justice Department to investigate the incident. Naturally, Gregory used the experience for material in his comedy routines. "When I was in Birmingham, Bull Connor told me to watch it or he'd give me a *white* eye," he joked. "I said if that was the case, then he'd be doing me a favor by hitting me all over."[115]

Meanwhile, after what appeared to be a devastating setback, Belafonte's work from his New York apartment proved crucial to the campaign's success. The negotiations spearheaded by Marshall finally came to a satisfactory conclusion. On Friday, May 10, Birmingham's business leaders agreed to all of the SCLC's demands for desegregation and for the hiring of black employees in exchange for an immediate halt to the protests. However, Alabama governor George Wallace denounced the settlement, and violence broke out in the streets. Connor used the hysteria as an excuse to crack down on demonstrators. Adding to these problems, at the hearing for an earlier march at which King and Shuttlesworth had been arrested, a local judge set new bonds for their appeal at the legal maximum of $2,500 each and sent them back to jail. The Kennedys feared that if King remained imprisoned, riots would prevail in Birmingham, but King refused to leave until the other demonstrators, especially the children, were also released. Robert Kennedy implored Belafonte to raise a spectacular $100,000, but at the time the banks in New York were closed. Belafonte ferried about the city to pick up loose cash from wealthy friends, and Kennedy arranged for a representative from the New York Transportation Workers Union to drop off $50,000 in cash at Belafonte's door. Then Belafonte arranged for Clarence Jones to meet Governor Nelson Rockefeller's assistant at the Chase Manhattan Bank vault to pick up the rest. Belafonte carefully avoided leaving a paper trail. The Kennedys could not afford for their heavy-handed role to become known to Southern Democrats, nor did King want them to discover his financial connection to the Republican governor. Whatever the risks, the cache of funds allowed for the demonstrators' release.[116]

Belafonte and King pressured Kennedy to enforce the Birmingham settlement, especially when violence threatened to overcome the city. When various Alabama newspapers and public officials denounced the agreement, Belafonte began mobilizing three thousand New Yorkers to picket the White House, and King threatened to bring planeloads of prominent supporters to Birmingham to encourage a strong stand by the president. In the meantime, two bombings against King and his family on the evening of May 12 led to all-night rioting. The result: six businesses, several houses, and a two-story apartment building burned to the ground, several dozen cars were destroyed, and nearly seventy people were taken to the hospital. Convinced that Wallace and Connor were working to sabotage the agreement signed by Birmingham's white business leaders, Kennedy acted. He authorized the deployment of US Army troops to the outskirts of Birmingham, both in the name of public order and to protect the desegregation settlement.[117] The agreement stood; Project C was over.

* * *

In the eyes of SCLC executive director Wyatt Tee Walker, Belafonte was able to "articulate better" than any other celebrity "what the movement was about." Prior to 1963, Belafonte often seemed to be working against the odds in a desperate struggle to raise money and awareness for the civil rights cause. The Birmingham campaign, however, would prove to be a turning point. In its immediate aftermath, President Kennedy, as well as a host of Hollywood stars, would take stronger stands on the issue of civil rights, strengthening the movement in its quest to break down segregation. Belafonte's championship of civil rights from his home in Manhattan strengthened the Northern liberal network and facilitated the movement's permeation of the mainstream, an acceptance which would allow him to make a resurgence in Hollywood as the decade proceeded.

Above: Ruby Dee with Richard Lane, Jackie Robinson, and Billy Wayne on the set of *The Jackie Robinson Story* (1950). Independent "message movies" provided improved roles for African American actors in the 1940s and 1950s and facilitated the careers of a new generation of black stars. *Library of Congress Prints and Photographs Division.*

Left: Harry Belafonte performing in an unidentified television program in 1965. Belafonte's form-fitting attire, handsome appearance, and dramatic expressions revolutionized the folk music scene and opened doors in Hollywood. *Photographs and Prints Division, Schomburg Center for Research in Black Culture, New York Public Library, Astor, Lenox, and Tilden Foundations.*

Right: Dorothy Dandridge arriving at the 27th Academy Awards on March 30, 1955. Nominated in the best actress category for *Carmen Jones* (1954), Dandridge was Hollywood's first African American leading lady and an early supporter of the civil rights movement. *mptvimages.com.*

Below: Sidney Poitier, Otto Preminger, Pearl Bailey, Sammy Davis, Jr., Samuel Goldwyn, and Dorothy Dandridge working on the script of *Porgy and Bess* (1959). Uncomfortable with material they considered demeaning, the cast demanded changes to the production that were unprecedented for an all-black cast on a major studio release. *mptvimages.com.*

The Rat Pack's Dean Martin, Frank Sinatra, and Sammy Davis, Jr., won notice for their interracial camaraderie both on . . . *David Sutton/mptvimages.com.*

. . . and offstage. Davis's affiliation with the Rat Pack helped him become the premier fundraiser for the movement, but he also drew criticism for his "clowning" and subservience to Sinatra. *Library of Congress Prints and Photographs Division.*

John F. Kennedy chats with Harry and Julie Belafonte at a private reception in
New York City in 1962. After campaigning for Kennedy in 1960, Belafonte remained
an administration insider, a position he leveraged for the Southern Christian
Leadership Conference and the Student Nonviolent Coordinating Committee.
John F. Kennedy Presidential Library.

Charlton Heston demonstrating against segregation in downtown Oklahoma City with his friends Dr. Chester Pierce and Dr. Jolly West in May 1961. Heston was the first major Hollywood star to participate in a Southern demonstration. *Photo courtesy of Fraser Heston.*

The actor and folk singer Theodore Bikel, photographed here in an undated publicity shot, partnered with the Student Nonviolent Coordinating Committee on voter registration and fundraising projects and was one of the few celebrities to go to jail for the movement. *Library of Congress Prints and Photographs Division.*

After his breakout performance at the Playboy Club in 1961, Dick Gregory became one of America's most popular comedians by the time of this 1964 interview. He hoped that his social satire would enlighten whites and embolden blacks on racial issues. *Library of Congress Prints and Photographs Division.*

The Arts Group
and the March
on Washington

The March in '63 proved that the artists indeed had a special place
in the struggle. We were out front, a part of the program.

—Ruby Dee

IN THE AFTERMATH OF THE BIRMINGHAM CAMPAIGN, A NEW ZEAL
for the civil rights cause emerged, and celebrities were not immune to
this fever. The stars that were involved continued serving as spokespersons, raising money, rallying crowds, and sometimes even participating in demonstrations. In the summer of 1963, the Leading Six and
their small cohort of allies expanded their range of activities and were
less wary of appearing too controversial. Furthermore, they became less
of isolated anomalies when some of Hollywood's most bankable stars—
such as Paul Newman, Burt Lancaster, and Marlon Brando—joined the
movement. This interest culminated in an Arts Group organized by
Brando and Charlton Heston for the March on Washington in August
that worked in tandem with Ossie Davis, who planned the program.
These stars' participation not only lent to the success of the overwhelmingly positive March but also played an important role in bringing Hollywood more conclusively into the movement's Northern liberal network
and renewing the black employment campaign in the film industry.

* * *

By the summer of 1963, one could sense an attitudinal shift among civil rights groups, their celebrity supporters, and the Kennedy administration. Heartened by the desegregation settlement at Birmingham, they emerged from the battle there notably hopeful and aggressive. Reassured that change could indeed come, they were more willing to risk controversy to achieve progress, an emboldened spirit that resulted in both cooperation and acrimony among them.

Martin Luther King, Jr., believed that a seismic mental shift took place among black Americans in the months after Birmingham. "They shook off three hundred years of psychological slavery and said: 'We can make ourselves free,'" he proclaimed. In the wake of Birmingham, the number of Southern Christian Leadership Conference (SCLC) affiliates grew from 85 to 110; 758 demonstrations occurred in 186 cities across the South; and at least 14,733 people were arrested.[1] Furthermore, the National Association for the Advancement of Colored People (NAACP) announced a shift in approach to include more direct action campaigns. Although the organization continued to focus on litigation, it more willingly embraced King's tactics of civil disobedience. On June 1, in Jackson, Mississippi, NAACP executive secretary Roy Wilkins himself was arrested, along with Medgar Evers and hundreds of other demonstrators.[2] The arrest of the firm yet prudent Wilkins indicated that the movement was growing increasingly defiant. Alarmed by this spirited pugnaciousness and fearful that a new wave of demonstrations would result in the full-scale riots that Birmingham almost became, Attorney General Robert Kennedy resolved to better understand "the Negro mood."

In this effort, Kennedy turned to black celebrities. Even though Harry Belafonte had warned John Kennedy in 1960 that celebrities have a slanted worldview, the administration still valued their perspective. The Kennedys believed that, unlike civil rights leaders, celebrities generally did not have a political agenda, in the sense that that they did not answer to an organization. Nor were they attempting to acquire political power. Furthermore, the administration had collaborated successfully with Belafonte. The Kennedys wanted to continue to learn insider perspectives without the demands that political leaders such as Wilkins and King would make of them. Robert Kennedy and his aide Burke Marshall turned to Dick Gregory, likely because of his participation in the Birmingham demonstrations.

During these confidential sessions, Gregory agreed that "the Negro mood" had, indeed, changed. He cracked that even his maid was "sassing" him, and Kennedy jokingly told the comedian to fire her. Gregory also seemingly shared the administration's suspicions of the movement's organizational leadership, as he led Kennedy and Marshall to believe that "competition and ill will among Negro leaders made it impossible" to deal with them reasonably. Gregory suggested that Kennedy consult with the author James Baldwin to further explore the question at hand.[3] *The Fire Next Time*, Baldwin's collection of essays articulating the angst and rage felt by many black Americans, had made him a leading voice for the civil rights movement. His position as both an intellectual and a celebrity made him an obvious choice for someone who was attempting to understand the black psyche.

After breakfasting with Kennedy at his Hickory Hill estate, Baldwin promised to bring together about a dozen individuals who would speak directly about civil rights. The premise: to find individuals who were not conventional politicians but were still people who "other blacks listened to."[4] Baldwin persuaded the singer Lena Horne, playwright Lorraine Hansberry, white actor Rip Torn (a friend of Baldwin's), psychologist Kenneth Clark, NAACP activist June Shagaloff, Freedom Rider Jerome Smith, and Baldwin's brother David, an actor, to participate. On May 24, the group gathered at Kennedy's Central Park South apartment, along with Marshall and Belafonte. They settled into their lush surroundings for what was expected to be a fairly pleasant meeting. One of the reasons Belafonte attended was that he feared that Kennedy would take advantage of the political naiveté and congenial natures of his artistic colleagues.[5] However, the meeting commenced on an angry note when Smith told the attorney general that sitting in the same room with someone who had the power to change things but had not made him want "to vomit."[6] The other guests rallied around the activist, who had been brutally beaten and jailed during the Freedom Rides. Angry denunciations were hurtled back and forth. The indignant mood was aggravated by derisive laughter; each side was incredulous at the misguided notions of the other. The painful exchange finally ended two and half hours later when Hornsberry defiantly led a walk-out.

Although Kennedy had purposefully sought out celebrities rather than political leaders for the consultation, he had not fully considered the consequences of dealing with an impassioned bunch of artists with nothing to lose. He certainly was not used to dealing with people who were ignorant of legislative policies or who were not looking for political gain. "They didn't really know, with a few exceptions, any of the facts," Kennedy commented. "James Baldwin couldn't discuss any legislation, for instance, on housing or any of these matters." Kennedy found himself regretting having deviated from normal political channels. "You couldn't talk to them as you can to Roy Wilkins or Martin Luther King, Jr.," he complained to one aide. "It was all emotion, hysteria." As the meeting unfolded, the guests' only political concerns became protecting their reputations as spokespersons for their race. No one wanted to be in the position of defending the White House. According to Kennedy, "Some of the statements that were made were completely untrue and [Belafonte] knew they were untrue. I asked him [why he didn't speak up], and he said, 'I'd lose my position with these people if I spoke up and defended you.'"[7] Baldwin leaked the meeting to the press and made clear the group's willingness to confront and criticize the attorney general. "He just didn't get the point," Baldwin told *Newsweek*. "He was naïve, he doesn't know pain. He just doesn't know."[8]

Angry as he was, Kennedy did not dismiss the contentious meeting from his mind. One aide says that he "pondered long and hard the meaning of the drama in that room—and in the country."[9] Kennedy concluded that the celebrities in his inner circle had deep-seated emotional issues. "A number of them, . . . I think, have complexes about the fact that they've been successful." He deduced, "The way to show that they hadn't forgotten where they came from was to berate me and berate the U.S. government."[10] Kennedy also determined that Belafonte's mixed marriage was an indication of his mental instability and exacerbated his feelings of guilt. Despite his rather negative psychoanalysis of the group, Kennedy took to heart the basic message: the federal government needed to do more, and if it refused, despair would deepen. Kennedy began demanding more African American hires in the federal government, snapping at colleagues for not doing so sooner.[11] He also became more supportive of his brother's growing inclination to go beyond calls for "law and order" and take a greater "moral stand" for civil rights.[12]

To what degree the celebrities had berated Kennedy to assuage their personal guilt is debatable, but it was clear that they became more comfortable speaking out for civil rights in the wake of Birmingham. Lena Horne had attended the Baldwin gathering because she felt ashamed for not having been in Alabama during the campaign. The sisters of Delta Sigma Theta had asked her to speak at a rally they staged there, but Horne had declined, worried that she would not be taken seriously or that she would be accused of making a publicity grab. The heated meeting with Kennedy had convinced her that despite her fears, she needed to become a more vocal supporter of the movement. Horne immediately called the NAACP and expressed her interest in going South. She learned about the rallies and arrests in Jackson and made arrangements to arrive there June 7, the city a veritable pressure cooker. Those involved with the NAACP's voter registration drives had found their names, addresses, and phone numbers published in the Jackson paper. Local hoodlums used this information to make harassing phone calls, to drive by the activists' homes with firebombs and other weapons, and even to drag individuals by lasso into cars to be beaten.[13] When Horne appeared in Jackson, she was volunteering for a mission few individuals—much less celebrities— had been willing to assume. But Horne's sudden volunteerism represented a larger trend among celebrities, as more stars began speaking out.

Only two days after the Baldwin meeting, a cohort of civil rights organizations in Los Angeles sponsored the Rally for Freedom to celebrate Dr. King and the successful conclusion of the Birmingham campaign. Fifty thousand people gathered at Wrigley Field, a stadium meant for twenty thousand. Onlookers crowded into the stands and onto the field, clutching pamphlets featuring a snarling police dog on the cover and eagerly awaiting the esteemed speakers. By the time the program started, Los Angeles had made history. This was the largest civil rights rally to date, and the one with the most Hollywood stars in attendance. The speakers included religious authorities and civil rights veterans, but the bulk of the program was devoted to Gregory, Paul Newman, Dorothy Dandridge, and King. The themes of the speeches revolved around the significance of Birmingham and the importance of capitalizing on its momentum. The stars involved in the rally tried to set an example as to how to carry the spirit of Birmingham even further.

With his twelve-minute slot, Gregory held the crowd longer than all of the other speakers except King. At this point in his career, Gregory's stand-up routines and his civil rights orations had become virtually indistinguishable. "I can't tell you what a pleasure it is being back up North again . . . of course, you know you're looking at a convict," Gregory cracked (he would be fined $100 and sentenced to 180 days in jail if he returned to Birmingham). He warned his listeners that if they planned to head South themselves, they ought "to brush up on your Uncle Tom lessons before you go 'cause it might save your life!" Downplaying his own bravery, he recounted being chased in Clarksdale, Mississippi. Even though "we might be ashamed of Ole Tom up North," he said, he was willing to assume that persona when being accosted in the South. He said he hopped in the car, rushed to the airport, and asked for a reservation for Mr. Gregory. When the attendant told him she had no such reservation, he replied, "Mr. Gregory sho gonna be mad!" The crowd laughed and cheered wildly at this, and Gregory went on in similar fashion about the subjects of black identity, black progress in American society, and the black image in American culture. He concluded seriously, saying that he believed the movement would benefit his children. "And I don't want no one helping my kids and I don't join in," he explained with forthright conviction.[14]

Newman and Dandridge emphasized the prominent newcomers to the movement. Although this was Newman's first public stand for civil rights, he told the crowd that it had been his job to gather other stars for the rally. He read the names of those supporters not in attendance, then introduced the Hollywood performers who were likewise new to the movement and seated with him onstage—Joanne Woodward (Newman's wife), Mel Ferrer, and Anthony Franciosa—as well as the regular supporters present, including May Britt, Sammy Davis, Jr., Rita Moreno, and Dandridge. Not wanting to overplay his role, Newman said, "I hope that in a very small way we represent conscientious Americans who are deeply concerned and who are personally committed to the fulfillment of your own aspirations." However, Dandridge noted the significance of these stars' participation, saying, "It really wasn't very long ago that it was considered dangerous for the people in show business to endorse anything more controversial than toothpaste. I don't know how dangerous it is today, but I do know that more and more of us are glad for the opportunity to stand up and be counted." She then urged, "We as actors and actresses should take part in the most important drama that his country has seen."[15]

A moving address by King concluded the rally. King, too, was thrilled with what he called "the largest and most enthusiastic civil rights rally that has ever been held in the history of this nation."[16] He focused on soliciting funds, and the crowd responded generously to King's call, donating $35,000 that afternoon. Davis proved the biggest donor. He pledged an additional $20,000, the equivalent of a week's salary from his upcoming engagement at the Sands Hotel in Las Vegas. "This should prove once and for all that my leader is your leader," he said defensively.[17] Although this statement was somewhat unbecoming, Davis did throw down the gauntlet of celebrity fund-raising, and his contribution inspired an A-list reception following the rally.

Invitations for the unprecedented gathering had been sent through the office of California governor Edmund G. "Pat" Brown, but the party itself took place at the home of the actor Burt Lancaster. Lancaster's wife Norma hosted the event, as her husband was out of town working on a film. All of Hollywood was abuzz about the couple's new stone mansion, and those in attendance were thrilled to finally see it. About 250 guests poured through the towering front door to press into the sunken library and atrium and the hallways and adjoining rooms. By opening their home to a civil rights event, the Lancasters were treading in new territory, but their interest was not entirely unforeseen. Lancaster's film career had built an image of him as a moral individualist. Freedom, according to one biographer, was his "secular religion." She explains, "By 1963, he was[,] in the public's mind, Elmer Gentry, the Birdman, the Nazi Janning who accepts the nation's guilt."[18] Meanwhile, Norma had become involved in California politics, particularly through the League of Women Voters. These activities facilitated her hosting the civil rights gathering at her home, which then inspired her husband's activism when he returned to Hollywood.

When King and his entourage arrived at the reception, they exuded a sense of passionate urgency that elicited surprisingly generous giving. Jack Tenner, an attorney in Hollywood, opened the meeting. "It takes about $1000 a day to keep Dr. King's organization operating. Who wants to pay for one day's operation?" he challenged. The stars responded in a competitive frenzy. Newman and Franciosa immediately wrote checks for $1,000, as did the actress Polly Bergen. Not to be outdone, Marlon Brando declared that he would sponsor an entire workweek, and he wrote out his check for $5,000. Lancaster and her friends hustled about the room, plucking checks written by a number of other guests, including the actor Lloyd Bridges, for a grand total of $20,000. King's eloquent concluding speech generated another round of competitive charity. Inspired by the reverend's insistence that "we are done with gradualism and are through with tokenism, and look-how-far-you've-come-ism," Brando took the microphone to say, "I think we should be concerned with what-have-we-done-ism." Already the top donor for the evening, Brando, as the world's highest paid actor, then pledged one day's pay to the SCLC. "And I would like to say to Dr. King," he added dramatically, "if he thought it would be of any benefit, I would be happy to go to Birmingham anytime he would ask me." Newman matched Brando's offer, saying "And if you go on a weekend when I'm not working, I'll go with you." He also pledged a day's pay. The spent crowd joined hands and swayed slowly as they sang "We Shall Overcome," the battle hymn of the movement.[19] This was King's first visit to Hollywood, and he could not have envisioned a better outcome. He raised a record $75,000 for his organization and pulled another major city into his Northern network. Brando and Newman would prove sincere in their pledges to travel South.

Events such as the Baldwin meeting and the Freedom Rally convinced President Kennedy that it was now time to take bold action on civil rights, and he was leaning toward a public accommodations bill. As revolutionary as the prospect of ending Jim Crow was, Kennedy hoped that it would not provoke white fears about class and status, as the issues of schools, jobs, and voting had done, and would therefore, be attainable.[20] Alabama governor George Wallace gave Kennedy an opening on June 11 when he blocked the door of the registrar's office to prevent two African Americans from enrolling in the state university. That very night the president went on television to announce his civil rights legislation, saying, "It ought to be possible . . . for American students of any color to attend any public institution they select without having to be backed up by troops." He argued that a century of delay had forced African Americans into the streets, as in Birmingham. Bemoaning the tension and violence in which such demonstrations often resulted, Kennedy demanded that Congress desegregate public accommodations.

Civil rights leaders did not stop to celebrate the introduction of this historic bill. Segregationist Congressional Democrats had the power and the tenacity to keep the bill bottled up in committee. Furthermore, only hours after Kennedy's speech, a gunman murdered Medgar Evers in his driveway. Although Jackson had a reputation for racial violence, news that the activist had been killed in front of his family at his own home sent shock waves of anguish among African Americans. Evers's death affirmed that bringing down segregation was going to be an uphill battle.

Evers's murder also inadvertently gave Lena Horne a leading voice in the civil rights movement. On the basis of her recent trip to Jackson, Horne had been scheduled to appear on the *Today Show* with Roy Wilkins to discuss the movement's progress. Just before her appearance, news came that Evers had died. Horne held up well against the unexpected strain. Her eloquent and tough bearing proved she could be an effectual spokesperson. She went on to perform in a benefit in Atlanta for King, to sing at a rally for the NAACP in honor of Evers, and to film a pair of "civil rights spots" sponsored by the Kennedy administration, among other activities that summer. No longer worried that she would not be taken seriously, Horne now, according to her biographer, "sang eagerly for any racial cause that might show the world she cared."[21]

Perhaps it was the newfound confidence exhibited by such celebrities as Horne, Newman, and Brando that led the NAACP to renew its drive against bigotry in the film industry in June 1963. The NAACP had long wanted to strengthen its position in Hollywood but had thus far been operating on the basis of cautious criticism. Still gun-shy after the contro-versial Walter White mission for improved roles for African Americans in the 1940s and the failed *Amos 'n' Andy* boycott in the 1950s, the NAACP leadership had not wanted to alienate its members with more contentious or weak campaigns. In fact, the leadership seemed more intent on clearing up past misunderstandings between the national office, the Los Angeles branch, and the studios than on launching a new initiative. Seemingly exasperated by the national office's lack of progress, Los Angeles branch president Edward D. Warren had spearheaded a series of meetings with the studios and the artists' guilds in 1961. The goal: to improve the hiring practices of the studios so that African Americans would be included, both onscreen and behind the scenes, in all pictures produced in Hollywood.[22]

This effort had met with mixed results. Even though the studios pledged their support, there was no enforcement mechanism to ensure their compliance. Furthermore, Warren had instigated these meetings without the knowledge or approval of the national office. Warren made no apology for his rogue behavior. "Any president of a branch who sits and waits for the National Office . . . to tell him what to do is a bad president and ought to get out," he proclaimed defiantly. He refused to file reports about the meetings and even referred to his superiors as "handkerchief heads."[23] Although the executive committee was displeased with Warren's attitude, his "Hollywood Activities Committee" had strengthened the NAACP's position within the film industry. Capitalizing on this momentum, the NAACP had established a permanent Hollywood–Beverly Hills chapter in 1962. In June 1963, this local chapter and the national office coordinated a newly aggressive campaign that demanded that the studios incorporate more African Americans into crowd and street scenes, pushed for more black middle-class characters, and threatened legal action against the discriminatory craft unions.[24] Apparently, based on King's recently successful visit to Hollywood, the NAACP asked King to return to try to open up negotiations with the unions.

King made minimal headway. Anticipating that the all-white craft unions would be hostile to his mission, he first broached the Screen Actors Guild (SAG), the artist union with the greatest number of black members. Since SAG allowed anyone of any race who obtained a job to become a member, it seemed the natural place to start, and Charlton Heston, whose civil rights activities in Oklahoma City were well-known to King, was the SAG president at the time. Heston arranged meetings between King and other craft guilds and producers to promote the use of antidiscrimination clauses in employment and an improved portrayal of blacks and Hispanics in films. Complicating King's effort, however, was the fact that the craft guilds discriminated against almost everyone outside their family circles, not just blacks, and had no intention of ending this tradition. Civil rights activists had encountered similar roadblocks among longshoremen, brewer, and auto worker unions since the 1940s.[25] Moreover, even Heston was not entirely comfortable with demands for more "black roles." Although he conceded that "films have borne [a responsibility] over the years in making this image [of minorities] an unjust and unsympathetic one," he believed that the best actor should be hired for a role, with little concern for race. The designation of "black roles," "white roles," or "Hispanic roles" seemed wrong to him, perhaps in part because the Anglo-Protestant Heston had played a Mexican police officer in *Touch of Evil* and, of course, Jewish roles in his biblical epics. Philosophically, Heston also drew a distinct line between civil rights and civil liberties, arguing that SAG "cannot deny the producer the right to cast the actor he thinks is right for the role."[26] When King privately told Heston about the idea of staging a mass demonstration in Washington in connection with Kennedy's proposed civil rights bill, however, the actor was much more

enthusiastic and offered to help form a supportive artist group.[27] King
flew east to plan the event.

*   *   *

Celebrities mobilized for the March on Washington with an arts contingent about seventy-five strong. This modest number reflected the overwhelming public skepticism of the event. Civil rights leaders envisioned
the participating stars serving not only as inspirational entertainment
during the March itself but as goodwill ambassadors who could convince
the public of the event's legitimacy.

The notion of a mass march for civil rights was certainly not a new
one. A. Philip Randolph had threatened to bring fifty thousand demonstrators to the capitol in 1941, leading President Franklin D. Roosevelt
to sign Executive Order 8802, which forbade discrimination by defense
contractors and established the Fair Employment Practices Commission.
Civil rights leaders had returned to this strategy in the 1950s with the
Youth March for Integrated Schools that Belafonte cochaired and the
Prayer Pilgrimage attended by Sidney Poitier, Belafonte, Ossie Davis, Dee,
and Sammy Davis, Jr. King hoped that another march would stoke the
summer's fiery civil rights spirit and told his aides that Brando, Newman,
and Heston had all pledged their support. The fact that they were all
"Kennedy men" seemed to give King added confidence in moving forward
with the idea. The same enthusiasm was true, King said, of many labor
leaders across the country, also Democratic supporters. King approached
the seventy-one year-old Randolph about staging a new march, and in the
meantime made the Kennedy administration aware of the possibility.[28]

Randolph was thrilled with the idea, and he would make numerous
adjustments to his original vision that would ensure that the March took
place and that would make it more amenable to celebrity participation.
The aging Randolph had originally wanted veteran activist Bayard Rustin
to oversee the event, a role that Rustin eagerly said he would accept. The
two men shared similar ideas for a two-day event that would include
demands for a universal jobs program, demonstrations on Capitol Hill,
and even sit-ins at Congressional members' offices. Roy Wilkins, however,
indicated that he would endorse neither Rustin's leadership nor civil disobedience. That Rustin was known as both a communist sympathizer and
a homosexual were great liabilities. The NAACP chief also feared that

untold acts of civil disobedience on Capitol Hill would result in more harm than good. Without the NAACP's participation, it is doubtful the event could have taken place. The leaders of the march—known as the Big Six—thus appointed Randolph as director. Rustin would serve as deputy, with the understanding that he was to work behind the scenes, where he would not invite negative publicity. The Big Six also eschewed civil disobedience and shifted the focus of the march away from a jobs program to Kennedy's civil rights bill. The bill was already in the forefront of the public mind, and Kennedy could hardly oppose a march in support of his own proposals. With these changes, the March became more of a public relations affair than a controversial demonstration, the aim being to sell the movement to the mainstream and thereby persuade Congress to turn the bill into law.

In the spirit of winning over white America, celebrities reflected the inclusiveness and nonviolence of the cause that Rustin wanted to emphasize. As King's aide Clarence Jones remembers, "Because of the nature of the movie industry, because of the nature, by definition, of who motion picture personalities were, Dr. King felt they could give his moral crusade a certain degree of authenticity and support from the mainstream media." Jones continued, "And who better to achieve that than a Burt Lancaster or persons like him?"[29] Rustin also reached out to labor and religious authorities; and Walter Reuther of the United Auto Workers and representatives of the Protestant, Catholic, and Jewish clergy, all of whom were white, joined the civil rights chieftains.[30] In addition to showcasing the broad moral reach of the civil rights cause, Rustin believed it imperative to have an incident-free march. With sixty days to plan, he worked doggedly from his headquarters in Harlem to make sure that the marchers would be comfortable, safe, and not prone to violence. He made arrangements for such amenities as portable toilets, temporary drinking fountains, first aid stations, a check-cashing facility, and sack lunches, while Ossie Davis organized the entertainment and programming for the March.[31] Since Davis was operating from his home in New York, however, the West Coast stars mobilized somewhat independently.

One of the most enthusiastic and renowned leaders of the so-called Arts Group was Marlon Brando. His portrayal of such characters as Stanley Kowalski in *A Streetcar Named Desire* (1951) and Terry Malloy in *On the Waterfront* (1954) had electrified audiences, winning Brando commercial success as well as critical acclaim. He had also proven to be one of Hollywood's most charitable stars. Brando had grown up in Nebraska with alcoholic parents, both abusive in their own ways. When he moved to New York as a young man in 1943, he described himself as deeply troubled and plagued by feelings of "depression, weakness, and worthlessness." These problems seemed to have created in him a deep sense of empathy toward others. Even as a moderately successful stage actor, he had donated the majority of his salary to such causes as food relief for war-torn Europe and Zionist efforts to establish the state of Israel.[32] However, it was not until King's visit to Hollywood that Brando became involved in the civil rights movement. "After the Los Angeles Freedom reception where I sat next to Dr. King and heard him speak, I was very moved by what he had to say and what he felt. Now, that was a stimulus to me," he commented. "That was the first time I had ever been to a meeting of that type."[33] It inspired Brando to mobilize an artists' contingent for the March on Washington, and he hosted the first meeting for this purpose at his home in Beverly Hills on July 26, 1963.

A small group of artists answered Brando's call. In addition to Brando, present at the meeting were Peter Brown, Tony Curtis, Mel Ferrer, Anthony Franciosa, Virgil Frye, Billy Wilder, Lancaster, and Heston. "When the dust settled," Heston recalled, the group elected him chair. He supposed it was "because of the time I put in with SAG . . . or maybe just because I'd gotten all those folks through the Red Sea." Indeed, as a long-time board member of the Screen Actors Guild, Heston had earned a reputation as a level-headed leader and negotiator that was underscored by his epic performance as Moses. Also a likely factor in his selection was Heston's previous involvement in the Oklahoma City demonstrations. Although he had only participated in a single campaign, that was one more march than any of Brando's other guests had experienced. Thus, he was a logical choice for chairman.

Belafonte claims that he suggested Heston as cochair, even though he was not at the meeting. Belafonte attests to working behind the scenes to help Brando line up celebrities, and says that King wanted them to reach "across the [political] divide." According to Belafonte, he pushed a reluctant Brando to include Heston, because he "was an insecure guy who yearned for the approval of his peers," and they could use his moral image to help their cause.[34] This is debatable, and seems rather vindictive on Belafonte's part, perhaps driven by Belafonte's disapproval of Heston's later involvement with conservative groups such as the National Rifle

Association. At this point, however, Heston was still a Democrat and considered by King a "Kennedy man" (his first endorsement of a Republican presidential candidate came in 1972). Furthermore, Heston already had a relationship with King and with the movement and was a proven leader in Hollywood. Whatever the case, the arts contingent worked doggedly over the coming days.

In a series of meetings, the Arts Group focused on recruiting other celebrities to join their ranks and on attracting, as Heston put it, "as much ink and TV time as possible.[35] On one occasion, they met in Brando's dressing room on a movie set. On another, a meeting was "staged" and reenacted for the benefit of network news cameras, who had missed a meeting on the previous night at Heston's home.[36] The group had direct access to the media. Brando reported on his calls to newsman David Brinkley and Mel Ferrer on his conversations with CBS-TV. These efforts paid off. Within about ten days, the group numbered sixty-one and all three major news networks had expressed interest in reporting on their activities. Meanwhile, Judy Francisosa made travel arrangements for the group, including chartering an airplane to fly to Washington, DC, reserving hotel rooms close to the National Mall, and figuring the costs for each participant (which they were expected to pay themselves). Since Ossie Davis was arranging the entertainment for the March, the Arts Group did not need to come up with programming ideas. Instead they focused their energy on educating their recruits about civil rights issues.

These efforts culminated in a large meeting on August 7 at the Lytton Center in Los Angeles. This was the only gathering for all of the participants before the March took place, and it illustrated the stars' sincere commitment. They barred the press and the public from the meeting, choosing to hold a simple press conference afterward. This decision, apparently made by Heston and his "Publicity Committee," insulated the Arts Group from accusations that they were trying to generate publicity for themselves. It also prevented the distractions that reporters and photographers were sure to provide, as well as any temptation for celebrity grandstanding. A serious tone prevailed. The group opened with the Pledge of Allegiance, and then Heston delivered the Arts Group "Statement of Purpose." Thomas Newsom explained the goals of the March; Peter Brown and Virgil Frye recited the Thirteenth, Fourteenth, and Fifteenth Amendments; and James Garner read a "digest of civil rights legislation." At the end of the meeting, Heston read aloud the list of committed

CHAPTER 4

artists, asking those in attendance to rise. At the press conference afterward, Heston downplayed their star status, stating that they were not operating on a partisan basis or acting as celebrities but attending the March simply "as citizens."[37]

Despite this momentum, several complications undermined the Arts Group. Recruitment proved difficult. Many celebrities who sympathized with the cause declined, saying that demonstrations were "not their style." The famed director George Stevens told Heston that he disliked group action and was so persuasive that he almost talked Heston out of it as well.[38] Such sentiments may have been a result of the negative publicity the March had already received. According to one Gallup poll, 63 percent of Americans opposed the March, and six out of ten believed that massive demonstrations hurt the civil rights cause. The rumor that agents and producers pressured "their" stars not to participate may have been another factor.[39] Divergent political leanings within the Arts Group also caused complications, sometimes along racial lines. Two weeks before the March, Eartha Kitt told the *Los Angeles Times,* "The white people do not really understand the problems of the Negro. How could they? They have been brainwashed their whole lives. But I believe in the sincerity of the white marchers."[40] Far more divisive were differing political philosophies about appropriate political action. Although the Arts Group ultimately agreed on "peaceful demonstrations," Heston recalled that "our meetings were studded with rousing speeches about chaining ourselves to the Jefferson Monument and lying down on Pennsylvania Avenue." The more conservative Heston was also chagrined to learn only a few days before the March on Washington that Brando, Newman, and Anthony Franciosa had attempted to intervene in civil rights demonstrations in Gadsen, Alabama. "This is the hook you hang on with a group," he lamented. "You can answer for what you do yourself, but how can you answer for what all the others do?" he asked, concerned that the three men's behavior would reflect negatively on the Arts Group.[41] The stars' intervention had had little effect in Gadsen—where they were called "rabble rousers"—and did not elicit a federal response.[42]

Despite these problems, the planning for the March came together well. Davis submitted his proposed program two weeks in advance. In the meantime, the Arts Group confirmed its participants.[43] News of the stars' involvement generated sympathetic press attention in the Hollywood trade papers and such newspapers as the *Los Angeles* and *New York Times.*

Particularly enthusiastic was *Jet* magazine, which hyped the celebrity contingent to encourage a large turnout. Days before the event, the magazine featured Marlon Brando, Eartha Kitt, and Lena Horne on its cover and proclaimed that "the cream of the nation's entertainment crop" would be at the March. "If you are one of the thousands of 'freedom marchers' in Washington, D.C., August 28, that heel you just stepped on could easily be movie star Marlon Brando, singer Nat King Cole, or dancer Gene Kelly," *Jet* offered enticingly. "The attractive lady marching beside you just might be Debbie Reynolds, Eartha Kitt, Lena Horne, or Ruby Dee."[44] Such enthusiasm likely helped minimize any qualms the stars may have felt about their involvement when FBI director J. Edgar Hoover ordered agents to call them at their hotels and urge them not to participate.[45] The stars had come too far at this point, indicating that for the first time, stars en masse had become comfortable supporting civil rights. As Diahann Carroll commented, "It was wonderful to be able to verbalize all this and not be afraid because there were so many of us doing it."[46]

* * *

When the March on Washington took place on August 28, 1963, never before had the nation seen such an impressive assemblage of integrated demonstrators. The estimated total number of marchers rose to two hundred thousand, far outnumbering what Rustin had anticipated. Delegations arrived from a number of major cities, including Chicago, Cleveland, and New York, and on seemingly every available mode of transportation, including trains, planes, bicycles, and even, in one instance, roller skates. That morning, buses clogged the highways into the nation's capital, and it was estimated that buses traveling through the Baltimore Harbor Tunnel brought one hundred people per minute.[47] The Arts Group arrived on their chartered plane, while the Student Nonviolent Coordinating Committee (SNCC) bused in African American sharecroppers from the Deep South "to show them that they were not alone, that people in America did care about them."[48] Belafonte and Sammy Davis, Jr., made a point to welcome these folks to the gathering. One contingent that was noticeably absent, however, was the Nation of Islam. Malcolm X had gone so far as to denounce the event as the "Farce on Washington." His attitude did not dissuade his celebrity supporters, however, the most notable being Ossie Davis, Dee, and Horne (who never really identified with King and considered Malcolm her "idol").[49] They understood that the March on Washington represented the most visible demonstration to date for, as Davis put it, "our desire to be included into American society," and they recognized the importance of participating in such an event. Rather than bemoaning Malcolm's rhetoric, however, they believed it could serve the purpose of sending a message to white America: "to escape Malcolm . . . deal with us."[50]

Such public relations concerns had escaped no one, particularly not President Kennedy, whose administration had taken the utmost precautions in preparing for the March. Robert Kennedy and Assistant Attorney General John Douglas had worked with Rustin in supplying amenities and had made arrangements for extra police protection, including four thousand troops assembled around the district and fifteen thousand paratroopers on alert in North Carolina. Kennedy also made it a point to monitor communist activity and worked with the NAACP to prevent communists from participating in the event. Following the administration's lead and apparently anticipating violence, local hospitals canceled elective surgery, district commissioners banned liquor sales for thirty-six hours, and the Washington Senators postponed two days' worth of games.[51] Kennedy feared that any violence or controversy associated with the March would not only hurt his proposed civil rights legislation but would also jeopardize his reelection campaign. According to his aide Harris Wofford, Kennedy worried that the March would "antagonize" Congress, and he nervously watched the polls that autumn. Gregory tried to reassure them, saying, "I know these senators and congressmen are scared of what's going to happen. I'll tell you what's going to happen. It's going to be a great big Sunday school picnic."[52]

Gregory's prediction proved correct, due in no small part to Ossie Davis's careful planning. Striving to provide "inspiration and uplift to the thousands of participants who will make up the body of the demonstration," Davis divided the areas of entertainment into three "stations," all of which functioned as one coordinating unit: the Washington Monument, the Line of the March (on the National Mall), and the Lincoln Memorial. Starting at 9:00 AM, recorded music "appropriate to the occasion" played at the Washington Monument. The edifice also served as the location for a warm-up concert that Davis planned and emceed, beginning at 10:00 AM. Joan Baez, Bob Dylan, Odetta, Josh White, the trio Peter, Paul, and Mary, and the SNCC Freedom Singers all performed. Dylan sang a new song he had written after Medgar Evers's death called

"Only a Pawn in Their Game." During interludes between songs, speakers such as the first black stewardess and the famed minister Norman Thomas addressed the crowds. When the March began at 11:00 AM, Davis hoped that the folk singers and song leaders he had placed strategically along the way would help maintain "speed and focus amongst the participants" until the program began at 1:00 PM.[53] The March was only eight-tenths of a mile and took about twenty-five minutes, so the demonstrators had plenty of idle time on the hot and muggy day.[54] Such entertainment served the important objective of occupying participants.

After the March, the Arts Group and other celebrities took their assigned places for the rally. Most of them gathered in a special section near the speakers' podium, although a few, including Newman and Sammy Davis, Jr., preferred to mingle with the crowd.[55] Horne, Belafonte, Heston, Poitier, Brando, and Ossie Davis ascended the stage along with over one hundred prominent civil rights veterans such as Daisy Bates (NAACP), John Lewis (SNCC), James Farmer (Congress of Racial Equality), and, of course Randolph, Rustin, Wilkins, and King.[56] Rustin and the March organizers had decided upon an official program (on which printed leaflets were based), but it served more as a guideline than a rigid agenda, given the overwhelming crowds and elated atmosphere at the event. In fact, the concert singer Marian Anderson was supposed to have opened the program with the national anthem but failed to get through the sea of people in time. She filled in after she arrived with the popular spiritual "He's Got the Whole World in His Hands."[57]

Remarks by participating celebrities comprised the majority of the additional unscheduled events. Ossie Davis, at Rustin's behest, had written a skit for Brando and Belafonte, but it was scratched due to time constraints. Nevertheless, Brando briefly took the microphone, wielding a cattle prod from Gadsden, Alabama, as an indictment of police brutality in the enforcement of segregation, and making a dramatic impression on the crowd.[58] Gregory, who originally declined Davis's invitation to help emcee, also spoke. He feared that he was too controversial among whites to play a major part in the program, but during the speeches, Rustin and Davis insisted he say a few words. Gregory brought some levity to the otherwise serious tone when he joked, referring to his arrests, "I'm very confused this year, because I never thought I'd see the day when I'd give out more fingerprints than autographs." Heston also came to the podium to read a brief statement written by James Baldwin on behalf of the Arts

Group.[59] Lancaster succeeded Heston. He had flown in from France to present a petition signed by 1,500 Americans in Europe, some of whom had staged their own small-scale march on the American embassy in Paris.[60] "All Americans traveling in the world today are in position of ambassadors and are very often made bitterly aware of our country's reputation," he professed, putting the March in a global context. "We are therefore forever indebted to those Americans represented by the March on Washington for giving us so stunning an example of what America aspires to become."[61] Traveling with Baldwin and Lancaster was the expatriate African American singer Josephine Baker, a surprise guest, who also spoke.

Born in Saint Louis, Baker had become a wildly popular nightclub entertainer in Paris during the 1920s and 1930s, and a Free France operative during World War II. She had attempted to gain stardom in the United States in the late 1940s and early 1950s. During that same time, she became a vocal critic of American racism and expressed her views to an international audience in magazines and on tour in Latin America. Her behavior gained notice by the US State Department, and although officials realized she had no communist sympathies, they still viewed her as a threat for provoking interest in America's racial discrimination. The government tried to limit Baker's activities through diplomatic channels, pressure that led several Latin American and Caribbean countries to cancel her visas and performance contracts, and the Immigration and Nationalization Service to ban her from the United States in 1955.[62] That she was able to return in 1963 for the March indicated the same shift in Cold War celebrity political culture that Dandridge and Carroll had commented upon, in terms of stars being less afraid to associate with controversial causes. Furthermore, the March itself filled Baker with a sense of optimism about the United States she had never before felt. Whereas she had once compared American racism to the Nazi's treatment of the Jews, her reception at the March "moved my heart," she said. "Negroes will be free within my lifetime," she proclaimed.[63]

The scheduled and unscheduled appearances set the stage for King's "I Have a Dream" speech, the undisputed highlight of the March. King described the "urgency" of the moment, the "determination of the Negro," and his dreams for a society that did not judge individuals for the "color of their skin but on the content of their character." He exalted repeatedly, "Let freedom ring!" CBS aired the March in its entirety, but ABC and NBC interrupted their programming to cut to King's speech. It was the first time that many Americans, including President Kennedy, heard one of King's addresses in its entirety.[64]

In light of King's triumph, the celebrities in attendance felt good about the March, but they did not want their participation overblown. Heston said, "It was a very stirring day. I'll never forget it, and I'm proud to have been a part of it."[65] Gregory reflected, "Oh, baby, to stand on the top of the Lincoln Memorial and look down, it was like everyone in the world was standing there . . . that day I felt like the Negro had been given his equal rights."[66] Sammy Davis, Jr., said, "I never had that feeling before or since . . . for that suspended space in time there was more love in the mall in Washington than the world has ever known."[67] Ossie Davis felt "euphoric" about the event, and Ruby Dee believed it "proved that the artists indeed had a special place in the struggle."[68] Nevertheless, they also saw the limitations of their presence. "So many of us were public faces that we seemed far more important to the undertaking than in fact we were," Heston noted. Likewise, Horne said, "I don't feel like a movie star particularly but I'm a New Yorker, and what happens in the South happens to my state and for my state, too."[69]

Veteran civil rights activists expressed similarly qualified praise of the stars' participation. "It was fascinating to see the collage of famous faces," SNCC chairman John Lewis said, "but what blew me away was the mass of the audience itself, the enormous size of the crowd, the nameless, faceless, everyday men, women, and children who were what we were all about in the first place." Even Rustin, who had recruited Ossie Davis and encouraged celebrity involvement, said, "It wasn't the Harry Belafontes and the greats from Hollywood that made the march. What made the march was that black people voted that day with their feet."[70] Nevertheless, having the celebrities at the Mall certainly boosted activists' morale. The Reverend Fred Shuttlesworth, in CBS's live coverage, praised the "movie stars," saying they made him and the other leaders feel "wonderful knowing that they're with us."[71] Other activists' encounters with celebrities created lasting memories of the day. The SNCC activist Julian Bond says that one of his tasks was handing soft drinks to movie stars. "I will remember forever [Sammy] Davis holding his hand like a pistol and saying 'Thanks, kid.'"[72]

Celebrities certainly did not "make" the march or give it legitimacy—it had President Kennedy's approval after all—but they helped make it successful and added value and meaning. Ossie Davis's handling of the entertainment significantly contributed to the "festival-like atmosphere" for which the March was so widely praised. The stars also brought a new sense of drama to the movement. As the scholar Taylor Branch asserts, "Even those who had attended a hundred mass meetings never had witnessed anything like Marlon Brando on the giant stage" with his cattle prod.[73] Lancaster unfurled his scroll with an impressive flourish, generating huge applause. Baker's presence also noticeably boosted the crowd's spirits. By and large, the stars' presence demonstrated both the popularity and urgency of the movement, factors that contributed to greater media interest in the March and in related civil rights issues.

Indeed, a "Hollywood Roundtable" televised on CBS in the immediate aftermath of the March illustrates this point. President Kennedy had agreed to meet with the Big Six after the March to discuss the prospects of his legislation, and the Arts Group had requested a meeting as well. They had been denied, however, despite Sammy Davis, Jr.'s appeals to Robert Kennedy. The attorney general told Davis, "The President's got a lot of advisors telling him he shouldn't meet with anybody, not Dr. King, nobody. If the performers come up, then it becomes a spectacle, the press would make it a farce."[74] However, the "Hollywood Round Table" resulted in an honest and earnest discussion. Moderated by journalist David Shoenbrun, the panelists included Baldwin, Belafonte, Brando, Heston, Poitier, and the writer-director Joseph L. Mankiewicz (best known for the 1950 film *All About Eve*). In an unrehearsed discussion, the group talked about their previous involvement with the movement, the significance of the March on Washington, and the future of civil rights in America. A clear theme emerged: despite their "hopeful" feelings about the day's events, hard work and "difficult days" lay ahead. Belafonte emphasized that the practice of nonviolence might soon expire. "If the Bull Conners continue to release dogs . . . there must come a point, if they're pushed to it, for retaliation." Heston agreed, saying that it would not be a "downhill coast" and that the "times ahead may be as difficult as the times behind." Having white stars on the panel helped emphasize the theme of the "white community's" responsibility going forward.[75]

The points on which the star panelists disagreed were perhaps the most instructive to the viewing audience. At one point, Shoenbrun asked, "Is the hope of our country the fact that we can have demonstrations of this kind, unlike the U.S.S.R. or China?" Baldwin said that the United

States was the "only country" where it could happen but also asserted that it was the only country "where such a demonstration was necessary." Belafonte, also undermining the question, argued that the United States "should not measure itself against dictator societies." Heston, however, disagreed, arguing that America had "conceived the idea of freedom" and that the movement was a "restatement of America's founding principles." Baldwin conceded, "The American Negro paradoxically has great optimism in the potential of the U.S." Disagreement also arose about how to frame racial issues henceforth. Whereas Poitier used the common term "the Negro question," Mankiewicz said it was more appropriate to call it the "white question," given the culpability of whites for the country's racial problems. Brando, speaking for other minorities, such as Native Americans, called it a "human question." When Heston argued that "calling it a 'white problem' denies the burning interest of every Negro citizen," the other panelists approved. Baldwin, to whom the others generally deferred, had the last word: "White America needs to ask itself why it was necessary to invent the nigger?"[76] This unvarnished exchange helped articulate the complexities of racial issues in the United States in an accessible way. It also served as a constructive follow-up to the March, the success of which posed the danger of insinuating that there was little left for white America to do.

That evening, Heston, Brando, Newman, Baldwin, and Belafonte attended a party hosted by Senator Jacob Javits (R-NY) in support of the legislation. All of the days' events, and the stars' participation in them, resulted in an overall consensus for the civil rights bill. Indeed, a new Harris poll for *Newsweek* revealed that two-thirds of Americans now approved of the bill, support that gave Kennedy and members of Congress added confidence in advocating for it.[77] The Stars for Freedom, in the unprecedented display of celebrity activism elicited by the March, played a significant role in swaying the public mood.

* * *

Despite the success of the March, related events in Birmingham brought despair. On September 15, 1963, arsonists bombed the 16th Street Baptist Church, where assorted meetings were held during the Birmingham campaign, and killed four young girls. Upon hearing the news, Gregory commented, "By now there were few things that you could tell me about a white racist system in the South that could stun me. But that stunned me, because even I was naïve enough to believe that the church was safe."[78] In fact, the bombing was one of twenty-eight such attacks, all crimes that remained unsolved. Furthermore, Birmingham officials had yet to enforce their desegregation agreements, and Kennedy refused to interfere. When Gregory arrived in Richmond, Virginia, to speak at the SCLC's annual convention, he found the mood there "low and divisive." Opinions differed among civil rights leaders as to whether or not they could afford a renewed campaign in Birmingham, either psychologically or financially.[79] Despair deepened after Kennedy was assassinated on November 22, 1963. As Belafonte says, the implications of Kennedy's death "extended far beyond the fight for civil rights," but with Lyndon Johnson's support for the movement unknown and the civil rights bill bottlenecked in Congress, he felt "bottomless grief."[80]

Such obvious setbacks did not dissuade celebrity supporters, however, and perhaps even spurred them on. In the weeks after the bombing, Jackie Robinson organized a fund-raiser in Harlem to help rebuild the church, and CORE organized a "cocktail sip" in support of the victims' families in a Bronx cabaret that featured Thelonious Monk and other jazz musicians.[81] In the autumn of 1963, a flurry of correspondence developed between various celebrities and the major civil rights organizations. This communication indicated celebrities' new level of comfort and familiarity with the movement. Meanwhile, Belafonte stayed in touch with Robert Kennedy, who remained attorney general for nine more months, and strategized with King about how to get the civil rights bill passed.

Soon after the March, civil rights organizations asked considerably more of their celebrity supporters than they had in the past. They pressed them to use their media and celebrity contacts to publicize aspects of the struggle. For example, SNCC executive secretary James Forman wanted to bring awareness to the violent conditions in Americus, Georgia, where he described "police and state trooper repression of local Negroes" as "almost absolute." He consulted with Marlon Brando on how to bring publicity to the region. Brando put Forman in touch with the actor Mel Ferrer and also pushed the SNCC leader to arrange an appearance for the Reverend Billy Graham on Jack Paar's weekly prime-time variety show to discuss the issue. Forman asked Dick Gregory, a frequent guest of Paar's and an acquaintance of Graham's, to help make this happen, and Graham appeared on the show on December 13, 1963.[82] Civil rights organizations also asked celebrities to make more appearances and to headline even more benefit shows. Only a week after Lena Horne and Frank Sinatra gave a benefit concert at Carnegie Hall that raised $32,000 for SNCC's voter education and registration program (totaling one-sixth of its projected yearly budget in that category), the organization again begged for Horne's assistance. The SNCC staffer Julia Prettyman requested that Horne attend two fund-raising parties, although she acknowledged that she felt "somewhat guilty imposing on you this way," given Horne's already extensive work.[83] Belafonte, who not only produced the Horne-Sinatra concert but gave a similar one himself with Miriam Makeba only a few weeks later, also received increased requests from SNCC to help bring attention to Americus and to help with a food drive, among other activities.[84]

Likewise, civil rights groups took on more fund-raising responsibilities themselves; this was especially true of the NAACP, which in October 1963 began plans for an expensive "Freedom TV Spectacular," a self-scripted program to be aired on closed-circuit television in various US cities in May 1964 and to involve over twenty-one Hollywood, Broadway, and musical performers. Freedom Network, Incorporated (originally Merit Productions) proposed the idea to the NAACP as a fund-raiser, promising to oversee the technical aspects of the production if the NAACP developed the programming. The national office would "sell" the spectacular to its branches, who would cover their costs by selling tickets for the program's viewing, presumably in theaters or auditoriums. Freedom Network estimated a potential income of between $140,000 and $546,500. Although the NAACP initially balked at the up-front costs and the "unknown" nature of the project, swayed by the projected returns, it ultimately decided to accept Freedom Network's proposal.[85]

By tapping its celebrity supporters and capitalizing on the shifting political culture in Hollywood, the NAACP put together an impressive program of East and West Coast talent. The organization asked its veteran supporters Sammy Davis, Jr., and Lena Horne to cochair the event, and tapped other familiar faces, such as Belafonte, Dandridge, Ossie Davis, Dee, Gregory, the revered gospel singer Mahalia Jackson, and Poitier to help provide the programming. It also recruited some newcomers. These individuals had been known sympathizers of the civil rights cause but had not spoken out explicitly in favor of the movement. One of these was Ed Sullivan, who had consistently invited African American entertainers onto his program in defiance of sponsors and studio executives, but who had never worked with the NAACP. He agreed to cochair the East Coast division with Davis, "because," he explained, "the NAACP has acted with such wisdom and dignity through the years."[86] Another sympathizer (and an example of the shifting Cold War environment) was the actor Edward G. Robinson, a well-known liberal whose near blacklisting in 1950 had driven him from politics for fourteen years.[87] Other significant recruits included the actors Elizabeth Taylor and Richard Burton. Taylor had starred in the films *A Place in the Sun* (1951) and *Giant* (1956), both of which advanced liberal messages for social justice, but the actress had not participated in any civil rights activities up to that point. Taylor was considered one of Hollywood's most beautiful and intriguing actresses, and her participation garnered huge headlines in the black press.[88]

A number of programming complications arose in the weeks leading up to the spectacular. While the shows were originally envisioned as a live "double-program" between an East Coast cast at Madison Square Garden and a Los Angeles cast at the Sports Arena, it soon became apparent that, due to the performers' schedules, both shows would need to be taped in advance. In the meantime, the Freedom Network fell apart, leaving the NAACP to assume responsibility for almost all aspects of the production and marketing, a task for which it was admittedly unprepared. At this point, however, enough of the planning was underway that it seemed prudent to carry forward. The organization managed to pull off a quality production with few technical failures. Wilkins had insisted that they avoid a "variety type show," an inclination that led the program to highlight the former NAACP lawyer and current judge Thurgood Marshall and to celebrate the tenth anniversary of the *Brown v. Board of Education* case. Indeed, the New York show consisted of a tasteful balance of historical context (which Poitier and the actor Robert Preston, best known as Harold Hill in *The Music Man* [1962], narrated), testimonies from civil rights activists, and entertainment by such performers as Belafonte, Horne, and the opera singer Camilla Williams.[89] The spectacular earned $258,982 in overall ticket sales and received generally positive reviews.[90]

The NAACP took great risks with the spectacular, with mixed results. Freedom Network's dissolution forced the organization to take over all of the costs of the show, and the expenses totaled a whopping $363,108, resulting in a $72,000 loss. This led to a financial crisis for the organization, especially since it had given $300,000 in bail money the year before.

In addition to the financial loss, the organization had lost time, as "many energies were tied up which could have been devoted to more routine fund-raising and membership campaigns."[91] John Morsell, chair of the planning committee, predicted, "I have the strong suspicion that it will be 1974 or later before we fully get free of all the ramifications and aftermath of the TV Spectacular."[92] Despite this devastating loss, the NAACP took comfort in the "considerable broad public relations gain . . . from the widespread national and local publicity" associated with the show, as well as the virtue and learning experience of delving into the technology with few resulting technical flaws.[93] The show also strengthened the organization's relationship with the arts community, illustrating the ongoing enthusiasm between celebrities and the civil rights movement after the March on Washington.

While the Freedom Spectacular proved the most extreme example, it certainly was not the only fund-raiser to lose money or barely break even. The primary reasons for low returns usually resulted from unexpected production and promotion costs, especially as civil rights organizations were inexperienced in show business. Celebrity performers often expected not only a certain level of expertise but also some reimbursement for fees and expenses, which were not often articulated until after the fact or were so extravagant (as with Sammy Davis, Jr.'s Waldorf-Astoria bill discussed earlier), that the organizations balked. On one occasion, Mahalia Jackson demanded to be paid a minimum of $1,500 for each performance, as well as a percentage of the gross, for a concert tour for the NAACP.[94] In a benefit for SNCC, the folk-blues singer Josh White performed a show that netted only $577, but White's fee of $300 and a car repair for his promoter left the organization with nothing.[95] Civil rights organizations took on some risks and other logistical problems with fund-raising benefits, but continued to pursue them due to the promise of great rewards.

In fact, the stars themselves proposed a number of their own ideas for fund-raisers, often conceived in such a way that the major civil rights organizations would share the proceeds equally. Until this time, the proceeds of each benefit show had almost always gone to one particular organization. However, perhaps inspired by the display of unity at the March on Washington, celebrities expressed a desire to divide the proceeds. The organizations, which did not always see eye to eye and sometimes even outright opposed one another, worked to achieve this goal. For example,

Josephine Baker, fresh from her triumphant appearance at the March, launched an American concert tour by playing a benefit show at Carnegie Hall for the NAACP, CORE, the SCLC, and SNCC. Although the show itself was a success, the NAACP lost money, as it was the only organization to commit staff members and to invest in the necessary expenses toward marketing and sales. NAACP administrators felt that "an even split across the board would hardly be fair under the circumstances." However, they ultimately decided not to press the issue. "Any suggestion that expenses ate up the proceeds, or that there was mismanagement, can be extremely damaging to subsequent fundraising . . . there is no doubt in my mind that all who were involved were proceeding in good faith and were sincerely desirous of aiding the cause of civil rights," one staff member explained.[96] Hereafter, however, the NAACP did insist that outside accountants handle such endeavors in order to allay financial differences.

This made for an easier distribution of funds when Sammy Davis, Jr., put together a committee called "Stars for Freedom" with Frank Sinatra, Dean Martin, and Count Basie for the primary purpose of civil rights fundraising. The committee's first event was a benefit show in December 1963 at the Santa Monica Civic Auditorium. Evoking images of Birmingham when promoting the show, Davis said, "It's easy to praise the accomplishments of the courageous workers in the great civil rights organizations, but in the face of police dogs, hoses and jails, the one kind of support that has real, practical meaning is money to keep it going." Similar to the King Tribute in 1961, patrons had the choice of a wide range of ticket prices and the option to attend a private after-party. The show netted over $25,000, and each organization received $8,563.[97] The Stars for Freedom committee would take on several other activities in the near future.

Sidney Poitier proposed an unprecedented fund-raiser when he offered to screen his new film *Lilies of the Field* (1963) for the combined civil rights organizations before its commercial release. Although Poitier had participated in a number of benefit shows, because he was neither a singer nor a comedian, he never served as a main draw. His film allowed him to give a benefit performance of his own. According to Poitier, the distributor for *Lilies*, United Artists, had never been particularly excited about the film, and its budget was only $240,000.[98] Therefore, the studio had little to lose by agreeing to Poitier's proposal. Poitier promised that if the civil rights organizations handled the logistics of the screening, neither he nor United Artists would require any profits and that he would also make a personal appearance at his own expense. A committee of representatives from the NAACP, CORE, the SCLC, and SNCC secured the Loew's Victoria Theatre in New York for half the price of its normal rate, developed promotional materials, and arranged for a "premier-like" atmosphere with spotlights, sound, and celebrity guests such as Lena Horne and Jackie Robinson. They emphasized the "combined effort and cooperation" of the civil rights groups in their literature, which had an effect on at least one observer, who wrote the NAACP, "I'm very glad to see that you are finally working together, instead of fighting amoung [sic] yourselves." Similar screenings were held in Chicago, Washington, DC, and Boston. It is unclear from the records how much money the *Lilies* benefit generated, but it does appear to have been profitable and to have required little upfront cost.[99] Poitier's magnanimity meant much personally to some of the activists who had been invited. As the SNCC worker Stokely Carmichael remembers, "A group of us in our jeans were standing in the lobby feeling a trifle uneasy amongst the affluent, elegantly turned out Washington players and wannabes . . . [until Poitier] saw us across the lobby, he stopped, took a second look, pointed at us, broke into that incandescent matinee idol smile, and strode over to hug and greet us, much to the amazement and envy of the assembled dignitaries."[100]

Cynics may wonder if Poitier offered up his film out of self-interest. *Lilies of the Field* starred Poitier as an itinerant worker who encounters an order of East German nuns in Arizona and ultimately builds them a new chapel. A relatively simple story with no other well-known actors, it certainly was not a guaranteed blockbuster. However, by the time of the benefit, favorable reviews for the film and for Poitier's performance were already pouring in. The benefit merely contributed to that buzz. This was certainly not the only time a civil rights group endorsed a celebrity supporter. In 1961, the NAACP sent a mass-mailing to its members, encouraging them to see Ossie Davis's Broadway play *Purlie Victorious*, and praising the way the comedy cleverly addressed racial issues. In 1964, the organization urged its members to demand that radio stations play Lena Horne's "sizzling freedom song 'NOW!'" Apparently sales had been brisk, but disc jockeys had been reluctant to play the controversial record on air. The NAACP suggested setting up letter-and-telephone committees to rectify "the broadcast freeze."[101] As far as both the celebrities and civil rights leaders were concerned, the success of one was beneficial to the other. Therefore, while celebrity benefits may have reflected an element of self-interest, the hope for the success of such groups and the contro-versies associated with them generally outweighed anything an individ-ual celebrity may have gained by the exposure.

It is fair to say that *Lilies of the Field* would have been a success with or without the benefit; it went on to gross over $2 million, and Poitier won an Academy Award for best actor in a leading role, the first African Amer-ican to do so. As Poitier tells it, he "went six feet up in the air!" when his name was announced.[102] His victory is considered a pivotal moment in Hollywood history. The award indicated that Hollywood had finally embraced African Americans in roles that were not stereotypical and demeaning but multidimensional and not necessarily race-specific. As one Poitier biographer argues, "To many, the Oscar was more than recog-nition of Poitier: it was a demonstration of interracial goodwill, an ana-logue to the March on Washington, even a symbolic absolution of Hollywood's complicity in racial prejudice."[103] The award also had a major effect on Poitier's career; in the aftermath, he received offers for multiple films, including *A Patch of Blue* (1965) and *To Sir, with Love* (1967), and was invited to cast his handprints at Grauman's Chinese Theater, cementing his status as a film icon. Poitier would host similar screenings for some of his other films in the future.

Individuals such as Poitier, Sammy Davis, Jr., Belafonte, Horne, Sina-tra, and Heston had managed to meld their careers and their activism into viable public personas, and the March on Washington had helped to solidify this image. However, it is important to note that most celebrities were still unwilling to embrace the civil rights movement. Even some of those who were loosely associated with racial liberalism balked at the notion of overt activism. Some worried about offending their white fan base and suffering the financial consequences. The singer Sam Cooke, for example, had an uneven relationship with the civil rights movement. On some occasions he played to segregated audiences; on others, he refused. He decided against attending the March on Washington, but in its after-math recorded "A Change Is Gonna Come" as an answer to Bob Dylan's "Blowin' in the Wind." Cooke was nettled that the unofficial anthem of the civil rights movement had been written by a white person.[104] Rather than social activism, the bulk of Cooke's civil rights work came in the form of passionate song and his black start-up music label All for One (A.F.O). Likewise, Nat King Cole, who had been attacked by members of the White Citizens' Councils during a show in 1956 and said he would continue to play to segregated audiences, was still uncomfortable with overt activism. "It's foolish to think a performer like me can go into a Southern city and demand that the audiences be integrated," he insisted. "The Supreme Court is having a hard time integrating schools. What chance do I have to integrate audiences?" However, Cole bought an NAACP lifetime membership, donated money to civil rights organizations, and occasionally performed in benefits.[105] Other artists, such as R&B and gospel groups that toured primarily in the South, avoided controversy in order to travel safely through the region from gig to gig.[106] Still others had experienced unhappy results in their efforts to collaborate with civil rights groups. The R&B artist Lloyd Price said, "We didn't count. They wanted high-profile artists like Sammy, Harry Belafonte, Louis Armstrong, artists like Nat 'King' Cole."[107] In 1963, Fats Domino went so far as to say he had lost "thousands and thousands" of dollars supporting the NAACP and that he refused to support them anymore.[108] The Stars for Freedom did not represent the majority of Hollywood stars or other branches of show business.

*   *   *

The March on Washington reflected a seismic shift in celebrities' relationship to the civil rights movement. Their success in helping stage the event and their increased activism in its aftermath indicated that Ruby Dee's wish for a prominent place for artists in the movement had indeed come true (at least for those who had similar activist inclinations) as had King's desire for a stronger Northern network. When the Civil Rights Act was finally signed into law on July 2, 1964, celebrities could take pride in their contribution to its passage. A landmark piece of legislation, the act outlawed segregation in public accommodations, prevented discrimination by government agencies, and more loosely highlighted voting rights and encouraged school desegregation. Title VII, which outlawed employment discrimination, would be an important weapon against the film industry itself, as the Stars for Freedom increasingly pushed Hollywood to hire black actors and crew members. They would also help publicize housing and voting rights, both of which were not enforced by the act, bringing the stars into greater contact with direct-action campaigns.

Dick Gregory
and Celebrity
Grassroots Activism

The only trouble we had was in one restaurant where the Grand
Dragon of the Ku Klux Klan was eating. We had fried chicken,
and he didn't like the way I wiped my hands on his sheet.
—Dick Gregory

IN DECEMBER 1964, DICK GREGORY ORGANIZED THE CHRISTMAS
for Mississippi campaign, which provided twenty thousand turkeys and
various trimmings and gifts to rural Mississippians. This "special delivery" reflected a shift toward more direct action by celebrities involved in
the civil rights movement. More stars willingly engaged in controversial
campaigns, such as California's Proposition 14 involving "open housing."
Others, like Harry Belafonte and Sidney Poitier, took greater personal
risks in their support of the Student Nonviolent Coordinating Committee
(SNCC). And Ossie Davis and Ruby Dee pushed political boundaries with
Malcolm X. Gregory epitomized these trends. Although he had been a
strong supporter of the civil rights movement since 1961, between 1963
and 1964 he consciously expanded his activism by engaging in more civil
disobedience in the urban North and rural South, publicizing the needs of
rural, black Southerners, and increasing his commitments to a number
of civil rights organizations. Gregory's actions and style presented both
opportunities and challenges to the civil rights organizations with which

he worked, as his spontaneity and self-described "loud mouth" sometimes led them in unexpected directions. Nevertheless, he proved an able fund-raiser, spokesperson, and tactician. Most importantly, he served a vital psychological function for rural Southerners, as reflected in the Christmas for Mississippi campaign, a creative endeavor that brought substantial aid to one of the most desperate sections of the region.

*　*　*

Gregory, more than any other celebrity in the 1960s, regularly risked arrest and served jail time for civil rights causes. He had been initiated into incarceration during the Birmingham campaign, and he went on to be arrested at least eight times during various demonstrations across the country. One such incident took place in Chicago, Gregory's home town. In August 1963, the comedian and his wife Lillian joined over one hundred demonstrators on Chicago's South Side to protest the installation of trailer classrooms in African American schools. The city was struggling to accommodate an overpopulation of students and had resorted to implementing "double-shift" programs and building mobile units. Since 1961, civil rights advocates had pushed for transferring black students to less-crowded all-white schools, only to be rebuffed by school officials. Parents concluded that the school district superintendent Benjamin Willis was favoring mobile units in an attempt to keep Chicago schools segregated. As Gregory explained, "The parents call them Willis Wagons because they are [his] personal methods for hauling little colored folks all over the city's Jim Crow ghetto to keep them from white kids." Several demonstrations had taken place in 1961, but the agitation reached new heights in 1963. Gregory joined protestors in Englewood who attempted to block construction crews, even going so far as to throw their bodies in front of bulldozers. When police attempted to strong-arm the demonstrators, the picketers regrouped for another rush. The near-riot ended when the police arrested over one hundred activists on disorderly conduct charges, including Gregory and his wife. Gregory refused to post the fifteen dollar bond and vowed to stay imprisoned for the month until his hearing, which won attention for the cause. Martin Luther King, Jr., visited the comedian in jail, as did *Jet* magazine.[1]

At this time, Gregory began to see himself more as a full-time activist and less as a professional comedian. As he said, "The press started saying that my demonstrating was interfering with my career. My response was that my career was interfering with my demonstrating."[2] Unlike performers such as Nat King Cole and Sam Cooke, who believed they made their best contribution to civil rights by setting examples as successful entertainers, Gregory felt that his stand-up routines had their limitations. "I've tried to relay the message through satire and comedy, but actions tell better than words and that's why I went down to that mobile school site," he explained. Not only did he forego approximately $20,000 in booking fees during his incarceration, but he also refused to perform for the inmates while he served time, saying, "I'm not here as an entertainer, but as a Negro fighting for the rights that every Negro should be fighting for."[3] This episode indicated an important shift in Gregory's perception of himself as a celebrity activist, and it reflected ongoing school desegregation efforts in other Northern cities, such as New York and Philadelphia, that, although overshadowed by the southern-based Southern Christian Leadership Conference (SCLC) and SNCC demonstrations, Gregory would continue to support. The school board canceled the mobile school project, and Gregory soon returned to the Deep South, but his dispute with Superintendent Willis was not over.[4]

SNCC activists asked Gregory to return to assist with their ongoing voter registration drives. By August 1963, SNCC had established projects in more than a dozen Mississippi communities, as well as other Southern cities, such as Danville, Virginia; Pine Bluff, Arkansas; and Selma, Alabama.[5] Because of the formidable conditions in Selma, SNCC decided to direct much of its resources there. Blacks made up about half of the voting population, but in 1961, only 156 of the approximately fifteen thousand registered voters, or .01 percent, were black.[6] SNCC workers canvassed black homes during the summer and fall of 1963 to determine by what means Dallas County officials had limited registrants. Local African Americans responded enthusiastically, working with SNCC activists to protest at the courthouse and to attend citizenship classes. The white community reacted harshly, however, by firing such "agitators" from their jobs and beating and jailing protestors who gathered downtown, all with the approval of Sheriff Jim Clark.[7] Such conditions threatened to halt SNCC's project at its crucial beginning stages, so the organization hoped that bringing Gregory to Selma would attract national publicity in its favor.

In fact, SNCC leaders made an increasingly concerted effort to cultivate outside contacts, and celebrities played an important role in that strategy. SNCC had learned the hard way that its access to the federal government would not keep it safe. The organization's isolation and lack of publicity since the Freedom Rides put them in an extremely vulnerable position. According to Casey Hayden, a founding member of SNCC, the activists remained "unprotected" and "terrorized." Although the group focused on grassroots activism, they did not feel that it was at odds with their mission to cultivate relationships with celebrities, because stars "had the public" and therefore offered "protection." Hayden asserts that although celebrities raised money and advocated for SNCC effectively with the press, their most important role was to act as a "buffer" against the isolation and danger SNCC faced.[8] Celebrities often approached SNCC first. As Dinky Romilly, who worked in SNCC's New York and Atlanta offices, notes, they did "not have to knock on doors or beg for help."[9] Nevertheless, the organization did need to maintain these relationships and give direction to celebrity volunteerism, duties SNCC executive director James Forman took the lead in expanding. He established twelve Friends of SNCC groups in Northern cities to improve the organization's fundraising and public relations efforts, and appointed Hayden as the "Northern coordinator" from the Atlanta office.[10] Forman, Hayden, and Romilly also spent considerable time writing celebrities with updates, invitations, and appeals for help, efforts that had borne fruit with Theodore Bikel, James Baldwin, and Marlon Brando, but Gregory proved the most responsive. He became an active member of Chicago Friends of SNCC and even attended SNCC executive meetings on an occasional basis.[11] That Gregory was willing to travel South and risk arrest meant that the publicity he received for these activities strengthened SNCC's connection to the outside world, and he became an increasingly reliable "buffer" for the group in the autumn of 1963.

When Gregory received SNCC's call in late September to help with voter registration drives, he was in the middle of an engagement at the Apollo Theater in New York City, so he asked his wife Lillian to go in his place. She had come to the same conclusion as her husband: that the civil rights struggle should be their number-one priority, even if that meant that there was less time for Gregory's career or even their children. Lillian, who was expecting, left her two daughters in the care of her sister when she traveled to Selma. Soon after her arrival, Lillian was arrested for "unlawful assembly" and "for contributing to the delinquency of minors" during her participation in a demonstration that included a number of adolescents. Although the latter charges were dropped, she was fined $300 and held on two bonds of $1,000 each. Lillian opted to stay in jail. "I am willing to stay here as long as necessary," she said, but "I don't know what this will do to my baby." Gregory completed his engagement at the Apollo but canceled two other shows at a substantial loss so that he could see his wife through a jailhouse window and help with further demonstrations.[12]

After discussing the situation with Forman, Gregory decided his talents would be best used if he remained out of jail so he could rally the African American community and help with SNCC's upcoming "Freedom Day." Hoping to embolden local blacks to participate in the event, Gregory spoke at a rally held at a church that had been tear-gassed only a few days earlier and was surrounded by a deputized posse of two hundred whites— "red necks" in Gregory's estimation. "I got up on stage in front of a crowd of scared Negroes," he recalled. "They needed some courage." A number of white policemen sat in the front row, pretending to be newspaper reporters and scribbling notes. "I directed my speech at those cops in the front row. I was mad," he said. "I told that audience how surprised I was to see a dumb Southern cop who knew how to write." Gregory continued in this manner for nearly an hour, and the crowd visibly responded. Giggling nervously at first, they began to sit up straighter until they finally felt confident enough to clap and cheer. "The white cops up front looked pale," Gregory claimed. "The crowd wasn't afraid of them."[13] Gregory's status as a comedian and celebrity allowed him to fulfill a distinctive and important psychological function for movement activists, boosting their morale and assuaging their fears. He spoke again the following night, trying to increase this spirit.

Forman also convinced James Baldwin to come to Selma in the hope that additional celebrity involvement would spur network news teams to send television cameras. "To involve people like Gregory and Baldwin was to involve many thousands more who could not come to Selma or Greenwood or whatever the place might be," explained Forman.[14] The presence of the news media and even the FBI did little to cow Sheriff Clark, however. Wearing a button on his lapel that read "NEVER," he arrested the SNCC workers, and the federal government refused to intervene. Thus, SNCC's voter registration drive stalled, and in 1964 a state judge would formally ban all marches and black meetings in Selma.[15] In many ways a failure, the campaign would be revived the following year, and it led the Gregorys to become more deeply involved with SNCC.

In the winter of 1963–64, the Gregorys worked with SNCC from its headquarters in Atlanta to target Southern restaurants that continued to enforce segregation. After SNCC activists had been denied service at a Toddle House restaurant in Atlanta—one in a chain of 255 restaurants in thirty states and Washington, DC, and owned by Dobbs House, Incorporated—the Gregorys strategized with SNCC chairman John Lewis about how to effectively target the business. They again decided that Lillian, who they now knew was pregnant with twins and whose condition "would lend a more powerful message," should risk jail while Gregory stayed on "the outside." Lillian was jailed eleven days over the Christmas and New Year holiday, during which time she and two other SNCC workers were placed in solitary confinement. In the meantime, Gregory purchased two shares of stock in both Dobbs House and Toddle House and brought the certificates with him to a sit-in organized by SNCC. As Gregory tells it, "As soon as we arrived and started demonstrating, in the presence of a cop the manager asked us to leave the premises. I stepped in front of the other demonstrators. 'I happen to own stock in this business. Do you?' I didn't tell him it was only two shares and I'm sure they thought I owned more." When the manager admitted he did not have any shares of stock, Gregory dramatically announced, "'Well, under these circumstances it appears that I represent more ownership than you do. So I'll have to ask you to leave my premises.' I turned to the cop and said, 'Officer, arrest this man!'"[16] Similar demonstrations led to the closing of twelve Toddle House restaurants and convinced the Dobbs House corporation to set up a meeting with the activists.

This was Gregory's first experience negotiating, and one that had meaningful results. He was struck "that when honesty sits around a conference table, black men and white men can understand and feel each other's problems, and help each other." In what Lewis called a "satisfactory agreement," Dobbs House consented to integrate more than fifteen of its restaurants in Atlanta and in cities in Florida, Texas, and Tennessee.[17] This victory led SNCC to undertake an "open city" drive in Atlanta, pressure that led the city's mayor, Ivan Allen, Jr., to push the business community to accept the desegregation of restaurants and hotels.[18] At least fifteen had already done so, but many continued to hold out, prompting SNCC to organize a series of demonstrations. During one such protest, Gregory joined five hundred demonstrators at the Atlanta University Center campus, where they began a march into downtown. They encountered robed and hooded Ku Klux Klan members picketing the desegregated establishments. The two groups came within inches of each other, both chanting slogans. "The Old KK, she ain't what she used to be," shouted SNCC activists. "We want a white mayor," yelled the Klansmen. Police arrested eighty-six SNCC activists, including Gregory and Forman.[19] Such demonstrations led to continued negotiations and further desegregation, and during the 1960s Atlanta won a reputation for coping with "the race issue" better than any other major city in America.[20] Perhaps because of the success Gregory had experienced in Atlanta, he seemed particularly emboldened on a visit to Pine Bluff, Arkansas, only two weeks later.

Gregory's behavior in Pine Bluff posed serious problems for the field staff there. After successfully desegregating downtown Little Rock, the leaders of Arkansas SNCC had moved its operation to Pine Bluff in the eastern part of the state. Considered the "heart of black Arkansas," most of the state's black population lived there, some of whom were trapped in the brutal cycle of sharecropping, while others attended the all-black Arkansas Agricultural, Mechanical, and Normal College.[21] SNCC's Atlanta office made arrangements for Gregory to make an overnight visit to Pine Bluff, where the movement was focused on its voter registration project, as well as desegregating some downtown restaurants in Helena and Pine Bluff. The purpose of the visit was for Gregory to speak at one of their weekly mass meetings. He was one of the most famous to reach their somewhat isolated project. However, the visit went in an unforeseen direction when Gregory insisted on stopping at Ray's Barbecue, an all-night whites-only truck stop on the outskirts of town. In the words of the SNCC field secretary William Hansen, it is where "the semi-insanity of working with Dick Gregory began."[22]

The small group of activists accompanying Gregory had gathered at the Elks Club north of Pine Bluff after the meeting and were driving in a three-car caravan to the SNCC Freedom House on campus in town. According to Hansen, "Gregory insisted he was hungry and that he had to go into that truck stop and get something to eat." The group tried to talk him out of entering the restaurant. They saw it as not only far too dangerous but also pointless. "The last thing we needed (the Arkansas Project) in the middle of our voter registration campaign was the hassle of a nondescript 'honky truck stop' out on a lonely highway." Before they could stop him, however, Gregory had started walking toward the restaurant, giving the local activists little choice but to act. "He was a celebrity and he was our guest," Hansen explains. "With that mouth of his he would have gotten himself killed." They decided that Hansen would accompany Gregory while one carload stayed on the highway as backup and the other went for the police. The two men were refused service, but the police arrived within a few minutes, and no violence erupted. When the police ordered the pair to leave or face arrest, however, Gregory refused. "For the same reason that we couldn't let him go into that place alone in the first place, we couldn't allow him to get arrested by himself," says Hansen, who thus went to jail, too.[23]

Gregory told the SNCC publication the *Student Voice* that the Pine Bluff jail was like a "secret torture chamber"; however, Hansen characterizes this statement as "the selected use of hyperbole" to bring national attention to Pine Bluff. Indeed, the *New York Times* covered the episode.[24] Hansen viewed the Pine Bluff jail as no better or worse than the dozens of Southern jails in which he had been incarcerated. The prison guards did not physically abuse the men, but they did put them in isolation. "That's when the fun began," Hansen notes dryly. Being imprisoned with a celebrity who told jokes for a living had its perks. While lying on his back on his bunk, Gregory discovered that kicking the sheet metal walls made a huge racket. He and Hansen kicked at it, keeping the entire station on edge, until they tired. At that point, Gregory would begin one of his monologues. "Only these were a cut above the normal TV/nightclub jokes," says Hansen. "These were absolutely guaranteed to drive the white police . . . into a frenzy. Plus, they were funny as hell. I couldn't stop laughing. He just went on and on and on with these withering racial insults and, good god, did he know how to let these zingers fly. Then we'd both bang on that tin wall again." The police occasionally prevailed upon the men to cease their behavior, but never used force. Hansen believed they had received orders "not to do anything at all to Gregory, nor to me since I was with him."[25] The two men posted bail soon thereafter, and Gregory's statements about the jail conditions brought added drama to the episode.

Gregory's impetuousness somewhat hijacked the Pine Bluff movement's agenda, but the consequences were not necessarily unfavorable. Hansen was frustrated with the "distraction" and publicity of the arrests, as Arkansas SNCC then felt compelled to continue trying to desegregate Ray's Barbecue. Even though it was not one of their priorities, Gregory's actions made it a symbol. "In other words," Hansen explains, "where earlier, no one really cared about it, now we had been challenged and there was no way we could allow that challenge to go unanswered."[26] This forced a shift in the group's focus away from its voter registration efforts, work that had gained considerable momentum. They had succeeded in doubling the number of black registered voters to roughly 40 percent of the entire black population in Pine Bluff and were involved in several campaigns for black candidates running for public office.[27] That Gregory discounted their priorities on a whim showed the hazards of working with celebrities, who, generally speaking, could be an egocentric lot. Nevertheless, Gregory's actions also brought several boons. "Folks could see that we weren't being ignored; that what happened in P[ine] B[luff] did make a difference," Hansen attests. He also saw Gregory's arrest as "key" to giving the group a renewed opening on campus, where organizing had collapsed after university administrators had expelled students for their involvement with SNCC. Dozens of students joined the pickets at Ray's Barbecue over the ensuing weeks, and the owner soon agreed to integrate. SNCC leaders valued the ability to deal with unexpected developments as a natural outgrowth of grassroots organizing. Still, Hansen wryly notes, "We continued to let obscure, lonely (not to mention very dangerous) all white/all night truck stops go their own way for the most part" as the group returned to its electoral efforts.[28]

Gregory's willingness to go to jail made a big impression on SNCC workers. They considered being arrested not only a badge of honor but a logical extension of nonviolence. As SNCC chairman, Lewis gratefully recognized Gregory's steadfast "commitment to the techniques and tactics of nonviolence" and also notes that, like the students, Gregory dressed in a suit and tie for all of their public demonstrations. Lewis felt that this was important to the organization's image, and one more way they could distinguish themselves from their "roughneck opponents." Likewise, Hansen comments that Gregory always looked exquisitely and expensively dressed when he came to Pine Bluff. Gregory joked, "A lot of white folks in Mississippi used to refer to me as 'that millionaire nigger,' and I didn't want to spoil their image."[29] That Gregory had embraced SNCC tactics so completely and endured jail enhanced his credibility with the activists. Of course, his stature as a celebrity meant that the actual danger he faced was less than that of a typical activist, but it was a real danger nonetheless, and one few other celebrities risked. According to Gloria Richardson, a SNCC leader who collaborated repeatedly with Gregory, "Everybody respected him because he was always putting his body on the line."[30]

*   *   *

Gregory's many jailings did more than interrupt his show-business career; they seemed to redirect it. During the same period as Gregory's increasing number of arrests, he reshaped and used his comedy routine to become more movement-oriented both in its content and purpose. Although Gregory had never shied away from racial topics, his performances became increasingly serious in tone and more focused on assisting the movement than on enhancing his own pocketbook.

Gregory became particularly concerned about needy sharecroppers in Mississippi when he began working with SNCC in rural Leflore County. The voter registration drives in such outposts as Greenwood had already met with arrests and violence. In the winter of 1962–63, county officials resorted to even harsher measures. They seized shipments of federally funded food commodities such as butter, milk, cheese, and potatoes. Nearly two-thirds of the county's population relied on this aid to survive the winter, leaving thousands, as one observer put it, "neckid, buck-barefoot, and starvin'."[31] When SNCC sent out appeals for help, two black students from Michigan State University tried to drive in a truckload of food only to be arrested in Clarksdale and charged with possessing "narcotics" for the aspirin and vitamins they carried.[32] Gregory worked with both SNCC and the NAACP to help deal with this seemingly intractable food crisis.

He took on an instrumental role in the Chicago area Friends of SNCC Food for Freedom campaign that winter. The organization pledged to send twenty-two thousand pounds of food to Leflore County, as well as to Sunflower and Coahoma Counties, where officials had taken similarly punitive measures. The Chicago group almost doubled its goal by collecting fifty thousand pounds of flour, corn meal, rice, cooking fat, canned food, and other items. Gregory paid the transportation costs for a fourteen-thousand-pound shipment destined for Clarksdale and personally accompanied it first by air then by truck to ensure its safety. A second delivery departed for Greenwood a few days later. According to one historian, these deliveries "averted a famine."[33] They also led to retribution. Arsonists burned four buildings in the black business district near the SNCC office. Not to be cowed, over one hundred locals attempted to register in the coming days, leading SNCC to link "food to the franchise."[34] In an emotional letter, Forman told Gregory, "The thousands of hungry Negroes in Leflore, Sunflower, and Coahama Counties . . . know, perhaps for the first time in their lives, that they are not friendless and that they do not have to be afraid to try to get their rights." Believing that the field workers had received a similar boost, he noted, "The number of workers has increased from 30 to 42, again, thanks to you." Forman concluded, "I hate to sound maudlin, but your efforts have really increased our determination to stay in Mississippi and get the job done." Still, one infant died of starvation, and two sharecroppers froze to death that winter.[35] These fatalities, along with the county's ongoing obstinacy, prompted Gregory to continue his efforts in the Mississippi Delta.

A fund-raising album that Gregory made for the NAACP reflected his more somber side. When Leflore County officials claimed they could no longer afford to pay the $37,000 required for the public relief rolls, Gregory arranged for the question-and-answer session of a performance at San Diego State College to be recorded, and the NAACP bought ten thousand copies of the LP. Titled *My Brother's Keeper*, the album consisted of Gregory's "seriously-funny" observations on such subjects as "southern 'liberals,'" "the Muslims," "the Negro's future," and "college kids." His response to one student who asked for Gregory's prediction for "Negroes in the South" especially generated whoops: "In the South, they don't care how close a Negro gets, as long as he don't get too big and in the North, they don't care how big a Nero grows as long as he don't get too close." However, Gregory mostly spoke seriously on the issues and even discussed the tragic fate of Clyde Kennard, a black man who had been imprisoned on trumped-up charges for theft after he repeatedly attempted to enroll in a Mississippi college. Stricken with cancer and having gone relatively untreated in prison, Kennard died in 1963.[36] The NAACP distributed the album to its chapters in twenty-six "key" cities, where it sold for $1.60. For each copy sold, sixty cents went toward Gregory's production costs, and one dollar went to Mississippi. Within less than a month, the NAACP had already sold nearly seven thousand copies.[37] The organization had attempted to cut similar fund-raising albums in the past but had experienced problems with performer's contracts and union regulations. Such issues were less binding for a comedian, and thus the album project was a relatively easy and lucrative one.

Gregory continued to tailor his comedic career to the movement's needs when he agreed to headline a national tour with the SNCC Freedom Singers to help launch Mississippi Freedom Summer in 1964. SNCC administrators had been receiving multiple requests from Friends of SNCC supporters who wanted to book the comedian for benefit shows and fundraising parties, and the organization's leadership had decided to revitalize its voter registration efforts in Mississippi with a mass summer project.[38] Sponsored by the umbrella group Council of Federated Organizations (COFO), the project primarily involved SNCC and CORE personnel, who ultimately invited white Northern student volunteers to attract greater national interest.[39] They planned to establish institutions responsive to the needs of rural black Southerners, including Freedom Schools focused on voter registration and community centers providing medical and legal services. Their ultimate goal was to elect an integrated slate of delegates for a Mississippi Freedom Democratic Party (MFDP) to replace the all-white Mississippi delegation at the Democratic convention in Atlantic City in August. COFO estimated that it needed $200,000 and one thousand workers for a successful project. Gregory agreed to a month-long tour to help offset these costs and to recruit volunteers.[40] This tour showed Gregory's deep level of commitment to the movement. Between April 19 and May 17, he performed twenty-six shows in as many Northern cities, starting in Boston and ending in Seattle. Romilly, who had replaced Hayden as Northern coordinator, worked with Gregory's staff to make the travel arrangements for the group. She also coordinated with a contact in each city regarding advance publicity and event logistics. Each day of the tour was exceedingly busy, even before taking travel time into consideration. A typical day included an early afternoon press conference, at least one reception or cocktail party at which guests could mingle with Gregory and the Freedom Singers for an additional fee, and the concert itself. The concert included songs, testimonies from the singers (most of whom had participated in the Freedom Rides), and Gregory's pontificating—all followed by a collection at the end. Occasionally, another cocktail fund-raiser followed the concert. Gregory did not have time for any other engagements during the tour, so he gave up one month of pay. By that time, Gregory's civil rights activities had already lost him $100,000 in canceled engagements.[41]

However, this tour was not a financial success. Some historians have mistakenly characterized it as profitable, but SNCC records show otherwise.[42] Several logistical problems may have compromised the profits. In one case, SNCC did not meet the permit deadline for the concert hall it had booked at Howard University, leading to the show's cancellation. In another instance, Harvard University regulations prevented the group from making a "fund pitch."[43] It is also unclear from SNCC's financial records if all of the Friends of SNCC groups sent their profits to Romilly as planned. Finally, competition between civil rights organizations complicated matters. In Minneapolis, the rumor emerged that Gregory was touring on behalf of CORE, during which time it was engaged in a controversial battle with the city mayor's office and school board and had also divided into rival factions. "To many people's mind, Gregory was coming here to support CORE, its demands here during the picketing," the Minneapolis contact explained, "and people were going to have no part of it."[44] Furthermore, the latter part of the tour conflicted with the NAACP's "Freedom TV Spectacular," which was cited for undercutting ticket sales in Minneapolis and Denver and which prevented the Los Angeles Friends of SNCC from hosting a Gregory booking at all. This must have been frustrating for Gregory, who had taped a segment for the spectacular, but it had been cut for time at the last minute.[45]

Despite these problems, Gregory's evolution from a comedian into a "seriously funny" spokesman may have also undercut profits. As Gregory increasingly saw himself as an activist first and an entertainer second, he seemed to consider direct-action protests even more important than the tour. He missed a press conference, two receptions, and a dinner in his honor before his engagement at Yale so that he could participate in the "stall-ins" coordinated by CORE at the World's Fair in New York, a controversial tactic endorsed by few in the movement. "This probably hurt the project because a good many moneyed people in New Haven were disappointed and because we lost publicity," the Yale contact explained.[46] Moreover, Gregory did not deliver a comedic performance. As one reviewer noted, "Gregory the Comic had given way to Gregory the Crusader; the wit had been replaced by militancy, the punch-lines by the drama of the human condition."[47] Such a routine ensured that only those already sympathetic to the cause were likely to attend the show. In fact, as many of the performances were held on college campuses, students comprised the vast majority of the overall audience. Therefore, tickets started at three dollars, with the highest going for only ten dollars. Some venues offered "patron subscriptions," but those cost a mere twenty-five dollars.[48] Even those venues with a large turnout did not net as much as coordinators had hoped. For example, overcapacity crowds attended the Yale performance, but due to low ticket prices, the event brought in only $850. In Philadelphia, where almost two thousand people attended the show, proceeds totaled only $4,000, but this exceeded any of the other events by far. The tour averaged $1,616 per show.[49] Although Gregory continued to command high booking fees for his comedic routines in nightclubs across the country, the social satire he presented on the tour did not draw a broad audience. He was, in a common expression, "preaching to the choir." Given that part of the tour's purpose was to recruit volunteers, such performances were certainly appropriate; nevertheless, a typical nightclub routine would probably have raised more money.

Despite the disappointing financial results of the tour, it was not a wasted effort. Gregory's involvement brought press attention to the summer project in Mississippi and piqued the interest of Drew Pearson, whose syndicated "Washington Merry-Go-Round" column drew an estimated sixty million readers. The two men kept in close contact thereafter, and Pearson regularly reported on Gregory's whereabouts and his perspective on various racial matters.[50] Many of the Friends of SNCC contacts also reported winning "new friends" to the organization. As the Athens coordinator in Ohio said, "We feel that the visit of the Freedom Singers and Mr. Gregory was very valuable in helping SNCC to recruit students for field work in Mississippi this summer."[51] The tour also gave the Freedom Singers more exposure, a useful perk, as their persistent performing and recording work brought in steady profits over the years. In Romilly's words, it was a "back-breaking and exhausting tour," but one in which "SNCC's exposure has increased greatly."[52] Although the results are difficult to measure, this was an important achievement on the eve of the voter registration project. SNCC raised $97,000 for Freedom Summer, collected thousands of books for Freedom Schools, and amassed dozens of cars to drive volunteers from site to site. CORE, SCLC, and the NAACP also made contributions. COFO had fallen short of its $200,000 goal, and SNCC was on the verge of a financial crisis, but it had recruited over one thousand out-of-state volunteers for the ten-week project.[53]

In the meantime, Gregory's performing career served as a useful "cover" when he visited the racially charged town of Cambridge on Maryland's Eastern Shore. A series of violent clashes between the Cambridge movement and local whites had prompted the governor to install the Maryland National Guard. By May 1964, the city had been occupied for almost eighteen months, and the guard enforced such measures as a moratorium on demonstrations and nightly curfews. After the Cambridge Nonviolent Action Committee (CNAC) staged a counterdemonstration against a rally featuring George Wallace (now a presidential hopeful), the National Guard used gas on the demonstrators, causing widespread injuries and one death.[54] This latest outbreak reinforced Cambridge's new reputation as a "war zone" and put Gregory in the position of being one of the few prominent civil rights activists welcome in the city. The CNAC had cut ties with both the NAACP and SCLC, even declining an offer from King to assist CNAC's efforts, in part because he had demanded a speaking fee. They did, however, reach out to Gregory. CNAC leader Gloria Richardson, who had worked with Gregory on the Toddle House campaign in Atlanta, says that her cohorts had "high esteem" for the comedian and hoped that he could help "reduce tension." His visit would also allow them to have a mass meeting at the Elks Hall, as Gregory had negotiated with the National Guard to make an exception to its ten-day ban by allowing him to "entertain" the group; in reality, he would charge black residents only one cent for entry.[55]

In the weeks that followed, Gregory's visit allowed him to mediate between the dueling parties. Richardson recalls that Gregory spent two or three days at a time attending meetings, and that Cambridge activists welcomed him in this role.[56] He and Richardson also met with the Justice Department's Burke Marshall, who told them that Cambridge would be included in a federal poverty program. Gregory explains, "So now I had more than jokes to tell the folks at the Elks Hall." He quipped, "My oldest daughter told me the other day she didn't believe in Santa Claus. She said, 'Dad you know darned good and well no white man's gonna come into our neighborhood past midnight!'" He also told the crowd, "I had a dream that [the federal government] would be here next week to look into the problems of Cambridge" and "we called off the demonstrations for tonight" and went straight home.[57] Gregory believed that being able to convey the news about the poverty program "kept things cool." Violence did cease for the foreseeable future. The withdrawal of the National Guard, the passage of the Civil Rights Act (which activists tested without incident), and Richardson's move to New York City further reduced tensions that summer.[58] While affairs may have improved without Gregory's visit, his involvement nevertheless deserves recognition. He managed to walk the line between moderation and radicalism, a balance that gave him authority with activists and law enforcement alike. He played a similar negotiating role in Cleveland and Philadelphia, but was once again called to Mississippi.

Soon after Freedom Summer commenced, James Chaney (a black CORE activist from Mississippi), Michael Schwerner (a white CORE organizer from New York), and Andrew Goodman (a white summer volunteer, also from New York) were reported missing after they left Meridian for Philadelphia, Mississippi. CORE director James Farmer's first reaction was to call Gregory. Farmer claimed he "wanted company," but he also likely hoped that Gregory's presence would bring media attention and perhaps some protection. Gregory says that Farmer "was scared."[59] The comedian handled the dangerous situation with aplomb. The local authorities who met them in Meridian discouraged the pair from driving to Neshoba County to meet the local sheriff, calling it "real red neck territory," where they would surely be killed. Farmer and Gregory refused to reconsider and ultimately received police protection and met with Neshoba County authorities. As the meeting proceeded, a crowd of "several hundred shirt-sleeved white men" stood outside the courthouse brandishing weapons. The deputy said he had arrested and jailed the activists but had released them around 7:00 PM; he and the others claimed to know nothing about what had happened after that. When Farmer suggested they undertake their own search, the officials refused, claiming it would be too dangerous. At this point, Farmer recalls, Gregory "rose to his feet. He began speaking to the assembled men, pointing his finger at them, looking at each one with sharp eyes, and speaking with an even sharper tongue." Says Farmer, "He made it clear that he thought someone there knew much more about the disappearance of the three men than was being told" and that we were "going to get to the bottom of it, and the guilty persons were going to pay for their crimes."[60]

Gregory's actions in the coming weeks arguably hastened the recovery of the activists' bodies. Convinced that the authorities were hiding something, Gregory suggested to Farmer that they offer a reward. CORE was broke, however, and Gregory could not afford to put up his own funds, because, as he says, "I'd spent more time fighting for equal rights than performing, and my gigs were fading away."[61] Gregory called Hugh Hefner, who had given him his first big break at the Playboy Club in Chicago. While by no means an activist, Hefner had proven to be racially progressive by including African American models and articles on racial matters in *Playboy* magazine. Gregory asked him for a $25,000 advance against his next gig, and Hefner immediately loaned him the money.[62] Gregory believed that his pushing helped further the case, as his bounty prompted the FBI to extend its own reward. Furthermore, he received an anonymous tip that included a cassette tape and a map, which he shared with Attorney General Robert Kennedy and the Department of Justice. Not satisfied that the FBI was actually pursuing the tip, Gregory called a press conference.[63] The bodies of Chaney, Schwerner, and Goodman were recovered soon thereafter, on August 4. It is not clear if Gregory's interference directly led to their discovery. The FBI called the letter and tape he provided "valueless." Indeed, in 2005 the informant was revealed to be a highway patrolman from Meridian. However, Freedom Summer director David Dennis says that Gregory had the correct information, and that by threatening publicly to release it, he provided the "key" pressure.[64] At the very least, Gregory's actions helped create a climate for federal interference, a necessary condition for finding the slain workers.

Gregory's seeming lack of fear in traveling South and dealing with authorities was unusual of the movement's celebrity supporters. Although the comedian perhaps felt safer due to his access to the media, Dennis adds, "it was just Gregory's personality" to be so bold. "If he was not a celebrity," Dennis attests, "he would have acted in much the same way, but he might not have been as involved." In contrast, when Belafonte and Poitier made a harrowing journey into Mississippi in 1964 to hand-deliver $50,000 that Belafonte had raised to sustain Freedom Summer, John Lewis says that they were "visibly frightened." The Ku Klux Klan had tailed them from the airport, and they had trouble sleeping during their overnight visit. At one point, Belafonte awoke from a fitful slumber to Poitier doing push-ups. "I can't sleep," he explained. "And when those motherfuckers come for us, I want to be sure I'm ready."[65] Likewise, field secretary Bob Zellner says that although SNCC always informed the stars that there would be no authorities protecting them, they "really couldn't believe it." When Zellner drove Marlon Brando from the airport, the actor asked, "Where's the FBI?"[66]

The stars' willingness "to show solidarity and moral support" in the face of danger made a big impression, because, as Zellner notes, activists and local residents were so "oppressed and put upon." Local residents who had ignored an appearance by King earlier in the year rushed to greet Belafonte and Poitier during their visit. By publicizing and bankrolling projects and traveling South to work directly with SNCC activists, Poitier, Belafonte, and Gregory all became part of the "beloved community" SNCC strove to establish. With Gregory's choice to put the movement before his career, and with his close encounters with the impoverished conditions in Mississippi, it is no wonder that his routine became more serious in tone. His politics would also soon evolve to become more radical.

*   *   *

As summer turned to fall, Gregory, Belafonte, and Poitier all became more emotionally invested in SNCC and urged unconventional tactics on the organization. Their increasingly radical stance represented a general trend among left-leaning celebrities to embrace civil rights measures that would have been politically inconceivable only a few years earlier.

Thanks to Belafonte and Poitier's cash delivery during Mississippi Freedom Summer, SNCC could now afford to charter buses to the Democratic National Convention in Atlantic City.[67] Sending an integrated delegation had been one of the original goals of Mississippi Freedom Summer, but it was a controversial tactic, in part because it ran the risk of offending President Lyndon Johnson. Johnson's successful passage of the Civil Rights Act in July had proven his sympathies to the movement, but it had also put him in a vulnerable position with his own party. Knowing that he had quite possibly delivered the white Southern vote to the Republican Party upon signing the bill, Johnson nervously anticipated a disastrous Democratic convention, with a Southern walkout or open fighting on the convention floor. To be seated, the Mississippi Freedom Democratic Party (MFDP) needed to convince the credentials committee of its legitimacy, and it had been making progress in swaying sympathies. Fannie Lou Hamer, with her vivid descriptions of the economic and physical abuse she had suffered for her voter registration efforts, had been a particularly effective MFDP spokesperson. However, LBJ had more resources at his disposal to put pressure on the credentials committee.[68]

The MFDP's celebrity supporters could do little to affect the credential committee's decision, but they did much to boost morale. Gregory performed at the Basin Street nightclub in town, and says his hotel room "became the headquarters for non-delegate activity." One hundred and fifty Freedom Democrats demonstrated on the boardwalk while waiting for what they hoped would be a favorable outcome. The mood was somber. Members of the mostly silent crowd held signs reading, "Stop hypocrisy, start democracy." They displayed artifacts from Mississippi, such as a charred church bell, photographs of destitute sharecroppers, and even a burned-out sedan representing Chaney, Goodwin, and Schwerner's vehicle. Gregory spoke to the crowd to "encourage their effort" and raise spirits. As MFDP chairman Lawrence Guyot remarked, "He played an indispensable role at a time that it was needed."[69] Word soon arrived that the MFDP could accept a compromise or go home: two delegates-at-large for the 1964 Democratic National Convention, with the promise, guaranteed by a permanent civil rights committee, that no all-white delegation would ever be seated again. Many observers, including a number of civil rights supporters viewed the deal as a victory, but the SNCC activists were crushed.[70] During his trip to Greenwood, Belafonte sensed that a number of activists "were on burnout," a mood compounded by the outcome in Atlantic City. Belafonte and James Forman had discussed a trip to Africa for SNCC leaders as early as June 1963, and Belafonte decided that now was the time to make the hiatus happen.[71] Those selected for the trip consisted of Robert and Dona Moses, Lewis, Forman, Prathia Hall, Julian Bond, Ruby Doris Robinson, William Hansen, Donald Harris, Matthew Jones, and Hamer. Belafonte footed the $10,000 bill.

Belafonte's experience and connections as an international celebrity allowed him to arrange a trip that SNCC could not have put together independently. None of the students had been to Africa, but Belafonte had "visited the continent with some regularity" and had chosen the newly independent country of Guinea as a fitting destination. His first visit there had been as a cultural ambassador for the Kennedy administration, and he had been "most taken by the young spirit of the country." Kennedy, however, had expressed skepticism at Belafonte's suggestions for closer relations due to President Ahmed Sékou Touré's relationship with the Soviet Union. Indeed, Touré had won the Lenin Peace Prize in 1961 for his socialist economic policies.[72] Belafonte made plans with his family to travel with the students and contacted the Guinean government to set up their accommodations and travel schedule. "The trip was arranged through those personal connections. There's no way SNCC could have done that on its own," Hansen attests, pointing out that "Most people, especially outside the U.S., had no idea who or what SNCC was." The group was treated like a celebrity entourage. They were guests of the Guinean government, stayed in a presidential villa akin to a palace, enjoyed breathtaking entertainment each evening, and partook of fine dining.[73] On the evening of their arrival, Touré dropped by unannounced to visit with the group, and they saw him again the following day at a state reception.

To be treated so respectfully moved Hamer to tears. As Belafonte explains, "For so long she and a lot of poor black folk had tried unsuccessfully to meet with the president of her own country . . . and we could never see him . . . but here in Africa . . . Touré came to see her with great words of encouragement and hope and a declaration that this Africa was their home and its people their family."[74] The activists were also impressed to see black people "in charge," whether politically, as with Touré, or in more mundane roles, such as airplane pilots.[75] For three weeks, they also felt safe. As Forman attests, "In the group we often talked about the tremendous pleasure of just being able to go to sleep at night without listening to every noise outside, worrying about bombings or racial attacks."[76] They even did some sightseeing on the way home, stopping in Casablanca, where they looked for "Rick's Café" from the Humphrey Bogart film, and in Paris, where Hansen and Bond happened to run into Miles Davis. The VIP treatment, camaraderie with African leaders, and sense of security all provided a psychological boost that few other than Belafonte could have bestowed. Gregory's public identification with the confrontational MFDP and Belafonte's handling of SNCC's trip to a country with a leftist government indicated a new willingness among celebrities to push political boundaries.

Also evident of this shifting mood was celebrity involvement in California's hotly contested debate over open housing. Paving the way was Marlon Brando, whose involvement in the movement continued to deepen as he strove to "have racial equality represented in [his] daily li[fe]" on a more widespread basis.[77] King's visit to Hollywood had made Brando more aware of employment discrimination in the film industry, and, believing he should improve his own hiring practices, Brando added an African American secretary to his payroll. He also met with studio chiefs about hiring more black actors and crew members, involvement that led him to CORE and its fair housing campaign. In addition to actions in such locales as Philadelphia, Detroit, Cleveland, and Chicago, the organization had been orchestrating a series of pickets at segregated-housing tracts in the city of Torrance outside Los Angeles.[78] Hoping to garner media attention for the issue, Brando joined that effort in July 1963. As one activist says, "There had been demonstrations, and arrests before our march. However, the presence of Marlon Brando sharply dramatized the situation and drew newspaper and TV reporters to the scene by the dozens." Brando was targeted by hecklers and arrested on at least one occasion. One youngster wielded a sign reading "Marlon Brando is a Nigger Loving Creep," and two Nazis carried a placard that read "Brando Stooge for Communist Race-Mixers." The first major Hollywood star to join demonstrations in Los Angeles, Brando received notice for his decorous behavior. He brushed off the hecklers and politely declined autographs. The publicity from the campaign led the developer to permit integration of the neighborhood.[79]

Hostility over residential integration was characteristic of many Northern states, but the issue of fair housing had become a particularly pressing concern for California's liberal establishment.[80] Even though the US Supreme Court had outlawed the enforcement of racially restricted covenants in the 1948 *Shelley v. Kramer* decision, realtors (as represented by the powerful California Real Estate Association, aka CREA), developers, and neighborhood associations continued to practice "informal" segregation by refusing to show, sell, or rent property to African Americans and other minorities.[81] Sammy Davis, Jr., had encountered this problem when he first moved to Hollywood in the 1950s, and it was the same phenomenon that Brando was protesting in Torrance. In April 1963, the Democratic governor Edmund G. "Pat" Brown signed the Rumford Fair Housing Act, which empowered the state's Fair Employment Practices Commission to handle claims of racial discrimination by realtors and owners of apartment houses and homes built with public assistance.[82] Significant exemptions (for investment property, for example) weakened the Rumford Act's coverage, but it nevertheless signaled an important policy shift that elicited an immediate response by the real estate industry. Through an organization called the Committee for Home Protection, CREA wrote and gathered signatures for Proposition 14, an initiative designed to repeal the Rumford Act, as well as earlier laws dealing with housing discrimination.

Brando's demonstrating foreshadowed greater celebrity involvement with the issue. Governor Brown made defeating Prop 14 the leading priority of his administration; he formed Californians Against Prop 14

(CAP), an umbrella group of "leading" figures in California politics and society, and worked with the Stars for Freedom committee formed by Davis, Frank Sinatra, and Dean Martin to organize CAP's Arts Division. Brown believed that the celebrities could provide "a unique gift—the gift of time, talent and the creative message to educate voters."[83] The Arts Division ultimately amassed over 150 celebrities and industry insiders, doubling the number who had participated in the Arts Group contingent for the March on Washington. Several participants from the earlier effort served in leadership roles. Burt Lancaster served as the chairman, along with Gordon Stulberg and M. J. Frankovich, both vice presidents of Columbia Pictures Corporation. Such familiar faces as Polly Bergen, Judy Franciosa, and James Garner served on the executive committee, while others, such as Poitier, Charlton Heston, Richard Burton, and Elizabeth Taylor volunteered general support. Nat King Cole and George Stevens, both of whom had been ambivalent about "group action" in the past, joined. Between the governor's personal appeals and the Arts Division's recruitment efforts, a significant number of stars who had thus far been absent from the movement lent their support, including such prominent film actors as Cary Grant, Steve McQueen, Tony Curtis, Peter Falk, and Gregory Peck. The committee also made a point to reach out to admired television personalities such as Art Linkletter, Carl Reiner, Dick Van Dyke, and Mary Tyler Moore. Ironically, Brando did not actively participate in the Arts Division, apparently due to his film schedule.[84]

It is surprising that an issue described by *Time* magazine as "the most bitterly fought issue" in the nation, one that even overshadowed LBJ's election campaign, would garner so much celebrity support, especially among first-timers.[85] Several complementary factors were at work here. At the time of the stars' recruitment, the issue likely did not seem that controversial. CAP had been formed with Governor Brown's endorsement, and the Rumford Act had passed, albeit narrowly, with little fanfare. Furthermore, Prop 14 could claim few prominent allies. Most Republicans refused to support the measure, and, according to one historian, "The large majority of the state's political, civic, and religious organizations opposed the initiative."[86] Ronald Reagan backed it, giving Prop 14 one celebrity friend, but even he did not give it much lip service during the 1964 campaign. The celebrities who had participated in the March on Washington and in the NAACP "Freedom TV Spectacular" provided an established base of support for CAP. And the presidential race also likely had a spillover effect. The Johnson administration recruited an unprecedented number of celebrity supporters for LBJ's election campaign, including Peck and Heston, and the president had endorsed the Rumford Act.[87]

The Arts Division capitalized on the stars' name recognition and communication skills in setting its priorities, namely "to raise money to help defeat Proposition 14, provide talent for producing television and radio commercials and shows, and assist local groups in fund-raising activities through personal appearances."[88] In fact, according to a report in *Variety*, by September the "showbiz arm" was compelled to "take over" the fund-raising for CAP because, perhaps in a foreshadowing of impending problems, "the party's big donors, bankers, and savings and loan cos. haven't been able to come thru on the campaign."[89] The Arts Division coordinated a letter-writing campaign for which Lancaster and Frankovich signed direct appeals for funds. The group also considered selling a television special to the networks and making an album, but ultimately aborted these efforts due to lack of interest.[90] The bulk of the organization's fund-raising energy went toward its "Night of Stars" benefit at the Hollywood Bowl on October 4, 1964. Taylor and Burton, the most famous couple in Hollywood at that time, signed on as the headliners. Cole and his producer, Ike Jones, handled the musical program, and Judy Franciosa and Milton Berle's wife Ruth arranged the rest of the itinerary, which included Lucille Ball, Milton Berle, Shelley Berman, Joey Bishop, Kirk Douglas, and The Kingston Trio, as well as Lancaster, Peck, and Van Dyke.[91] That the executive committee consisted of individuals already well-connected in show business gave it an advantage in maximizing profits for the benefit. The public relations coordinator, Maury Segal, made arrangements with various publicity and public relations offices to donate their services, and George Schlaff dealt with the tax procedures. It was arranged that all performers and musicians would play at scale, and that the rental would cost merely 15 percent of the gross, which the Arts Division hoped would be $115,000. They could then anticipate about $85,000 for their coffers.[92] All told, they raised $104,457, about 20 percent of the $500,000 that CAP raised overall.[93]

Its fund-raising success allowed the Arts Division to buy widespread advertising that targeted fellow actors, as well as the general public. The group took out two full-page ads in *Variety* articulating their opposition to Prop 14.[94] They also produced a number of TV spots, again using their show business connections to cut production costs, and employed "personalities like Art Linkletter in whom the public has a faith in matters of this kind."[95] Whereas the Hollywood Bowl show focused on glamour and entertainment to raise money, the TV spots played more like political ads. Since Linkletter was a popular television host with a scandal-free personal life, the executive committee apparently felt that he would be more likely to shore up the Arts Division's political credibility. They increased the frequency of these spots in the last week of the campaign "to make full use of all the movie and television personalities who are working with us."[96]

The Arts Division also provided ways for the stars to talk directly with voters. It furnished fact sheets and set up speaking engagements with community groups, asking Peck to deliver a speech to a civic association in the Thousand Oaks neighborhood, for example. In a speech written in his own hand, Peck told the audience that if a sense of "righteousness" did not convince them to oppose Prop 14, "then the practical side of discrimination and bigotry in the loss to the nation of the vast reserve of widespread talent, ingenuity, [and] genius" should. Other stars participated in radio call-in shows or made themselves available at designated times when citizens could call them at a phone bank. Wives of the stars, such as Marjorie Van Dyke and Rita Wade Davis (married to Sammy Davis, Sr.) did door-to-door campaigning and distributed "No on Prop 14" literature.[97] This activity resulted in unprecedented grassroots campaigning among the Hollywood set.

Going into election day, it seemed that CAP had the edge, one historian calling it "a mismatch of David and Goliath proportions."[98] However, 65 percent of California voters approved Prop 14, even while they voted for President Johnson in almost equal numbers. The reasons for Prop 14's stunning victory have been rigorously analyzed by scholars, and how the governor's office managed the Arts Division exemplifies the problems with CAP's overall approach. Following CAP's leadership, the Arts Division used increasingly moralistic language when speaking of Prop 14, eschewing the more logical approach it had emphasized early in the campaign. Its first *Variety* ad had focused on the proposition itself and had warned that its broad implications would "actually legalize housing discrimination" and "prevent the State and all Cities and Town from ever passing any laws to prevent such discrimination." The second ad read much more dramatically. "The globe on which we spin needs a bath," it began. "An old-fashioned Saturday night scrubbing to cleanse it of the dirty stains of hatred and indecency that now despoil a planet." This approach annoyed voters, who were more interested in how fair housing affected them personally.[99] CAP had been concerned that specific references to racism or identification with minority groups would hurts its efforts, and so it had focused on white voters in its campaign. Likewise, although the Arts Division included a number of African Americans on its committee, there was little outreach to black or Hispanic groups.[100] Finally, CAP had underestimated the reach of CREA and its vast network of developers, brokers, and other real estate partners, as well as its political sophistication. Instead of appealing to crass racism, CREA used civil rights language to frame the issue as one of "owners rights," of a choice between "freedom of choice" and "forced housing.[101] By failing to address these problems, the Arts Division, while not causing CAP's defeat, reflected the missteps in its approach.

In determining the lessons of Prop 14's passage, historians have emphasized its relation to the splintering of liberalism, the conservative ascendance, and urban unrest, but its importance to celebrities, civil rights, and politics has not been appreciated. The Arts Division's self-characterization as "the most important group of performing artists, executives, directors, writers, and craftsmen from the broadcast and movie industries ever assembled for a single, political purpose" was not an exaggeration.[102] Not only did more celebrities become involved in fair housing than on any other issue until that point, they did so by taking on myriad responsibilities and participating in politics in a personal manner. They went beyond acting as spokespersons to organizing an all-out fund-raising and media effort and stumping on the campaign trail. Although the Arts Division was deeply disappointed in Prop 14's passage, in the wake of the election, celebrities proved increasingly willing to take on political responsibilities, including controversial issues.

Interestingly, Lancaster proved the exception to this trend. His biographer asserts that he increasingly avoided "mass, celebrity-strewn forums" like the March on Washington, and reasons that "some kind of reluctance, a sense of his own limitations, and a respect for the efforts of the those much more substantively involved than himself kept him away from the political limelight.[103] The Prop 14 fight also facilitated Lancaster's withdrawal. Not only was the work exhausting, but the actor's highly visible role as the Arts Division chair elicited controversy and retaliation. According to one report, "Some crafty joker had a Negro answer a 'vacancy' sign in one of Lancaster's apartment buildings and report that he had been turned away."[104] However, two years later the California Supreme Court deemed Prop 14 unconstitutional (a decision affirmed by the US Supreme Court in 1967), and most celebrities continued to delve into the political fray. Gregory in particular evolved into a more sophisticated political force.

*   *   *

Between 1964 and 1965, Gregory crisscrossed the country as an activist, driven by concerns for what he called "the little Negro," that is, the impoverished and likely angry African American. Gregory simultaneously grew more radical and more committed to nonviolence, tendencies that led him to experiment with the leftist elements of the movement and to plead for peace on the front lines of urban unrest. These activities reflected a diversity within the movement and showed how celebrities could open "back channels" between various individuals or constituencies. They also killed Gregory's chances for a film career and complicated his relationship with the national office of the NAACP.

Gregory developed a more coherent political philosophy during the spring and summer of 1964. His early activism came largely out of instinct and a desire to help via his celebrity status, but his consistent work gave him a larger sense of the movement and of his place in it. Not only had he confronted the enemy firsthand and met a variety of activists, but the "seriously funny" discussion he developed for the NAACP fund-raising album and the SNCC tour forced him to reflect on and articulate his own viewpoint. Gregory's relationship with Drew Pearson gave him a forum in which to express his beliefs. Gregory told the columnist that he supported public demonstrations, including the controversial "stall-in" at the World's Fair, in large part because they gave the average African American an outlet to "let off steam." Not only did the demonstrations give average blacks a greater sense of ownership in the movement, but they prevented violence. "What you white people don't know is that there are elements of my people with knives and guns who are ready to go to work. We have trouble restraining them right now," Gregory explained. "If we didn't let off steam with some of these demonstrations in Brooklyn and at the New York World's Fair, we would lose control."[105] Gregory believed that antiwhite sentiment in the North was growing. "How can I hate white boys who went to jail with me?" Gregory asked. "But the Negro up North doesn't know this. That's why the situation in Northern cities can be so tense." Furthermore, he added, "The Southern system at least is honest. They tell you down there, 'You can't mingle with us.' The Northern system is dishonest," he said, referencing the housing campaigns. "They tell you you can live side by side in the North but they don't mean it."[106] He feared that even an innocent incident could touch off a riot.

Gregory's concerns about Northern cities led him in new political directions. Despite his good relationship with many of the major civil rights organizations, he did not believe that they had the capacity to deal with the unrest among Northern blacks. He told Pearson, "The NAACP and the Urban League have passed them by"—and seemingly castigated their leadership. The "little Negro," he argued, "wouldn't recognize Roy Wilkins" and "can't afford membership in the NAACP and if he did come to an NAACP meeting he'd embarrass them," alluding to the class divisions Gregory believed the organization reflected. He also asserted that King would have minimal effect. "King, God bless his heart, can't stop trouble today . . . in the North the Negro considers him a conservative." "Malcolm X is getting to be about the only man who can stop a race riot," Gregory concluded, because he was the only one left with credibility to a constituency tired of whites.[107] This belief led Gregory to make public alliance with Malcolm X. Although the two men had known each other for several years, their different approaches and alliances had prevented their political collaboration. Gregory's recent evolution and Malcolm's break with the Nation of Islam (NOI) offered new opportunities. In March 1964, the two men met in Chester, Pennsylvania, with Lawrence Landry from Chicago SNCC, Cambridge's Gloria Richardson, and Stanley Branche, chief of the local NAACP chapter and a fervent protester against racist police practices and de facto segregation in schools and housing. Soon thereafter, Gregory and Malcolm agreed to serve as consultants to ACT, a new committee founded by Landry out of the belief that the major civil rights organizations had grown overly occupied with passing civil rights legislation and pleasing the white community. The organization never gained traction but nevertheless reflected Gregory's evolving approach.[108]

Gregory likely overestimated Malcolm's ability to prevent rioting, but his trumpeting of the leader came at a time when Malcolm himself was reaching out to celebrities to fulfill his political aspirations. According to one historian, after Malcolm broke with NOI, he became "more positive towards grassroots leaders who focused on goals beyond civil rights."[109] Ossie Davis and Ruby Dee, longtime admirers of Malcolm, worked with Poitier's wife Juanita to organize a summit of prominent civil rights activists at the Poitier home, so they could "meet in an informal atmosphere, talk, map strategy without press participation, without cameras—let down our hair." An unprecedented array of individuals with a variety of perspectives attended the meeting. Hoping to build a common agenda between them, the group endorsed Malcolm's proposal for bringing the black freedom struggle to the United Nations, a strategy he would pursue by cultivating his contacts in the Middle East and Africa, and by establishing the Organization of African American Unity (OAAU).[110] However, African heads of state had indicated during Malcolm's recent visit that they considered King the leader of the struggle and Malcolm a latecomer. According to one of Malcolm's aides, "He needed people of stature and substance that would allow him to have that kind of dialogue with Africa, or with the UN, or international bodies. And people like Ossie Davis or Ruby Dee or Sidney Poitier are people who are well known."[111] Organizers targeted these celebrities for a rally establishing OAAU's founding. Juanita Poitier attended, as did a representative for Davis and Dee.[112] Given that Malcolm's reputation derived from his defense of the urban poor, it is compelling that he behaved much like the NAACP, SCLC, and SNCC in shoring up celebrity supporters at this stage in his career. It is also noteworthy that through their associations with Malcolm, these celebrities eschewed concerns about appearing too radical. Gregory insisted, for example, on letting the media snap his picture at events. Malcolm "was so pleased, and he really wanted a picture of my appearance," says Gregory.[113]

In working with Malcolm X, Gregory did not necessarily reject his old allies, but he did show a willingness to experiment with political options in his concern for "the little Negro." Like many in the movement, he could not be neatly characterized by any one label. Gregory also did not abandon his nonviolent beliefs. Malcolm continued to call for armed self-defense, but even the FBI noted that ACT rejected Malcolm's advocacy of that policy. Likewise, after his visit to Cambridge, Gregory convinced Gloria Richardson of his commitment to nonviolence even as she had given up on preventing bloodshed.[114] Gregory's dedication to pacifism increased, a fervency likely deriving from his concerns about rioting and in reaction to the rising skepticism of nonviolence within the movement. Nevertheless, his work in the spring and summer of 1964 did indicate that Gregory could no longer be characterized simply as a civil rights supporter. He had become a political force in his own right. Gregory's 1964 Christmas for Mississippi showed his growing influence and capacities as a leader.

The sophistication of this campaign is evident when compared to Gregory's similar relief efforts in the winter of 1962–63. Indeed, the overall goal of the project proved much more ambitious: getting twenty thousand turkeys to needy Mississippians—blacks, whites, and Native Americans alike—on Christmas morning. At thirty-nine cents per pound, the birds alone cost $93,600, not to mention the costs of distributing them or any additional trimmings.[115] Ultimately, Gregory needed to raise upward of $100,000, and this time he brought in more heavy-hitting allies, including his new media champion Drew Pearson, who served as cochair. Due to his experience with other charitable causes, Pearson arranged for the project to get tax-exempt status. Not only did Pearson plug the campaign at least five times in his column, but he did so with the dramatic flourish that was his style. Pearson lamented the bigotry in Mississippi, and his frequent references to the Ku Klux Klan cast Gregory in a heroic light. "Probably there is no man in America . . . who is hated more by the Ku Klux Klan," he postulated.[116] The *New York Times* and other major papers also picked up the story, and the project received extensive coverage in *Jet* magazine, in no small part because of Sammy Davis, Jr.'s involvement. Another early supporter of the initiative, Davis headlined a benefit show at McCormick Place in Chicago on December 20 that drew an audience of five thousand and raised an impressive $70,000.[117]

This project was also more professional and organized than his previous efforts. Instead of working through an existing civil rights organization, Gregory established an ad hoc committee with he and Pearson as cochairs, Mahalia Jackson as honorary chair, and Lawrence Landry as vice-chair. The group created its own stationery and polished fund-raising fliers for reaching out to various sponsors and donors. That Gregory did not need the backing of a civil rights organization to solicit funds is an indication of the reputation he had established as an activist. The project's connection with the movement was apparent; the drive was dedicated to the memory of Medgar Evers and the slain Freedom Summer Workers, and leaders such as Roy Wilkins spoke at the benefit show. However, because the project was developed independently and received favorable media coverage guaranteed by Pearson, it attracted more outside sponsorship. Four major grocery store chains, including Food Fair, Giant, Safeway, and Daitch-Shopwell, donated one thousand turkeys each. Pearson praised their "generous" support, proclaiming, "It looks as if the bombs of bigotry might be offset by Christmas dinners."[118] The project also received substantial union support. The International Ladies Garment Workers Union, United Steelworkers, American Meat Cutters, and the International Union of Electrical Workers all made donations, the last of which, on behalf of the AFL-CIO, even lent the project $18,000 when, as reported by Pearson, "the turkey market was going up and we had to buy in a hurry." A taxi drivers union in Chicago raised $3,500 to help pay transportation costs.[119]

Gregory relied on his grassroots network to complete his mission. He asked for donations from individuals across Chicago and told of "a magnificent grass-roots response on the street corners, in church collections, donations by club groups, and individual replies to radio appeals."[120] A campaign flyer targeting individual donors proclaimed, "From the heart of Chicago to Mississippi for Christmas, $5 Buys a Family Christmas Dinner."[121] Most importantly, it was the civil rights activists and religious figures whom Gregory had come to know in Mississippi who helped with the distribution of food. Gregory coordinated with Charles Evers and Aaron Henry (president of Mississippi NAACP) to establish ten major distribution centers and a number of minor ones. SNCC activists volunteered, as did a number of individual priests, rabbis, and black and white ministers. However, the Salvation Army refused to cooperate, and Pearson reported that most white religious institutions also declined. In at least one case, a local rabbi was forced out by his congregation after volunteering.[122] Nevertheless, Gregory could proudly reflect on the successes of the campaign. He said that at least 90 percent of the recipients had never eaten a turkey before, and they accepted the donations with "pure joy and gratitude. It was such a beautiful sight."[123]

The mission showed the attraction of working independently. Not only was Gregory able to control the donations from beginning to end, but he could join forces with a diverse set of partners and promote the project without getting bogged down in some of the political concerns that beset established organizations such as the NAACP and the SCLC. That he won support from both corporate and union sponsors was unusual for a civil-rights action. And while Wilkins and King felt it prudent to keep a public distance from Malcolm X to protect their organizations, Gregory performed with Malcolm at an OAAU meeting in New York that same December, joking for forty minutes after Malcolm's featured speech.[124] Gregory was also able to use humor more freely in promoting and publicizing the project. In a caustic sympathy tug, one fund-raising flyer asked, "Did you give thanks that your Thanksgiving was not spent in Mississippi?" Likewise, Gregory encouraged Davis to play up his Judaism in order to emphasize the project's diversity. Davis appeared on the cover of *Jet* magazine dressed in a white beard and a red suit. "Whoever heard of a Jewish Santa Claus?" he joked. Gregory had created a versatility for himself through his extensive activism and celebrity status that gave him an influential voice in civil rights issues without his necessarily being a spokesperson for any one organization.

Gregory's determination to preserve that independence put him at odds with the norm. He continued to embrace tactics that a number of moderates rejected. For example, when Gregory learned that Superintendent Benjamin Willis's contract had been renewed in the summer of 1965, he led a series of demonstrations targeting City Hall that brought traffic to a standstill in downtown Chicago.[125] Mayor Richard Daley refused to replace Willis and repeatedly ordered the arrest of the demonstrators. At one point, Gregory, Lillian, and their two daughters (ages four and six) were all held by the police. Over forty-eight demonstrations and 700 arrests took place during the next two months. By the end of the summer, the Chicago movement focused on Daley himself, and Gregory led 120 demonstrators in a silent vigil to the mayor's home only to be pummeled with food by thousands of white hecklers. One scholar asserts that the demonstration brought little change and was criticized by both city officials and civil rights sympathizers.[126]

In fact, during this same period, the NAACP distanced itself from Gregory. Although one NAACP insider had groused about Gregory's affinity for black nationalism and irreverence toward the NAACP as early as 1963, Wilkins had not taken the complaint seriously.[127] Wilkins likely recognized that the NAACP couldn't "control" Gregory, and did not necessarily need to, since he was an entertainer with a reputation for confounding wit. As Pearson once commented, one "couldn't quite be sure just where the Negro comedian's humor began and where it ended."[128] However, Wilkins's tolerance ended in August 1965 when Pearson reprinted Gregory's comments about "the Little Negro." Wilkins had apparently not been aware of the comments the previous year, and sent a firm rebuttal to Pearson and a separate telegram to Gregory reading, "It is inconceivable to us that you could have made any such flatly untrue statements about the NAACP." Wilkins especially objected to Gregory's characterization of the organization as elitist and as being "embarrassed" by poor blacks. As with his visit to Pine Bluff, the comedian had not carefully considered the political ramifications of his behavior. After this flap, Gregory and the NAACP no longer collaborated closely.

Gregory also turned his back on an acting career. His fame as a comedian had piqued the interest of the film industry, and in 1965 the director Herbert Danska cast him in the independent film *Sweet Love, Bitter*. Gregory soon learned that "when you are on a movie set, every minute counts and every minute costs." He could not cancel or reschedule a scene the way he had given up club engagements, a realization that nettled him when conditions heated up in Selma. The low-budget film received mediocre reviews and was not a commercial success. However, critics praised Gregory's engaging performance, and it is certainly plausible that he would have won more acting roles in bigger films if he had wanted them. He clearly had different priorities. "I could never be an actor," he concluded. "You can't schedule filming around the Movement."[129]

*　*　*

The Christmas for Mississippi campaign reflected the fascinating trajectory of Gregory's activism. He evolved from a comedian with activist inclinations to a radical whose public persona depended more on his politics than on his comedy. His work proved vital to SNCC in terms of publicity and morale, while he provided important financial resources to the NAACP and to Mississippi locals. By going to jail and forgoing a movie career, Gregory represented the extreme end of celebrity civil rights activism, but his behavior contributed to the development of a more liberal celebrity political culture. The Arts Division's involvement in Prop 14, Belafonte's trips to Greenwood and Guinea, and celebrity interest in Malcolm X all indicated an energetic fervor for grassroots activism that increasingly ran less of a risk of inviting anticommunist backlash or pressure from concerned studio chiefs. This shift would allow for a true cadre of celebrity civil rights support as the Selma campaign came to a head in 1965.

6

Stars for Selma

The march was almost over, and the marchers were ready for a good
laugh. I tried to give it to them: "I read in the paper a week ago where
Sheriff Jim Clark said, 'They'll make that march to Montgomery
over my dead body!' And I thought that wouldn't be a bad route."
                                                        —Dick Gregory

WITH THE LEADING SIX AT THE FOREFRONT, AN OUTPOURING OF
celebrity civil rights supporters backed the 1965 Selma, Alabama, campaign for voting rights. Harry Belafonte made arrangements for scores of
stars to assemble in Montgomery to join marchers on the historic trek
from Selma. Sammy Davis, Jr., broke fund-raising records in the march's
aftermath with his biggest benefit yet. Meanwhile, the Leading Six continued to pursue stage roles, television work, and nightclub engagements,
and to live primarily on the East Coast, indicating that they still did not
feel comfortable in Hollywood, largely as a result of their continued
struggles for film roles. The schedules and residential patterns of the
Leading Six shaped the fund-raising arms of the Student Nonviolent
Coordinating Committee (SNCC) and the Southern Christian Leadership
Conference (SCLC) during this period. SNCC focused on its New York
"friends" office, and the SCLC seemingly depended on Belafonte and
Davis's participation for benefits. The National Association for the
Advancement of Colored People (NAACP) returned to focusing primarily
on its grassroots fund-raising drives and recruited Davis to lead a massive
membership drive. Such collaboration reflected the stars' importance in
the Northern liberal network, yet the paradoxes of celebrity activism also

became apparent. While Selma proved to be the high point of celebrity activism, it was the point at which the stars' involvement in the movement became more closely scrutinized by friends and foes alike.

*   *   *

Although film and television stars had proven their willingness to publicly embrace the civil rights movement, Hollywood continued to be a challenging industry for African American actors. During a series of congressional hearings regarding discrimination in the performing arts in 1962, Sidney Poitier testified, "I'm probably the only Negro actor who makes a living in the motion picture industry, which employs thirteen thousand performers. It's no joy to me to be a symbol."[1] Poitier did not exaggerate. Opportunities for black actors in film had actually dwindled after 1960. The "message movie" had largely been exhausted, and few studios hired blacks in leading roles except for "racial dramas." Most of the leading black stars from the previous decade found fewer film opportunities in the early 1960s. The only films Sammy Davis, Jr., did during this period were two mediocre Rat Pack projects, *The Sergeants 3* (1962) and *Robin and the 7 Hoods* (1964), and the independent drama *Convicts 4* (1962), in all of which he played supporting roles. Belafonte's banishment continued. Dorothy Dandridge completed her last film in 1962. Ossie Davis, Ruby Dee, and Diahann Carroll also found intermittent work in supporting roles but not frequently enough to support themselves on such work alone.

The television industry provided little alternative, as neither the quality nor quantity of TV roles had expanded since the 1950s. The fact that TV had grown into a billion-dollar industry by 1960 possibly made it even more averse to risk taking. The networks strove to be as neutral as possible with their programming by not offending blacks or whites. CBS canceled *The Grey Ghost* (1957–58), a syndicated series about the heroic exploits of a Confederate Army officer, during the Little Rock crisis, while ABC refused to air Poitier's film *The Defiant Ones* in the 1962–63 season out of fear of a hostile reaction from its thirty Southern affiliates. As one television historian explains, "With several notable exceptions, [during the early 1960s], African Americans continued in TV as infrequent guest stars on variety shows, or as occasional stars in filmed or live dramas, still cast in traditional roles." According to a report by the New York

Ethical Society, on an average evening in April 1963, a television viewer in New York City would see only three blacks, and only one of them for longer than a minute.[2]

However, between 1963 and 1964 the television industry did show promising signs. Echoing earlier critiques of the medium, in 1961 the Federal Communications Commission chair Newton Minnow had called network television a "vast wasteland."[3] This federal pressure, combined with the NAACP's 1963 campaign for improved roles and the increased involvement of stars in the civil rights movement, seemingly shamed studio executives into providing better programming. All of the major drama programs on the primetime networks ran at least one racial story during the 1963–64 season, a trend that brought liberal racial messages to television audiences. It also brought guest appearances for a host of black actors, including Sammy Davis, Jr., on *Ben Casey* (ABC 1961–66); Ossie Davis on *The Defenders* (CBS 1961–65); Ruby Dee on *The Great Adventure* series (CBS 1963–64), and, along with James Edwards, on *The Fugitive* (ABC 1963–67); James Earl Jones on *Channing* (ABC 1963–64); Diahann Carroll on *Eleventh Hour* (NBC 1962–64); and Diana Sands on *Breaking Point* (ABC 1963–64), *Outer Limits* (ABC 1963–65), and *The Nurses* (CBS 1962–65). Even more promising, two dramatic series featured African Americans in permanent roles, with Hilda Simms on *The Nurses* and Cicely Tyson on *East Side/West Side* (CBS 1963–64). An unusual series about the dismal conditions of the inner city, *East Side/West Side* included guest turns by Dee, Earle Hyman, Jones, and Sands that year as well.[4] In another heartening trend, black actors received unprecedented recognition, as Sands, Dee, and Jones all received Emmy nominations in 1963.[5] Such rewards and appearances, however, generally did not lead to financial solvency, and most black performers relied on stage work for their annual incomes.

Such work came in part from concerts and nightclub performances. Belafonte's earnings came primarily from his huge concert performances in such venues as the Greek Theater in Los Angeles and Carnegie Hall in New York. He also performed on the nightclub circuit, as did Sammy Davis, Jr., Carroll, Lena Horne, and Dorothy Dandridge, at the Copacabana in New York City, the Riviera in Vegas, and the Cocoanut Grove in Los Angeles, among other legendary stages. A nightclub contract could allow a performer to exercise a wide range of talent and to earn huge profits. Belafonte convinced Carroll that "touring, regardless of how inconvenient it was, could be very lucrative."[6] He received $200,000 per month at the Riviera; Davis signed a contract with Harrah's Club in Nevada for $1 million for eight weeks of work over a four-year period, tantamount to $125,000 per week.[7] The nightclub circuit also represented a creative alternative to Hollywood, although not always a welcome one. Whereas it served as a refuge for Horne and Carroll, it was a symbol of decline for Dandridge. Divorced, bankrupt, and without any film roles, Dandridge had taken to singing in smoke-filled lounges to pay off her debts and was living in a small apartment in West Hollywood before she died of an overdose of antidepressants in September 1965.[8]

Theatrical stage productions were another possibility. Many film actors returned to the stage to exercise their craft. For someone like Charlton Heston, for example, stage work was a luxury he could afford. For many black actors, however, it was a necessity to help make ends meet between their scarce film roles. Ossie Davis and Ruby Dee proved to be two of the most successful black stage performers during this period. However, they often felt frustrated with the overall messages their work presented. For example, Davis played in a Broadway revival of *Green Pastures*, a play he considered "offensively sentimental and condescending in the same class as any blackface minstrel show." Dee was also unhappy with *Raisin in the Sun*, as she believed its warning about the frustrations experienced by African American men had been watered down into a "comedy-drama about a family's urgent need for decent housing." Davis rationalized of *Green Pastures* that "it was a job," and he tried to "infuse the stilted, childlike language with revolutionary fire and brimstone." Likewise, Dee accepted the importance of *Raisin's* message, even in its tempered form. But these frustrations drove Davis to pen his own work.[9] He brought *Purlie Victorious* to Broadway in September 1961, one of the most significant plays of the 1960s and one in which Davis felt he truly embraced his "blackness" and his "manhood."[10]

Set in Georgia, the play stars Purlie Victorious Judson, who seeks to build an integrated church and manipulates the oligarchic Ol' Cap'n, a "colonel" from the Southern elite, into paying for its construction. Through the setting, characters, and dialogue, Davis uses satire to deliver dual social messages: first, to ridicule segregation, and second, to assert black liberation from the economic and psychological confines of Southern society. As Davis explains, "Purlie is a stereotype minister, only instead of talking about hamhocks and watermelon Purlie is talking about liberation and freedom and revolution. . . . I took the stereotype . . . and loaded him with protest and correction."[11] Davis infuses the dialogue with such farcical lines as "Running have saved more Negroes' lives than the Emancipation Proclamation" and "Being colored can be fun if nobody's looking."[12] Using satire to address racial matters was not new, as Dick Gregory had proven on the stand-up circuit; it was in the theatrical setting that *Purlie* broke new ground.

Davis had fretted that his attempt to make fun of stereotypes, the first such attempt on Broadway by a black playwright, would be "misunderstood or destructive, an act of betrayal."[13] Multiple readings with fellow actors and friends from the civil rights struggle, who howled with laughter at the script, eased Davis's mind. In fact, Malcolm X "loved" *Purlie*, and Roy Wilkins strongly pushed it via NAACP outlets. "See the funniest of Uncle Toms who finally turns up on a definite side," Wilkins urged. "Help the point get over to more and more people . . . by keeping the play on Broadway through a heavy attendance by you and your friends."[14] The play took off, with 964 Broadway performances and three national tours. Although some white critics seemed confused by the production, others, like Howard Taubman of the *New York Times*, effusively praised it, and black patrons flocked to the theater in record numbers. *Purlie* ushered in a new phase of black Broadway productions, such as *Day of Absence* in 1965, that used humor as a weapon against racial oppression. As one theatrical historian puts it, they liberated "humor until blacks could dare come on the commercial stage and demand that the white audience pay to laugh at itself." Davis became the leading African American figure in theater.[15] Soon thereafter Dee, who costarred in *Purlie*, won the roles of Catherine in *The Taming of the Shrew* and Cordelia in *King Lear* at the renowned American Shakespeare Festival in Connecticut, the first black actress to play in a major role there.[16]

For Diahann Carroll, all of the touring and television guest appearances paid off when she won the lead in the new musical *No Strings* in 1961. Composer Richard Rodgers cast her after seeing her in a guest appearance on *The Jack Paar Show*. Carroll played opposite Richard Kiley in Broadway's first integrated love affair. Besides being proud to present this groundbreaking storyline, Carroll was thrilled to be playing an American model living in Paris. "It meant the world to be able to depict a black woman with some sophistication," she remarks. The show ran on Broadway for 580 performances before it went on tour, and Carroll won a

Tony Award. Warner Brothers bought the film rights and, to Carroll's consternation, cast the Asian-American actress Nancy Kwan in the female lead, although the project never went into production. "I wasn't too old for the part in the movie, just too black," Carroll concluded, indicating why many African American performers felt the stage continued to present more opportunities.[17]

Sammy Davis, Jr., returned to Broadway in 1964 to star in the musical *Golden Boy*, one of the biggest smashes of the decade, with the most substantial role of Davis's career. Based on the 1937 play of the same name, *Golden Boy* focuses on Joe Wellington, a Harlem youth who, despite his family's objections, is seduced into prizefighting to escape the slums. Set in the 1960s, this updated version incorporates civil rights issues into the storyline and includes an explicit interracial romance and an urban jazz score. Wellington is someone who "can't survive in the ghetto because he is repulsed by it. He resents his dad, who he considers an Uncle Tom, and resents his brother, a civil rights worker, because he sees the fight as useless," Davis explained. "I thought it important showing this kind of frustration within the American Negro."[18] Davis broke Broadway records with his $10,000 per week salary for the show, but, with ten songs, four dances, and varying comedic, dramatic, and fight scenes, he *was* the show.[19] *Golden Boy* made an incredible run, with 568 performances, stellar reviews, and four Tony nominations. Such acclaim belies the personal and financial risks Davis took with the musical. During tryouts in Philadelphia and Boston and rehearsals in Detroit, Davis and his producer received multiple death threats, and Davis's record salary was a substantial pay cut from what he normally made in Las Vegas. Furthermore, the demands of the storyline, which intricately paralleled Davis's own life, sent him into an emotional tailspin.[20] The plot's focus on integration alludes to the deferential side of Davis's persona, but *Golden Boy* ushered in a new phase of stardom for Davis, more independent of the Rat Pack. Among other things, it proved his ability as a dramatic lead and gave him more leverage in Hollywood. In the meantime, the show kept him in New York.

Indeed, the necessity of stage work and the inimical nature of Hollywood led many black artists to reside in or spend considerable time in New York, often making it easier to come together there for civil rights events. This ease had been demonstrated in the gatherings at Belafonte's apartment and the summit with Malcolm X organized by Dee and Juanita Poitier. This summit had advanced a celebrity connection with Malcolm that became even more apparent with his death. Few were surprised to learn of Malcolm's assassination. Ruby Dee says that he seemed "hunted," "haunted," and "running for his life."[21] She had even tried to convince her husband that they provide Malcolm with a secret hiding place. Such foresight made Malcolm's assassination no less tragic. On February 21, 1965, three gunmen later identified as Nation of Islam conspirators shot Malcolm during a speaking engagement in Harlem, and he died soon thereafter. For Gregory, who, with President John Kennedy's death, had begun to believe in conspiracy theories, the murder only deepened this belief, and he concluded that it was "a government hit."[22]

Ossie Davis and Dee helped make the arrangements for Malcolm's funeral and presided over the service. They read aloud notes of sympathy from those not in attendance, and Davis delivered a powerful eulogy. "Many will ask what Harlem finds to honor in this stormy, controversial and bold young captain," he remarked. "Malcolm was our manhood, our living, black manhood! . . . And we will know him then for what he was and is—a Prince—our own black shining Prince!" Gregory was one of the few other prominent African Americans in attendance. He expressed his admiration for Davis's involvement, especially because "he was at the height of his career. Most entertainers were afraid to attend Malcolm's funeral, and they definitely would not have given the eulogy."[23] One scholar contends, "Davis's soliloquy on the meaning of Malcolm's life to the black people of Harlem . . . captured the public's imagination, and in subsequent decades would dwarf everything else that occurred that day."[24]

Dee's and Juanita Poitier's efforts to rally around Malcolm's widow, Betty Shabazz (who was pregnant with twins at the time), further shaped the slain leader's legacy. They formed the Committee of Concerned Mothers to provide housing and education funds for Shabazz and her daughters. Dee, who was not well acquainted with Shabazz at that point, explained, "It was something we did out of love and passion for the movement. All of us were very much connected to Malcolm, and that's something that he would have done." They used the now-familiar strategies of garnering publicity, staging benefit shows, and appealing to an interracial liberal audience. Days after Malcolm's death, Davis pleaded for money on the *Barry Gray Show*, a popular late-night talk radio show in New York, while Dee and Poitier made personal solicitations. They also organized a midnight benefit show at the Apollo featuring Sammy Davis, Jr., Gregory, and the singer Nina Simone, and another concert on Poitier's lawn in

Mount Vernon, New York, that summer. All told, they raised $22,000. These efforts came at a pivotal time. According to Shabazz's biographer, most of the African American establishment viewed her "as a pariah's widow, and ignored or shunned her." In the meantime, Malcolm's Organization of African American Unity was in disarray. The stars' support for Shabazz, who had begun to abandon some Islamic strictures, put her in a stronger position to promote Malcolm's legacy in an ecumenical fashion with more widespread appeal. The concert on Poitier's lawn indicated that Malcolm's image had already begun to change, as several white neighbors and corporate executives were in attendance.[25] The stars grew close with Shabazz and collaborated on events, such as Davis's recitation of his "black shining prince" eulogy at the Apollo on the 1969 anniversary of Malcolm's death, that helped promote a more positive public image of Malcolm than he had enjoyed during his lifetime.[26]

The New York Friends of SNCC office recognized the virtue of having these socially conscious artists in such proximity. In 1964, it shifted its fund-raising strategies to hold more "house parties" in the private homes of wealthy individuals in the New York area. The twelve Friends of SNCC (FOS) offices that James Forman had established in 1962 had grown into a multicity network. Sixty Northern cities and two hundred college campuses boasted FOS groups by late 1964.[27] Due to the influence of Dick Gregory and Lawrence Landry, the Chicago office engaged in some direct-action campaigns, but Forman instructed FOS groups to focus on raising money for general support and bail funds, publicizing SNCC, recruiting volunteers for field work, and putting political pressure on federal authorities.[28] The New York office proved by far the most successful at raising money by focusing on "special gifts" or "high-level" fund-raising with house parties. These events included a wealthy patron who served as the host; at least one well-known SNCC activist such as Forman, John Lewis, or Gloria Richardson; two or three high-profile "special guest" celebrities; and approximately one hundred potential donors, drawn to the event by the prospect of mingling with the activists and stars in a relatively intimate environment.

SNCC held what appears to be its first house party at Davis and Dee's home in 1962, and threw two more in 1963 at the homes of wealthy New Yorkers. Sidney Poitier, Carroll, and Theodore Bikel attended both of the latter parties, and SNCC netted $13,105 from the events.[29] However, at that point (seemingly because of Sinatra and Horne's successful concert at Carnegie Hall, discussed in chapter three), SNCC envisioned benefit shows as its future fund-raising mechanism. The Northern coordinator Casey Hayden wrote to the New York FOS office, "We want each city and college area where we have responsible people to do the job to stage a . . . benefit concert—like the one at Carnegie Hall but minus all of the SNCC staff. But," she continued, "New York will have to take major responsibility, since most of the artists are located there and you all have last year's concert to draw on." Hayden also indicated that she preferred benefit shows in which only SNCC received the profits. "Someone will have to contact people like Belafonte, Cole, others who are friendly but haven't performed for us alone yet," she suggested.[30] The New York office proved willing to take the lead in pursuing artists for SNCC-only affairs but eschewed benefit concerts in favor of house parties, believing them more profitable.

New York FOS proved aggressive in its new approach. It organized a "special gifts staff," trained by a volunteer committee of professional fund-raisers, whose first task was to break supporters of the benefit concert mentality. In describing negotiations with a contact in South Orange, New Jersey, a SNCC staffer explained that a "primary factor . . . was to convince the interested person that the function, which he had conceived of as a benefit concert, should not be one in which SNCC and CORE would split the proceeds," and that "our type of house party would prove more profitable." After one successful event, it became easier to find other potential backers and "to persuade them to try our approach."[31] New York FOS soon developed a systematic and professional approach to formal invitations to events, follow-up and thank you letters, party favors, and bookkeeping practices.

A house party could be more profitable and perhaps easier to organize than a benefit concert, but it, too, depended on celebrities for its success. As one SNCC report stated, "talent is key." Another concluded, "One of the most difficult and frustrating jobs is that of obtaining talent."[32] SNCC struggled to negotiate the stars' busy schedules. "High-level fundraising requires a top name artist and since top name artists are always working it is extremely difficult to obtain their services," one report lamented. New York FOS at least had a sizable pool of interested artists to call upon. Other FOS offices frequently complained about "a talent problem" in terms of recruitment, including the Los Angeles group. It began reaching out to Burt Lancaster, Charlton Heston, and Marlon Brando in 1964, but simply did not have access to a reliable base of interested stars.[33] This situation derived in part from the group's fairly new status but also speaks to the residential patterns of the Leading Six. Between June 1962 and August 1964, Davis and Dee attended at least three New York–area house parties, Poitier three, Belafonte three, and Sammy Davis, Jr., one, along with Carroll and Bikel, who attended three, and the actors Rod Steiger, Claire Bloom, and Robert Ryan, who attended at least one. Belafonte, Poitier, Bikel, and Sammy Davis, Jr., all agreed to help mobilize more artists. Bikel sat on the executive committee of the New York FOS steering committee. Chaired by the New York lawyer Michael Standard, the committee concentrated on drawing in artists and celebrities. Bikel lent his apartment for the weekly planning meetings and press conferences, sent numerous letters to associates encouraging their support, and provided SNCC with the "guarded" phone numbers of potential Hollywood-based supporters.[34]

The SNCC house parties soon became, in the words of the activist Bob Zellner, "legendary."[35] Their allure was their informal and relatively intimate nature. About one hundred people typically pressed into a Long Island home or Manhattan apartment. They could expect to hobnob with the special celebrity guests over cocktails and hors d'oeuvres, hear a short civil rights presentation, and possibly enjoy some entertainment, depending on the performer. Belafonte and Bikel were likely to sing a couple of songs, and Davis to tell jokes; however, the emphasis was on mingling.[36] Gloria Richardson, the acclaimed veteran of the Cambridge movement, remembers her mixed feelings about meeting Brando at a house party. A friend had warned her about his reputation as a womanizer, and she acknowledges, "He did just sit there and look at the women." When he asked her to dance, she was both "flattered" and "petrified. I don't know how my limbs worked."[37] The potential for such direct encounters helped boost the parties' attendance, as well as their earnings. The SNCC staffer Dinky Romilly attended virtually all of the house parties and notes that their intimate nature made for "public giving." People tended to donate more money in such an environment, because it became a "competition," much like an "auction."[38]

The SNCC house parties proved very lucrative indeed. A typical event raised between $5,000 and $10,000. Between mid-May and mid-October 1964, New York FOS made $56,000 from eight house parties. During the next two months, the group raised an astounding $48,000 from one party with Sammy Davis, Jr. (there were possibly more parties but the records are not clear). Such events required a fair amount of legwork on behalf of the staff but very little financial investment from the organization beyond stationery and mailing costs. Between 1963 and 1964, fund-raising expenses increased a mere 30 percent (from $9,888 to $12,749), while contributions increased over 400 percent (from $69,184 to $363,443).[39] In other words, while spending only $3,000 more, New York FOS put an additional $294,000 into SNCC's programs. The New York office far outpaced the other FOS groups during that time, as the next highest earnings came from Chicago, with $18,000. Los Angeles came in fifth, with $2,500.[40] This money helped fund SNCC during Mississippi Freedom Summer and, in its aftermath, allowed SNCC to pay a staff of 225 people with a payroll of $15,000 every two weeks to expand voting rights projects in the Deep South.[41] Pleased with their momentum, the FOS groups planned a large fund-raising workshop for the winter of 1965, just as the Selma campaign was also heating up.

*   *   *

The SNCC chairman John Lewis felt that it was during the Selma to Montgomery March that the civil rights movement finally had a "true cadre" of celebrity support.[42] Although stars participated in numbers comparable to those at the March on Washington, they were not as instrumental to the 1965 event. The terrible violence inflicted upon the civil rights workers in Selma garnered more national attention than any celebrity supporter could have produced. The stars' participation proved more valuable in reflecting the national backing for voting rights legislation in the face of such violence, energizing weary protesters, providing valuable media copy, and perpetuating the spirit of Selma for further publicity and fund-raising.

Voter projects continued to face difficulties in the Deep South. Between 1958 and 1964, African American Southerners had made only incremental progress in registering to vote. The number of registered blacks increased only 4.8 percent in Alabama (to 19.4 percent of the total African Americans in the state), 2 percent in Mississippi (to 6.4 percent), and a pitiful .1 percent in Louisiana (to 31.8 percent).[43] Even after Mississippi Freedom Summer, the Council of Federated Organizations registered fewer than one thousand new black voters, an impressive number given the circumstances, but statistically insignificant all the same. Voting statistics remained dismal in Selma. Only seventy-one African Americans had successfully registered since 1961, and those resulted from suits brought by the Justice Department.[44] Movement efforts had repeatedly stalled in Selma against the formidable opposition of Sheriff Jim Clark, who baldly expressed his racism and regularly arrested protesters with little legal grounding. Martin Luther King, Jr., had come to believe that Clark could serve the movement well. As one scholar explains, Clark "had come straight out of central casting. He often sported a white crash helmet, a swagger stick, and had at his disposal a motley crew of amateur lawmen."[45] If civil rights activists could provoke an extreme reaction from Clark, they hoped it would gain media attention and force a federal response. In late December, the SCLC announced its intention to kick off the Selma campaign on January 2, 1965.[46]

In the meantime, President Lyndon Johnson had already decided on the necessity of federal action on voting rights. Although the 1964 Civil Rights Act had been in effect for less than six months, Johnson knew it would be relatively inadequate for voting rights, as it relied on litigation to address discrimination and intimidation during the registration process. Such a strategy was slow and burdensome, relied on judges who were often unfriendly, and did little to correct the terrifying conditions in the South for those who demanded the ballot.[47] Johnson announced his intention to pursue voting rights legislation in his State of the Union address on January 4, 1965, just as the SCLC's campaign was beginning. Within a few weeks, Sheriff Clark played into King's strategy when he and his posse arrested hundreds of marchers, garnering national headlines for their rough handling of women and youngsters in particular. In late January, Clark roughed up a black woman named Amelia Boynton. The media noted that he grabbed her by "the collar of her fur-trimmed coat" before wrestling her down with a billy club.[48] A week later, Clark arrested 165 teenagers and sent them on a forced run through the countryside, using cattle prods and nightsticks to make them keep up the pace. In a night march later that month, during which the streetlights suddenly went dark, Clark's men severely broke up the crowd of five hundred, beating members of the press and shooting a young black man named Jimmie Lee Jackson, who died several days later. In the course of these events, President Johnson gave his tacit support to the SCLC, continued to tout the need for voting legislation, and began lining up congressional support for a bill.[49]

The worst violence and most media attention came with "Bloody Sunday." On Wednesday, March 3, the SCLC had announced its plans to walk from Selma to Montgomery that coming Sunday to stage a protest at the state capital building. However, Governor George Wallace's refusal to permit the event and numerous threats of violence altered plans for the march. SNCC decided not to participate as an organization, but said that individual members could join of their own accord, and King opted to stay in Atlanta. SNCC's John Lewis and SCLC's Hosea Williams led six hundred marchers out of Selma, but when they reached the Edmund Pettus Bridge spanning the Alabama River, they met opposition. Clark, his posse, and the Alabama state troopers, some of whom sat astride horses, ordered the marchers to turn around; when they refused, the authorities attacked with clubs, whips, teargas, and fists while white locals cheered them on. As the marchers retreated, the lawmen chased them into downtown Selma, some all the way to their homes. Approximately one hundred marchers were treated for injuries, including Lewis, who suffered a concussion. The three major networks ran footage of the sickening melee, including ABC, who interrupted, in an ironic coincidence, its Sunday night movie *Judgment at Nuremburg* (1961) to air the scene. Forty-eight million viewers had tuned in that night to see the film, giving the civil rights movement unprecedented prime-time coverage of a single event. Likewise, the march was heavily covered by the national papers, who printed dramatic headlines and grainy, yet vivid, photos.[50]

King and the SCLC wrestled with how best to move forward after "Bloody Sunday." Feeling they must press on, King announced he would return to Selma and lead a new walk to Montgomery on Tuesday, March 9. However, the SCLC had requested an injunction against state interference of the march, and the trial would not begin until Thursday, March 11. Not only did the judge strongly urge the SCLC against pursuing its plans until after he had ruled on the injunction, but so did President Johnson, who was close to submitting his bill and was also planning a criminal prosecution of Clark. Ultimately, King compromised by leading a group of activists back to the Pettus Bridge and, when ordered to retreat, kneeled and prayed before backtracking to Selma. Known as "Turnaround Tuesday," King's actions were held in contempt by a number of SNCC activists who were unaware of the compromise. Still, the march quickly got back on track. The next week, Johnson delivered the most moving speech of his presidency in which he explained the need for a voting rights bill and concluded by adopting the mantra of the movement: "We *shall* overcome." He sent his bill to Congress the same day that the judge ruled that the demonstrators had the right to complete their trek to Montgomery.[51]

The now sanctioned march was set to begin March 21. The demonstrators planned to follow Highway 80, which, with the exception of the immediate vicinities of Selma and Montgomery, consisted of two lanes. The judge allowed for unlimited marchers on those sections of the highway with four lanes, but placed a three-hundred-person limit on those with only two. SCLC made arrangements for a kick-off rally, support services (such as communication, food, and security) and campgrounds at churches and farms for each of the four nights on the road, and a final concert at the city of St. Jude, a Roman Catholic Conference Center outside of Montgomery, where participants would stay before the last few miles' march into the state capitol. All told, the core marchers would walk fifty-four miles over a five-day period; 3,200 people participated in the walk out of Selma; and 30,000 made the procession into Montgomery.[52] Most celebrity supporters participated in the final leg, but Gregory, Sammy Davis, Jr., and Belafonte gave their support throughout.

Gregory had a vested interest in Selma due to his long-standing voter registration efforts, as well as to another run-in with the law he had experienced there. Gregory had willingly gone to jail again in February 1965 (about two weeks before Bloody Sunday). While attempting to check into Selma's Holiday Inn Hotel, he had been arrested on disorderly conduct charges. He and his party had reservations but had arrived late and were refused rooms. According to Gregory, other guests had also arrived late but were allowed to check in. He confronted the manager, was arrested, and jailed. He took the arrest in stride, saying, "I didn't have any obligations until my weekend engagement at the Village Gate, and I needed a few days rest, soul food, and Kool Aid."[53] Although the arrest received media attention, it did not make headlines, as stories about the voting rights campaign and related violent altercations eclipsed Gregory's.[54] These incidents nevertheless put Selma on Gregory's radar well before the violence on the Pettus Bridge and made him a natural choice to help represent the SCLC during the campaign.

Prominent individuals like Gregory received media attention for their involvement in launching the march. As thousands of people from all over the country surged into Selma, the *New York Times* reported on the mood of "festivity and chaos" permeating the city and identified the "notables" participating. However, for the first leg, Gregory and the film and television actor Gary Merrill (also famous as the ex-husband of Bette Davis) were the only celebrities publicized. Gregory joined such veteran activists as Lewis, Diane Nash, James Bevel, and Andrew Young in making speeches at a small meeting the night before at Brown's Chapel. Gregory focused on "preaching to the preachers," but Lewis noted that he "couldn't help working a little routine into his speech." Gregory joked, "It would be just our luck to find out that Wallace is colored" upon arriving in Montgomery. The next day, three thousand people gathered outside of the chapel, and Gregory joined with King and other movement activists to lead the column out of the city. Local Selmans immediately followed the leaders, and most out-of-towners walked further back. "We were all very sensitive about this," Lewis explains, "about keeping the focus as much as possible on the people who had brought this historic day about, the everyday men and women of Selma."[55] Thus, unlike the March on Washington, the SCLC purposefully avoided relying on celebrities to stage the event. Gregory's leadership role was a reflection of his previous devotion to the movement. He walked to the first campsite, then flew to Philadelphia, where he was filming *Sweet Love, Bitter,* with plans to regroup with the marchers at St. Jude's.

Before the march had begun, Sammy Davis, Jr., had initiated a huge benefit show that would connect a dizzying array of stars to events in the South. On March 18, Davis announced his intention to produce "Broadway Answers Selma" at the Majestic Theater on April 4 to benefit the family of the slain activist Reverend James J. Reeb, as well as SCLC, CORE, and SNCC. Davis, with the help of *Golden Boy* producer Hilly Elkins, quickly secured everything needed to deliver a spectacular show with maximum profit. At the time of the show's announcement, Davis had already lined up sixty performers, including Robert Preston, Dick Shawn, Steve Lawrence, Victor Borge, Carol Burnett, Carol Channing, Sir John Gielgud, Buddy Hackett, Chita Rivera, Barbra Streisand, Eli Wallach, and Ann Jackson, as well as all of the technicians. Everyone agreed to donate their services, and the Majestic's owner, the Schubert Organization, contributed the use of its theater, most likely due to Davis's fabulous success with *Golden Boy* there. Indeed, it was Davis's charisma and connections, not only as a celebrity but as a Broadway star, that allowed him to put together this kind of event. According to Elkins, they sent telegrams to every star currently appearing on Broadway, and within twenty-four hours all had agreed to participate, representing an impressive $1 million worth of talent. New York mayor Robert F. Wagner, Jr., who was invested in the success of the city's theatre district and was himself a liberal, purchased the first ticket, with much media fanfare. His was one of several tickets sold for $100; a select few were offered at $1,000, and the rest of the house ranged from $5 to $50 per ticket. With this scaling, a sold-out show would net $150,000.[56] Despite Davis's obvious enthusiasm for assisting with the Selma campaign, he had no intention of actually traveling to Alabama.

In fact, Merrill and Parnell Roberts, star of TV's *Bonanza* (NBC 1959–73), were the only celebrities to complete the entire fifty-four-mile journey, but as the march continued stars joined to participate in a large concert Belafonte had put together. King had anticipated that the weary travelers would need "pumping up" for the final leg into Montgomery. According to Belafonte, recruiting was easy, because "the cause was so compelling, the news photos of violence on the Pettus Bridge so fresh."[57] Such luminaries as the singers Nina Simone, Tony Bennett, the trio Peter, Paul, and Mary, Johnny Mathis, and Odetta; the actors Anthony Perkins, Mike Nichols, Elaine May, Shelley Winters, and Davis and Dee; and the comedians Nipsey Russell, George Kirby, and Gregory all agreed to come. So would Sammy Davis, Jr., but only after intense pressure from Belafonte. "I couldn't possibly have expressed how strongly I didn't want to go, how scared I was," he explained.[58]

Davis certainly had reason to fear. Individuals who completed the march noted the intense hostility expressed by Alabama whites. Passersby waved placards with threatening messages, cursed and spat upon the demonstrators, and yelled racial insults, leading the marchers to fear snipers and planned attacks on the campsites.[59] Gregory admitted that plenty of people feared for their lives, and although he did not identify anyone in particular, he said that some marchers secretly carried weapons and some stars brought bodyguards. Acknowledging the electric atmosphere, Lewis noted that at one point during the concert the stage cracked, and Mathis "flew up into the air" out of fright.[60] President Johnson had called 1,800 Alabama National Guardsmen into federal service to protect the marchers, but many troopers openly expressed their hostility. One took pictures of the marchers in an effort to intimidate them. This palpable fear highlights the significance of staging such an impressive event with a large contingent of stars in the South.

CHAPTER 6

Indeed, it was the Southern setting and the potential for violence that made the stars' involvement so significant in Lewis's mind. Fewer Hollywood stars participated in the Selma march than in the March on Washington. Certainly, fewer A-listers turned out. The last-minute nature of the event reduced attendance, as there were stars in support of the march who were unable to attend because of their work and other public service schedules. For example, Charlton Heston believed the march to be "meaningful" and "necessary" but could not fit it into his schedule. He sent a telegram of support, as did Carroll, who wrote, "My heart, my thoughts, all my emotions will be with you in Montgomery tomorrow. I am deeply distressed I can't be there in person."[61] Poitier, Paul Newman, and Marlon Brando were likewise busy. In Lewis's estimation, those who could make the trip "helped to say to the rest of the country that these people were willing to be part of the struggle" and that "the movement was not something to be scared of."[62]

One noteworthy newcomer was Shelley Winters. Winters had won an Academy Award for her work in *The Diary of Anne Frank* (1959) and was one of Hollywood's most acclaimed actresses. Although she had campaigned for liberal Democratic candidates and contributed to the Committee to Defend Martin Luther King, Jr. (discussed in chapter three), she had not become actively engaged in the civil rights movement until 1965. She credits her friendship with the Belafontes and her work on *A Patch of Blue* (1965) with leading her to Selma. In this dramatic romance between a black journalist played by Poitier and a white blind woman, Winters played the girls' mother, a bigoted and angry prostitute opposed to the couple's relationship. Winters found the role extremely "challenging" due to her friendship with Poitier. After filming, she recalls, "I found I no longer could retreat to my Shelley Winters position of 'take care of number one.'" She, too, had difficulty adjusting to the obvious fear in Selma, but from a different perspective than many of the black stars. "Harry Belafonte carefully briefed us not to go near any southern policemen," she remembers, "but rejecting your life condition comes hard." As Winters left the airport and was for a waiting bus, she recalled, "a jovial Alabama sheriff said, 'Oh, Shelley Winters my longtime favorite.'" He took her arm, almost wrenching it out of its socket. "All I could think to do was point to a national guardsman and yell weakly, 'Mr. Soldier!' He came over quickly with his bayoneted rifle, and the jovial sheriff held his hands up in the air innocently, looking bewildered."[63]

The concert itself proved haphazard yet triumphant, and Winters's participation helped bring it off. Belafonte spent countless hours and thousands of dollars making travel arrangements for the entertainers, but he had given little thought to actually staging the concert. "I'd thought the crowd would be much smaller, that we'd set up on some nearby hillside," he admitted.[64] By the time the marchers reached St. Jude, they numbered ten thousand; at the end of the night, close to twenty-five thousand had squeezed into the compound and were nearing pandemonium. Support staff improvised a makeshift stage of stacked coffin crates loaned by a local black funeral parlor. Rain had shorted out the sound system, and there were no lights set up. A friend of Winters's husband, who was there filming, loaned the crew his microphones and speakers. For lights, Winters called the commanding officer at Maxwell Air Force Base and threatened to notify President Johnson, for whom she had campaigned, if he refused to help them. "The Southern colonel was so angry he almost came through the telephone at my throat," she recalls, "but he delivered the lights himself with the line: 'Mizz Winters, your water boy's here.'" She received praise from the *Pittsburgh Courier* for bringing "the H'wood touch."[65]

These difficulties delayed the show by two hours and prompted the crowds to press even closer to the stage. Fifty-seven people collapsed from illness, exhaustion, or injury.[66] Ossie Davis, in a role similar to the one he had filled at the March on Washington, took over the emceeing. According to one observer, he "kept the crowd in good spirits until the main body of performers found their way to the entertainment area."[67] John Lewis, himself worn from the grueling march, gratefully described the scene: "It was a spectacle, a salute to Selma, with more than four hours of songs, speeches, and sketches." Winters spoke about filming *Patch of Blue*. She told the audience how difficult one particular scene, in which she was required to hit Poitier and shout "Nigger!" repeatedly, had been for her. "The black audience at the rally seemed to find this uproarious," she remarks, "and the kids yelled back at me that was one of the *nice* names they were called in the South."[68] Harris Wofford, Belafonte's former colleague from the Peace Corps, remembers Gregory eliciting the most laughter. Gregory cracked: "Now don't you believe that Communist propaganda about the great experiment of a Russian spaceman climbing out of his rocket. What really happened is that they had engine trouble and the radio told them they were to make an emergency landing. 'We're going to put you down in Selma, Alabama,' their radio orders said. That's when the Russian decided to climb out."[69] The "midnight gala" was a success; it revived the core marchers and fortified the new arrivals for the walk into Montgomery.

The celebrities' position in the parade reflected their important but modest role in the Selma campaign. As the marchers gathered that morning, disagreement arose as to the order of the marchers, especially who should be out front—the core marchers, the movement leaders, or the celebrities. Odetta and Roy Wilkins, whose NAACP Legal Defense Fund had been an important resource to jailed Selmans, insisted that the core marchers go first.[70] A smattering of movement leaders and the celebrities immediately followed. A crowd of thirty thousand filled out the ranks. As the procession slowly snaked its way through town on the three-mile walk, celebrity marchers engaged with black supporters and white bystanders. One CBS news correspondent marveled that the celebrities were not cloistered off "with important persons" but just "walking along in the group! It was quite interesting." Gregory recalls, "It was a beautiful sight to see the kids hanging out the windows" of a black elementary school, "smiling and waving at Belafonte. Harry joined in the fun, waving back to his little fans and saying, 'come on down and join us.'"[71] Many hostile whites also watched, some of whom shouted epithets at the participants, including the celebrities. Belafonte looked "right at them, one after another silently. Many just looked away, or met my gaze with hate, but some seemed startled and shamed. A few even waved and smiled."[72]

At the plaza that marked the march's final destination, the celebrities took on a more prominent role in entertaining the crowds while the cameras rolled. Belafonte, Baez, the Chad Mitchell Trio, Peter, Paul and Mary, and others spontaneously jumped on stage as CBS News, which provided live coverage, showed hundreds of marchers standing and sitting around with nothing to do but wait for the crowd to fill in. "Great day! Great day! Great day! And there's millions on the way," Belafonte exclaimed, peering out into the throng. Picking their songs and the key as they went along, the singers crooned such patriotic and movement anthems as "Go Tell It On the Mountain," "Michael Row Your Boat Ashore," and a rousing rendition of "You Got to Move When the Spirit Says Move." The impromptu concert provided easy "filler" for the news media as it waited for the speeches to begin, as well as important images for the movement. The crowd clearly enjoyed the songs as they clapped, swayed, and sang along.

One performer waved a huge American flag throughout the concert, counteracting the many Confederate flags atop the state capitol. The amity among the interracial group was striking, as they linked arms and hugged one another during their songs.[73] One marcher remembered thinking, "If I were Otto Preminger and this were a movie set, this is probably the way I would stage it." "It is all very cornball," he admitted, but it was effective.[74] Belafonte and Mary Travers (of Peter, Paul, and Mary) seemed especially close, with their arms around one another, sharing a water cup and even a kiss. Southern callers besieged CBS corporate headquarters in protest.[75] The media praised the "magnificent array" of celebrities on hand and credited them with adding "the trappings of triumph" to a march that had begun against huge odds.[76]

King delivered the stirring concluding address, and the stars, having boosted the morale of the marchers, dispersed with the rest of the crowd to return home. The core marchers had traveled under such difficult conditions that the celebrity guests had provided welcome distractions. As Richard Leonard, a white minister who had traveled from New York to participate in the campaign, recalls, by the third day of the trek, "I was rapidly reaching the most depressed moment for me in my eighteen days in the South." After walking in the rain all afternoon, their campsite was a muddy "quagmire" that immediately absorbed the hay brought in for stability and bedding. With no place to sit or lie down, a fellow marcher compared the campsite to being stationed in New Guinea during World War II. After Leonard learned that Parnell Roberts and his wife were there, "things began to look up," he says. "I managed to talk to the two of them for fifteen or twenty minutes and got his autograph, knowing that his would make my absence from home almost justified in their [his family's] eyes."[77] Roberts, along with Merrill, had volunteered to erect and break down the huge tents at each camp. That these two celebrities volunteered for this difficult job impressed the marchers. "Unsung," *Jet* magazine praised, they "performed dirty, necessary, work."[78] The onerous weather conditions sometimes overwhelmed the stars. Odetta arrived at the muddy campsite ready for a planned "community sing" to lift morale only to find Pete Seeger asleep and no appropriate place to perform.[79] Indeed, Leonard felt so filthy and worn out by the fourth night of walking that he skipped the concert at St. Jude's altogether. However, for another marcher, who pushed his way up front and gave Odetta a shoulder massage, it was "the high point of his evening." Joan Baez even sang over the public address system on a return flight to New York, continuing to raise spirits.[80]

Davis's "Broadway Answers Selma" show on April 4 helped keep this positive spirit alive. In the immediate aftermath of the march, Klansmen gunned down two SNCC volunteers who had just dropped off marchers in Selma. One, Viola Liuzzo, a white housewife from Detroit, died instantly; the other, Leroy Moton, a black SCLC volunteer from Selma, escaped by feigning death. The FBI quickly apprehended the murderers, but the violence disheartened civil rights supporters.[81] The naturally slow legislative process also dampened the press coverage of voting rights. "Broadway Answers Selma" renewed the elated spirit of the march and brought the movement back into the news cycle. Davis managed to nab multiple headlines from a host of activities related to the show. That morning, at a breakfast forum meeting of the men's club of Temple Emanu-El in Manhattan, he spoke of his experiences in Selma. Davis said he was "proud" to have stood up against the "Southern extremists," and compared the circumstances of blacks in the South to "probably like the Jews in Germany" under the Nazis, a common comparison after the *Judgment of Nuremberg* coincidence. A rally preceding the show won media attention due largely to the surprising sight of uniformed New York City policemen linking arms and singing "We Shall Overcome" with some of the performers, several New York City councilmen, and five thousand others in the theater district.[82] Two months later, Davis ceremoniously deposited $77,000, about half of the show's proceeds, in the newly formed Freedom National Bank in Harlem in an effort to bolster its deposits. This nod to black capitalism would become more instrumental to Davis's activism in later years, but at this point it served as a clear reminder of the Selma campaign.[83]

Broadway Answers Selma boosted both the movement and Davis personally. It brought a new array of stars to the cause. Beyond those identified in the initial announcement were such "names" as Walter Matthau, Ethel Merman, Diana Sands, Lou Gossett, Alan Alda, Alan Arkin, and a young Martin Sheen. These stars performed for over four hours to a full house and received positive reviews, as much for the material presented as for the incredible profits. The show was reported as raising the "highest [proceeds] for a single benefit performance in theater history," and Davis reached his $150,000 goal.[84] Having spent $50,000 on the Selma march, the SCLC gratefully accepted its portion of the returns. CORE used some of its proceeds to offer ten CORE field fellowships for volunteers in the Deep South.[85] Davis had once again shown his ability to bring white liberal artists into the civil rights fold with an important fund-raising endeavor, and this time he achieved it without the umbrella of the Rat Pack. "Governor Wallace . . . count your days!" he challenged at the show's end.[86]

* * *

On August 6, 1965, President Johnson signed the Voting Rights Act, and Dick Gregory commemorated the event at the Sumter County Courthouse lawn in Americus, Georgia, with a group of avid African American registrants. Surrounded by a cordon of white state troopers in white helmets who were dispatched to protect them, Gregory observed, "When everybody gets to voting, we are going to get us some black faces under those white helmets. And it ain't going to be from no suntan neither."[87] He foretold of the dramatic effect voting rights would have on the daily lives of African Americans.

Only one week later, the comedian rushed to the Watts district in Los Angeles, where a race riot was threatening to destroy the city. Sparked by the arrest of a young black man for drunk driving, the altercation had grown into a widespread armed confrontation with the Los Angeles police and the National Guard. Wanting "to help in any way I could," Gregory drove into the riot area near a housing project and was shocked by the "stark and horrible expression of raw violence." He started to walk between law enforcement and the rioters when "the bullets started to fly." When he was shot in the leg, Gregory rushed into the street, yelling "Alright goddamn, it. You shot me, now go home!" With a burning wound, Gregory was in disbelief that "after all the times I'd been arrested by red neck deputies in the past four years, here I was shot by a black man in California." He charged forth, believing "somebody had to stop it." On that street corner at least, the rioters retreated.[88] Across town, Belafonte, already booked at the Greek Theater, continued to perform nightly when most other public venues were closed. Admittedly "apprehensive" about potential problems in an audience of five thousand, he also saw it "as a challenge" to show a capacity for unity in such dreadful circumstances. Belafonte even brought in youngsters from Watts to give them safe haven.[89] The riot lasted six days and resulted in thirty-four deaths and $40 million in property damage. Gregory and Belafonte's activities in

August 1965 foretold of the movement's impending "crisis of victory" and of the stars' varying roles in its progression.

For the time being, however, the leading civil rights organizations optimistically planned their futures, and celebrities were instrumental in their efforts. In March 1965, the New York FOS office held a workshop emphasizing their new fund-raiser of choice: the house party. Although such events were admittedly "small, exclusive receptions," the group still called their efforts "a grassroots public relations program." They instructed workshop attendees to ask themselves "Is the money there?" before planning a party. "Regardless of their goodwill, a constituency must be people of means or the funds realized will be commensurately small," the literature explained. The program emphasized cultivating "prominent" and "wealthy" individuals, as well as members of the media, and highlighted obtaining artists for the parties. Another development from the conference included the creation of a contact information sheet (with addresses and phone numbers) for the artists willing to sponsor SNCC events.[90] This long-awaited list could be distributed among the FOS groups and made for more streamlined planning. It also reflected the importance of Selma to bringing more celebrities into the movement on a more permanent basis. The list included the regulars from the 1964 house parties, as well as those individuals, such as Tony Bennett and Shelley Winters, who had marched in Selma, and those, such as Alan Arkin and Eli Wallach, who had participated in Davis's Broadway benefit. FOS groups went on to hold an unprecedented number of star-studded house parties in the coming months.

The successful house parties led to benefit concerts devoted to SNCC alone. With the help of Julie Belafonte and Diahann Carroll, the New York FOS organized an elegant black-tie dinner and dance at the New York Hilton Grand Ballroom on April 25, 1965, to benefit freedom schools and voter registration drives in the South. The program featured Harry Belafonte, Brando, Carroll, Sammy Davis, Jr., Streisand, Sonny Terry, and Brownie McGhee. Tickets cost $100 per person, and a number of celebrities and wealthy New Yorkers sponsored entire tables at $1,000 each. SNCC netted an estimated $80,000 from the event, and held a similar dinner, again hosted by Julie Belafonte and Carroll, the following year.[91]

The organization also succeeded at having more parties in Los Angeles. Brando headlined one party at a Hollywood home in June 1965.[92] Poitier cohosted a SNCC fund-raiser with Belafonte, Elizabeth Taylor,

Richard Burton, Burt Lancaster, Paul Newman, and Mike Nichols at a posh Beverly Hills discotheque in August. The event resembled a movie premiere. Such guests as the actors James Garner, Lauren Bacall, and Lee Marvin, and the filmmakers Stanley Kramer, Arthur Penn, and Robert Blumofe arrived wearing tuxedoes, long gowns, and lavish jewelry. The event was held only a few days after the Watts riot, and Poitier used it to plead for funds, arguing the disturbances were "only a symptom of the underlying social diseases eating away at the fabric of society." The stars shouted their pledges, challenging one another until they reached $50,000. The party was written up in the *New York Times* for the "surprising number of Hollywood luminaries" willing to publicly support the "most radical and controversial of all the major civil rights organizations."[93]

Since the parties targeted only a select few, "for the balance of the community," SNCC used "broadside direct mail appeals for money," but it employed celebrities for this task as well.[94] Belafonte penned a series of letters in the spring and summer of 1966, alerting recipients of the continued impoverished and terrorized conditions of the rural South and pleading for funds.[95] Ultimately, the organization raised $637,736 in 1965, its highest income to date, and double what it had raised in 1963 before house parties and close collaboration with celebrities became routine.[96]

Despite this impressive fund-raising record, SNCC did not always manage its celebrity supporters effectively. This largely stemmed from a lack of organization outside of the New York office. FOS groups failed to coordinate with the New York staff members, and wealthy supporters complained of being inundated with requests for parties and benefits. Betty Garman, a fund-raiser in the New York office, admitted, "I don't know they are sending letters off and thus can't explain that this is not the way to obtain talent for concerts, etc." She expressed confidence only in the Bay Area (San Francisco), Boston, and New York groups as being "competent" to handle major events; Chicago, Los Angeles, and Washington was "where smaller events could be planned."[97] A Philadelphia FOS volunteer, however, complained, "We cannot understand how it is that New York can easily have a dozen top stars where not one can be available for Philadelphia." She reported that they had started plans for parties, "*but on one condition. We must* have top name stars like Harry Belafonte, Sammy Davis, Jr., [opera star] Leontyne Rice, Marlon Brando, Charlton Heston" or "big fund raising in Philly is a dead issue."[98] Meanwhile, a report on fund-raising at the Baltimore FOS office expressed disappointment that despite its proximity to Washington and its potential to obtain "big-name people," the full-time staffer there "somehow . . . does not follow up."[99]

Moreover, SNCC bungled some lucrative opportunities. A celebrity billiard tournament to be chaired by James Garner, cochaired by Steve Allen, Milton Berle, and Sammy Davis, Jr., and held in Los Angeles in May 1966 had to be aborted within a week of the event due to disorganization and friction among the Los Angeles FOS activists. One embarrassed SNCC organizer admitted, "I feel very badly about this because I have had contact with all these stars in the past and as you can understand, it can leave a feeling of ill-will." The event would have brought in a number Hollywood's white stars, such as James Coburn and Dennis Hopper, and rising black entertainers such as Bill Cosby and Ivan Dixon, who were rather new to the movement, as well as many others who had done little civil rights work since the Prop 14 campaign. Fifty-seven celebrity participants had to be notified of the cancellation.[100] SNCC likewise failed to follow through on a benefit concert with Frank Sinatra and benefit screenings of the short film *Ivanhoe Donaldson* (1964) about one of its own activists. The film's distributor offered to screen previews in New York, Los Angeles, and Washington, but after seeing little follow-through, complained about "the lack of any action at SNCC."[101] These lapses resulted largely from SNCC's unusual makeup as an organization without a membership or a traditional hierarchical structure.

They also perhaps reflected a growing discomfort within SNCC about its connection to wealthy liberals. In a Northern staff meeting in 1965, several activists raised concerns that SNCC was becoming "elitist" due in part to its income stream.[102] Indeed, after the fund-raiser in Beverly Hills, Belafonte acknowledged, "The irony of partying at a discotheque was not lost on anyone." Stokely Carmichael became SNCC chair that same year. He was openly critical of nonviolence, and Belafonte felt Carmichael and his cohorts had begun to view him as "part of the establishment," which in the 1960s was tantamount to treason.[103] James Forman denied that guilt-ridden liberals constituted SNCC's support. "I think they are sophisticated people who understand the importance of what we are doing," he asserted. "These are people who have been red-baited, who pulled out of politics in the late '40s, and have been waiting for a new generation of political activists." He cited Belafonte as an example, saying, "Harry Belafonte, who is wealthy, is more radical than anyone in

SNCC. He really understands the social forces involved."[104] Longtime activist Bob Zellner said, "Most SNCC folks were grateful for all political and financial help from whatever the source." Betty Garman, another SNCC activist engaged in fund-raising, concurred, saying that the fund-raisers were "helping us to tap resources we could never reach ourselves because of who we are and how we work. On the other hand," she continued, "there is some concern that the people who give wouldn't give to us if they knew more about who we are and how we work."[105]

SNCC attempted to deal with these contradictions and critiques. Under pressure from New York FOS volunteers to hire a salaried professional fund-raiser, Forman repeatedly refused, saying "that would destroy the philosophy of the organization."[106] When those at the winter 1965 fund-raising conference continued to insist on such a position, Forman took on the responsibilities, but not a pay increase, himself.[107] Meanwhile, Betty Garman encouraged FOS offices to reach out to "all sections of a community" in broader programs. She challenged the advice pushed at the fund-raising conference in terms of pursuing elite donors. Acknowledging that "house parties work," she also insisted "they work on *all* levels of a community. Some people think of a house party as a way to raise BIG money—which means a fancy house and a star and expensive food and free drinks and NAME people. But there is no reason to feel," she continued, "that a house party cannot be successful if it raises $50 or $100 or $200," as long as SNCC held many such parties. Thus, SNCC could *"involve people,"* meaning a broad cross-section of average folks.[108] Others in the organization expressed concern that if students wanted to begin direct action in the urban North, they could well find themselves in conflict with the very liberals that supported the Southern projects. This anxiety led SNCC activists to brainstorm how to reach more blacks in Northern ghettoes and in the South, and, ironically given SNCC's suspicion of the NAACP, the black middle class.[109] This debate would come to naught later in the decade due to radical policy changes within SNCC, but it foreshadowed a growing critique of liberal celebrity activism and its paradoxes.

The SCLC, which also did not have a membership and relied on outside income, proved equally capable of using the constructs of celebrity to raise cash, but perhaps relied on it too heavily, given its large operating budget. The SCLC raised $1.6 million in 1965 but nevertheless faced a "financial crisis." Outstanding expenses from Selma, a growing staff, and money tied up in bail bonds and court procedures made the organization unable to reasonably plan for future campaigns.[110] King returned to familiar celebrity-driven ideas to try to rectify the situation. His own public image had grown with his receipt of the Nobel Peace Prize in 1965, and he earmarked royalties from the sales of his publications to the SCLC. He brainstormed with Belafonte, hoping that he could coax Sammy Davis, Jr., into arranging a benefit at Madison Square Garden with Burton and Taylor, who were newly remarried and hotter than ever. The SCLC also tried to secure Davis for a series of concerts between March 1965 and December 1966. When the ever-busy Davis balked, SCLC operatives grumbled about the entertainer's "unreliability and failure to carry out his commitments."[111] This sentiment says more about the growing frustration with SCLC's finances and unrealistic expectations of its supporters than about Davis's failures.

However, Belafonte's bold suggestion to look "beyond our borders for allies" in spring 1966 once again put his celebrity connections to effective use for the SCLC. Daddy King resisted Belafonte's plan to do a fund-raiser at the American Church in Paris, arguing that "going global" might invite a backlash. Belafonte viewed his "almost pathological patriotism" with pity, but Daddy King's prediction bore out when, after interference from the State Department, the church canceled the show.[112] In response, Belafonte made arrangements with the French actors Yves Montand and Simone Signoret for a concert at the Palais des Sports in Paris and brought over his entire company at his own expense for the show. Furthermore, King Gustav VI of Sweden met privately with Belafonte and King and agreed to be a "patron" for a similar performance with Swedish stars at the Royal Opera House in Stockholm. The monarch established a special account with the Bank of Sweden for the SCLC and arranged for the show to be broadcast throughout Scandinavia and northern Europe. Not only did money from ticket sales go straight into the account, but Swedish citizens could deposit funds directly, even by mail. Sweden soon presented a $100,000 check to the SCLC. The *Chicago Defender* hailed Belafonte as "the one person most responsible" for the contribution, and there did not seem to be the media backlash that Daddy King had feared. It was the biggest gift the SCLC had received thus far. Yet it did not resolve the organization's financial problems, in part because King had committed to an expensive campaign in Chicago for the summer of 1966.[113]

The NAACP also faced financial difficulties, and it sought to bolster its membership in collaboration with Davis. In April 1966, the board of directors appointed the star chairman of the Life Membership Committee. Life Memberships, which cost $500 each, constituted one-third of the organization's $1.3 million income in 1965, but a loss of twenty thousand members, higher operating costs (including the loss from the television spectacular discussed in chapter four), and about $265,000 tied up in bail bonds had put the NAACP in a precarious position. Hoping Davis could sell Life Memberships "to friends in the limelight as well as to fans on the darkened side of the footlights," the NAACP ambitiously announced its intention to augment the list of 18,500 Life Members to one hundred thousand. At Davis's disposal were five full-time staff members and thirty-five volunteers. He used a variety of strategies, including using the honorariums that he had previously refused from civil rights, civic, and philanthropic groups as payment for those groups' memberships, and hosting cocktail parties for the program. Davis's wife May and three children all received memberships, and he began pressing campaign pamphlets into the hands of friends and colleagues. The celebrated actor Yul Brynner was one of the first to sign up.[114]

Davis's appointment marked the first time the NAACP had offered the job to a performer, which indicated both the significant role celebrities had played in the movement, and the movement's esteem for Davis—especially since the organization considered the role a "vital" one. Although Davis did not reach the one-hundred-thousand-member goal, the organization welcomed twenty thousand new members and improved revenues during a time when the other major civil rights organizations were losing members and funds.[115] Indeed, Davis earned the reputation as a man who could save the fiscal day. He was pressed upon to raise funds for any number of NAACP projects, including establishing a staff for the Los Angeles branch, reforming the Baton Rouge police department, and assisting a youth project in Danbury, Connecticut.[116]

Clearly, the major civil rights organizations had made celebrities an integral part of their agendas. They made frequent appeals to the same group of celebrities, and although the competition for stars did not seem to cause problems among them, conflicts over competing strategies and ideologies did. Belafonte, who had already eased frictions between SNCC activists and King in 1963, found himself playing a similar role in 1965. The festering tension between the groups had reignited with Selma's "Turnaround Tuesday" incident, as allegations of King's timidity reflected a rising militancy among student activists. Belafonte presided over two meetings between Forman and King in Atlanta in which the two men aired their differences. They ultimately issued a cooperative statement, and King credited Belafonte with playing a vital role in "preventing a serious cleavage."[117] The SNCC-SCLC agreement, however, would not last, and the last time the major organizations came together in public cooperation was with the James Meredith march.

On June 5, 1966, Meredith, of Ole Miss fame, launched his "March Against Fear" from Memphis, Tennessee, to Jackson, Mississippi. When he was shot and hospitalized, celebrity involvement helped transform the march from a one-man affair into what he called "the last great march of the civil rights era in the South."[118] Meredith had instigated the march to inspire black voting. Although Mississippi had begun quietly complying with the new voting rights legislation, many blacks feared the registration process. Meredith had walked only fourteen miles when a sniper ambushed him. The first visitor at Meredith's bedside, Dick Gregory had already released a statement to the press that he and his wife Lillian would continue the march. "I was determined to get to the scene of the crime as quickly as possible," Gregory explained. "I felt there was a lot at stake for the civil rights movement."[119] King and CORE's Floyd McKissick visited Meredith the next day. Although the black press had praised Gregory for "stepping forward," the two leaders were apparently unaware of his actions and, in Meredith's estimation, "they seemed upset" upon hearing the news.[120] By simply picking up the march, the Gregorys were being faithful to Meredith's original vision. They walked alone at first. "Genuinely scared," Gregory realized that taking Meredith's place "had really been a march against my own fears and apprehensions."[121] Meredith told King and McKissick, "I don't want the march turned into a publicity stunt or fund-raising contest among civil rights organizations." However, King's own celebrity status and recruitment of entertainers would turn it into an event much like Selma.

After the attack on Meredith, the march could not conceivably continue as a one-man enterprise. Meredith himself became "an icon," he admits, as people across the country sent him get-well wishes, spoke out in protest, and flocked to Mississippi. About three hundred people joined Gregory, who rotated out when King stepped in. Although no entertainer completed the 220-mile trek, King was enough of an attraction to draw press interest and black participation along the way. Unfortunately, the lack of a specific legislative goal, haphazard planning along the route, and the clear differences among the civil rights groups regarding nonviolence and the emerging "Black Power" slogan led the United Press International to portray the marchers as a bunch of "kooks." King privately thought that the march was "a mistake."[122] Although march leaders vowed it would be "bigger than Selma," this negative vibe is perhaps what led King to reach out to Belafonte to arrange a rally for the evening before the last leg of the trek, and to Davis to recruit Hollywood stars.[123]

Davis's efforts in particular received press attention. The *New York Times* reported that Davis, Lancaster, and Brando would all be arriving on a plane chartered by Davis. "I'm not going down there to get shot, but we can't all sit around Beverly Hills talking about it," Davis said. "Marlon and I and Burt Lancaster are going to Mississippi to show the Negroes there that other[s] . . . aren't afraid to give them spiritual and moral support to get out and vote." Privately, Davis was afraid, even more than he had been in Selma. Robert Kennedy had told him that there was a contract out on his head. He nevertheless committed to the trek. Lamenting that "more Hollywood people aren't able to join us," Davis recruited only a few, including the Olympic decathlete turned film actor Rafer Johnson.[124] Belafonte, Poitier, and the R&B/funk singer James Brown, relatively new to movement events, met them in Jackson.

The rally at Tougaloo College provided a festival-like atmosphere similar to Selma. About 500 marchers arrived from Canton to be met near campus by 500 additional protesters, but a crowd of more than eight thousand turned out for the concert, which served as a staging area for the final leg into Jackson.[125] Brown, Belafonte, and Davis all sang, but Davis performed scat songs a capella, without his usual piano. The entertainers also acknowledged the cries for "Black Power" expressed by SNCC's Stokely Carmichael along the route. King had indicated his discomfort with the term, but Brando wore a sticker on his forehead with a picture of a lunging black panther that young activists had been selling for a dollar. The sticker also included the slogan "We're the Greatest," in reference to the boxing champion Muhammad Ali. Ali's bold assertions of racial pride had made him an icon to SNCC students and foreshadowed the trend of celebrity athletes expressing Black Power. Gregory had fun with the term. "I get on a crowded bus the other day, and there were no seats. I just shouted 'Black Power!'" he cracked, "and two little old ladies got up to give me their seats. And they were colored ladies!"[126]

Ultimately fifteen thousand marchers poured into Jackson. Gregory observed that more people, including whites, handed out refreshments and posted supportive signs on the walk the next day, an observation that was also reported in the news coverage.[127] During the march, some six thousand Mississippians registered to vote. What is more, some of the proceeds from Belafonte's European benefits went toward setting up thirty-five organizers in Mississippi in the aftermath of the Meredith march.[128] Hundreds of thousands more registrants would follow in the coming years. Although the aspects of celebrity that had helped achieve this may have bothered Meredith, he felt proud that the "beast of fear had been slain."[129]

SNCC's internal discussions and James Meredith's attitude revealed concerns that celebrity fund-raising and star-studded events betrayed their grassroots efforts and fomented a carnivalesque atmosphere that undermined their message. Others simply disliked the distraction. Although the CORE activist David Dennis greatly appreciated Belafonte, Gregory, and the rest of the Leading Six, he found the presence of other celebrities "awkward." Stars who attended house parties often made arrangements with the civil rights organizations to travel South so they could "see [the conditions] for themselves." Dennis understood how this bolstered fund-raising, but said, "You couldn't really tell [celebrities] what to do," and they did not understand the projects or their dangers. Likewise, the SCLC's Reverend Wyatt Tee Walker felt that most celebrities could not strategize for the movement, as they "had no idea what day-to-day the movement required," nor did they grasp the "depravity" of many Southern white authority figures. Not wanting to "name names" because they all seemed sincere, Dennis nevertheless got the impression that they felt, "'I'm doing my civic duty' and that was enough."[130]

No matter how sincere the stars, the fact remained that they were celebrities and could occasionally behave in egocentric ways. Casey Hayden recalled Brando "grabbing my ass in the elevator" during a tour of Gadsden, and Bob Dylan passing out drunk at a concert in Greenwood.[131] William Hansen says that during the SNCC trip to Guinea, Belafonte indulged in a fair bit of "preening." However, no activist seemed to have regretted working with the stars. They could forgive celebrity excesses and appreciated the need to let off steam, especially given the favorable results of collaborating with them.[132] They also enjoyed the admiration they received from the stars. SNCC activist Bob Zellner believes that actors like Brando and Newman, who played roles for a living, appreciated the "real" lives the activists led and the work they did. "We all realized we were stars to them," says Zellner. Indeed, at one benefit concert, Walker says Poitier asked for *his* autograph.[133]

* * *

The civil rights movement drew the Stars for Freedom into grassroots politics, and American involvement in Vietnam would prompt them to expand their activism even more. The studios generally distanced themselves from the war. Unlike during World War II, when the industry churned out dozens of films, no major studio was willing to make a movie about Vietnam soldiers or about the conflict at large to avoid alienating either war supporters or opponents.[134] The major civil rights organizations took a similarly neutral stance. However, celebrity supporters within the movement began asserting their own beliefs as matters of conscience. A few actively supported the war. Heston appeared in advertisements for war bonds, twice traveled to South Vietnam to meet with troops, and even confronted a war critic in the White House Rose Garden at a National Endowment for the Arts function.[135] Sammy Davis, Jr., also spoke out in favor of the war, out of patriotism and a respect for the troops serving.

However, Gregory, Ossie Davis, Dee, and Belafonte all spoke out against the war, well before King, who famously asserted his disapproval in April 1967 at the Riverside Church in New York. Gregory participated in a "teach-in" at University of California, Berkeley, in May 1965, making the link between civil rights and his antiwar stance before an audience of ten thousand. "I'm not about to fight them Red Chinese [allied with North Vietnamese communists]," he proclaimed. "When you stop and think that Red China got 688 million people, if them cats ever start singing 'We Shall Overcome,' they gonna do it, baby!"[136] Davis and Dee participated in a mass demonstration in Washington, DC, later that fall.[137] During his European fund-raising tour for the SCLC in 1966, Belafonte aligned himself with the antiwar movement and told the press, "We think that it's not to the best interest of the people of the United States that it continue its adventures in Vietnam."[138] These stars would continue to criticize the war and sometimes helped organize demonstrations, although they saw it as an extension, not a replacement, of their civil rights work. Nevertheless, the demonstrations took their toll. Gregory decided not to cut his hair until the war ended, and he undertook a series of highly publicized thirty-day fasts, shrinking to 103 pounds at one point.[139] After King's Riverside speech, Belafonte launched an eight-city benefit tour. An onstage spat between Sammy Davis, Jr., and Joan Baez on the Oakland stop reflected the general problems of the tour. Davis warned his audience not to deviate from civil rights issues and promoted his upcoming goodwill tour to Vietnam, whereas Baez snapped that Davis should help bring the soldiers home. With similar problems in other cities, the series actually lost $8,000, also likely a result of "benefit fatigue."[140]

A number of new political interests also captured the attention of the Stars for Freedom. Gregory ran as mayor of Chicago in 1967, and as president of the United States in 1968, both times as a write-in candidate. He, along with Marlon Brando, also championed Native Americans and participated in fish-ins, as well as strategy sessions with the American Indian Movement.[141] Poitier began supporting the Progressive Liberal Party (PLP) in his native Bahamas that challenged the white-controlled United Bahamian Party for control of the island's government. Poitier provided financial support and political advice, taking satisfaction in the PLP's victory in 1967 and the Bahamas independence from Britain in 1973, and becoming personal friends with the prime minister.[142] Both Heston and Poitier became heavily involved with the National Endowment for the Arts and its offshoot, the American Film Institute. Heston also worked on a gun-control task force, before he later concluded that such legislation was misguided and became a spokesperson for the National Rifle Association. Indeed, the civil rights movement had drawn celebrities back into politics, allowing them to comfortably take on a host of controversial issues, whether liberal (as much of Hollywood now proved to be), or conservative.

Black Celebrities
and Black Power

I rolled my cameras for the first time. I want to tell you, after three
or four takes of that first scene, a calm came over me. A confidence
surged through my whole body . . . and I, as green as I was, had a
touch for this new craft I had been courting from a distance for
many, many years.

—Sidney Poitier, on directing *Buck and the Preacher*

IN 1971, SIDNEY POITIER AND HARRY BELAFONTE FIRED THE DIREC-
tor Joseph Sargent from their film *Buck and the Preacher*, a black western
they were coproducing through Poitier's E & R Productions and Belafonte
Enterprises and starring in with Ruby Dee. Feeling that Sargent's failure
to share their artistic vision had "racial consequences," Poitier opted to
direct the film himself, thus, in a single instant, ridding himself of the
anxieties that had hamstrung him on the set of *Porgy and Bess*. Now,
fourteen years later, he had achieved a position of power in Hollywood as
a director. Poitier, one of several black directors working in the 1970s,
proved the most successful. *Buck* also epitomized the Leading Six's
approach to the changing social and cultural norms shaped by calls for
Black Power. It brought "blackness" to viewing audiences in a commer-
cially viable form but without the graphic, antiwhite nature of the Blaxploitation genre. Indeed, the Leading Six pursued cultural politics after
the civil rights movement irreparably fractured in 1968, and, with the
exception of Sammy Davis, Jr., abstained from presidential politics

entirely. *Buck* illustrated how the civil rights movement had come full circle in Hollywood and, as is the fickle nature of celebrity culture, brought new challenges for the black stars who supported it.

*   *   *

Poitier's directorial debut evolved from a growing commitment to film-making that he shared with much of the Leading Six. Although Belafonte's film production company remained dormant, Ossie Davis and Ruby Dee had also begun their own projects. In 1963, they brought *Purlie Victorious* to the big screen in the retitled *Gone Are the Days*. Davis adapted the screenplay from his Broadway folk-fantasy satire, and he and Dee also coproduced and starred in what he described as the "independent, independent, independent" film. They worked with a local distributor for the premiere in New York but struggled to find a national one. *Gone* received generally enthusiastic reviews in the black press and the *New York Times*, but in an all-time low in the movie industry, only one person purchased a ticket for the opening performance. Attendance picked up after several civil rights organizations urged their members to support the film.[1] However, it still fell flat with audiences. The lampooning of the Tom, pickaninny, mammy, and white liberal stereotypes that had succeeded before a live audience did not successfully transition to film, perhaps because of the production quality, the uneven acting, or the timing. The film's release came on the heels of the 16th Street Baptist Church bombing, when few felt like laughing, and likely too soon for audiences to be able to distance themselves from the film stereotypes of old. The "Amos 'n' Andy burlesque," as one critic called it, closed after five weeks.[2]

Sammy Davis, Jr.'s efforts with *A Man Called Adam* (1966) proved more successful. Davis had failed to sell any of his film ideas until his Broadway hit *Golden Boy* gave him the clout to establish his own Trace-Mark Productions (named after two of his children) in 1965. He worked with the independent studio and distributor Embassy Pictures (a subsidiary of Paramount Pictures) to put together *Adam*, which told the melancholy story of a self-destructive jazz musician and costarred Cicely Tyson and Ossie Davis. "As far as I'm concerned," the overjoyed star told the press, "this is my first picture. I'm grateful for 'Anna Lucasta,' the three Sinatra pictures and 'Porgy and Bess'—but this one is about a man," he explained, referring to the somewhat frivolous characters he played with his supporting roles.[3] Davis exercised impressive authority as an executive producer. He hired Ike Jones, known for his work with Nat King Cole until Cole's death in 1965, to produce the film, making Jones the first African American to hold that title for a major motion picture.[4] Davis also stood up to political pressure when the studio objected to Ossie Davis's anti–Vietnam War activism. "They were going to fire me," Ossie recalled. "Sammy said [to them], 'If you lose one Davis, you'll lose another.' I have a great deal of admiration for Sammy."[5] The storyline itself broke new ground as the first film about the world of jazz artists. *A Man Called Adam* received mixed reviews but earned solid returns and is considered a "transitional" film that generated more opportunities for black filmmakers in Hollywood.[6]

Poitier first indicated an interest in making his own films in 1967 when he formed E & R Productions (named after his parents Evelyn and Reginald). He simultaneously inked a three-year nonexclusive contract with Columbia Pictures, making him Hollywood's first major black producer.[7] However, for his first film effort in 1968 he worked with the ABC subsidiary Palomar Pictures International to write and star in *For Love of Ivy*. This allowed him to significantly shape the picture while paving the way for his later directorial efforts. Like Ossie and Sammy Davis, Jr., he wanted to break new ground while broadening his range of acting roles. Poitier had starred in three of the top films of 1967, all interracial dramas: *To Sir, with Love*; *In the Heat of the Night*; and *Guess Who's Coming to Dinner*. However, these films' emphasis on equal citizenship and racial harmony at a time of unprecedented social strife seemed out of touch. In *To Sir, with Love*, Poitier played a teacher in a London inner-city school bent on reforming white juvenile delinquents; in *Heat*, he was a police officer navigating the racist social structure, and ultimately befriending the white sheriff, to solve a murder in the Deep South; and in *Guess Who's Coming to Dinner*, an esteemed doctor who wants to marry a white girl. A "Super Negro," Poitier's supreme intelligence and unending patience promoted tolerance in the white world but also prevented audiences from appreciating his cultural identity and sexual edge. By bringing his own films to the screen, Poitier hoped to overcome these limitations. As he told the *New York Times*, he would be "sexless Sidney" no more.[8]

Poitier wrote *For Love of Ivy* so he could play against an African American lead in what would be Hollywood's first black romance. He plays Jack

Parks, owner of a truck-driving business who also runs a gambling operation, leading him to be blackmailed into romancing Ivy Moore (Abbey
Lincoln) by a family who wants to keep her as their maid. In this light
tale, Jack and Ivy predictably foil their plan by falling in love. Poitier
defended his earlier film choices as being "interesting" stories that made
"a positive contribution," but he yearned for more lifelike heterosexuality.
"I never worked in a man-woman relationship that was not symbolic," he
pointed out. "Either there were no women, or there was a woman but she
was blind, or the relationship was of a nature that satisfied the taboos."
A romance with a black character was more authentic and sent an important message about black women. As the father of four daughters, Poitier
said, "I want them glamorized and idolized and put on a pedestal and
spoiled rotten."[9] *Ivy* also allowed Poitier's character a sophisticated ward-
robe and sharp sense of humor more akin to his own style and personality.[10] While some reviews lamented the lack of powerful social messages
that were central to Poitier's other films, they nevertheless appreciated
his desire to evolve as an actor. As one critic said, *Ivy* "marks the final step
in the metamorphosis of Sidney Poitier . . . into a Hollywood superstar,
with all of the mythic cool and sexual prerogatives of a Clark Gable."[11]

That Sammy Davis, Jr., and Poitier had finally moved into film production reflected their years of hard work in show business, as well as the
growing influence of the civil rights movement in Hollywood. The
National Association for the Advancement of Colored People (NAACP)
renewed its pressure on the industry in 1965. NAACP representatives
acknowledged that the studios employed more black actors and clerical
workers, but lamented that the craft unions, including those for electri-
cians, carpenters, propmen, and cameramen, were still "lily white" and
that as "closed shop" entities seemed impenetrable by any outsider.

Union leaders, with a fair bit of hostility, contended that during a time
of industry unemployment they could not be expected to expand their
memberships to inexperienced upstarts.[12] So the NAACP took more
forceful action. After meeting with industry representatives in the winter
and spring of 1965, the NAACP issued a host of demands. It called for
studios to offer a greater ratio of roles for black performers; that for every
"stereotypical" (servile or menial) black role, a "nonstereotypical" character also be presented; and that all new pilots for the 1964–65 season
include African Americans "in the permanent and continuing roles." The
NAACP also demanded that the unions implement apprenticeship train-

ing programs and make a "special effort" to recruit black trainees to achieve integration. The organization threatened to boycott any studio that failed to comply.[13] However, the training programs failed to get off the ground, and the Motion Picture Producers Association (MPPA) employment surveys showed little progress. In 1961, African Americans comprised only 1.19 percent of the payroll for extras employed by the studios; by 1965, the number had risen to a lowly 2.25 percent. Meanwhile, employment for African Americans who were not actors or extras had actually decreased from twenty-three positions before 1963 to twenty-two afterward.[14] The NAACP began plans to file lawsuits against the studios and unions for violating the Civil Rights Act's Title VII, which barred employment discrimination.[15]

This legal pressure yielded results. After the NAACP joined with the Urban League and the California State Employment Bureau to coordinate hiring and employment programs, the league's Floyd Covington reported enthusiastically in 1966 that the studios had begun to hire "hundreds" of African Americans. He credited Universal Studios, Desi-Lu Productions, and Metro-Goldwyn-Mayer Studios with leading the way.[16] The unions also started to recruit some African American apprentices. Charlton Heston (who was Screen Actors Guild president at the time) commented, "There's a huge wave of employment reform surging through the movie industry these days, especially behind the camera, and the civil rights movement deserves much of the credit."[17] In front of the camera, however, African Americans had made few collective gains. Between May 1965 and December 1967, of the total income paid to actors, African American earnings fluctuated between a dismal 1.71 and 3.34 percent.[18] Such statistics indicate the noteworthy yet limited significance of stars such as Davis and Poitier, as well as white actors such as Frank Sinatra, Marlon Brando, and Heston, whose contracts gave them a say in the casting, in employing African Americans in their films. In Heston's *Planet of the Apes* (1968), *Omega Man* (1971), and *Soylent Green* (1973), for example, he insisted on showing interracial relationships and casting black actors in a variety of roles. Believing his efforts to be "a step in the right direction," Heston also noted, "I don't claim for a minute that this is going to make a shattering impression on the movie industry."[19]

Bill Cosby's debut in 1965 in *I Spy* as the first African American lead in a television series since *Amos 'n' Andy* also reflected the gradual changes taking place onscreen; he remained the only black lead for the next three years. Cosby, an up-and-coming comedian in the early 1960s, had been a regular guest on television variety shows. Not wanting to tell "racial jokes to white people," Cosby became the master of the "nonethnic anecdote."[20] One popular bit involved him playing a referee calling the Revolutionary War during the painstakingly slow process of loading a musket.[21] A variety show appearance caught the eye of Leonard Sheldon, one of the creators of *I Spy*. Sheldon had not been intentionally looking for a black lead, but seeing Cosby on-camera inspired him to cast the comedian. Cosby played Alex Scott, a CIA agent who travels undercover as an athletic trainer to his partner Kelly Robinson (Robert Culp), who poses as a wealthy amateur tennis player. Cosby's role had originally been written for an older actor, who mentored Culp's character, but Sheldon rewrote the pair as equals, a move that generally characterized the show.

The international setting allowed the show's creators to avoid dealing directly with American racial strife, but Cosby's presence pushed clear racial messages. Scott appeared as not only a "friend and buddy" but, in the role of a federal agent, as a defender of American principles.[22] Furthermore, Cosby convinced the producers to implement several significant changes. In an early episode titled "Danny Was a Million Laughs," Scott is forced to protect an American witness who repeatedly calls him "boy" and even demands a shoe shine. Reminiscent of a 1950s "message movie," Scott stoically ignores his behavior. However, Cosby and Culp protested this portrayal, and a more upbeat approach in "Affair in T'Sien Cha" aired two months later. Scott meets a Chinese youngster who is fascinated by his dark skin and tentatively rubs his cheek. "No, it doesn't rub off," Scott says affectionately. "It's not war paint." At the end of the episode, the villagers playfully hail Scott as "a living legend whose skin doesn't rub off."[23] Cosby also successfully pushed the writers and producers to give him romantic storylines and to add more black extras and supporting characters.[24] While the show toed a safe line, it was a huge ratings success. Only three stations (all Southern) refused to carry the program, and it consistently achieved top-twenty status. Cosby won three Emmy Awards for outstanding actor in a drama for his role, paving the way for more dramatic actors. After *I Spy*'s debut, *Daktari* (CBS 1966–69), *Mission: Impossible* (CBS 1966–73), and *Star Trek* (NBC 1966–69) all featured black characters as series regulars.[25]

For every television success, there were also failures. One of the most devastating was *The Sammy Davis, Jr., Show*. Davis continued to parlay his

Golden Boy triumph into new projects and achieved a longtime dream when NBC signed him to host and produce a weekly variety series, to debut in January 1966, the first such program since Nat King Cole's short-lived series. Writers in the black press hoped this would mark a turning point at which African American entertainers would no longer be "'guests' in television's glass house."[26] Unfortunately, Davis never acquired a national sponsor, and the program faced tough Friday night competition against *Gomer Pyle, USMC* (CBS 1964–69), *Hogan's Heroes* (CBS 1965–71), and *The Addams Family* (ABC 1964–66). Davis's ratings, though good, did not meet expectations, and NBC cancelled the series after four months.[27] The competitive nature of television made any new show a gamble, but that Davis's experience had been similar to Cole's—including the lack of a sponsor and a small production budget—was discouraging. It also meant that network programming continued to be devoid of consistent black producers during this period. Even without a steady television forum, Davis and Belafonte both took on multiple special programs and guest host appearances, and they used these platforms to address racial matters in new ways.

In February 1966, Belafonte produced *The Strollin' Twenties* for CBS, a stylized version of Harlem culture in the 1920s. In the wake of Watts and other urban northern riots, Belafonte wanted to show a more positive side of ghetto life. Written by Langston Hughes and narrated by Poitier, Belafonte also recruited Sammy Davis, Jr., Diahann Carroll, Nipsey Russell, Duke Ellington, and other entertainers for the all-black production. Presented in a dreamlike sequence as Poitier saunters through Harlem, the show points to the hardships African Americans experienced, particularly unemployment and poverty. However, it particularly emphasizes the rituals that helped them cope with and even escape their troubles, such as a "rent party" to save a family from eviction, street corner song-and-dance routines, card games, flirting, and an elaborate Savoy Ballroom finale featuring Ellington. The poetic narration gives viewers insight into African American language and praises black womanhood. "Brown sugar lassie, caramel treat, honey gold babies, good enough to eat," Poitier recites. Numerous musical numbers reflect Harlem's important role in the development of blues and jazz during this period. Calling the neighborhood itself "a song with a minor refrain," Poitier repeatedly expresses his "love" for "that dusky sash" Harlem. *The Strollin' Twenties* received considerable media coverage, including a large photo spread in

Life magazine with captivating images of the actors in their exquisite costumes.[28] This lush approach differed from Belafonte's 1959 *Revlon Revue*, as he eschewed social realism to emphasize how black culture thrived in separate enclaves.

In a similar special for ABC the following year, Belafonte brought comedy from the "chitlin' circuit" to mainstream audiences in *A Time for Laughter: A Look at Negro Humor in America*. The show was reminiscent of Ossie Davis's aspirations with *Purlie Victorious*. Belafonte explained, "I wanted the jokes and routines Negroes told one another, the humor they shared away from white folk, the humor that came directly from the severity of their lives: poverty, joblessness, prejudices. And I wanted white audiences as well as black to hear it." All of the sketches were performed among blacks, whose comedy came from their everyday experiences in segregated settings such as pool halls, funeral parlors, and barber shops and between married couples. Belafonte knew it was "risky."[29] As scholars have noted, black comics historically struggled to "cross over" out of fear of being misunderstood by white audiences or shunned by the black middle class.[30] "Our humor—our history—is a heady wine rarely tested by the outside world" because it was so often "a caricature," Belafonte explained.[31] He gathered a wide variety of comedic performers, including "senior statesmen" such as Redd Foxx, Moms Mabley, George Kirby, and Pigmeat Markham, as well as younger stars such as Dick Gregory, Godfrey Cambridge, Nipsey Russell, and Richard Pryor, along with Carroll and Poitier, who again narrated.

The special includes a range of comedic styles. It particularly highlights "signifying" or "dissing" (what the *Chicago Defender* called "ghetto talk") in sketches with Moms Mabley and Red Foxx, as well as more contemporary political satirists such as Gregory. These sketches include commentary on the mundane, such as "ugly folks" and superstitions, and on such relevant issues as whether or not to join civil rights demonstrations, straighten one's hair, or take the Nation of Islam seriously. One skit takes on the "hang-ups" of integration as experienced by a suburban black couple who disdain Harlem "niggers" and fear they are "reverting to type" by eating watermelon. Moms Mabley, who plays their maid, says pointedly, "If this is what they call integration, then maybe it ain't worth it," expressing the viewpoint of many black activists who had given up on housing integration not only because of the hostility they had faced but also due to the cultural adaptations integration required.[32]

Particularly powerful is Belafonte's effort to distinguish between minstrelsy and the "authentic" vaudeville of African American culture.[33] The program opens with a scene from the antebellum South in which the black slave "Jim Crow" practices a dance that he is paid by his master to perform. A white bystander called "Daddy Rice" kinks his hair, blackens his face, and dons tattered clothes. And then steals the dance. Shots of famous white performers in blackface—including Al Jolson and the *Amos 'n' Andy* radio duo Freeman Gosden and Charles Correll—flash on screen while whites in hideous blackface makeup sang in obvious irony, "And that's how Darkies are born." Belafonte disdained such minstrelsy but celebrated black vaudeville.

The show features Pigmeat Markham, who developed his "Here Comes De Judge" routine about a comically amateurish justice of the peace while working the vaudeville circuit in the 1920s. He wore a graduation cap and gown on the bench in order to look more "official," frequently slapped his defendants with a rubber bladder, and ruled his courtroom with bewildering logic.[34] In a long sketch between Markham and a married couple played by Belafonte and Carroll, an oily Belafonte strolls in donning a pencil moustache and a slick suit. "I'm a self-made man," he proclaims. Markham replies, "That's the result of unskilled labor." After similar banter and a comedic song by Carroll, "the Judge" finally sentences Belafonte with this rapid exchange:

Markham: Do you work?
Belafonte: Yes and no.
Markham: What do you do?
Belafonte: This and that.
Markham: Where do you work?
Belafonte: Here and there.
Markham: When do you work?
Belafonte: Now and then.
Markham: That's it. Lock him up!
Belafonte: But judge, when you gonna let me out?
Markham: Sooner or later.[35]

Markham actually took issue with the presentation of his act as "some sort of historical thing." "I was *funny*. Not historical—*funny*," he says.[36] Even so, that Belafonte featured a vaudeville performer known for his injudicious characters marked a new comfortableness with the "ethnic humor" that he had once avoided. It also foreshadowed a revival of "de Judge."

Soon after *Rowan and Martin's Laugh-In* (NBC 1968–73) debuted on television in 1968, Sammy Davis, Jr., whom Markham had "carried around in my arms" backstage when Davis was only a baby, became a regular guest star and propagated "de Judge."[37] Hosted by the nightclub comics Dan Rowan and Dick Martin, the show itself had vaudeville roots in its zany humor and rapid-fire one-liners. It also incorporated timely material about race relations, the sexual revolution, and the antiwar movement. Davis used his guest appearances to address such topics with gusto, in part with the humor exemplified by "de Judge." The show featured a stuffy British magistrate played by Roddy Maude-Roxby, who harassed his hapless defendants. In his first guest appearance on *Laugh-In* on March 25, 1968, Davis introduced the sketch. Wearing an oversized judicial wig and black robe, he broadly struts across the stage chanting, "Here comes de Judge!" He offers variations of the character throughout the program, as if drunk, stoned, or effeminate, sounding like James Brown in one version and an elderly woman in another. Davis and "de Judge" became a cultural sensation and catapulted *Laugh-In* to the number-one ratings slot (where it stayed for over two years). The episode won the series its first of two Emmy Awards, and the phrase "Here comes de Judge," according to one historian, "earned a permanent niche in the glossary of American showbiz phraseology." This led to Markham joining the cast for a season to assume the character he had created. Davis continued to reprise the role, with four more guest appearances and three cameos in subsequent episodes.[38]

Davis's turns on *Laugh-In* showcased a broad range of racially neutral humor, but also included numerous ethnic quips in the tradition of the show's jaunty zingers. He sometimes referenced vaudeville, often as *Amos 'n' Andy*'s Kingfish. "Josephine, stash the jewels. Here comes the Judge!" was one familiar phrase. Other quips made fun of racism and racial identity, as in "You know, my ancestors picked so much cotton I still hate to open an aspirin bottle" and "I just can't win. Last night I dreamt I was white and a colored kid beat me up." Davis also referenced black radicalism. After singing at such a high pitch that a vase breaks, he says pointedly, "Now that's black power."[39] In a March 1969 episode devoted entirely to ethnic humor, Davis plays a Japanese geisha, a Mexican stag film director, and an Irish tap dancer. He and his "brother," played by Arte Johnson, joke about a seven-course Irish meal.

> Johnson: "Six mugs of beer and a potato?"
> Davis: "No, a six-pack and a watermelon."
> Johnson: "You black Irishmen are all alike!"

Flip Wilson, who frequently guest starred on the program, and Dick Gregory, who appeared once, took a similar approach.[40] Their performances on *Laugh-In*, combined with Belafonte's *A Time for Laughter*, foreshadowed a revival in ethnic humor that would become a hallmark of the 1970s.

Davis and Belafonte also developed a greater platform to explore racial matters as guest hosts on *The Tonight Show Starring Johnny Carson* (NBC 1962–92). Davis filled in for the comedian multiple times, and in one episode in March 1968, the celebrated runner Jesse Owens appeared as a guest. He and Davis discussed the upcoming Summer Olympic Games that young black athletes were boycotting as a protest against American imperialism abroad and racism at home. Owens argued that "participating" was the best way to promote "brotherhood," and Davis agreed. "Everybody is very, totally aware of our blackness today," he said. "If our cats could go over there and wrap it up [win], that would be the best thing in the world in terms of blackness, you dig what I mean?"[41] When Belafonte took over for a full week for a vacationing Carson, he booked guests in an effort to fulfill his liberal, racial agenda. He bantered with friends Robert Kennedy and Paul Newman in order to show blacks and whites "relating to one another on a friendly level." Belafonte and his guests denounced US policy toward the inner cities, American Indians, and Vietnam. Martin Luther King, Jr., also made an appearance. He and Belafonte strongly asserted their politics, even endorsing Eugene McCarthy as the Democratic nominee for the presidency. "Belafonte was an unusual host," Carson's sidekick Ed McMahon observed, "He didn't go for one laugh." Even so, the New York ratings for Belafonte's week topped the average ratings of Carson himself.[42]

As the Leading Six persistently moved into production, they not only reflected the changes in Hollywood but helped shape them. No longer content to merely prove themselves as equals, they offered more complex narratives in their various projects that attempted to show a more human side of African American life and culture. Not everyone appreciated their approach. Ossie Davis's *Gone Are the Days* was an unmitigated failure, and Belafonte received his fair share of criticism. Like the *Porgy and Bess* film, *The Strollin' Twenties* generated so much heat for its "spic and span" portrayal of the ghetto, a place the vast majority of blacks wanted to escape, that CBS refused to collaborate with Belafonte again.[43] Thus *A Time for Laughter* appeared on another network. This, too, was denounced. The *New York Times* bemoaned the "all-Negro presentation" and the "flat" writing, while the more forgiving *Chicago Defender* questioned the wisdom of showcasing performers and techniques designed for 1930s vaudeville or the contemporary "chitlin' circuit" to network audiences. As for "de Judge," many considered its popularity an embarrassment and marveled at Markham's resurgence. It is ironic that only six years after Belafonte had refused to do an all-black revue for Revlon, he proceeded to produce two such shows. Since stereotypical caricatures were no longer the sole means of portraying African Americans, the Leading Six became more comfortable engaging in the humor of vaudeville or in all-black settings as part of a broader context of representation. With the rise of Black Power and the election of Richard Nixon in 1968, the group would continue to reshape their pursuit of racial and cultural politics.

* * *

On April 4, 1968, a white supremacist shot and fatally wounded Martin Luther King, Jr., in Memphis, Tennessee. Sammy Davis, Jr., made arrangements to return to *The Tonight Show*, as well as to appear on the evening news networks, to plea for nonviolence. Gregory, Belafonte, Davis, Dee, and just about anyone else with a public forum took similar measures, but to little avail.[44] Riots broke out in sixty-eight American cities over the next few days. The vision of interracial brotherhood that King and his celebrity allies represented, already in decline, experienced a devastating blow with his death. As one scholar remarks, it was "the end of the age of Sidney Poitier."[45]

King's funeral brought out the differences between his celebrity supporters. Gregory, Lena Horne, Sammy Davis, Jr., Cosby, Diana Sands, Poitier, Ossie Davis, and Dee, among others, attended the service. The national media noted that, except for President John F. Kennedy's funeral, no event had brought out so many prominent mourners.[46] Belafonte

assumed a special place at Coretta Scott King's side, a result of his atten-
tiveness to her family throughout the decade. For those who had grown
disenchanted with the potential of the movement, King's murder was the
last straw. Horne, for example, said she had attended King's funeral to
see if "the sadness would soften me up a little." But she left more cynical
than ever and felt that her activism had accomplished little.[47] Henceforth she avoided the movement. For the majority of the stars, even
Gregory, who believed that the FBI was responsible for King's death, it
was a matter of determining the best method of moving forward. The
day before the funeral, Belafonte proposed staging a huge rally at Atlanta
Stadium reminiscent of the March on Washington. Hoping that it would
"turn the nation from violence," he gathered a group of political figures
and celebrities to sell the idea. Poitier balked, arguing that it would
deflect attention from the funeral and, if it failed to prevent more violence, would further mar King's legacy. When their disagreement turned
ugly, Belafonte's idea was discarded and the two men stopped speaking
for two years.[48] Their falling out, while driven by their personal rivalry,
also reflected a larger problem within the movement itself as it splin-
tered near the end of the decade.

The movement's dissolution made it difficult for celebrities to continue
supporting the cause of civil rights. The Reverend Ralph Abernathy
assumed the leadership of the Southern Christian Leadership Conference
(SCLC) and continued with the Poor People's Campaign (PPC) that King
had begun planning in 1967. The PPC sought an economic bill of rights
from the federal government through employment and housing programs. To pressure Congress, five thousand protesters descended on
Washington, DC, in the summer of 1968 and lived in tents on the National
Mall in "Resurrection City." Sammy Davis, Jr., raised $17,800 for the PPC
through a benefit performance of *Golden Boy* in Chicago.[49] He and a host
of other celebrities visited Resurrection City to boost the morale of the
"residents." Poitier, Brando, Barbra Streisand, Eartha Kitt, Culp, and Cosby
all provided entertainment, performing at a bandstand on the grounds.[50]
However, Congress failed to take up a bill, and the public grew repulsed
by the five thousand squatters. After a six-week occupation, police drove
out the protesters, and bulldozers demolished Resurrection City. Disappointed in Abernathy's leadership, Belafonte "felt tired of fighting, tired
of the movement." He questioned how he could continue to support civil
rights in King's absence.[51] Indeed, the SCLC began to splinter, and after

a falling out with Abernathy, the young operative Jesse Jackson left the organization to found Operation PUSH (People United to Save Humanity) in Chicago. While this new group worked with celebrity supporters, Jackson never gained King's stature. Meanwhile, the SCLC lost its cohort of stars amid the infighting.

SNCC adopted enough policy changes that it, too, drove away its celebrity allies, including Theodore Bikel, one of its earliest supporters. Under Stokely Carmichael's leadership, SNCC marginalized whites in the organization and dropped nonviolence in favor of "defensive violence." Furthermore, during the Arab-Israeli War in 1967, a number of SNCC workers strongly criticized Israel.[52] This marked a "turning point" for SNCC, as a number of Jewish and mainstream organizations withdrew their support. Bikel, who was also the national vice president of the American Jewish Congress, publicly "resigned" from the organization. He described SNCC's position on Israel as the "latest in a long line of missteps" in a pattern that "made a mockery of the word 'nonviolent' in your name."[53] SNCC's actions deeply bothered Bikel—even more so when some activists claimed he had not been an important ally to begin with.[54] Belafonte also grew uncomfortable with SNCC under Carmichael's leadership and decided to support only various members' individual projects as opposed to the organization at large.[55] However, when the group changed its name to the Student *National* (emphasis added) Coordinating Committee to officially reflect its rejection of nonviolence, Belafonte "lost heart." He broke off his relationship with the organization as well, and SNCC dissolved soon after.

One scholar asserts that those stars who had been most crucial to the movement found that their reputations "withered, or were systematically destroyed, by the peculiar demands of the black power era."[56] It is mistaken to say that the careers of the Leading Six were "destroyed." However, stars were presented with new political and artistic choices, choices made more complicated by the variety of interpretations of the meaning of "Black Power." Malcolm X's influence on grassroots organizers and the growing emphasis on economic and political power after the passage of the Civil Rights and Voting Rights Acts helped facilitate the rise of Black Power. At its base was the desire for self-determination and racial pride, which were rather broad concepts. However, militant groups generally repudiated the "moderation" and liberal integration pursued by mainstream organizations. SNCC, the Congress of Racial Equality, and the

Black Panther Party (BPP) were the most visible organizations to reflect this militancy.[57] For the Leading Six, a separatist stance was anathema to their careers and their years of dedication to integrationist groups. They nevertheless empathized with cries for Black Power. Gregory perceived Black Power not as a "color" but as "an attitude" that elicited pride. Belafonte proclaimed Black Power to be "psychologically" important to black people to help "liberate" them from the self-hatred inculcated in them by white society.[58] Such sentiments had drawn Ossie Davis, Dee, and Gregory to Malcolm X. Poitier and Sammy Davis, Jr., the two celebrities most readily associated with integration, both publicly defended Back Power in terms of ethnic identity.[59] Thus, while the Leading Six never symbolized the politics of Black Power, they identified with its cultural goals.

The group's relationship with the Black Panther Party exemplifies these guarded sympathies. Founded in Oakland, California, in 1966, the Black Panthers dedicated themselves to self-determination through community economic programs and self-defense, and had won media attention for carrying weapons. By 1968, Black Panthers numbered one thousand members in twenty-five chapters nationwide, but the party also seemed under siege.[60] In 1968, Ossie Davis asserted the right of the BPP to exist, a declaration prompted by the shooting death of the seventeen-year-old activist Bobby Hutton by Oakland police.[61] Davis's belief that the Black Panthers experienced "constant police harassment" only deepened when, by 1969, twenty-two members of the party (known as the Panther 22) had been arrested on various charges of plotting to kill policemen and to bomb public facilities. Ruby Dee called the treatment of the Panther 22, including that of BPP cofounder Bobby Seale, "outrageous" and predicted their "ultimate triumph."[62] After police shot BPP member Fred Hampton in his Chicago home in December 1969, Davis and Gregory convened a National Emergency Conference to Defend the Right of the Black Panther Party to Exist with a cross-section of civil rights, peace, religious, and labor movement activists. Believing a national plan to "annihilate" the Black Panthers was at work, the conference formed a Panther Defense Fund cochaired by Davis and Gregory and tried to raise awareness about the Black Panthers' "genocide."[63] In that vein, in 1970 Sammy Davis, Jr., quietly met with BPP representatives and agreed to finance the film *The Murder of Fred Hampton*, about the violent police raid of Hampton's residency in Chicago, which was released in 1971.[64] Their suspicions proved warranted, as it would later be revealed that Federal Bureau of Investigation director J. Edgar Hoover had begun a new phase of COunter INTELigence PROgram (COINTELPRO) against BPP in 1968 in an effort to discredit and disrupt its activities.[65]

Ultimately, Dee, Gregory, and Ossie and Sammy Davis, Jr., hoped to facilitate constructive dialogue between black militants and the mainstream movement. For example, Gregory and Ossie Davis convinced Ralph Abernathy and Coretta King, who were still with the SCLC, to endorse their efforts to defend the Black Panthers.[66] Likewise, Sammy Davis, Jr., felt that "without contact," the militants and "middle-of-the-road groups were wasting effort." He set up a private meeting with Ron Karenga, a Black Panther affiliate and sometimes rival, and SCLC's Jesse Jackson at his home "so there could be a cross-action." Afterward, Davis said, "[I felt that] I had done something more tangible than just another benefit, or being seen at a march."[67] When Diahann Carroll held a fundraiser for Congressional candidate Shirley Chisholm, the actress made a point of inviting Black Panther cofounder Huey Newton. These efforts demonstrate an empathetic skepticism of the militants' approach. Gregory remained an advocate of nonviolence and continued to work with integrationist groups. Sammy Davis, Jr., felt that the militants relied too much on fear and intimidation and that some of their demands were "ridiculous." Carroll admits that although she admired the BPP's community work, camaraderie, and sense of purpose, she felt that their macho rhetoric and devotion to guns were "bound to entice a lot of innocent people into suicidal confrontation that could not possibly be won."[68] Belafonte and Poitier appear to have steered clear of the group.

The white actors Marlon Brando, Shirley Sutherland, Jean Seberg, and Jane Fonda become more intricately involved in the Black Panthers' daily activities. Brando was one of Hollywood's earliest supporters of the BPP. He provided money and spoke at Bobby Hutton's memorial service. Although Bobby Seale considered Brando "a friend," others in the organization "lambasted him for 'poking his nose' into their world."[69] Brando kept his distance henceforth. The Canadian-born Sutherland (then wife of the actor Donald Sutherland) cofounded Friends of the Black Panthers in Los Angeles in 1968 to raise money for the group. Sutherland says that she initially began simply supporting a breakfast program, but that it was "easy to get sucked in." In 1969, police arrested and jailed her for allegedly buying ten grenades for the BPP.[70] Meanwhile, Hakim Abdullah Jamal, an erstwhile Black Panther who ran a community program in his own right, reached out to Seberg, who was known for her work in French "new wave" films and her roles in *Saint Joan* (1957) and *Paint Your Wagon* (1969). Seberg threw fund-raising parties for the BPP, though with little success. One party attended by Fonda, Paul Newman, Joanne Woodward, Lee Marvin, James Baldwin, and Vanessa Redgrave raised only $2,000, indicating a general discomfort among the Hollywood elite toward the organization. Seberg grew more reckless when she began a passionate affair with Jamal and a fling with another BPP member, occasionally hiding guns or providing safe harbor for them.[71] Although Fonda describes her own involvement with the Black Panthers as "brief" and as consisting "wholly of raising bail money," in reality she also demonstrated a deeper commitment.[72] She lent her apartment for BPP news conferences, spoke at rallies for the organization, and when Newton arrived in New York to attend Seale's murder trial, welcomed him at the airport. She ardently defended BPP to the press, saying, "Of course I like the Panthers; of course I totally support the Panthers."[73]

Because of these entanglements, white celebrity supporters received more recrimination for their involvement with the Black Panthers than did Ossie Davis or Gregory. In fact, after Davis received a death threat, the police provided him with protection.[74] Conversely, due to the grenade incident, the US government refused to renew Sutherland's work permit. After she and Donald divorced, she had little choice but to return to Canada in 1977. In the meantime, the FBI began monitoring both Seberg and Fonda as part of its COINTELPRO operation. When phone surveillance revealed that Seberg was pregnant, the FBI launched a smear campaign in which it falsely leaked to the press that she was carrying a Black Panther's baby. In reality, the FBI did not know the child's paternity but saw an opportunity to scare away other celebrities who might have supported the party.[75] The agency also attempted to discredit Fonda, whom it had begun to investigate in May 1970. However, the effort lost momentum, in part because Seberg went into premature labor and her baby died, leading the FBI agent in charge of Fonda's case to back off. Besides, Fonda was not as easy a target; she was not intimately involved with any of the Black Panthers, and her support of the group was public knowledge. She also had the emotional wherewithal to deal with the surveillance, whereas Seberg, who never fully recovered from the experience, returned to France and committed suicide in 1979.[76]

The most likely repercussion of white celebrity involvement with the

Black Panthers, however, was public mockery, an outcome facilitated, but not fabricated, by Hoover's agents. In June 1970, the journalist Tom Wolfe wrote an essay for *New York* magazine in which he coined the term "radical chic," that is the trend of wealthy white liberals throwing fancy fundraisers for radical groups, after he learned about a cocktail fete thrown by Leonard and Felicia Bernstein for the Black Panthers at their elegant Park Avenue home. The *New York Times* first reported the affair, which raised $10,000 for the Panther 22, in mid-January. "Black Panthers from the ghetto" and wealthy whites such as the directors Otto Preminger and Sidney Lumet debated the organization's philosophies on capitalism and violence "over cocktails and the silver trays of canapés." The hosts and their liberal friends received widespread criticism for their "elegant slumming" and their obliviousness of the hypocrisy of wealthy "jet setters" giving money to an avowed socialist organization. Hoover instructed his agents to build on these critiques. The FBI sent letters signed "a concerned Jew" to the Bernsteins' guests, pointing out the anti-Semitism the BPP espoused. Hoover complained to the press about the "well-intentioned but uninformed" celebrities who had given them money.[77] But it was the nature of the fund-raiser itself and Wolfe's acerbic details of its many contradictions that allowed "radical chic" to take hold.

In some ways, the Bernstein's party resembled a typical SNCC house party. James Forman, one of the organization's original promoters of such fund-raisers, had himself joined the Black Panthers. The SNCC parties had not been without their paradoxes. The activist David Dennis felt that the parties could generate a romanticism that he found off-putting. Guests liked to "hear the stories and see the activists in their overalls," as if they were "from the jungle," foreshadowing the reaction to the Black Panthers at the Bernsteins' party.[78] However, Wolfe points out that, before 1968, civil rights did not have much social cachet, in part because of the middle-class earnestness of such individuals as Roy Wilkins, King, and the early SNCC students. Thus, SNCC's house parties did not carry the baggage of radical chic, in which the guests of honor were "hip" and "funky" in their black leather outfits, dark shades, and large Afros, and the patrons absurd. "I've never met a Panther—this is a first for me!" gushed one guest upon arriving at the Bernstein's apartment. Hand-wringing over such questions as whether or not Black Panthers ate Roquefort cheese and where one could find white servants infuse Wolfe's description. He cuttingly declares it "pointless to debate their sincerity." Promoters of radical chic, he says, displayed an "honest outrage," just as they showed a "sincere concern" for having "a proper address, a proper scale of interior decoration," and a weekend home by the shore.[79] Although the Bernsteins were roundly ridiculed in New York circles, harassed by the press, and chastised by the Jewish Defense League, in the long run they suffered little more than "bitter unpleasantness."[80]

Of the many questions raised by Black Power, one of the most significant to black celebrities was the role of the artist in the shifting political culture. By 1972, the trend among black activists had moved more decisively to electoral politics.[81] The number of black office holders would more than triple between 1969 and 1975, from 1,125 to 3,503.[82] Even the Black Panthers began "exchanging guns for ballots," as former members ran for office and party leaders renounced the gun in favor of voter education and registration drives.[83] These trends both validated the political efforts of black stars and led them to question their own place in the political landscape. Whereas celebrities had once been among the few voices to speak for black concerns, this was no longer the case. In a 1971 speech for the Congressional Black Caucus, Ossie Davis suggested that it was time for black politicians to represent black interests and for artists to step aside.[84] Increasingly, black political groups concluded that working within the system, as opposed to operating a separate black political party, would lead to the most constructive gains. For the vast majority of African Americans, this meant supporting the Democratic Party. As the 1972 presidential campaign got underway, the Leading Six turned their attention to black-oriented artistic endeavors and to supporting black and Democratic candidates. Sammy Davis, Jr., however, bucked this trend.

Davis continued to construct his public image as a blend of edgy and old-fashioned. May Britt had divorced him in 1966 due to his frantic schedule and their nonexistent home life. Davis married the black dancer Altovise Gore in 1970. At thirty years his junior, Gore accepted Davis's "swinging" lifestyle and possessed a youthful vibe that helped give Davis the confidence to embrace the latest trends and to assert his "blackness." He grew his hair somewhat longer, wore "mod" jackets, and donned flashier jewelry. Despite these changes, Davis's appearances on *Laugh-In* perpetuated the "clowning" and "Tomming" for which he had been criticized with the Rat Pack. Indeed, after enduring a barrage of barbs in one episode, Davis scratches at his skin and says, "We gonna rub this stuff off." Furthermore, his film and recording choices remained similar to his

1950s stylings. He made the comedic films *Salt and Pepper* (1968) and *One More Time* (1970) with Peter Lawford. After an aborted attempt to record with Motown, Davis began working with MGM Records, where he continued to record standards and ballads, as well as the novelty tune "Candyman," his only number-one song. As the 1972 presidential campaign got underway, Davis joined many in the Old Hollywood establishment who endorsed Nixon, which was both a deferential and daring decision.

A few months after Nixon's election, special assistant to the president Robert J. Brown approached Davis about working with the administration. A White House liaison to minority groups, Brown briefed Davis on Nixon's initiatives, which, in a sense, embraced Black Power by promoting capitalism, education, and cultural pride for African Americans. The president established the Office of Minority Business Enterprise in the Department of Commerce with the intention of shoring up minority-owned businesses and banks. Likewise, Nixon doubled aid to black colleges to more than $600 million.[85] Davis was impressed and, in fact, had fond memories of an encounter with Nixon in 1954, when he was vice president and had visited Davis backstage at the Copacabana club. Nevertheless, Davis was reluctant to commit to a political partnership with the Nixon administration due to his longstanding relationship with the Democrats. He called various civil rights leaders, including Jesse Jackson, to solicit their advice, and claimed that they all encouraged him to try it. Davis met with Nixon for the first time at the White House on July 1, 1971.[86]

The two men hit it off. To be sure, Davis was "honored and thrilled" to visit the Oval Office. He had never enjoyed such access before, certainly not with John F. Kennedy. More importantly, the two men shared similar philosophical beliefs about the power of hard work—they were both "self-made men"—and the danger of a disillusioned underclass, especially among the nation's youth.[87] Nixon impressed Davis with his follow-through in subsequent months. After appointing Davis to the National Advisory Council on Economic Opportunity, the administration awarded $100 million in contracts to minority businesses and pumped over $1 billion into minority-owned banks through a combination of private and public efforts, leading to the doubling of such institutions by 1974.[88] Nixon also asked Davis to go to South Vietnam in spring 1972 on a fact-finding mission to investigate reports of heavy drug use among the soldiers and racial discrimination in the treatment centers. Davis shepherded a group of twenty-five show folks through eighteen performances in ten days to audiences ranging from twenty-two to twenty thousand. Between performances, he talked with enlisted men and officers and visited a number of drug treatment facilities. Davis identified twenty concerns in a report to Nixon, including the prison-like atmosphere of the hospitals and racial discrimination in enforcement. The army presented Davis with an award of appreciation, and Nixon implemented ten of his proposals.[89] Soon thereafter, the president surprised Davis by dropping in at an honorary dinner for Brown that Davis helped sponsor. Davis praised Nixon, "Your extemporaneous speech, I thought, was so sincere and heart-felt for Bob and I'm so glad the people that night got a chance to see a rare picture of a great man saluting his friend." He felt that Nixon's appearance especially "had a positive effect on all of the 'soul brothers' in the audience."[90]

This begs the question of motive. There is no shortage of critics who view Nixon's efforts as "token" programs meant to win black votes, especially in light of his "Southern strategy," a racially divisive plan to win white Southern votes. As the historian Robert E. Weems, Jr., notes, however, the 1968 Democratic presidential candidates Robert F. Kennedy and Hubert Humphrey would have, "like Nixon," given precedence to economic tools for community development programs over the increased social spending President Lyndon Johnson favored.[91] Furthermore, the same critics who dismiss Nixon's economic programs also bemoan their demise during the Reagan administration, indicating that perhaps they were not "tokens" after all. Davis was certainly not the only African American involved; in addition to Bob Brown, the civil rights activists Roy Innis and Floyd McKissick also worked as advisors on these programs, and all have been derisively called "negrocons," "accommodationists," and even "political prostitutes" due, in part, to the federal grants some of their own initiatives received.[92] However, recent scholarship on Nixon's record suggests that black appointees were not simply being used. Such historians argue that Nixon did not think programs such as minority enterprise would necessarily win votes. He backed them because he believed in them—as both a tool of social mobility and for discouraging urban riots—and ensured that the programs received funding and strong administrative support.[93]

As for Davis's motive, Nixon certainly treated Davis more respectfully than had any other office holder, and the men's interactions had allowed them to forge a personal bond. Perhaps this personal validation partly drove Davis to campaign for Nixon's reelection. It is also possible that Sinatra's endorsement of Nixon influenced Davis, although there is nothing in the archival record that indicates this, and Davis had become more independent of the Rat Pack since 1965. Nixon's work with African Americans and his record on minority issues seemed the most important factor. Indeed, one administration staffer noted that Davis was most interested in "'what is in it'—which was spelled out to mean something 'for the people'—not for himself." Nixon's appearance at the Brown dinner seemed to be the tipping point, showing Davis Nixon's sincerity. As Davis wrote the president, "If you want an old ex-democrat, you've got him!"[94] Despite this enthusiasm, Davis did not publicly endorse Nixon for another four months, likely due to the fallout from his controversial appearance on TV's *All in the Family* (CBS 1971–79).

"Sammy's Visit" appeared in the program's second season. Davis was an ardent fan of the show—even planning his nightclub performances around its 8:00 PM start time—because of "the metamorphosis of television" he believed it engendered.[95] In a historic moment in the 1970–71 season, three television shows featuring black central characters had succeeded simultaneously: *Julia* (1968–71), starring Diahann Carroll; *The Bill Cosby Show* (1969–71); and *The Flip Wilson Show* (1970–74), all on NBC. By 1972, however, Wilson was the only one still on the air. *Julia*, about a widowed nurse raising a young son, had been a breakthrough hit as the first to feature a black female lead in an average household. Yet the show's emphasis on middle-class notions of integration and the lack of a father figure proved inflammatory for social critics, including Belafonte, who urged Carroll to turn it down. She was so exhausted and frail from "dealing with the criticism" that she asked for her release at the end of the second season.[96] Meanwhile, network analysis showed that audiences had grown weary of real-life dramas with social relevance, preferring situation comedies and escapist themes. Black employment once again fell off in Hollywood; by autumn 1971, only ten prime time network shows featured blacks.[97] *Laugh-In* and Flip Wilson brought ethnic humor to the airwaves, especially with Wilson's popular sketches "The Church of What's Happening Now," which poked fun at the incongruities of the black church, and "Geraldine," in which he donned a wig and dress to play a flirtatious character. However, neither program directly dealt with social issues, and Wilson purposefully avoided "any messages on my show."[98] When Norman Lear created *All in the Family*, it was the first network program to consistently address relevant social themes, but it did so in a way that appealed to audience tastes at the time. As for Davis, guest-starring roles continued to be the only way to work on television.

All in the Family starred Carrol O'Connor as Archie Bunker, an old-school, working-class conservative given to racist, sexist, and homophobic behavior he does not recognize as offensive. His liberal daughter and son-in-law challenge him to little avail, yet Archie is characterized as foolishly out of touch, making him the foil for the liberal message intended by Lear. Davis's guest appearance played into this comedic cultural conflict. After having left his briefcase in Archie's cab, Davis stops by the Bunker household to retrieve it. Thrilled by the star's presence, Archie proclaims Davis a "credit to his race." Davis replies, "Well, thank you very much. I'm sure you've done good for yours, too." This type of banter continues, and in a reference to Davis's recent appearance on a nightly talk show with Raquel Welch, Archie's wife Edith interjects, "Archie said he never thought he'd see the day when coloreds and whites would be hugging and kissing coast to coast." Davis sarcastically claims there is a "kissing clause" in his contract. "It's those white celebrities. You see, this year we're 'in,' and they all want to jump on the bandwagon." Archie is aghast that Davis is forced to "intersex" on the air. Such ignorance makes Archie the butt of every joke, but his cluelessness allows him to feel vindicated. Archie asks Davis if he, like his family, considers Archie a racist. "If you were prejudiced," Davis responds, "you'd walk around thinking you're better than anyone else in the world, but I can tell after having spent these marvelous moments with you, you ain't better than anybody." Satisfied, Archie suggests they take a photograph together. Davis agrees and kisses him on the cheek when the camera clicks. Stunned, Archie sheepishly concedes, "Well, what the hell, he said it was in his contract."[99]

The reaction to "Sammy's Visit" indicated that Davis's ability to use his controversial persona for the movement's gain had lost some of its effectiveness. For many black viewers, Davis had crossed an unspoken line. Whereas his kowtowing to Sinatra and his interracial romances had been tolerated, kissing a "lovable bigot" like Archie was not. One biographer characterizes the kiss as "a joke so majestically cruel" that it left black viewers in a position of "disbelief." Another calls it "absolutely traitorous." Indeed, Davis received an onslaught of negative mail from African Americans and was baldly labeled a sell-out.[100] However, "Sammy's Visit" also drew one of the largest viewing audiences in television history. With *All in the Family* being set in Queens, it helped educate audiences about an insidious form of racism common in Northern cities—prejudiced but not forthrightly so, and not always negatively. After the civil rights movement shifted North and the enemy was no longer easily identified by a KKK uniform or a policeman's nightstick, this perspective was important to share. Bob Zellner, a former SNCC activist who founded the antiracism project Grass Roots Organizing Work in the Deep South's white community, admired the show's ability to "bring out the 'know-nothing' racist," and he employed that theme, and Davis's episode in particular, as a "good talking point" during his fieldwork.[101] With the movement itself in disarray, Davis provided constructive dialogue for a national audience of upward of sixty million people on a medium that was still largely conservative.

Davis became gradually more involved in Nixon's campaign throughout the summer of 1972, advising the administration on how to recruit the "now" generation of younger celebrities and African American stars. Nixon won the support of Pearl Bailey and James Brown, as well as a fair number of black athletes, but Davis made little headway with his number-one target Flip Wilson, reporting, "Wilson is not for Blacks, whites, or even his relatives . . . he just doesn't communicate with anyone and is extremely insecure." Over the next several months, Davis and Altovise attended six events on behalf of the Nixon campaign. Davis also donated $10,000 to a National Black Committee dinner for the Republican Party, landing a coup when Nixon agreed to attend his first all-black event.[102] These activities led to Davis taking on a number of responsibilities at the Republican National Convention in August, including appearing on NBC's *Today Show* and emceeing and performing at the nomination rally, the Women of Achievement brunch, and a Republican youth rally.[103] That same week, Davis's music producer learned that "Candyman" had gone gold, and Nixon agreed to surprise Davis at the youth rally to present the award. The president expressed his admiration of the entertainer and defended his public persona: "You can't buy Sammy Davis, Jr. You can only buy Sammy by doing good things for America." Overwhelmed by Nixon's words, Davis enfolded him in an embrace.[104]

That hug, like Archie's kiss and "de Judge's" joviality, undercut Davis's broader civil rights work. Contemporaries such as the former SNCC activist Julian Bond condemned it as "unbelievable, an irrational act." Davis's biographers have been no less forgiving, chalking up it up to a childlike need "to be loved."[105] At the root of this perspective is the belief that Davis no longer needed to pursue a daring and deferential approach, as if the civil rights gains and rise of Black Power no longer made it necessary. By this way of thinking, Davis's continued effort to "please whitey" seemed an old-fashioned habit at best and a deep-rooted psychological problem at worse. However, these critics do not recognize the limitations faced by Davis, particularly the conservative nature of television in the early 1970s. Nor do they give credence to Davis's reasonable notion that African Americans would be better served if the two national parties competed for their support. Davis perceived Nixon's economic programs through that lens. Soon after the election, he agreed to serve on the executive board of Floyd McKissick's National Committee for a Two-Party System.[106] He also organized a welcome home gala with Bob Hope for returning prisoners of war, and made arrangements with Jesse Jackson to present $25,000 at a PUSH rally, only to be loudly booed until Jackson intervened. His Sammy Davis Jr. Greater Hartford Open in 1973 was the first corporate-sponsored golf tournament hosted by an African American. However, "After Nixon" one biographer says, "not a lot of blacks were mindful of Sammy's history-making ventures."[107] Davis's risks did not pay off as they had in earlier years, and this was an emotionally devastating time for him. It also put him somewhat out of step with the rest of the Leading Six, who had made considerable headway on economic and cultural issues in New Hollywood.

* * *

By the late 1960s, the trend toward independent film production had become so commonplace that the term itself had been rendered meaningless. Ongoing financial difficulties led the major studios to be absorbed by large conglomerates, who increasingly favored the use of market research to make predictably profitable blockbuster films all while retaining a monopoly over the industry with "negative pickups," films made independently and then picked up by a studio for distribution. In 1966, 75 percent of the films released were "pick-ups"; in 1967, eighty percent.[108] When the studios dropped the Production Code Administration in favor of the MPAA rating system, filmmakers now had the freedom to explore topics that had previously been taboo. An "auteur renaissance" took place with such films as *Bonnie and Clyde* (1967), *Easy Rider* (1969), *MASH* (1970), and *The Godfather* (1972). Directed by such fresh young talent as Arthur Penn, Dennis Hopper, Robert Altman, and Francis Ford Coppola, these top box-office earners explored new variations on American themes with graphic sexuality, intense violence, and unexpected conclusions. A similar approach would characterize racially oriented films. The rise of Black Power and growing unease with Poitier's interracial dramas gave way to the ultramacho black hero who transcended, rather than integrated, white society. Thus, New Hollywood presented opportunities for young black filmmakers and actors but appeared inhospitable to Poitier's brand.

"Bashing the Poitier icon became high fashion," says one biographer. The prestigious psychologist Alvin Poussaint argued that Poitier's heroes "placed undue burdens" on black youth, and even Lincoln Perry (better known as Stepin Fetchit) chimed in, claiming that *Guess Who's Coming to Dinner* "served the purpose of white supremacy." Poitier went against type in *The Lost Man* (1968) by playing a militant who turns to robbery and murder to help imprisoned revolutionaries, but it seemingly tried too hard to be "newsworthy" without any of the cathartic energy vital to the success of other black films of the era. Roundly panned as a "liberal white fantasy of a black revolutionary," Poitier's career bottomed out, and he was labeled a "lickspittle."[109] Mindful that much of this criticism stemmed from "a resentment of my success," Poitier nevertheless reacted bitterly to accusations that he had not adequately supported the black point of view. He vented to Ruby Dee about the number of black writers he had financed who had come up "with nothing," aspiring filmmakers who failed to understand the financial aspects of the industry, and those who had publicly trashed him without ever attempting to meet with him. "Well fuck them," he lashed out, "if their failures have to be reflected in my success, that's their problem."[110] He withdrew to his native Bahamas, where he built a mansion and stewed about his paradoxical situation. It did not help that the estrangement between Poitier and Belafonte (about the scuttled King rally) continued or that Poitier fundamentally disagreed with the types of black-oriented films succeeding at the box office. "To be accepted," he complained, "you have to be appropriately hostile and obviously militant, and sufficiently anti-white."[111]

Such militant films had taken Hollywood by storm, starting with Melvin Van Peebles's *Sweet Sweetback's Baadasssss Song* in 1971. "Rated X by an all-white jury," the film chronicles the exploits of a wrongfully arrested sex show performer who teams up with the Hells Angels motorcycle gang to escape to Mexico. Van Peebles wrote, produced, scored, directed, starred in, and financed the film on a $150,000 budget, supplemented by a loan from Bill Cosby and a soundtrack by the R&B band Earth, Wind & Fire. Black audiences, including the Black Panthers' Huey Newton, embraced Sweetback's resistance of the establishment and his sexual prowess. One film critic explained the film's success by describing it as a "fantasy that fully plays into the needs of the black mass audience" with "a viable, sexual, assertive, arrogant black male hero."[112] With box office returns totaling an astonishing $15 million, the studios took notice. They began financing projects with similar themes and hiring black directors to film them.

One of the most triumphant of these was MGM's partnership with the still photographer Gordon Parks for *Shaft* in 1971. Starring the formidable Richard Roundtree as a private detective in Harlem who adroitly navigates a corrupt police force and the New York underworld, the low-budget production earned over $18 million, and the soul artist Isaac Hayes won an Academy Award for the title song. The film's success spawned two sequels and a "black movie boom" that incorporated a shared set of characteristics: a bold, black protagonist, graphic sexuality and violence, a desire to stick it to "the man," and a funky soundtrack. Between 1970 and 1975, Hollywood churned out over sixty such films, and black audiences flocked to the theaters. The professional athletes Jim Brown, Fred Williamson, and Jim Kelly, already well-known to the public for their athletic feats, starred in such films as *Slaughter* (1972), *Black Caesar* (1973), and *Black Belt Jones* (1974), respectively, and the striking actresses Pam Grier and Tamara Dobson played similarly robust characters in *Foxy Brown* (1974) and *Cleopatra Jones* (1973).[113] However, the genre seemed increasingly exploitative as white directors and producers tried to do what Van Peebles and Parks had pioneered. Their success "went to everybody's head and now they're all doing the same thing," one black producer noted. "White filmmakers aren't really seeing black; they're seeing black and green."[114]

Soon after the trend had begun, Julius Griffin of the Beverly Hills–Hollywood branch of the NAACP called the films "Blaxploitation," a term that has since categorized the genre. Charging that the "forced diet of violence, murder, drugs, and rape" served as "a cancer . . . gnawing away at the moral fiber of our community," Griffin formed the Committee Against Blaxploitation (CAB) with a coalition of civil rights groups in 1972.[115] Griffin also argued that the films presented black youth with "false heroes" and revived old stereotypes. CAB implemented its own rating system and threatened to hold demonstrations at studios, on location, and in movie houses. "We're prepared to go all the way with this, even to the extent of running people out of theaters," said one CAB member. The group soon fell apart under considerable pushback from the black directors, stars, and producers, who, reminiscent of the *Amos 'n' Andy* debate, emphasized the jobs the films provided, their harmless elements of "fantasy," and the "elitism" of the critics. Ron O'Neal, who starred as a drug pusher in *Superfly* (1972), lamented, "I'm so tired of handkerchief-head Negroes moralizing on the poor black man." Gordon Parks, his director, argued that the audience enjoyed seeing "superheroes with fast cars and fancy clothes," and that the characters did not, as some intellectuals had argued, damage their self-esteem. "White people don't go home upset because they aren't James Bond or John Wayne." A group of actors took out a full-page ad in *Variety* disavowing CAB's actions.[116] Fans soon tired of the formulaic films, and the Blaxploitation fizzled by the mid-1970s. The genre nevertheless showed the importance of black moviegoers to the health of the industry; Ossie Davis, Poitier, and Belafonte took advantage of such interest, but shunned the excesses of Blaxploitation in their own projects.

Davis emerged as a leading voice against the hypersexualized representation of black men when Twentieth Century Fox bought the film rights to William Stryon's Pulitzer Prize–winning 1967 novel *The Confessions of Nat Turner*. Based on the true story of a slave uprising in rural Virginia, Styron took considerable historical liberties to present Turner as a sex-crazed maniac bent on bedding white women. Davis joined the Black Anti-Defamation Association (BADA), an ad hoc group formed by the story analyst Louise Meriwether and the actor and set designer Vantile Whitfield, two of Hollywood's first black studio hires. As BADA sought endorsements from a cross-section of civil rights groups and met with studio representatives, one historian says that Davis emerged as "their most eloquent celebrity spokesman."[117] In one such discussion, Davis told Styron that an emphasis on "black male lusting" had provided the rationale for over 3,500 lynchings and that he feared that more violence against blacks would follow the release of the film. He proposed an absurd yet insightful solution: let "Hollywood choose one of its outstanding white matinee idols and have him play Nat Turner in blackface. If they do it that way, everybody's off the hook."[118] BADA generated enough press that the studio finally agreed to meet with Meriwether, Whitfield, and Davis to reconceptualize the project. It agreed to drop the sensational sexuality and incorporate other source material in order to portray Turner in a positive light, leading James Earl Jones to accept the starring role. Sudden financial difficulties led Twentieth Century Fox to declare a "feature film hiatus," however, and *Nat Turner* was never made.[119]

The other studios also faced financial problems, and, ironically, the Blaxploitation genre was an answer to their woes. United Artists received a financial boost when Samuel Goldwyn, Jr., hired Davis to rewrite the script for *Cotton Comes to Harlem* (1970), based on the book by Chester Himes. Goldwyn was so pleased with Davis's work on the screenplay that he hired Davis to direct the film as well. The film tells the story of two cops, played by Godfrey Cambridge and Raymond St. Jacques, who investigate an armored car robbery in Harlem. To solve the case, they contend with a dishonest Garvey-esque preacher, their own racist boss, a hostile community who call them "nigger pigs," the Italian mob, and a junk dealer played by Redd Foxx in a forerunner to his *Sanford and Son* television role. Since it is set in Harlem, features a majority black cast, and—much like in *Gone Are the Days*—pokes fun at a number of racial stereotypes, the film is often mistakenly labeled "Blaxploitation." While Cambridge and St. Jacques do engage in a fair number of action sequences, there is no graphic violence or nude scenes. Unlike most Blaxploitation flicks, it is *meant* to be a comedy. Most importantly, although there are plenty of derogatory references to "the man," the primary message of the film is that blacks need a leader to promote their collective interests, but the existing figures are disappointing shysters. There are no condemnations of the man or brutal revenge taken by the protagonists, both key features of Blaxploitation.

Cotton Comes to Harlem succeeded where *Gone Are the Days* had failed. Its dynamic plot came alive onscreen, and the jabs at racial stereotypes mostly worked. For example, the Garvey-esque preacher claims he had been "down on my knees in a white man's jail" and argues that this makes him "black enough" to lead his people. The line reappears throughout the film. At one point, Redd Foxx sells a bale of cotton that had fallen out of a truck during the theft for twenty-five dollars. He buys it back for thirty, quipping, "Is that black enough?" In another scene, a black eyewitness tells the cops that the thieves were white men wearing masks. When the cops question how he could know their racial identity if they wore masks, he replies, "They ran white, dammit." Another scene shows a dancer at the Apollo Theater who refuses to perform with such "Uncle Tom props" as balloons and feathers. Instead, she dons a sharecropper costume and then stripteases down to a bikini made of cotton balls. The humorous discovery at the film's conclusion is that $87,000 is hidden in the bale that Foxx acquired. Indeed, an African American finally makes money from the Southern crop. Some of the stereotypes seem too obvious, such as the wagon full of watermelons in a chase scene, leading some critics to question the overall taste of the film and once again revealing the difficulty of exploring ethnic humor onscreen. Nevertheless, the film received generally positive reviews, made $5.2 million, prompted a sequel, and led to more directing projects for Davis with such films as *Black Girl* (1972) and *Gordon's War* (1973).[120]

Most importantly, Davis founded Third World Cinema as a result of *Cotton*. During the filming, a group of activists engineered a number of obstructive activities. "Sure," admits Davis, "there was a black director, and a lot of black actors were working, but about the crew—the gaffers, the carpenters, the propmen, the scenic designers, the set dressers, and the drivers?" Davis had already tried to integrate the crew but encountered union obstinacy, a problem shared by both Poitier and Belafonte with their recent films.[121] During the making of *The Lost Man*, Poitier personally worked with each department at Universal Studios to ensure black hires. Belafonte starred in *Angel Levine* in 1970, and although the film would flop miserably at the box office, he pressured United Artists to include more minority crewmen. Both men secured grant money through liberal foundations to pay for the "apprenticeship" programs in order to circumvent union restrictions.[122] While these were important steps, they were also short-term solutions dependent upon grant money. Davis established Third World Cinema in 1971 with Cliff Frazier, then chair of New York's Film Workshop Council, who had also administered the apprenticeship program on *Angel Levine*. The studio produced a handful of film projects in the 1970s, including the critically acclaimed *Claudine* (1974), starring Diahann Carroll as a single mother in Harlem. Carroll garnered an Academy Award nomination for best actress in a leading role. Furthermore, Third World Cinema established the Institute for New Cinema Artists, a training arm for minorities and women in filmmaking jobs that remained in existence until 1986.[123]

This type of mentoring reaped almost immediate results when Drake

Walker, an apprentice from *Angel Levine*, approached Belafonte about a story he had written for a black-oriented Western called *Buck and the Preacher*. Fascinated by the two lead characters—a wagon master and a swindling reverend—Belafonte called Poitier. Not only did he want to pitch the script, but after not seeing each other for two years, Belafonte says, "I missed my friend." They took up where they left off and, making no mention of their rift, agreed to a 50-50 split between their production companies, with Columbia Pictures as the distributor, the first of Poitier's three-picture deal. Poitier worked on revising the story with screenwriter Ernest Kinoy. They raised $2 million for the budget and agreed on Durango, Mexico, with its starkly beautiful scenery and cut-rate costs, for the location.[124]

Poitier and Belafonte shared similar racial and artistic goals for the picture. The story centered on freed slaves after the Civil War being stalked by bounty hunters hired by Southern planters to return them to gang labor in the fields. Says Poitier, "We thought that black people played an important part in the building of the west; we want black children to see that."[125] Despite the gunslinging and potential to become a revenge story, the two also purposefully avoided the characteristics of Blaxploitation. They were "not turned on by pictures that seduce an audience with the use of violence in the name of race," Belafonte explained, saying that the shootouts in their film were "not violence for violence's sake." The only nudity is a humorous scene in which Buck (Poitier) steals the Preacher's (Belafonte) horse while he is bathing in a river. Belafonte mischievously emerges from the water with a strategically placed cowboy hat and then treats the audience to a quick glimpse of his backside.

Poitier and Belafonte also grew equally dismayed with their choice of director. Joseph Sargent, whose experience came mostly from working in television at that point, did not bring the sense of gravitas they wanted. The daily rushes failed to impress the executives at Columbia Pictures, as well. "If the nature of the subject wasn't such that it was working and dealing as deeply with the black psyche," Belafonte explained, "it might not matter." Feeling a special sense of responsibility, however, they fired Sargent, and Belafonte convinced Poitier to assume the director's chair. Although Poitier had always wanted to direct films, it was a daunting task, with a seventy-five member crew and hundreds of extras, many of whom did not speak English. Ruby Dee, who played Buck's wife Ruth, remembers being both "surprised" by and "impressed" with Poitier. She says, "He gave all his actors a great sense of confidence in his vision and in his direction. It was immediately obvious that he knew what he was doing."[126] The studio representatives who flew in to check on the situation agreed.

With Poitier at the helm and in frequent conference with Belafonte, Dee commented, "It felt like old times," referring to their American Negro Theater days.[127] Despite the extreme weather conditions, poor housing, and bad food during their nine-week shoot, the group enjoyed being together. Ossie Davis was a frequent visitor, and Belafonte's wife Julie played an Indian chief's wife named Sinsie in the film. Just as in the past, some tension remained between the two producers. Rumors emerged about Belafonte irritating Poitier by always being late to view the daily rushes, and of Poitier having miffed Belafonte by leaving the singer's birthday party early.[128] However, an absence of friction between the old friends would have been even more unusual. In any case, the tension did not negatively affect the finished film and perhaps may even have enhanced it, given that Buck and the Preacher were written to be somewhat antagonistic. Buck is a socially conscious man of the land, and the Preacher an unscrupulous, leering reverend of the questionable High and Low Order of the Holiness Persuasion Church who appears eager to make a quick buck.

Poitier's first directorial effort resulted in a creditable, lively film that expressed black desires in the wake of the Civil War. When the bounty hunters try to violently force the settlers to return South and to kill Buck, Ruth laments the "poison in the land" and her desire to give up on the United States for Canada. Especially poignant is that Buck could have presumably led a quiet farming life but risks death to lead black settlers to a better place. After the "night riders" steal the migrants' money, Buck and the Preacher put their antagonism aside to steal back the cash and hand-deliver it to the wagon train, which results in two massive shootouts. Buck's relationship with the local Indian tribe gives their escape an added complexity. Buck pays the tribe in gold for safe passage, but the Indians refuse to fight for him, reminding Buck that he once served in the US Army. Buck acknowledges this and the camera pauses in awkward silence. Ultimately, the Indians do provide backup, and Buck and the preacher emerge bloody yet triumphant. Belafonte's performance brought valuable levity to the film. He appears unusually relaxed under Poitier's direction and clearly had fun with his part, relishing the rascally side of his character and going all out to appear believably grubby; unkempt hair and rotten teeth—which he blackened with eyeliner and coated with nail polish—rounded out his look. It is a delight to see Clarence Muse, who came out of retirement once again to play Cudjo, a conjure man. The blues musicians Sonny Terry and Brownie McGhee play a gripping soundtrack, skillfully punctuated with Terry's signature harmonica.

Buck marked the beginning of Poitier's lucrative directorial career, although the film itself was only somewhat successful. It earned disappointingly modest profits and received mixed reviews. Generally considered an "amiable" and "delightful" film, it received criticism for not pushing the boundaries of the Western genre. Although it offered black heroes, it did not, as the progressive African American critic Clayton Riley argued, "bring [any] discernable dimension to cowboy flicks that the genre did not already possess." Riley identified Buck's "muddled" response to the Indians as particularly troubling and lambasted Poitier and Belafonte's "chauvinism" for not giving more screen time to Dee. "Women rarely play substantial roles in Westerns," he notes. "Their male egos notwithstanding, Poitier and Belafonte could have managed more than this."[129] Although Riley has a point, expecting Poitier to revolutionize the Western genre in his directorial debut is rather unrealistic. The Indian scene was the very first that Poitier printed.[130] *Buck* accomplished what was needed, and Poitier went on to direct four more films in the 1970s, including *Uptown Saturday Night* (1974) and *A Piece of the Action* (1977), both highly profitable black-oriented comedies costarring Bill Cosby. Such films gave Poitier bankability and allowed him to outride the Blaxploitation fad. In 1980, he directed Richard Pryor and Gene Wilder in the wildly successful *Stir Crazy*, an interracial buddy film that grossed over $100 million. Not only did Poitier emerge as the most successful black director of all time at that point, but he did so in a way that reflected the ideals and sensibility that had made him one of the civil rights movement's most important celebrity supporters.

* * *

With the dissolution of the civil rights movement, the Stars for Freedom pressured Hollywood through both individual and collective action and attempted to deal with some of the important unfinished issues, as with economic and job training programs, but they faced ongoing challenges.

CHAPTER 7

The stereotyping of African Americans and black underemployment (especially in production and for black women) persisted in the 1970s. Politically active celebrities who had seen the end of McCarthyism and the decline of the House Un-American Activities Committee now faced new hazards. Jane Fonda faced an "unofficial blacklist" as a result of her radical political causes. Sammy Davis, Jr., withdrew from social activism and began partying heavily with porn stars, drug users, and even, for a short time, devil worshippers. Always one step away from bankruptcy, his debt finally caught up with him, and he became the target of an IRS audit, which eventually led to the much-publicized seizure of some of his assets. To what degree this self-destructive behavior resulted from the public shaming in the Archie Bunker and Richard Nixon controversies is anyone's guess. Davis could have been having a "midlife" crisis or may simply have wanted to indulge in the excesses of the decade. Whatever the case, his behavior did little to restore his reputation. He fought to keep his career together for the next few years, eventually making a respectable comeback in the 1980s. Nevertheless, the Stars for Freedom helped create a far better film industry for minorities in the 1970s than they had encountered upon first arriving in Hollywood.

As a result of their efforts, Hollywood showcased a wide variety of black perspectives and opened up more jobs behind the camera to minorities. Network television portrayed African Americans in multiple ways. *All in the Family* launched the spin-off *The Jeffersons* (CBS 1975–1985), starring Sherman Helmsley as the cantankerous George Jefferson who deals with integration on his own terms. *Sanford and Son* (NBC 1972–77), *Good Times* (CBS 1974–79), and *What's Happening!!* (ABC 1976–79) portrayed a variety of family structures in America's inner cities. By the end of the decade, a number of "integrationist" shows had debuted, including *Diff'rent Strokes* (NBC 1978–85), *The White Shadow* (CBS 1978–81), and *Benson* (ABC 1979–86). In 1975, Sammy Davis, Jr., finally achieved his dream of hosting his own variety series. *Sammy and Company* aired for three seasons, although Davis's health problems cut the show short. The made-for-television movies *The Autobiography of Miss Jane Pittman* (1974) and *Roots* (1977), both historical dramas that explored the effects of slavery in unprecedented fashion, were two of the most-watched programs of the decade. Although the stars generally did not feel comfortable with the Blaxploitation approach, Poitier noted that such films "represent diversified creative attitudes and ideas."[131] Indeed, the films of the 1970s proved that both black and white moviegoers would pay to see African Americans in leading roles that went beyond the interracial drama. The Stars for Freedom helped pave the way for such stars as Eddie Murphy, Wesley Snipes, Denzel Washington, and Danny Glover, as well as director Spike Lee, in the 1980s. In a 1989 interview with the *New York Times*, Poitier noted that "historical circumstances had changed," allowing for an "impressive number of very good actors working with regularity." He asserted, "I view it as wonderful."[132]

Left: Lena Horne with the NAACP's Medgar Evers at the start of a civil rights rally in Jackson, Mississippi in June 1963. This visit marked a turning point in Horne's engagement with the movement. *Library of Congress Prints and Photographs Division.*

Below: Charlton Heston, Judy Garland, Eartha Kitt, and Marlon Brando at an Arts Group meeting for the March on Washington on August 8, 1963. Heston and Brando cochaired the effort to bring over seventy-five stars to the demonstration. *Library of Congress Prints and Photographs Division.*

Right: Ossie Davis emceeing the preliminary concert for the March on Washington on the National Mall on August 28, 1963. Davis's careful planning of the program and entertainment kept the marchers engaged and upbeat throughout the long, hot day. *National Archives.*

Below: Sammy Davis, Jr., and National Association for the Advancement of Colored People executive secretary Roy Wilkins speaking with a reporter at the March on Washington. Davis took on multiple projects for the NAACP in the 1950s and 1960s. *National Archives.*

Sidney Poitier and Burt Lancaster at the March on Washington. Lancaster and his wife Norma raised money for the Southern Christian Leadership Conference and helped organize Hollywood celebrities against California's Prop 14. *Library of Congress Prints and Photographs Division. © The Estate of Roosevelt Carter.*

Josephine Baker conversing with Lena Horne. Baker launched a concert tour and a benefit show for the major civil rights organizations in the aftermath of the March on Washington, which ended Baker's long exile from the United States. *Library of Congress Prints and Photographs Division. © The Estate of Roosevelt Carter.*

Right: Dick Gregory under arrest in 1963 for "disorderly conduct" while protesting segregated schools in Chicago. This was the first of Gregory's many arrests, and his incarcerations brought publicity to issues in the urban North and Deep South that would otherwise have been ignored by the national media. *Library of Congress Prints and Photographs Division.*

Below: When civil rights organizations renewed efforts for open housing near Los Angeles in July 1963, the added publicity brought by Marlon Brando helped integrate a housing development in Torrance. Brando was the first Hollywood star arrested during civil rights demonstrations in California, and his involvement paved the way for a strong Arts Division in the Californians Against Prop 14 campaign. *Bettmann/CORBIS.*

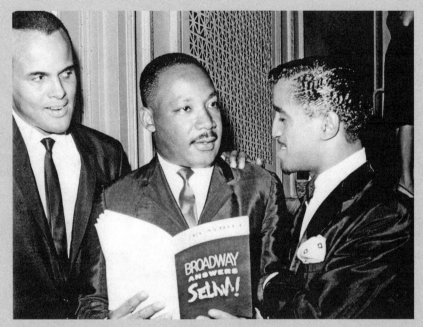

Harry Belafonte, Martin Luther King, Jr., and Sammy Davis, Jr., at the "Broadway Answers Selma" benefit show at the Majestic Theatre on April 4, 1965. The event raised an unprecedented $150,000 but also marked the peak of celebrity involvement in the civil rights movement. *Bettmann/CORBIS*.

Ossie Davis and Ruby Dee at the premiere of their film *Gone Are the Days* (1963) in New York City. Although a critical and commercial flop, the film facilitated Davis's emergence in the 1970s as a successful director, writer, and producer. *AP/Corbis*.

Sammy Davis, Jr., in his appointment to President Richard Nixon's National Advisory Council on Economic Opportunity on July 1, 1971, with Nixon aide Robert J. Brown looking on. This meeting began Davis's relationship with Nixon, one driven by Davis's belief that the federal government would be more responsive to racial issues if more African Americans worked with the administration. *Richard Nixon Presidential Library and Museum.*

Sammy Davis, Jr., vulnerable to accusations of "accommodationism" throughout his career, received unprecedented criticism for embracing President Richard Nixon during a youth rally at the 1972 Republican National Convention in Miami in August. Davis's relationship with Nixon, and especially the image of this hug, undermined his civil rights work in the historical record. *Richard Nixon Presidential Library and Museum.*

Sidney Poitier directing the 1977 film *A Piece of the Action*. Poitier became Hollywood's most successful black director in the 1970s, helping integrate the film industry both in front of and behind the camera. *Photographs and Prints Division, Schomburg Center for Research in Black Culture, New York Public Library, Astor, Lenox, and Tilden Foundations.*

EPILOGUE

THE STARS FOR FREEDOM PAVED THE WAY FOR AN ACTIVIST CELEB-
rity culture that continues to the present day. Although celebrities had
been regular fixtures in wartime and presidential campaigns since the early
days of Hollywood, the studio system, the House Un-American Activities
Committee's investigations of the film industry, and McCarthyism inhibited many Hollywood stars from engaging in social activism. The civil
rights movement drew stars into grassroots politics, including the anti–
Vietnam War movement, the battle over the Equal Rights Amendment in
the 1970s, the "nuclear freeze" movement in the 1980s, global warming and
gun rights debates at the turn of the twenty-first century, and the anti–Iraq
War demonstrations during George W. Bush's presidency, as well as a host
of new controversial causes. High-profile celebrities, some of whom had cut
their teeth on the civil rights movement, used their public personas and
media connections to bring attention to and shape these debates. They also
became increasingly involved in electoral politics, not just as supporters
but also as advisors and important figures in fund-raising networks. Of
course, several celebrities, such as Ronald Reagan and Arnold Schwar-
zenegger, have become elected officials themselves, but most are reluctant
to give up their lucrative day jobs for full-time public service. As Oprah
Winfrey, an entertainment mogul in her own right, demonstrated in her
2008 endorsement of Democratic presidential candidate Barack Obama,
stars can lend credibility as well as help build a national audience. This
partnership, in which a black woman who was one of America's most powerful celebrities helped elect the first black president of the United States,
vividly illustrates the influence of the Stars for Freedom.

Many of the Stars for Freedom endorsed Obama as well, a continuation of their lifetime commitment to racial advancement. Even without the organizational infrastructure of the 1960s, many of the Stars for Freedom continued to engage in civil rights activism throughout their lifetimes, often focusing their efforts on global issues. Theodore Bikel, Ossie Davis, Ruby Dee, Dick Gregory, Sidney Poitier, and Harry Belafonte all engaged in antiapartheid campaigns against the South African government in the 1980s.[1] Belafonte co-organized the interracial "We Are the World" song project in 1985, which resulted in one of the best-selling singles of all time and raised over $63 million for humanitarian aid in Africa.[2] The Leading Six stayed in touch with many civil rights activists and supported their grassroots initiatives. When the former Congress of Racial Equality activist David Dennis launched the Algebra Project, a public education initiative in Mississippi in the 1990s, Belafonte and Poitier toured schools and helped raise money through community outreach. Gregory remained as unpredictable as ever. Dennis recalls that the comedian met him in Shreveport, Louisiana, on another matter, but when Gregory noticed shop owners selling drug paraphernalia in a black neighborhood, he held an impromptu sit-in at the stores. Gregory held demonstrations in a nearby park every day for months, staying in a tent, until he was satisfied that the neighborhood had cleaned up.[3] Starting in 1993, Ossie Davis and the actor Mike Farrell cochaired the Committee to Save Mumia Abu-Jamal, a former Black Panther who had been sentenced to death for killing a police officer in Philadelphia, in an effort to raise money to achieve a stay of execution and a new trial.[4] Today's celebrities, such as Jamie Foxx, who led the National Association for the Advancement of Colored People's (NAACP) Hurricane Katrina Relief Fund in 2005, have clearly been inspired by these stars' examples.

Although celebrity politicking has become the norm, and numerous African American artists have achieved megasuccess in the mass market, these trends have not resulted in a greater obligation to social activism by black stars. It is possible that their success has even inhibited activism, disconnecting them from real-life problems. Alternatively, their reluctance to get involved may evidence the same philosophical views shown by Nat King Cole and Sam Cooke, as illustrated by a recent flap between Belafonte and the hip hop icon Jay Z. After Belafonte accused the rapper of "turning his back on social activism," Jay Z responded that he provided more opportunities for African Americans as a businessman than as an activist, claiming that his "presence was charity." He addressed this issue on his multiplatinum album *Magna Carta Holy Grail* (2013) in the song "Nickels and Dimes." He rapped, "Mr. Day O, major fail / respect these youngins boy, it's my time now" and "You don't know all the shit I do for the homies."[5] By this way of thinking, the focus on political pressure in the 1960s may have been necessary, but now an economic focus achieves better results. Not to be cowed, Belafonte insisted that the lack of black stars willing to engage in the "political struggles concerning the issues of race, poverty, and the disenfranchisement of the poor is disappointingly evident."[6]

Many veteran activists agree. The former Student Nonviolent Coordinating Committee activist and NAACP chair Julian Bond finds it problematic that "movie stars always precede their victory statements at the Oscars by saying 'I want to thank the Academy' while the black performers who appear at the NAACP's Image Awards always say 'I want to thank God' but never the NAACP." He continues, "Black celebrities—with some exceptions—are notorious lax as donors to civil rights organizations."[7] Congressman John Lewis acknowledges this anemic activism but also says, "It is not entirely their fault." The current political climate is different, and, most importantly, many of the civil rights organizations of the 1960s are not in existence or are "shells of their former selves." Therefore, it is hard for celebrities to "relate to them."[8] It is also possible that some black stars do not agree with liberal remedies regarding racial issues and do not want to risk the same fate as Sammy Davis, Jr., after the Archie Bunker and Richard Nixon fracases. Since Davis's death in 1990, his effect on the civil rights movement has been greatly undervalued in the historical record, and overshadowed by the deferential side of his public image.

Bill Cosby's conservative cultural critique of the inner city has generated considerable pushback from African Americans and white liberals. In 2004, at an NAACP event honoring the fiftieth anniversary of *Brown v. Board of Education*, the comedian spoke passionately about the failures of the black community to take advantage of the changes brought on by the Supreme Court decision. "The lower economic and lower middle economic people are not holding their end in this deal," he argued, pointing to the need for responsible parenting in getting kids to school, demanding they speak proper English, encouraging chastity and proper dress, and avoiding violence and drug use. Saying "we cannot blame white people," he encouraged the audience to "take back the neighborhood."[9] Cosby continues to make similar statements to youth groups, civil rights organizations, and the media. To many observers, Cosby has "crossed a line" with his conservative analysis of the black inner city, much as Sammy Davis, Jr., did. Recent allegations that Cosby drugged and assaulted more than a dozen women, starting in the 1970s, has further undermined his credibility.

Disagreements about the appropriate screen images for African Americans and about black humor in mixed settings also continue. For example, the comedian Cedric Kyle, aka Cedric the Entertainer, joked about the civil rights leadership in several memorable scenes of the film *Barbershop* (2002). Playing a crotchety barber, he scoffs at Martin Luther King, Jr.'s promiscuity and says that other African Americans had refused to give up their bus seats in Montgomery before Rosa Parks's famous arrest, but that she got the attention due to her NAACP affiliation. The other characters protest this "disrespectful" attitude. "You better not never let Jesse Jackson hear you talkin'," one warns. Cedric replies, "Fuck Jesse Jackson!"[10] At the time of the film's release, Jackson demanded an apology, which he received, and requested that the filmmakers delete the scenes from future releases, which they refused. The controversy reignited when the film received multiple nominations at the NAACP annual Image Awards and the organization invited Cedric to host the event. Parks, who was to receive a special tribute, boycotted the show.[11] The Image Awards marks the NAACP's continuing efforts to monitor Hollywood, but the *Barbershop* controversy illustrated the ongoing challenges of balancing the cultural politics of its various constituents. Similar to the disputes regarding *Amos 'n' Andy*, the *Porgy and Bess* film, and the Blaxploitation trend, the NAACP was caught between the crosscurrents of those seeking job opportunities in Hollywood and cultural critics concerned about the consequences of negative portrayals. *Barbershop* made $75 million and spawned two sequels. Not only did it feature an almost entirely black cast, but the writer, producers, and director were all black filmmakers who believed they were promoting a multidimensional portrayal of African Americans. Although the practice of lampooning racial stereotypes was no longer as controversial, poking fun at civil rights heroes obviously proved inflammatory.

These ongoing disagreements about the appropriate roles for race artists in social and cultural politics should not detract from the progress African Americans have made in Hollywood, although the effect of the civil rights movement was not wholly felt until as late as 2001, when the Academy Awards were considered a "turning point." Denzel Washington and Halle Berry both won Oscars, and Poitier received a Lifetime Achievement Award. In his acceptance speech, Poitier said that when he arrived in Hollywood in 1949, his success "would have been considered almost impossible." He "respectfully shared" his award with the independent filmmakers and producers responsible for the message movies that launched his career. Since then, numerous African Americans have received Academy Award nominations, including Jamie Foxx and Forest Whitaker, who won best actor in a leading role; Morgan Freeman, best actor in a supporting role; and Jennifer Hudson, Mo'Nique, Octavia Spencer, and Lupita Nyong'o, best actress in a supporting role. Several actors, such as Washington, Freeman, Whoopi Goldberg, and Will Smith, have earned A-list status, and African Americans currently comprise about 15 percent of film roles. Still, black directors continue to face an uphill battle. Only three—John Singleton, Lee Daniels, and Steve McQueen—have been nominated for best directing in the history of the Academy Awards, and, as of 2008, about 5 percent of the directors of the one hundred top-grossing films were black.[12] They have brought a wide variety of stories to the screen from historical epics to romantic comedies to inner-city tales. The threat of stereotypes persists, whether in white-made films such as *The Blind Side* (2009) or films with black directors, such as Tyler Perry's *Madea* franchise, in which Perry dresses in drag to play a title character who is strangely reminiscent of a mammy. Actress Viola Davis explained her decision to play in 2011's *The Help* as a tribute to black women (including her mother and grandmother) who worked as domestics, but she recently announced, "I'll never play a maid again."[13]

The Stars for Freedom helped achieve integration and greater opportunities for blacks in Hollywood and in American life. For those hoping to pass down the mantle of the Left, the Belafonte/Jay-Z, Cosby, and *Barbershop* controversies all indicate that this goal has gone unrealized. Whatever disappointment this failure may have caused progressives, the Stars for Freedom paved the way for celebrity politics in the Cold War era and beyond, even as the changing nature of the civil rights movement has made the stars' roles less defined. They provided early, consistent support when it was a risk to their careers and blazed the path for today's stars. According to *Forbes*, seven of the top ten "most powerful celebrities" today are African Americans, including Jay Z, who is at number six on the list. While Belafonte may not know all that the rapper does for his "homies," it is imperative that we not forget what the Stars for Freedom did before Jay Z.

NOTES

NOTES TO PREFACE

1   Jamie Foxx in Stephanie Chan, "Jamie Foxx: Will Smith, Jay Z Should
     Be Next Civil Rights Leaders," video, *Hollywood Reporter*, August 28, 2013,
     accessed October 14, 2014, http://www.hollywoodreporter.com/news/
     jamie-foxx-will-smith-jay-616846.

2   "The SCLC Story in Words and Pictures," booklet (Atlanta, Georgia: SCLC,
     1964), 40–42, F. "M. L. King #3736," George Stevens Papers, Special Collec-
     tion, Margaret Herrick Library-Academy of Motion Pictures Arts and
     Sciences, Beverly Hills, California.

3   Brian Ward, *Just My Soul Responding: Rhythm and Blues, Black Consciousness,
     and Race Relations* (Berkeley: University of California Press, 1998), 293–303;
     and Ingrid Monson, *Freedom Sounds: Civil Rights Call Out to Jazz and Africa*
     (Oxford: Oxford University Press, 2007), 201–22.

4   Thomas Sugrue, *Sweet Land of Liberty: The Forgotten Struggle for Civil Rights
     in the North* (New York: Random House, 2008), xiv–xvi; and Martha Biondi,
     To Stand and Fight: The Struggle for Civil Rights in Postwar New York City (Cam-
     bridge, MA. And London: Harvard University Press, 2003), 279.

5   See also Douglas Flamming, *Bound for Freedom: Black Los Angeles in Jim Crow
     America* (Berkeley: University of California Press, 2005); Matthew J. Country-
     man, *Up South: Civil Rights and Black Power in Philadelphia* (Philadelphia: Uni-
     versity of Pennsylvania Press, 2006); Colleen Doody, *Detroit's Cold War: The
     Origins of Postwar Conservatism* (Urbana, Chicago, and Springfield: Univer-
     sity of Illinois Press, 2013); James R. Ralph, Jr. *Northern Protest: Martin Luther
     King, Jr., Chicago, and the Civil Rights Movement* (Cambridge, MA: Harvard
     University Press, 1993); and Daniel Martinez Hosang, *Racial Propositions:
     Ballot Initiatives and the Making of Postwar California* (University of California
     Press, 2010).

6   Sidney Poitier, *The Measure of a Man: A Spiritual Autobiography* (San Francisco:
     Harper, 2007), 108–9.

7   Gloria Richardson in Ward, *Just My Soul*, 314.

8   Stokley Carmichael, with Ekwrieme Michael Thelwell, *Ready for Revolution: The Life and Struggles of Stokley Carmichael (Kwame Ture)* (New York: Scribner, 2003), 256.

9   Richard deCordova, *Picture Personalities: The Emergence of the Star System in America* (Urbana: University of Illinois Press, 1990), 51–81; Charles L. Ponce de Leon, *Self Exposure: Human Interest Journalism and the Emergence of Celebrity in America, 1890–1940* (Chapel Hill: University of North Carolina Press, 2002), 42–43; and Chris Rojek, *Celebrity* (London: Reaktion Books, 2001), 189.

10   Donald Bogle, *Toms, Coons, Mulattoes, Mammies, and Bucks: An Interpretive History of Blacks in American Films* (New York: Continuum, 2001), 3–18; and Joshua Gamson, *Claims to Fame: Celebrity in Contemporary America* (Berkeley: University of California Press, 1994), 18.

11   Thomas Cripps, *Slow Fade to Black: The Negro in American Film, 1900–1942* (New York: Oxford University Press, 1977), 8; and Aram Goudsouzian, *Sidney Poitier: Man, Actor, Icon* (Chapel Hill: University of North Carolina Press, 2004), 67.

12   Jill Watts, *Hattie McDaniel: Black Ambition, White Hollywood* (New York: Amistad, 2005), 223–25.

13   Arthur Knight, "Star Dancers: African-American Constructions of Stardom, 1925–60," in *Classic Hollywood, Classic Whiteness*, ed. Daniel Bernardi (Minneapolis and London: University of Minnesota Press, 2001), 402–5.

14   Walter White in Watts, *Hattie*, 227.

15   James Gavin, *Stormy Weather: The Life of Lena Horne* (New York: Atria Books, 2009), 93–105.

16   "White Answers Stars' Blast at 'Interference,'" *Pittsburgh Courier*, March 2, 1946, 17; and Watts, *Hattie*, 223.

17   Norman Corwin, *Trivializing America: The Triumph of Mediocrity* (Secaucus, NJ: Carol Publishing Company, 1986); Neil Postman, *Amusing Ourselves to Death* (New York: Penguin, 2005); and Darrel M. West and John Orman, *Celebrity Politics* (Upper Saddle River, New Jersey: Prentice Hall, 2003), 119.

18   Robert D. Benford and Scott A. Hunt, "Dramaturgy and Social Movements: The Social Construction and Communication of Power," *Sociological Inquiry* 62, no. 1 (Feb. 1992): 36–55; Steven J. Ross, *Hollywood Left and Right: How Movie Stars Shaped American Politics* (Oxford University Press, 2011); Donald T. Critchlow, *When Hollywood Was Right* (Cambridge University Press, 2013); Kathryn Cramer Brownell, *Showbiz Politics: Hollywood in American Political Life* (Chapel Hill: University of North Carolina Press, 2014); and Rojek, *Celebrity*, 198.

NOTES TO CHAPTER 1

Epigraph: Diahann Carroll, *The Legs Are the Last to Go* (New York: Amistad, 2008), 117.

1   Izzy Rowe, "Izzy Rowe's Notebook," *Daily Defender*, October 31, 1959, 22, F. "Porgy Publicity #1636," Samuel Goldwyn Papers, Special Collections, Margaret Herrick Library–Academy of Motion Pictures Arts and Sciences, Beverly

Hills, California (hereafter referred to as MHL-AMPAS); James Baldwin, "On Catfish Row: *Porgy and Bess* in the Movies," *Commentary* 28 (Sept. 1959): 247–48; and Sidney Poitier in Frederic Morton, "The Audacity of Sidney Poitier," *Holiday,* June 1961, 105, Core Collection–Sidney Poitier, MHL-AMPAS.

2   George H. Roeder, Jr., *The Censored War: American Visual Experience during World War II* (New Haven: Yale University Press, 1993), 47.

3   John Nickel, "Disabling African-American Men: Liberalism and Race Message Films," *Cinema Journal* 44, no. 1 (Fall 2004): 25.

4   Thomas Cripps and David Culbert, "*The Negro Soldier* (1944): Film Propaganda in Black and White," *Hollywood as Historian: American Film in a Cultural Context,* ed. Peter C. Rollins (Lexington: University Press of Kentucky, 1983), 132.

5   Labor Code Section 2855, known as "the seven-year rule," is also referred to as the de Havilland rule for the actress Olivia de Havilland, who successfully sued Warner Brothers after the studio repeatedly extended her contract after suspending her for rejecting the roles it demanded of her.

6   Joshua Gamson, *Claims to Fame: Celebrity in Contemporary America* (Berkeley: University of California Press, 1994), 41; and Richard Dyer Maccann, "Independence, with a Vengeance," *Film Quarterly* 15, no. 4 (Summer 1962): 15.

7   Donald Critchlow and Emilie Raymond, eds., *Hollywood and Politics: A Sourcebook* (New York: Routlege, 2009), 200.

8   Jon Lewis, *American Film: A History* (New York: W. W. Norton and Company, 2008), 195–97.

9   Thomas Cripps, *Making Movies Black: The Hollywood Message Movie from World War II to the Civil Rights Era* (New York: Oxford University Press, 1993), 215–20.

10   "$20,000 Box Office Payoff for H'Wood Negro—Tolerance Pix," *Variety,* November 30, 1949, 1, 18, in Nickel, "Disabling African-American Men," 25.

11   Leonard Courtney Archer, *Black Images in American Theater: NAACP Protest Campaigns—Stage, Screen, Radio and Television* (Brooklyn: Pageant-Poseidon, 1973), 19 and 24; and Aram Goudsouzian, *Sidney Poitier: Man, Actor, Icon* (Chapel Hill: University of North Carolina Press, 2004), 43–46.

12   Sidney Poitier in Henry Louis Gates, Jr., "Belafonte's Balancing Act," *New Yorker,* combined issue, August 26, 1996, and September 2, 1996, 134.

13   Sidney Poitier in Tom Prideaux, "Poitier's Search for the Right Corner," *Life,* April 27, 1959, 142.

14   Goudsouzian, *Sidney Poitier,* 70.

15   Ossie Davis and Ruby Dee, *With Ossie and Ruby: In This Life Together* (New York: William Morrow and Company, 1988), 21–45, 73–87.

16   Ibid., 57–65, 91–94.

17   Ibid., 164, 199.

18   Harry Belafonte in Eleanor Harris, "The Stormy Success of Harry Belafonte," *Redbook Magazine,* May 1958, 47, Core Collection–Harry Belafonte, MHL-AMPAS.

19   Marguerite Byrd in Harris, "Stormy Success of Harry Belafonte," 102.

20 Genia Fogelson, *Belafonte* (Los Angeles: Holloway House, 1980), 35.

21 Harris, "Stormy Success of Harry Belafonte," 103.

22 Fogelson, *Belafonte*, 54.

23 Cripps, *Making Movies Black*, 244; and Donald Bogle, *Toms, Coons, Mulattoes, Mammies, and Bucks: An Interpretive History of Blacks in American Films* (New York: Continuum, 2001), 179.

24 Dorothy Dandridge and Earl Conrad, *Everything and Nothing: The Dorothy Dandridge Tragedy* (New York: Abelard-Schuman, 1970), 121.

25 Foster Hirsch, *Otto Preminger: The Man Who Would Be King* (New York: Knopf, 2007), 169–70.

26 Otto Preminger, *Preminger: An Autobiography* (Garden City, NY: Doubleday, 1977), 135.

27 Hirsch, *Otto Preminger*, 213.

28 Anna Everett, *Returning the Gaze: A Genealogy of Black Film Criticism, 1909–1949* (Durham, NC: Duke University Press, 2001), 303.

29 Brock Peters in Hirsch, *Otto Preminger*, 214.

30 Dandridge and Conrad, *Everything and Nothing*, 158; and Hirsch, *Otto Preminger*, 218–19.

31 John H. Johnson, *Succeeding Against the Odds* (New York: Warner Books, 1989), 160.

32 Hirsch, *Otto Preminger*, 222

33 "A New Beauty for Bizet," *Life*, November 1, 1954, 87–90.

34 Marguerite H. Rippy, "Commodity, Tragedy, Desire: Female Sexuality and Blackness in the Iconography of Dorothy Dandridge," in *Classic Hollywood, Classic Whiteness*, ed. Daniel Bernadi (Minneapolis: University of Minnesota Press, 2001), 179–201.

35 Donald Bogle, *Brown Sugar: Eighty Years of America's Black Female Superstars* (New York: Harmony Books, 1980), 130–33; and Steven J. Ross, *Hollywood Left and Right: How Movie Stars Shaped American Politics* (Oxford: Oxford University Press, 2011), 196.

36 Martha Biondi, *To Stand and Fight: The Struggle for Civil Rights in Postwar New York City* (Cambridge, MA: Harvard University Press, 2003), 67.

37 Davis and Dee, *With Ossie and Ruby*, 232–33; Sidney Poitier in Goudsouzian, *Sidney Poitier*, 88.

38 Emilie Raymond, *'From My Cold, Dead Hands': Charlton Heston and American Politics* (Lexington: University Press of Kentucky, 2006), 104.

39 Paul Robeson in David Falkner, *Great Time Coming: The Life of Jackie Robinson, from Baseball to Birmingham* (New York: Touchstone Books, 1995), 195–96.

40 "Hearings Regarding Communist Infiltration of Minority Groups—Part I and II," *Hearings Before the Committee on Un-American Activities House of Representatives*, 81st Cong., 1st sess., July 13, 14, and 18, 1949, 479–83; Falkner, *Great Time Coming*, 198–202; "Hearings Regarding Communist Infiltration," 516.

41 Goudsouzian, *Sidney Poitier*, 89; and Davis and Dee, *With Ossie and Ruby*, 232–33.

42   Poitier, *Measure of a Man*, 88–92.

43   Goudsouzian, *Sidney Poitier*, 115–17.

44   Ossie Davis, *Life Lit by Some Large Vision: Selected Speeches and Writings* (New York: Atria Books, 2006), 3–7, 42–44; and Davis and Dee, *With Ossie and Ruby*, 276–78.

45   *Counterattack* 8, no. 2 (Jan. 8, 1954), 4; *Counterattack* 8, no. 7 (Feb. 12, 1954), 4; and Harry Belafonte in *Scandalize My Name: Stories from the Blacklist*, ed. Doug Rossini (Thousand Oaks, CA: Urban Works Entertainment, 1999).

46   DuBose Heyward, *Porgy* (New York: George H. Doran Company, 1925).

47   Hollis Alpert, *The Life and Times of Porgy and Bess: The Story of an American Classic* (New York: Alfred A. Knopf, 1990), 187–88

48   Ibid., 245, 258, 260.

49   Sammy Davis, Jr., *Yes, I Can: The Story of Sammy Davis, Jr.* (New York: Farrar, Straus and Giroux, 1965), 72.

50   Wil Haygood, *In Black and White: The Life of Sammy Davis, Jr.* (New York: Alfred A. Knopf, 2003), 125, 196, 278.

51   Biondi, *To Stand*, 186–90.

52   Haygood, *In Black and White*, 235.

53   Davis, *Yes, I Can*, 151, 408–9.

54   Sammy Davis, Jr., *Hollywood in a Suitcase* (New York: William Morrow and Company, 1980), 53.

55   Alpert, *Porgy and Bess*, 261.

56   Harry Belafonte in Arnold Hirsch, "Belafonte Blasts 'Porgy,'" *Detroit Times*, October 16, 1959, 24, F. "Porgy Publicity #1636," Samuel Goldwyn Papers, Special Collections, MHL-AMPAS.

57   Harry Belafonte in "Harry Belafonte a Tough Critic," *Variety Weekly*, July 10, 1957, Core Collection–Harry Belafonte, MHL-AMPAS.

58   Fogelson, *Belafonte*, 114.

59   Harry Belafonte in "Harry Belafonte a Tough Critic."

60   Harry Belafonte in Richard W. Nason, "Evaluating the 'Odds': Harry Belafonte Tries Broad Racial Approach in Locally Made Feature," *New York Times*, March 15, 1959, X7; and Harry Belafonte in Jesse Zunser, "Young Man in a Hurry: Harry Belafonte Talks about Movies—Tells Why He Wants to Make His Own," *Cue Magazine*, April 25, 1959, 19, Core Collection–Harry Belafonte, MHL-AMPAS.

61   Gondsouzian, *Poitier*, 146–48.

62   Alpert, *Porgy and Bess*, 261.

63   Melvin Patrick Ely, *The Adventures of Amos 'n' Andy: A Social History of an American Phenomenon* (New York: Free Press, 1991), 213–40.

64   "Statement to Time Magazine by Roy Wilkins, November 22, 1957," F. "NAACP, Wilkins, Roy, 1957–58, 1964–64," Box 4, Jackie Robinson Papers, Manuscript Division, Library of Congress.

65   Dick Williams, "Film Career Widens for Sammy Davis, Jr." *L.A. Mirror News*, November 3, 1958, 4, Core Collection–Sammy Davis, Jr., MHL-AMPAS.

66 Haygood, *In Black and White*, 285–86.

67 Alpert, *Porgy and Bess*, 261.

68 Letter from Samuel Goldwyn to Sammy Davis, December 22, 1958, F. "Porgy Correspondence #1495," Samuel Goldwyn Papers, Special Collection, MHL-AMPAS.

69 Pearl Bailey, *The Raw Pearl* (New York: Harcourt, Brace & World, 1968), 77.

70 Diahann Carroll in *Porgy and Bess: An American Voice,* dir. Nigel Noble (Princeton, NJ: Films for the Humanities and Sciences, 1999).

71 Dandridge and Conrad, *Everything and Nothing*, 187–88.

72 Goudsouzian, *Sidney Poitier*, 117.

73 Letter from Lillian Schary Small to Samuel Goldwyn, May 15, 1957, F. "Porgy Correspondence #1501," Samuel Goldwyn Papers, Special Collection, MHL-AMPAS.

74 Letter from Lillian S. Small to Samuel Goldwyn, October 30, 1957, F. "Porgy Production Memoranda #1567," Samuel Goldwyn Papers, Special Collection, MHL-AMPAS.

75 Letter from Lillian S. Small to Sidney Poitier, November 11, 1957, F. "Porgy Correspondence #1501," Samuel Goldwyn Papers, Special Collection, MHL-AMPAS.

76 Leonard Lyons, "The Lyons Den," *New York Post,* November 21, 1957, M8, F. "Porgy Publicity #1574," Samuel Goldwyn Papers, Special Collection, MHL-AMPAS.

77 Poitier, *This Life*, 203–4.

78 Ibid., 203–10.

79 Dandridge and Conrad, *Everything and Nothing*, 187–88.

80 Poitier, *This Life*, 210.

81 Press Conference with Samuel Goldwyn and Sidney Poitier, December 10, 1957, F. "Porgy Production Memoranda #1567," Samuel Goldwyn Papers, Special Collection, MHL-AMPAS.

82 Donald Bogle, *Dorothy Dandridge: A Biography* (New York: Amistad, 1997), 404.

83 Contracts between Sidney Poitier, Dorothy Dandridge, Sammy Davis, and Pearl Bailey and Samuel Goldwyn Productions for *Porgy and Bess,* F. "Porgy Legal #1548," Samuel Goldwyn Papers, Special Collection, MHL-AMPAS.

84 Poitier, *This Life*, 211.

85 Gates, "Belafonte's Balancing Act," 139.

86 Sidney Poitier, interview with Hedda Hopper, May 23, 1958, 1, Hedda Hopper Papers, Special Collection, MHL-AMPAS.

87 "Statement Issued by Screen Directors Guild," July–August 1958, F. "Porgy Production Memoranda #1569," Samuel Goldwyn Papers, Special Collection, MHL-AMPAS.

88 Press release by Leigh Whipper, n.d. (c. August 5, 1958), F. "Porgy Correspondence #1502," Samuel Goldwyn Papers, Special Collection, MHL-AMPAS.

89 Press release by Sammy Davis, Pearl Bailey, Brock Peters, and Loren Miller,

August 6, 1958, F. "Porgy Correspondence #1502," Samuel Goldwyn Papers, Special Collection, MHL-AMPAS; and Bailey, *Raw Pearl*, 79.

90   Telegram from Noble Sissle to Samuel Goldwyn, August 13, 1958, F. "Porgy Correspondence #1502," Samuel Goldwyn Papers, Special Collection, MHL-AMPAS; and Joseph Horowitz, *"On My Way": The Untold Story of Rouben Mamoulian, George Gershwin, and Porgy and Bess* (New York: W. W. Norton and Company, 2013), 189–92.

91   Poitier, *This Life*, 218

92   Alpert, *Porgy and Bess*, 274.

93   Goudsouzian, *Sidney Poitier*, 163.

94   Bogle, *Dorothy Dandridge*, 420.

95   Letter from N. Richard Nash to Samuel Goldwyn, February 8, 1958, F. "Porgy Production Memorandum #1569," Samuel Goldwyn Papers, Special Collection, MHL-AMPAS.

96   Telegram from Otto Preminger to Samuel Goldwyn, September 27, 1958, F. "Porgy Production Memorandum #1567," Samuel Goldwyn Papers, Special Collection, MHL-AMPAS.

97   "Porgy, Bess Film Presents Problems," *Dayton Daily News,* January 26, 1958, sect. 2, p. 11, F. "Porgy Publicity #1574," Samuel Goldwyn Papers, Special Collection, MHL-AMPAS.

98   Ellen Noonan, *The Strange Career of Porgy and Bess: Race, Culture, and America's Most Famous Opera* (Chapel Hill: University of North Carolina Press, 2012), 263; and Carol Eastman, *The Search for Sam Goldwyn* (New York: William Morrow and Company, 1976), 278–79.

99   Porgy Second Revised Screenplay, February 17, 1958, F. "Porgy Second Revised Screenplay, #1470," pp. 13 and 43, Samuel Goldwyn Papers, Special Collection, MHL-AMPAS.

100   Morton, "Audacity of Poitier," 106.

101   Williams, "Film Career Widens," 4.

102   "Pearl Wins Her Battle to Strip 'Porgy' of Dialect," *Daily Defender,* September 4, 1958, 4, F. "Porgy Publicity #1591," Samuel Goldwyn Papers, Special Collection, MHL-AMPAS.

103   Davis says, "There's no Uncle Tom. The dialogue is no more offensive than Sidney's is in *The Defiant Ones*"'; Williams, "Film Career Widens," 4. Nash says that Poitier complained to him that "some of the characters seemed dumb"; Eastman, *Search for Sam Goldwyn*, 280.

104   See Porgy Fourth Revised Screenplay, June 12, 1958, F. "Porgy Fourth Revised Screenplay #1491," pp. 6 and 31–48, Samuel Goldwyn Papers, Special Collection, MHL-AMPAS; and *Porgy and Bess*, Dir. Otto Preminger, Columbia Pictures, 1959, Film.

105   See Porgy Fourth Revised Screenplay, June 12, 1958, F. "Porgy Fourth Revised Screenplay #1491," p. 88, Samuel Goldwyn Papers, Special Collection, MHL-AMPAS; and *Porgy and Bess* film.

106   See Porgy Fourth Revised Screenplay, June 12, 1958, F. "Porgy Fourth Revised

Screenplay #1491," p. 28, Samuel Goldwyn Papers, Special Collection, MHL-AMPAS; and *Porgy and Bess* film.

107 Letter from N. Richard Nash to Samuel Goldwyn, January 17, 1958, F. "Porgy Correspondence #1500," Samuel Goldwyn Papers, Special Collection, MHL-AMPAS.

108 See Porgy Fourth Revised Screenplay, June 12, 1958, F. "Porgy Fourth Revised Screenplay #1491," Samuel Goldwyn Papers, Special Collection, MHL-AMPAS; and *Porgy and Bess* film.

109 Bailey, *Raw Pearl*, 77.

110 Irene Scharaff in A. Scott Berg, *Goldwyn: A Biography* (New York: Knopf, 1989) 482.

111 Bogle, *Dorothy Dandridge*, 407.

112 Porgy First Draft Screenplay, December 24, 1957, F. "Porgy First Draft Screenplay #1466," p. 9, Samuel Goldwyn Papers, Special Collection, MHL-AMPAS.

113 Porgy Third Revised Screenplay, February 28, 1958, F. "Porgy Third Revised Screenplay #1481," p. 44, Samuel Goldwyn Papers, Special Collection, MHL-AMPAS.

114 Davis, *Hollywood in a Suitcase*, 55–57.

115 "A Poker Hand Changed the Destiny of Clarence Muse," *Philadelphia Independent,* January 31, 1959, 16.

116 Noonan notes Goldwyn's "thorough" publicity and promotional efforts in the black press, and Eastman characterizes Goldwyn's efforts as "a promotional orgy." Noonan, *Strange Career*, 269; and Eastman, *Search for Sam Goldwyn*, 281.

117 "American Classic Sings Anew," *Life* 46 (Jun. 15, 1959: 70–82): 70–82.

118 Noonan, *Strange Career*, 269.

119 *Porgy and Bess* opening, New York City, Hearst Vault Material, June 24, 1959, University of California–Los Angeles Film and Television Archive.

120 "Negro Beauties Are Next in Hollywood Vogue," *Pittsburgh Courier*, n.d. (c. June 1959), 23, F. "Porgy Publicity #1636," Samuel Goldwyn Papers, Special Collection, MHL-AMPAS.

121 Leonard Lyons, "Lyons Den," *Daily Defender,* March 11, 1959, 5, F. "Porgy Publicity #1637," Samuel Goldwyn Papers, Special Collection, MHL-AMPAS.

122 "*Porgy and Bess* More Glamorous as Film; Misses Personalized Singing," *Daily Defender,* July 22, 1959, 18, F. "Porgy Publicity #1637," Samuel Goldwyn Papers, Special Collection, MHL-AMPAS.

123 "And Nuttin's Plenty for Me," *Commonweal* 70 (Aug. 14, 1959): 424; and "The New Pictures," *Time* 74 (July 6, 1959): 57.

124 Ed Hocura, "A Sleeper Misses Its Mark but a Negro Comes Through," *Hamilton Spectator,* August 24, 1959, 49, F. "Porgy Publicity #1628"; and "'Porgy N Bess' Film Near $2 Million Net," *Daily Defender,* October 21, 1959, 7, F. "Porgy Publicity #1636," Samuel Goldwyn Papers, Special Collection, MHL-AMPAS.

125 "Izzy Rowe's Notebook: The Goldwyn I Met," *Pittsburgh Courier,* October 31, 1959, 22, F. "Porgy Publicity #1636"; "*Porgy and Bess* Stars Worthy of Nomination," *California Eagle,* November 19, 1959, 11, F. "Porgy Publicity #1636";

"*Porgy and Bess* Film Near $2 Million Net," *Daily Defender,* October 21, 1959, 17, F. "Porgy Publicity #1636"; and "*Porgy and Bess* Topped Sepia Participation in Films Last Season," *Daily Defender,* December 26, 1959, 19, F. "Porgy Publicity #1636," Samuel Goldwyn Papers, Special Collection, MHL-AMPAS.

126 "Two Preminger Pictures," *New Republic* 141 (Jul. 13, 1959): 22; and "The New Pictures," *Time* 74 (Jul. 6, 1959): 57.

127 "'Porgy and Bess' Dustily Out of Focus, Tribune Reader Finds," *Los Angeles Tribune,* October 9, 1959, 11, F. "Porgy Publicity #1636," Samuel Goldwyn Papers, Special Collection, MHL-AMPAS.

128 Hazel A. Washington, "This Is Hollywood," *Daily Defender,* August 26, 1958, 17, F. "Porgy Publicity #1591," Samuel Goldwyn Papers, Special Collection, MHL-AMPAS.

129 "New Pictures," *Time,* 57.

130 Robert Hatch, "Films," *Nation* 189 (July 4, 1959): 19.

131 Dandridge and Conrad, *Everything and Nothing,* 189.

132 Baldwin, "On Catfish Row," 247–48.

133 Diahann Carroll and Darlene Clark Hine in *Porgy and Bess: An American Voice.*

134 Philip T. Harteng, "The Screen: 'Nuttin's Plenty For Me,'" *Commonweal* 70 (August 14, 1959): 425.

135 Haygood, *In Black and White,* 291.

136 Peters in Hirsch, *Otto Preminger,* 302.

137 Rippy, "Commodity," 190–200; and Knight, "Star Dances," 400–406.

NOTES TO CHAPTER 2

Sammy Davis, Jr., in Dick Gregory, *Up from Nigger* (New York: Stein and Day, 1976), 73.

1 Douglas Flamming, *Bound for Freedom: Black Los Angeles in Jim Crow America* (Berkeley: University of California Press, 2005), 153, 175, 349–50.

2 Wil Haygood, *In Black and White: The Life of Sammy Davis, Jr.* (New York: Alfred A. Knopf, 2003), 177; and Sammy Davis, Jr., *Yes, I Can: The Story of Sammy Davis, Jr.* (New York: Farrar, Straus and Giroux, 1965), 185 and 278.

3 See "Jerry Lewis Surprises Sammy Davis, Jr.," Dailymotion, accessed September 10, 2009, http://www.dailymotion.com/video/x83n75_jerry-lewis-surprises-sammy-davis-j_music.

4 Haygood, *In Black and White,* 155.

5 Sammy Davis, Jr., in Alex Haley, "*Playboy* Interview: Sammy Davis, Jr.," *Playboy* (Dec. 1966): 118.

6 Tina Sinatra, with Jeff Coplon, *My Father's Daughter: A Memoir* (New York: Simon and Schuster, 2000), 95.

7 Davis, *Yes, I Can,* 214.

8 Ibid., 186, 214.

9 Sammy Davis, Jr., *Why Me? The Sammy Davis, Jr., Story* (New York: Farrar, Straus and Giroux, 1989), 195.

10 Haygood, *In Black and White,* 185.

11   Davis, *Why Me?*, 195.

12   Christine Acham, *Revolution Televised: Prime Time and the Struggle for Black Power* (Minneapolis: University of Minnesota Press, 2004), 20; and J. Fred MacDonald, *Blacks and White TV: Afro-Americans in Television since 1948* (Chicago: Nelson-Hall Publishers, 1983), 11–21 and 47.

13   "Ed Sullivan Leads TV Blast at Gov. Talmadge," *Pittsburgh Courier*, January 19, 1952, 13.

14   Tino Balio, *Hollywood in the Age of Television* (Boston: Unwin Hyman, 1990), 30–32; and Christopher Anderson, *Hollywood TV: The Studio System in the Fifties* (Austin: University of Texas Press, 1994), 2–4.

15   In 1955, Interstate Television syndicated the *Our Gang* film short series, produced by Hal Roach between 1927 and 1938, and renamed the series *The Little Rascals*. It remained on television, on various channels, for the next three decades. MacDonald, *Blacks and White TV*, 21–31.

16   *The Steve Allen Show*, May 5, 1957, and *The Colgate Comedy Hour: Eddie Cantor Show*, March 16, 1952, Paley Center for Media, New York (hereafter referred to as PCM).

17   Sammy Davis, Jr., interview, *Edward R. Murrow: The Best of Person to Person*, November 4, 1955, disc 3, CBS Broadcasting 2006, University of California–Los Angeles Film and Television Archive (hereafter referred to as UCLA-FTA).

18   *What's My Line?*, May 26, 1957, UCLA-FTA.

19   Gerald Early, ed., *The Sammy Davis, Jr., Reader* (New York: Farrar, Straus and Giroux, 2001), 205–6.

20   Davis, *Yes, I Can*, 259.

21   Ibid., 329, 372.

22   Ibid., 440.

23   Chris Rojek, *Frank Sinatra* (Cambridge, MA: Polity Press, 2004), 121.

24   Davis, *Why Me?*, 54.

25   MacDonald, *Blacks and White TV*, 52.

26   Soon thereafter, she abandoned Hollywood for Europe. Dwayne Mack, "Hazel Scott: A Career Curtailed," *Journal of African American History* 91 no. 2 (Spring 2006): 153–70.

27   "Studio Space Out, WOR-TV Axes 'Harlem Detective,'" *Pittsburgh Courier*, June 23, 1954, 8.

28   "Sammy Davis, Jr., Says Satchmo No Spokesman," *Pittsburgh Courier*, October 12, 1957, in Early, *Sammy Davis, Jr., Reader*, 231–33.

29   Frank Sinatra in "Sammy Davis," *Life*, November 13, 1964, 89.

30   Davis, *Yes, I Can*, 184.

31   Haygood, *In Black and White*, 252.

32   Ibid., 382; and Gerald Early, *This Is Where I Came In: Black America in the 1960s* (Lincoln: University of Nebraska Press, 2003), 45.

33   Taylor Branch, *Parting the Waters: America in the King Years, 1954–63* (New York: Simon and Schuster, 1988), 186, 222.

34   "NAACP Uneasy Over Rights Unit," *New York Times,* January 7, 1958, A22; and Branch, *Parting the Waters,* 222.

35   "Memorandum from Mr. Current to Mr. Wilkins, April 6, 1956," F. "Civil Rights, Madison Square Garden Rally, 1956," III: A64, NAACP Papers, Manuscripts Division, Library of Congress (hereafter referred to as MD-LOC).

36   Letter from Roy Wilkins to "NAACP Member," April 18, 1956; and flyer, "Salute and Support the Heroes of the South!" F. "Civil Rights, Madison Square Garden Rally, 1956," III: A64, NAACP Papers, MD-LOC.

37   Nelson Arsenault, *Freedom Rides: 1961 and the Struggle for Racial Justice* (Oxford: Oxford University Press, 2006), 75.

38   Adam Fairclough, *To Redeem the Soul of America: The Southern Christian Leadership Conference and Martin Luther King, Jr.* (Athens: University of Georgia Press, 1987), 31–32.

39   Barry Gray column, June 7, 1956, *New York Post*, n.p., F. "Civil Rights, Madison Square Garden Rally, 1956," III: A64, NAACP Papers, MD-LOC.

40   Letter from Henry Lee Moon to Barry Gray, June 8, 1956, F. "Civil Rights, Madison Square Garden Rally, 1956," III: A64, NAACP Papers, MD-LOC.

41   FBI File, Sammy Davis, Jr., 100-450712 (hereafter referred to as Davis FBI File).

42   Ossie Davis and Ruby Dee, *With Ossie and Ruby: In This Life Together* (New York: William Morrow and Company, 1998), 249–51.

43   Branch, *Parting the Waters,* 185.

44   August Meier and John H. Bracey, Jr., "The NAACP as a Reform Movement, 1909–1965: 'To Reach the Conscience of America,'" *Journal of Southern History* 59, no. 1 (Feb. 1993): 22.

45   Minnie Finch, *The NAACP: Its Fight for Justice* (Mituchen, NJ: Scarecrow Press, 1981), 202.

46   Pamphlet, c. 1957, F. "Benefits, General, 1956–1963," General Office Files, III: A44, NAACP Papers, MD-LOC.

47   Letter from Sammy Davis, Jr., c. 1957, F. "Benefits, Apollo," III: A44, NAACP Papers, MD-LOC.

48   Letter from Marion R. Stewart (of the Lifetime Membership Campaign) to Sammy Davis, Jr., July 25, 1957, F. "Benefits, Apollo Theatre Benefit, 1957–58," III: A44, NAACP Papers, MD-LOC.

49   See www.actorsequity.org/Benefits/theatreauthority.asp, accessed October 9, 2014.

50   Memos from "Ellen" to Roy Wilkins, February 17, 1958, and February 20, 1958, F. "Benefits, Apollo Theatre Benefit, 1957–58," III: A44, NAACP Papers, MD-LOC.

51   "Sidney Poitier Begins Work on Porgy, Bess Pix," *Chicago Daily Defender,* April 8, 1958, 18.

52   "Sammy Davis and Trio in Benefit for NAACP," NAACP press release, April 10, 1958, F. "Benefits, Apollo," III: A44, NAACP Papers, MD-LOC.

53 "Apollo Theatre Benefit" financial report, n.d. (c. May 27, 1958), F. "Benefits, Apollo," III: A44, NAACP Papers, MD-LOC.

54 "Memorandum from Richard W. McClain to Herbert Hill Regarding Apollo Theatre Benefit, May 27, 1958," F. "Benefits, Apollo," III: A44, NAACP Papers, MD-LOC.

55 See letter from V. Jean Fleming (secretary to Sammy Davis, Jr.) to Roy Wilkins, July 24, 1958, and letter from John A. Morsell (assistant to Roy Wilkins), August 18, 1958, F. "Benefits, Apollo," III: A44, NAACP Papers, MD-LOC.

56 Letter from Frank Schiffman to Mr. McClain [of NAACP], May 20, 1958, F. "Benefits, Apollo," III: A44, NAACP Papers, MD-LOC.

57 Citation for Sammy Davis, Jr., April 17, 1958, F. "Davis, Sammy, Jr., 1958–65," III: A94, NAACP Papers, MD-LOC.

58 Letter from John A. Morsell (assistant to Roy Wilkins) to Sammy Davis, Jr., April 25, 1958, F. "Benefits, General," 1956–63, III: A44, NAACP Papers, MD-LOC.

59 Haygood, *In Black and White*, 381–82.

60 Al Monroe, "So They Say," *Chicago Daily Defender,* February 17, 1959, 18.

61 "Mission," *Dick Powell's Zane Grey Theatre*, CBS, November 12, 1959, PCM.

62 "Blue Boss and Willie Shay," *Lawman*, March 12, 1961, UCLA-FTA.

63 Early, *This Is Where I Came In*, 45.

64 Haygood, *In Black and White*, 151.

65 Ibid., 243–44.

66 Davis FBI File.

67 Davis, *Why Me?*, 107.

68 Sociologist Chris Rojek argues, "In the 1950s and early 1960s, there is no parallel for a star of Sinatra's stature working over a prolonged period on stage, film, and recordings with a person of color. Sinatra's example in fostering multiracial attitudes should not be underestimated." Rojek, *Frank Sinatra*, 138.

69 Gay Talese, "Frank Sinatra Has a Cold," in *Smiling Through the Apocalypse: Esquire's History of the Sixties*, ed. Harold Hayes (New York: McCall Publishing Company, 1969), 303.

70 See *The Rat Pack's Las Vegas*, White Star Studio, 2002.

71 Ibid.

72 Haygood, *In Black and White*, 301.

73 Davis, *Why Me?*, 110–11.

74 Davis, *Yes, I Can*, 538.

75 See *Life* Magazine, June 20, 1960, 42, for coverage of their engagement, and November 28, 1960, 117–19, for coverage of their wedding.

76 Haygood, *In Black and White*, 299–300.

77 Davis, *Yes, I Can*, 579.

78 Davis, *Why Me?*, 121.

79 Ibid., 117.

80   Davis in Haley, "*Playboy* interview," 124.

81   Jack Carter in Haygood, *In Black and White*, 413–14.

82   Sinatra, *My Father's Daughter*, 96.

83   Rojek, *Frank Sinatra*, 138.

84   Donald Bogle, "*A Man Called Adam* and the Son of Sunshine Sammy," in Early, *Sammy Davis, Jr., Reader*, 382.

85   Davis, *Why Me?*, 148.

86   Sammy Davis, Jr., in Early, *Sammy Davis, Jr., Reader*, 33.

87   Shirley Rhodes in Haygood, *In Black and White*, 303.

88   *The Frank Sinatra Timex Show*, May 12, 1960, UCLA-FTA.

89   *Ocean's 11*, dir. Lewis Milestone, 1960.

90   Rojek, *Frank Sinatra*, 127; Mike Mallowe, "The Selling of Sinatra," in *The Frank Sinatra Reader*, ed. Steven Petkov and Leonard Mustazza (New York: Oxford University Press, 1995), 205; Martha Weinman Lear, "The Bobby Sox Have Wilted, but the Memory Remains Fresh," in Petkov and Mustazza, *Sinatra Reader*, 49; and James Wolcott, "When They Were Kings," in Early, *Sammy Davis, Jr,. Reader*, 192.

91   Letter from C. Chuck Williams to Hedda Hopper, January 13, 1960, F. "Sammy Davis, Jr.,#513," Hedda Hopper Collection, Margaret Herrick Library-Academy of Motion Pictures Arts and Sciences, Beverly Hills, California.

92   Brown and Byrnes were both associates of the Rat Pack.

93   "Sammy Davis, Jr., Brought Friends to Chicago Jazz Bash," *Pittsburgh Courier*, September 10, 1960, 23. See also Don DeMichael, "Urban League 'Festival,'" *Downbeat* 27, October 13, 1960, 20.

94   Wyatt Tee Walker, interview with the author, Chester, Virginia, August 6, 2014; and Fairclough, *To Redeem the Soul*, 58. See also Branch, *Parting the Waters*, 327.

95   Harry Belafonte in Haygood, *In Black and White*, 404.

96   Davis, *Why Me?*, 134.

97   "Tribute to Dr. King," *New York Times*, January 6, 1961, 12.

98   Harry Belafonte in "A Tribute to the Rev. Martin Luther King, Jr.," *Ebony* (Apr. 1961): 92.

99   Letter from Maya Angelou to Bernice Wilds, December 7, 1960, F. "Martin Luther King Tribute," Box 24, A. Philip Randolph Papers, MD-LOC.

100 Letter from A. Philip Randolph and Harry Belafonte to "Brother" (form letter to labor leaders), January 3, 1961, F. "Martin Luther King Tribute," Box 24, A. Philip Randolph Papers, MD-LOC.

101 Harry Belafonte in "A Tribute to Rev. King," 92.

102 Stanley Levison to A. Philip Randolph, c. December 12, 1960, F. "Martin Luther King Tribute," Box 24, A. Philip Randolph Papers, MD-LOC.

103 Letter from Stanley Levison to Martin Luther King, Jr., October 13, 1960, in Carson Clayborne, *The Papers of Martin Luther King, Jr.*, vol. 5 (Berkeley: University of California Press, 1992), 518–20.

104 Branch, *Parting the Waters*, 348.

105 Ibid., 359, 369.

106 Ibid., 378.
107 Davis, *Why Me?*, 121.
108 Early, *This Is Where I Came In*, 49.
109 Letter from Stanley Levison to A. Philip Randolph, January 10, 1961, "Martin Luther King Tribute," Box 24, A. Philip Randolph Papers, MD-LOC.
110 Letter from Martin Luther King, Jr., to Sammy Davis, Jr., January 20, 1961, Clayborne, *Papers of Martin Luther King*, vol. 5, 582–83.
111 Sinatra, *My Father's Daughter*, 76.
112 Davis, *Why Me?*, 132.
113 "Tribute to MLK," 91.
114 George F. Brown, "Inside Sammy Davis, Jr.," in Early, *Sammy Davis, Jr., Reader*, 229.
115 "Tribute to MLK," 94.
116 George E. Pitts, "Sammy Davis, Jr., Sounds Off," in Early, *Sammy Davis, Jr., Reader*, 228.
117 "Tribute to MLK," 94.
118 Branch, *Parting the Waters*, 385.
119 Wyatt Walker in Fairclough, *To Redeem the Soul*, 85; and Walker interview.
120 Fairclough, *To Redeem the Soul*, 70.
121 Early, *Sammy Davis, Jr., Reader*, 41.
122 Ingrid Monson, *Freedom Sounds: Civil Rights Call Out to Jazz and Africa* (Oxford: Oxford University Press, 2007), 157.
123 Raymond, *From My Cold, Dead Hands*, 66–67.
124 "$60,000 Worth of Fun!" *Pittsburgh Courier*, April 22, 1961, 2.
125 Early, *This Is Where I Come In*, 45.

NOTES TO CHAPTER 3

Nelson Arsenault, *Freedom Riders: 1961 and the Struggle for Racial Justice* (Oxford: Oxford University Press, 2006), 265.
1 Harry Belafonte in *King: Go Beyond the Dream to Discover the Man*, dir. Tim Beacham, Tom Keenan, and Shoshana Guy, dist. New Video (New York: A & E Television Networks), 2008.
2 Harry Belafonte in Henry Louis Gates, Jr., "Belafonte's Balancing Act," *New Yorker*, combined issue, August 26, 1996, and September 2, 1996, 134.
3 Harry Belafonte in M. Cordell Thompson, "Belafonte Bounces Back Big and Black," *Jet*, July 6, 1971, 59.
4 Harry Belafonte, interview with Etta Moten Barnett, NBC Radio, MIRS Sc Audio C-558, Schomburg Center for Research in Black Culture, Harlem, New York.
5 Harry Belafonte, *My Song: A Memoir* (New York: Knopf, 2011), 192; and James Gavin, *Stormy Weather: The Life of Lena Horne* (New York: Atria Books, 2009), 254.
6 Harry Belafonte, recorded interview with Vicki Daitch, May 20, 2005, 5, John F. Kennedy Library, Oral History (hereafter referred to as JFKOH).

7   Harry Belafonte in Thompson, "Belafonte Bounces Back," 59–60.

8   Clayborne Carson, *The Papers of Martin Luther King, Jr.*, vol. 3 (Berkeley: University of California Press, 1992), 514.

9   Belafonte, *My Song*, 189.

10 Letter from Gretl Steinberger to A. Philip Randolph, October 19, 1958, "Youth March for Integrated Schools, Correspondence," Box 5, A. Philip Randolph Papers, Manuscripts Division, Manuscripts Division (hereafter referred to as MD-LOC).

11 Harry Belafonte in "Harry Belafonte, Jack Robinson Lead Integrated Schools March," (journal not evident), "Youth March for Integrated Schools, Clippings," Box 35, A. Philip Randolph Papers, MD-LOC.

12 Letter from Ellen Lurie and Preston Wilcox (from The East Harlem Project) to A. Philip Randolph, May 18, 1959, "Youth March for Integrated Schools, Correspondence," Box 35, A. Philip Randolph Papers, MD-LOC.

13 Belafonte, *My Song*, 189.

14 See materials in F. "African Affairs, African-American Students Foundation, Project Airlift America, Scrapbook, 1959," Box 3, Jackie Robinson Papers, MD-LOC.

15 Sidney Poitier, *Measure of a Man: A Spiritual Autobiography* (San Francisco: Harper, 2007), 182.

16 Genia Fogelson, *Belafonte*, (Los Angeles: Holloway House, 1980), 153–61; and Sally K. Marks, "How to Interview Poitier, Man in a Hurry," *L.A. Times*, August 14, 1961, n.p. Core Collection—Sidney Poitier, Margaret Herrick Library–Academy of Motion Pictures Arts and Sciences, Beverly Hills, California (hereafter referred to as MHL-AMPAS).

17 Belafonte, *My Song*, 199.

18 Ibid., 207; and Harry Belafonte in Gates, "Belafonte's Balancing Act," 140.

19 Gavin, *Stormy Weather*, 289.

20 Harry Belafonte in "I Wonder Why Nobody Don't Like Me," *Life*, May 27, 1957, 85, 86, 89, 90, Core Collection–Harry Belafonte, MHL-AMPAS.

21 Bill Attaway in Gates, "Belafonte's Balancing Act," 139.

22 See Taylor Branch, *Parting the Waters: America in the King Years, 1954–63* (New York: Simon and Schuster, 1988), 275–77; and Stephen B. Oates, *Let the Trumpet Sound: The Life of Martin Luther King, Jr.* (New York: Harper and Row, 1982), 152–53.

23 "The Revolving Bail Fund," Committee to Defend Martin Luther King, Jr. (CDMLK), n.d. (c. February 1960), F. "Martin Luther King, Jr., Committee to Defend," Box 24, A. Philip Randolph Papers, MD-LOC.

24 Branch, *Parting the Waters*, 288–89.

25 "Heed Their Rising Voices," *New York Times*, March 29, 1960, 25.

26 Minutes for April 4, 1960, p. 1, CDMLK, F. "Martin Luther King, Jr., Committee to Defend," Box 24, A. Philip Randolph Papers, MD-LOC.

27 Harry Belafonte, board meeting minutes, March 7, 1960, CDMLK, F. "Martin

Luther King, Jr., Committee to Defend," Box 24, A. Philip Randolph Papers, MD-LOC.

28 See letters between George Stevens, Harry Belafonte, and Sidney Poitier in F. "Charities #3522," George Stevens Papers, Special Collection, MHL-AMPAS. For publicity and armory comments, see F. "Martin Luther King, Jr., Committee to Defend," Box 24, A. Philip Randolph Papers, MD-LOC.

29 Branch, *Parting the Waters*, 289 and 296.

30 See "Telenews [vol. 13, issue 103—excerpt. New Yorkers Rally for MLK Defense—NYC]," May 18, 1960, roll number 1128, University of California–Los Angeles Film and Television Archive; and "15,000 Attend Garment Center Civil Rights Rally," *New York Times*, May 18, 1960, 22.

31 "The Spirit of the 60's," *New York Amsterdam News*, May 21, 1960, 1.

32 "15,000 Attend," 22.

33 "The Spirit of the 60's," 1.

34 Letter from Stanley D. Levison to Martin Luther King, Jr., March 1960, Carson, *Papers of Martin Luther King, Jr.*, vol. 5, 381.

35 Adam Fairclough, *To Redeem the Soul of America: The Southern Christian Leadership Conference and Martin Luther King, Jr.* (Athens: University of Georgia Press, 1987), 66.

36 Harry Belafonte in *King;* and Wyatt Tee Walker, interview with the author, Chester, Virginia, August 6, 2014.

37 Branch, *Parting the Waters*, 209–11; and "Statement of Income and Expenditures for Period Ended July 31, 1960," CDMLK, F. "Martin Luther King, Jr., Committee to Defend," Box 24, A. Philip Randolph Papers, MD-LOC.

38 Fairclough, *To Redeem the Soul*, 66.

39 Memo from "emb" to Roy Wilkins, June 29, 1960, F. "King, Martin Luther, Jr., General, 1956–61," III: A175, NAACP Papers, MD-LOC.

40 Belafonte, JFKOH, 7.

41 David Falkner, *Great Time Coming: The Life of Jackie Robinson, from Baseball to Birmingham* (New York: Touchstone Books, 1995), 277.

42 Belafonte, JFKOH, 7.

43 Falkner, *Great Time Coming*, 279.

44 Belafonte, JFKOH, 8.

45 Branch, *Parting the Waters*, 314.

46 Louis Martin, interview with Ronald J. Grele, March 14, 1966, JFKOH, 9, 29.

47 "The Living Room Candidate: Presidential Campaign Commercials, 1952–2012," Museum of the Moving Image, accessed October 9, 2014, www.livingroomcandidate.org/commercials/1960/harry-belafonte.

48 Belafonte, JFKOH, 9.

49 Ibid., 10–11.

50 Belafonte, *My Song*, 221.

51 John Lewis, interview with the author, Washington, DC, September 11, 2013.

52 John Lewis, *Walking with the Wind: A Memoir of the Movement* (New York: Simon and Schuster, 1998), 110.

53 See Falkner, *Great Time Coming*, 273–75; and "Dear Friend" letter from John Armstrong and Jackie Robinson, May 18, 1960, F. "Civil Rights Student Emergency Fund, 1960–61, n.d.," Box 4, Jackie Robinson Papers, MD-LOC.

54 See Harris Wofford, *Of Kennedys and Kings: Making Sense of the Sixties* (New York: Farrar, Straus, Giroux, 1980), 124; and Belafonte, JFKOH, 13.

55 Robert Kennedy, *In His Own Words: The Unpublished Recollections of the Kennedy Years* (New York: Bantam Books, 1988), 102.

56 Branch, *Parting the Waters*, 480.

57 Arsenault, *Freedom Riders*, 330; and "Mammoth L.A. Rights Rally Attracts 20,000, Raises $30,000," *Jet*, July 6, 1961, 58–59.

58 Harry Belafonte, JFKOH, 13.

59 Belafonte, *My Song*, 237; and Stokley Carmichael, with Ekwrieme Michael Thelwell, *Ready for Revolution: The Life and Struggles of Stokley Carmichael (Kwame Ture)* (New York: Scribner, 2003), 222.

60 Arsenault, *Freedom Riders*, 330.

61 Lewis, *Walking with the Wind*, 181–82.

62 Branch, *Parting the Waters*, 382 and 481. COFO member organizations also included the NAACP, CORE, and SCLC.

63 Emily Stoper, *The Student Nonviolent Coordinating Committee: The Growth of Radicalism in a Civil Rights Organization* (Brooklyn, NY: Carlson Pub., 1989), 186.

64 Carmichael, *Ready for Revolution*, 222.

65 Belafonte, *My Song*, 237.

66 Stoper, *Student Nonviolent Coordinating Committee*, 191–92.

67 Branch, *Parting the Waters*, 512–14.

68 Fraser Heston, telephone interview with the author, January 21, 2011.

69 Clara Luper, *Behold These Walls* (Oklahoma City: Jim Wire, 1979), 134–36.

70 Heston's son says that these civil rights activities "became a cornerstone of the foundation of our family" because of the basic sense of "duty and decency" that his father established for them. It was as important to him as his World War II service, and he was "glad he did it." Heston interview.

71 Emilie Raymond, *'From My Cold, Dead Hands': Charlton Heston and American Politics* (Lexington: University Press of Kentucky, 2006), 74.

72 Theodore Bikel, interview with the author, Westwood, California, January 13, 2011.

73 Ibid.

74 Bob Zellner, telephone interview with the author, February 5, 2014.

75 August Meier, *CORE: A Study in the Civil Rights Movement, 1942–1968* (New York: Oxford University Press, 1973), 149.

76 Zellner interview.

77 Theodore Bikel, "Civil Rights Remembered," memoirs prepared for the author.

78 Bikel interview.

79 Zellner interview.

80 Dick Gregory with Robert Lipsyte, *Nigger: An Autobiography* (New York: E. P. Dutton and Company, 1964), 158.

81 Christine Acham, *Revolution Televised: Prime Time and the Struggle for Black Power* (Minneapolis: University of Minnesota Press, 2004), 9–18; and *Bell and Howell Close-Up: What's So Funny?*, June 12, 1962, Paley Center for Media, New York City (hereafter referred to as PCM).

82 "Gregory Puts Niteries on Freedom March," *Chicago Daily Defender,* May 29, 1963, 16.

83 Dick Gregory in *What's So Funny* and *Bell and Howell Close Up!: Walk In My Shoes*, ABC, September 19, 1961, PCM.

84 Dick Gregory on *The Jack Paar Show,* March 1, 1963, PCM.

85 Dick Gregory, *Callus on My Soul: A Memoir* (Atlanta: Longstreet Press, 2000), 53–61.

86 John Dittmer, *Local People: The Struggle for Civil Rights in Mississippi* (Urbana: University of Illinois Press, 1995), 147–52.

87 David Dennis, telephone interview with the author, January 29, 2014.

88 Claude Sitton, "Mississippi Town Seizes 19 Negroes: Dick Gregory, Not Held, Leads Greenwood March," *New York Times,* April 4, 1963, 22.

89 "Tonight with Belafonte," *Revlon Revue,* CBS, December 10, 1959, PCM.

90 Michael Curtin, *Redeeming the Wasteland: Television Documentary and Cold War Politics* (New Brunswick, NJ: Rutgers University Press, 1995), 19 and 24.

91 Belafonte, *My Song,* 208–20.

92 Harry Belafonte in "Belafonte's Upcoming Battle," *Pittsburgh Courier,* May 26, 1962, 14. See also Branch, *Parting the Waters,* 592.

93 James Forman, *The Making of Black Revolutionaries* (Seattle: University of Washington Press, 1997), 293.

94 Clayborne Carson, *In Struggle: SNCC and the Black Awakening of the 1960s* (Cambridge, MA: Harvard University Press, 1981), 71.

95 Branch, *Parting the Waters,* 705.

96 Arsenault, *Freedom Riders,* 446.

97 Fairclough, *To Redeem the Soul,* 82; Vanessa Murphree, *Selling of Civil Rights: The Student Nonviolent Coordinating Committee and the Use of Public Relations* (New York: Routledge, 2006), 28; Stoper, *Student Nonviolent Coordinating Committee,* 184–85; and Carson, *In Struggle,* 70.

98 Branch, *Parting the Waters,* 558.

99 Ibid., 579.

100 Ibid., 691; and Aldon Morris, *Origins of the Civil Rights Movement: Black Communities Organizing for Change* (New York: Free Press, 1984), 253.

101 For voter registration and Meredith, see Branch, *Parting the Waters,* 640, 672. Martin Luther King, Jr., *Why We Can't Wait* (New York: Signet Classics, 2000), 8–9.

102 Lee White, interview with Milton Gwirtzman, 1964, JFKOH, 104; Branch, *Parting the Waters,* 694–98; "Ticker Tape USA, *Jet,* March 6, 1963, 12.

103 Walker interview.

104 William Kuntsler, *Deep in My Heart* (New York: Morrow, 1966), 173.

105   King, *Why We Can't Wait*, 58–59.

106   Ibid., 59.

107   "'Bull' Threatens Negro Stars," *Chicago Daily Defender,* April 8, 1963, 2.

108   King, *Why We Can't Wait,* 71.

109   Kuntsler, *Deep in My Heart*, 173; and Sammy Davis, Jr., *Why Me? The Sammy Davis, Jr., Story* (New York: Farrar, Straus and Giroux, 1989), 135.

110   "Ray Charles Denies He'll Join Birmingham Fight," *Chicago Daily Defender,* April 13, 1963, 1.

111   Adam Fairclough, "Martin Luther King, Jr. and the Quest for Nonviolent Social Change," *Phylon* 47, no. 1 (Spring 1986): 6.

112   Bill Lane, "Nat Cole Defends Stars Who Shun Dixie Racial Picket Lines," *Chicago Defender,* May 11, 1963, 10.

113   Gregory, *Callus on My Soul*, 69–70.

114   Claude Sitton, "Birmingham Jails 1,000 More Negroes: Waves of Chanting Students . . .," *New York Times,* May 7, 1963, 1.

115   "Dick Gregory Accuses Police of Brutality in Alabama Jail," *New York Times,* May 10, 1963, 14; "U.S. Probes Assault on Gregory in Alabama Jail," *Chicago Daily Defender,* May 13, 1963, 3; and "Gregory Puts Niteries on Freedom March," *Chicago Daily Defender,* May 29, 1963, 16.

116   See Branch, *Parting the Waters,* 784–88; Robert Weisbrot, *Freedom Bound: A History of America's Civil Rights Movement* (New York: Norton, 1990), 71; Belafonte, JFKOH, 16; and Belafonte, *My Song*, 261–64.

117   Branch, *Parting the Waters,* 795–800.

NOTES TO CHAPTER 4

Ossie Davis and Ruby Dee, *With Ossie and Ruby: In This Life Together* (New York: William Morrow and Company, 1998), 306–7.

1   Martin Luther King, Jr., *Why We Can't Wait* (New York: Signet Classics, 2000), 135, 144; and Aldon Morris, *Origins of the Civil Rights Movement: Black Communities Organizing for Change* (New York: Free Press, 1984), 274.

2   Thomas Gentile, *March on Washington: August 28, 1963* (Washington, DC: New Day Publications, 1983), 23.

3   Taylor Branch, *Parting the Waters: America in the King Years, 1954–63* (New York: Simon and Schuster, 1988), 808.

4   Robert Weisbrot, *Freedom Bound: A History of America's Civil Rights Movement* (New York: Norton, 1990), 73.

5   Branch, *Parting the Waters,* 275–77, 811.

6   Ibid., 811.

7   Robert Kennedy, *In His Own Words: The Unpublished Recollections of the Kennedy Years* (New York: Bantam Books, 1998), 224–25; and Harris Wofford, *Of Kennedys and Kings: Making Sense of the Sixties* (New York: Farrar, Straus, Giroux, 1980), 172

8   James Baldwin in "Kennedy and Baldwin: The Gulf," *Newsweek,* June 3, 1963, 19.

9   Wofford, *Of Kennedys and Kings*, 172.

10   Kennedy, *In His Own Words*, 225.

11   Branch, *Parting the Waters*, 813, 854.

12   Wofford, *Of Kennedys and Kings*, 172.

13   James Gavin, *Stormy Weather: The Life of Lena Horne* (New York: Atria Books, 2009), 315–17.

14   Gregory in *We Want to Be Free*, BB4745b, Pacifica Radio Archive.

15   Newman and Dandridge in ibid.

16   King in ibid.

17   Sammy Davis, Jr., in Louie Robinson, "50,000 Jam L.A. Ball Park for Biggest Rights Rally," *Jet*, June 14, 1963, 58.

18   Kate Burford, *Burt Lancaster: An American Life* (New York: Alfred A. Knopf, 2000), 234.

19   Robinson, "50,000 Jam L.A. Ball Park," 57–60.

20   Branch, *Parting the Waters*, 809.

21   Gavin, *Stormy Weather*, 320–25; and Thomas Sugrue, *Sweet Land of Liberty: The Forgotten Struggle for Civil Rights in the North* (New York: Random House, 2008), 296.

22   Special report of Althea T. L. Simmons (field secretary, Southern and Southwest Areas West Coast Region, NAACP), n.d. (c. November 1961), F. "Films, Movie Industry, 1960–1961," III: A119, NAACP Papers, Manuscripts Division, Library of Congress (hereafter referred to as MD-LOC).

23   "Report on Conference with Edward D. Warren, Los Angeles Branch President, Re: Reported Meeting of NAACP and the Movie Industry," n.d. (c. November 1961), F. "Films, Movie Industry, 1960–1961," III: A119, NAACP Papers, MD-LOC.

24   Murray Schumach, "Stars Join Drive Against Bigotry," *New York Times*, July 15, 1963, 25.

25   See Martha Biondi, *To Stand and Fight: The Struggle for Civil Rights in Postwar New York City* (Cambridge, MA: Harvard University Press, 2003); and Colleen Doody, *Detroit's Cold War: The Origins of Postwar Conservatism* (Urbana, Chicago, and Springfield: University of Illinois Press, 2013).

26   Emilie Raymond, *'From My Cold, Dead Hands': Charlton Heston and American Politics* (Lexington: University Press of Kentucky, 2006), 119–20.

27   Gentile, *March on Washington*, 209.

28   Branch, *Parting the Waters*, 816.

29   Clarence Jones in Burford, *Lancaster*, 234.

30   Jerald Podair, *Bayard Rustin American Dreamer* (Lanham, MD: Rowman & Littlefield Publishers, 2009), 58.

31   Gentile, *March on Washington*, 114.

32   Marlon Brando, *Songs My Mother Taught Me* (New York: Random House, 1994), 125.

33   "Brando Fights for Civil Rights," *Ebony* 18 (Oct. 1963): 64.

34   Harry Belafonte, *My Song: A Memoir* (New York: Knopf, 2011), 277.

35   Charlton Heston, *In the Arena: An Autobiography* (New York: Simon and Schuster, 1995), 316.

36   Gentile, *March on Washington*, 210.

37   For press releases, committee meeting minutes, Lytton Center program, and the article "Sixty Showbiz Personalities Going to Wash'n to Appear for Civil Rights Legislation," *Hollywood Reporter*, August 9, 1963, see F. "Hollywood March on Washington #468," Charlton Heston Papers, Special Collection, Margaret Herrick Library–Academy of Motion Pictures Arts and Sciences, Beverly Hills, California (hereafter referred to as MHL-AMPAS).

38   Gentile, *March on Washington*, 210; and Charlton Heston, *The Actor's Life: Journals, 1956–1976* (New York: E. P. Dutton, 1978), 178.

39   David Lawrence, "'March Will Go Down as a Disgrace," *Citizen News*, August 2, 1963, B7, F. "Hollywood March on Washington #468," Charlton Heston Papers, Special Collection, MHL-AMPAS; and Gentile, *March on Washington*, 208–9.

40   "Top Film Group Plans to Join Rights March," *L.A. Times*, August 8, 1963, 2, 7, F. "Hollywood March on Washington #468," Charlton Heston Papers, Special Collection, MHL-AMPAS.

41   Heston, *Actors Life*, 178–79.

42   Gentile, *March on Washington*, 211; and Adam Fairclough, *To Redeem the Soul of America: The Southern Christian Leadership Conference and Martin Luther King, Jr.* (Athens: University of Georgia Press, 1987), 148.

43   Ossie Davis, March on Washington program prospectus, August 14, 1963, Rustin Papers, Reel 8, MD-LOC.

44   "Stars March for Freedom," *Jet*, August, 29, 1963, 60–61.

45   Gentile, *March on Washington*, 212.

46   Diahann Carroll in Gavin, *Stormy Weather*, 326.

47   "March on Washington NBC," August 28, 1963, University of California–Los Angeles Film and Television Archive.

48   Stephen B. Oates, *Let the Trumpet Sound: The Life of Martin Luther King, Jr.* (New York: Harper and Row, 1982), 257.

49   Gavin, *Stormy Weather*, 329, 345.

50   Ossie Davis in Henry Hampton and Steve Fayer, *Voices of Freedom: An Oral History of the Civil Rights Movement from the 1950s through the 1980s* (New York: Bantam Books, 1990), 162.

51   Branch, *Parting the Waters*, 872; "No Booze During March—Except for Lawmakers," *Jet*, September 12, 1963, 10; Kennedy, *In His Own Words*, 227.

52   Wofford, *Of Kennedys and Kings*, 174; and Dick Gregory in Hampton and Fayer, *Voices of Freedom*, 161.

53   Davis, March on Washington program prospectus, 2.

54   "March on Washington NBC."

55   John Lewis, *Walking with the Wind: A Memoir of the Movement* (New York: Simon and Schuster, 1998), 221; Burt Boyar, *Photo by Sammy Davis, Jr.* (New York: Regan, 2007), 250.

56 "March on Washington Platform Guests—Lincoln Memorial," F. "March on Washington, Plans, Material Related to, 1963," n.d., NAACP, III: A227, NAACP Papers, MD-LOC.

57 "March on Washington NBC."

58 Lewis, *Walking with the Wind*, 221; and Branch, *Parting the Waters*, 877.

59 "March on Washington NBC"; and Heston, *Actor's Life*, 179.

60 Burford, *Lancaster*, 234.

61 Burt Lancaster in CBS News special report: "March on Washington," part 1 of 2, August 28, 1963, Paley Center for Media, New York City.

62 Mary L. Dudziak, "Josephine Baker, Racial Protest, and the Cold War," *Journal of American History* 81, no. 2 (Sept. 1994): 556, 565. Baker had become a French citizen in 1937. Dudziak also notes that the "INS action was probably not necessary to keep Baker from performing in the United States in the mid-1950s. Theater owners were unlikely to book such an 'un-American' figure" (565).

63 Baker compared American racism to the Holocaust on several occasions, saying at one point, "Negroes throughout the world entirely rightly are looking upon the United States in the same way the Jewish people pointed a short time ago to the land where they had been sentenced to extinction." Dudziak, "Josephine Baker," 556; and Allan Morrison, "Josephine Baker Flies from Paris for D.C. March," *Jet*, September 12, 1963, 40–41.

64 Branch, *Parting the Waters*, 883.

65 Heston, *Actor's Life*, 179.

66 Dick Gregory with Robert Lipsyte, *Nigger: An Autobiography* (New York: E. P. Dutton and Company, 1964), 211–12.

67 Boyar, *Photo*, 253.

68 Davis and Dee, *With Ossie and Ruby*, 306–7.

69 Heston, *Actors Life*, 177; and Horne in CBS "March on Washington."

70 Lewis, *Walking with the Wind*, 221; Rustin in Hampton and Fayer, *Voices of Freedom*, 169.

71 Fred Shuttlesworth in CBS "March on Washington."

72 Julian Bond, e-mail interview with the author, March 10, 2014.

73 Branch, *Parting the Waters*, 877.

74 Boyar, *Photo*, 250.

75 "Hollywood Round Table—Civil Rights, c. 1963," U.S. Information Agency, Record Group 306, ARC Identifier: 48311, Motion Picture, Sound, and Video Records, National Archives, College Park, Maryland.

76 Ibid.

77 Gentile, *March on Washington*, 257–60.

78 Dick Gregory, *Callus on My Soul: A Memoir* (Atlanta: Longstreet Press, 2000), 82.

79 Fairclough, *To Redeem the Soul*, 156; and Branch, *Parting the Waters*, 898–909.

80 Belafonte, *My Song*, 284–85.

81 David Falkner, *Great Time Coming: The Life of Jackie Robinson, from Baseball to*

Birmingham (New York: Touchstone Books, 1995), 302; and Ingrid Monson, *Freedom Sounds: Civil Rights Call Out to Jazz and Africa* (Oxford: Oxford University Press, 2007), 202–4.

82 Letter from James Forman to Marlon Brando and Dick Gregory, September 5, 1963, Student Nonviolent Coordinating Committee Papers, reel 5 (hereafter referred to as SNCC Papers).

83 Letter from Julia Prettyman to Lena Horne, October 13, 1963, SNCC Papers, reel 27.

84 Letter from Clarence Jones to Harry Belafonte, October 18, 1963, SNCC Papers, reel 6; and letter from James Forman to Harry Belafonte, December 4, 1963, SNCC Papers, reel 5.

85 Merit Productions, "A Proposal for National Association for Advancement Colored People," n.d. (c. 1962), F. "Freedom TV Spectacular," "Closed Circuit TV, Related Matter"; and "Memorandum from Henry Lee Moon to Mssrs. Wilkins, Morsell and Current," October 31, 1962, F. "Freedom TV Spectacular" Correspondence General 1962–63"; III: A136 NAACP Papers, MD-LOC.

86 Letter from Ed Sullivan to Roy Wilkins, March 2, 1964, "Freedom TV Spectacular," "Correspondence General 1964, January–March," III: A136, NAACP Papers, MD-LOC.

87 Steven J. Ross, *Hollywood Left and Right: How Movie Stars Shaped American Politics* (Oxford: Oxford University Press, 2011), 177–25.

88 M. G. Lord, *The Accidental Feminist: How Elizabeth Taylor Raised Our Consciousness and We Were Too Distracted by Her Beauty to Notice* (New York: Walker and Company, 2012), 44–45, 50–53, 166; and "Super Cast of 30 Led by Poitier, Liz Taylor: NAACP Will Reap Million from May 14 TV-Spectacle," *Pittsburgh Courier,* May 9, 1964, 16.

89 "The NAACP Presentation: *Freedom Is the Word,* tape: May 11, 12, 1964, F. "Freedom TV Spectacular," script, 1964, III: A138, NAACP Papers, MD-LOC.

90 "Memo from John Morsell to Members of the Board on Freedom Spectacular, December 29, 1964," "F. Freedom TV Spectacular," "Correspondence, General, 1964 September–December," III: A137, NAACP Papers, MD-LOC.

91 "Memo from John Morsell."

92 Letter from John A. Morsell to Leonard H. Carter, December 7, 1964, F. "Freedom TV Spectacular," "Correspondence, General, 1964, September–December," III: A137, NAACP Papers, MD-LOC.

93 "Memo from John Morsell."

94 Memo to Reverend Odom from Roy Wilkins, F. "Benefits, General, 1956–1963," III: A44, NAACP Papers, MD-LOC.

95 Brian Ward, *Just My Soul Responding: Rhythm and Blues, Black Consciousness, and Race Relations* (Berkeley: University of California Press, 1998), 329.

96 Letter from Roy Wilkins to "Friend of Civil Rights," n.d. (c. October 1963);

letter from John A. Morsell (assistant to the executive secretary of the NAACP) to Howard Burney (chairman, Committee of Friends of Josephine Baker), n.d. (c. October 1963); and letter from John A. Morsell to Felix G. Gerstman, October 16, 1963, F. "Benefits, Josephine Baker, 1963," III: A44, NAACP Papers, MD-LOC.

97   Letter from Pauline Marshall (secretary, "Stars for Freedom"), November 4, 1963, F. "MCA Artists," Howard Fleming Papers, Special Collection, MHL-AMPAS; and "Stars for Freedom Benefit Performance—December 5, 1963, Santa Monica Civic Auditorium, Statement of Income and Expenditures, September 27, 1963 to March 18, 1964," F. "Benefits, General, 1956–1963," III: A44, NAACP Papers, MD-LOC.

98   Sidney Poitier, *The Measure of a Man: A Spiritual Autobiography* (San Francisco: Harper, 2007), 200.

99   Memo to Mildred Bond from William C. Jones (Life Membership assistant, NAACP), "Sidney Poitier in 'Lilies of the Field,'" August 8, 1963; letter to Sidney Poitier from Bernard L. Moore, September 10, 1963; "NAACP Expense 'Lilies of the Field' Benefit," receipt for K. H. Costa and attached not written by K. H. Costa, October 4, 1963; all in F. "Civil Rights Benefits, *Lilies of the Field*, 1963," III: A63, NAACP Papers, MD-LOC. Letter to "Friend" from Val Coleman, CORE, Bernard Moore, NAACP, Ruth Bailey SCLC, and Julia Prettyman, SNCC, September 16, 1963, F. "Benefits, General, 1956–1963," III: A44, NAACP Papers, MD-LOC. The expenses for the New York film totaled little more than $2,000.

100   Stokley Carmichael, with Ekwrieme Michael Thelwell, *Ready for Revolution: The Life and Struggles of Stokley Carmichael (Kwame Ture)* (New York: Scribner, 2003), 267.

101   Letter to "NAACP Member" from Roy Wilkins, December 18, 1961, F. "Davis, Ossie, 1961–65," III: A94; and Special Memorandum from the Executive Secretary [Roy Wilkins], "The Hottest Thing UNDER OFF The Air," F. "Horne, Lena, 1956–63," III: A184, NAACP Papers, MD-LOC.

102   "Sidney Poitier Oscar Awards," April 21, 1967, United States Information Agency, "Voice of America," sound recordings, RG 306-EN-X-T-9103, Motion Picture, Sound, and Video Records, LICON, Special Media Archives Services Division, College Park, Maryland.

103   Aram Goudsouzian, *Poitier: Man, Actor, Icon* (Chapel Hill: University of North Carolina Press, 2004), 218.

104   Daniel J. Wolff, *You Send Me: The Life and Times of Sam Cooke* (New York: W. Morrow, 1995), 215, 274–75, 290–92; and Peter Guaralnick, *Dream Boogie: The Triumph of Sam Cooke* (New York: Little, Brown, 2005), 272, 368, 512.

105   Daniel Mark Epstein, *Nat King Cole* (New York: Farrar, Straus, and Giroux, 1999), 252–61; Cole quote ibid., 332.

106   Guaralnick, *Dream Boogie*, 139.

107   Lloyd Price in Guaralnick, *Dream Boogie*, 513.

108   Fats Domino in Richard Iton, *In Search of the Black Fantastic: Politics and*

Popular Culture in the Post-Civil Rights Era (Oxford: Oxford University Press, 2008), 70.

NOTES TO CHAPTER 5

Dick Gregory, *Up from Nigger* (New York: Stein and Day, 1976), 83.

1   James R. Ralph, Jr., *Northern Protest: Martin Luther King, Jr., Chicago, and the Civil Rights Movement* (Cambridge, MA: Harvard University Press, 1993), 14–19; "Gregory Arrested in Protest, Says Cops Reminds Him of B'ham," *Jet,* August 1963, 6–7; "50 Racial Pickets Seized in Chicago," *New York Times,* August 13, 1963, 22; and Dick Gregory, "Dick Gregory Tells of Jail Experiences," *Jet,* September 5, 1963, 58–61.

2   Dick Gregory, *Callus on My Soul: A Memoir* (Atlanta: Longstreet Press, 2000), 83.

3   "Gregory Arrested in Protest," 7; and "Dick Gregory Tells of Jail Experiences," 60.

4   See Ralph, *Northern Protest,* 19, 25, 37; Martha Biondi, *To Stand and Fight: The Struggle for Civil Rights in Postwar New York City* (Cambridge, MA: Harvard University Press, 2003), 241–49; Thomas Sugrue, *Sweet Land of Liberty: The Forgotten Struggle for Civil Rights in the North* (New York: Random House, 2008), 163–199; and Matthew Countryman, *Up South: Civil Rights and Black Power in Philadelphia* (Philadelphia: University of Pennsylvania Press, 2006), 228–39.

5   Clayborne Carson, *In Struggle: SNCC and the Black Awakening of the 1960s* (Cambridge, MA: Harvard University Press, 1981), 71.

6   David Garrow, *Protest at Selma: Martin Luther King, Jr., and the Voting Rights Act of 1965* (New Haven: Yale University Press, 1978).

7   Robert Weisbrot, *Freedom Bound: A History of America's Civil Rights Movement* (New York: Norton, 1990), 129.

8   Casey Hayden, telephone interview with the author, July 30, 2013.

9   Dinky Romilly, telephone interview with the author, August 13, 2013.

10   Vanessa Murphree, *Selling of Civil Rights: The Student Nonviolent Coordinating Committee and the Use of Public Relations* (New York: Routledge, 2006), 38; and Hayden interview.

11   Letter from James Forman to Dick Gregory, April 18, 1963, Student Nonviolent Coordinating Committee Papers, reel 6 (hereafter referred to as SNCC Papers).

12   Larry Still, "Dick Gregory's Pregnant Wife Tells of Treatment in Selma Jail," *Jet,* October 17, 1963, 20–22.

13   Dick Gregory with Robert Lipsyte, *Nigger: An Autobiography* (New York: E. P. Dutton and Company, 1964), 215–16.

14   James Forman, *The Making of Black Revolutionaries* (Seattle: University of Washington Press, 1997), 349–50.

15   Weisbrot, *Freedom Bound,* 129.

16   "Workers Spend Xmas in Jail," *Student Voice* 4, no. 10 (Dec. 30, 1963):, 1–3; and Gregory, *Callous on My Soul,* 90–91.

17 Gregory, *Nigger*, 223; and "Agreement Reached with Dobbs House," *Student Voice* 5, no. 2 (Jan. 14, 1964): 3–4.

18 Matthew T. Lassiter, *The Silent Majority: Suburban Politics in the Sunbelt South* (Princeton: Princeton University Press, 2006), 100–101.

19 "In Atlanta: Jails Fill as Protests Rise," *Student Voice* 5, no. 3 (Jan. 27, 1964): 1, 3; and Claude Sutton, "Negroes and Klansmen Clash in Atlanta as U.N. Group Visits City," *New York Times*, January 26, 1964, 1.

20 Lassiter, *Silent Majority*, 100–118; and Ivan Allen, *Mayor: Notes on the Sixties* (New York: Simon and Schuster, 1971), 81–90. However, as Lassiter points out, resistance to school desegregation eventually resulted in Atlanta developing a middle-class, multiracial suburbia with a hypersegregated poor minority in the city.

21 Brent Riffel, "In the Storm: William Hansen and the Student Nonviolent Coordinating Committee in Arkansas, 1962–1967," *Arkansas Historical Quarterly* 63, no. 4 (Winter 2004): 410.

22 William Hansen, e-mail interview with the author, July 1, 2013.

23 Ibid.

24 "In Pine Bluff: Leaders Call 72 Hour Truce," *Student Voice* 4, no. 7 (Feb. 25, 1964): 1–2; "Gregory Held in Arkansas," *New York Times*, February 18, 1964, 21; and "Dick Gregory Found Guilty in Arkansas Demonstrations," *New York Times*, February 26, 1964, 14.

25 Hansen interview.

26 Ibid.

27 Riffel, "In the Storm," 412; and Randy Finley, "Crossing the White Line: SNCC in Three Delta Towns, 1963–1967," *Arkansas Historical Quarterly* 65, no. 2 (Summer 2006): 123–28.

28 Hansen interview.

29 John Lewis, interview with the author, Washington, DC, September 11, 2013; Hansen interview; and Gregory, *Up from Nigger*, 74.

30 Gloria Richardson, telephone interview with the author, August 26, 2013.

31 Bruce Watson, *Freedom Summer* (New York: Penguin, 2010), 9.

32 John Dittmer, *Local People: The Struggle for Civil Rights in Mississippi* (Urbana: University of Illinois Press, 1995), 145.

33 Letter from Dick Gregory to Howard Schomer, January 22, 1963, F. 4, "SNCC Miss, Leflore Co., 1963–65," Box 38, James Forman Papers, Manuscript Division, Library of Congress (hereafter referred to as MD-LOC); letter from Laurence Landry to "Contributor toward Freedom," n.d. (c. February 1963), SNCC Papers, reel 6; and Watson, *Freedom Summer*, 10.

34 Dittmer, *Local People*, 147–52.

35 Letter from James Forman to Dick Gregory, March 5, 1963, SNCC Papers, reel 6; and Watson, *Freedom Summer*, 10.

36 Dick Gregory, *My Brother's Keeper*, accessed October 15, 2014, https://archive.org/details/DickGregory-MyBrothersKeeper.

37 Letter from John A. Morsell (assistant to Roy Wilkins) to Dick Gregory,

March 13, 1963; press releases "NAACP to Sell 10,000 Dick Gregory Records to Help Bias Victims," March 15, 1963; "NAACP Begins Moving Gregory Records," March 22, 1963; "D. Gregory Recording Selling Well—NAACP," April 12, 1963; all in F. "Gregory, Dick, Record—Order for 1963–65," III: A 148, NAACP Papers, MD-LOC.

38 Letter from Sandra Hayden to Nancy Stearns, April 15, 1963, SNCC Papers, reel 27; and letter from Dinky Romilly to Julie Prettyman, January 17, 1964, SNCC Papers, reel 27.

39 Emily Stoper, *The Student Nonviolent Coordinating Committee: The Growth of Radicalism in a Civil Rights Organization* (Brooklyn, NY: Carlson Pub., 1989), 61–62.

40 Henry Hampton and Steve Fayer, *Voices of Freedom: An Oral History of the Civil Rights Movement from the 1950s through the 1980s* (New York: Bantam Books, 1990), 185; and press release, "Dick Gregory and Freedom Singers to Appear at Howard University Civil Rights Group to Benefit," April 15, 1964, SNCC Papers, reel 27.

41 See daily schedules for Gregory Tour, SNCC Papers, reel 27; and program, "Detroit Friends of SNCC Present Dick Gregory," April 26, 1964, SNCC Papers, reel 27.

42 Brian Ward claims the tour made $35,000, while Bruce Watson insinuates that it made $20,000. See Brian Ward, *Just My Soul Responding: Rhythm and Blues, Black Consciousness, and Race Relations* (Berkeley: University of California Press, 1998), 313; and Watson, *Freedom Summer*, 66.

43 Cordelia Ruffin, "Rights Benefit Has Permit Problem," (journal not evident), SNCC Papers, reel 27; and daily schedule for Gregory Tour—Boston, SNCC Papers, reel 27.

44 William D. Ware, "Commentary on the Dick Gregory Concert," May 25, 1964, SNCC Papers, reel 27.

45 Letter from Dennis Leonard to Dinky Romilly, May 28, 1964, SNCC Papers, reel 27; and letter from Jayne Cortez and Bob Rogers to Dinky [Romilly] and Betty [Garman], April 21, 1964, SNCC Papers, reel 27.

46 James Farmer called the stall-ins "hare-brained" and noted that by 1964 the organization had begun to "cannibalize." James Farmer, *Lay Bare the Heart: An Autobiography of the Civil Rights Movement* (Fort Worth: Texas Christian University Press, 1998), 258; Ruffin, "Rights Benefit"; letter from Steve Bingham to Dinky Romilly, April 24, 1964, SNCC Papers, reel 27.

47 Joe Eszterhas, "Gregory Looks to Ohio for Prejudice Examples," *The Post* 53, no. 96 (May 1, 1964): 1.

48 Letter from Harold Bleich to Friends of SNCC, April 11, 1964, SNCC Papers, reel 27.

49 Letter from Bingham to Romilly; letter from Mrs. Jerome L. (Naomi) Bernstein to Dinky Romilly, April 28, 1964; and notes from daily schedule— Gregory Tour, SNCC Papers, reel 27.

50 See "Biography of Drew Pearson" and "Washington Merry-Go-Round"

columns, American University Library-Special Collections, Washington, DC (hereafter referred to as AUL-SC).

51   Letter from Victor Goedicke to Dinky Romilly, May 8, 1964, SNCC Papers, reel 27.

52   Letter from Dinky Romilly to Dick Gregory, May 18, 1964, SNCC Papers, reel 27.

53   Watson, *Freedom Summer*, 67–69; Stoper, *Student Nonviolent Coordinating Committee*, 62; and Doug McAdam, *Freedom Summer* (New York: Oxford University Press, 1988), 40.

54   Peter B. Levy, *Civil War on Race Street: The Civil Rights Movement in Cambridge, Maryland* (Gainesville: University Press of Florida, 2003), 92–109; and Cleveland Sellers, *The River of No Return: The Autobiography of a Black Militant and the Life and Death of SNCC* (Jackson: University Press of Mississippi, 1990), 66–80.

55   Levy, *Civil War*, 96–99, 109; Richardson interview; and "Gregory Charges 1c for Freedom," *Chicago Defender*, June 2, 1964, 2.

56   Drew Pearson, "The Washington Merry-Go-Round," August 18, 1965, AUL-SC; and Richardson interview.

57   Gregory, *Up from Nigger*, 44–50.

58   Ibid., 46–50; and Levy, *Civil War*, 114–15.

59   Gregory, *Up from Nigger*, 53.

60   Farmer, *Lay Bare the Heart*, 276.

61   Gregory, *Callous on My Soul*, 93–94.

62   Steven Watts, *Mr. Playboy: Hugh Hefner and the American Dream* (Hoboken, NJ: Wiley and Sons, 2008), 195–97.

63   Gregory, *Callous on My Soul*, 95.

64   "Tipoff Message Held Valueless," *New York Times*, August 7, 1964, 13; Watson, *Freedom Summer*, 210; and David Dennis, telephone interview with the author, January 29, 2014.

65   Harry Belafonte, *My Song: A Memoir* (New York: Knopf, 2011), 8–11.

66   Bob Zellner, telephone interview with the author, March 26, 2014.

67   Watson, *Freedom Summer*, 226.

68   Ibid., 243–50; and John L. Bullion, *Lyndon B. Johnson and the Transformation of American Politics* (New York: Pearson Longman, 2008), 98–100.

69   Lawrence Guyot in Ward, *Just My Soul*, 313.

70   Walter Mondale, Joseph Rauh, Courtland Cox, Unita Blackwell, and Victoria Gray in Hampton and Fayer, *Voices of Freedom*, 200–204.

71   Letter from Harry Belafonte to James Foreman [sic], June 3, 1963, F. 13, "Correspondence 1963 Feb.–Aug.," Box 16, James Forman Papers, MD-LOC.

72   Belafonte, *My Song*, 228–32; Belafonte in Hampton and Fayer, *Voices of Freedom*, 204; and Lansine Kaba, "From Colonialism to Autocracy: Guinea under Sékou Touré, 1957–1984," in Prosser Gifford and William Roger Louis, eds. *Decolonization and African Independence: The Transfers of Power, 1960–1980* (New Haven: Yale University Press, 1988), 225–44.

73   Lewis claims that the fish they were served is still the best he has ever eaten.

Lewis interview and William Hansen, e-mail interview with the author, August 11, 2013.

74 Harry Belafonte in Hampton and Fayer, *Voices of Freedom*, 204–5.

75 John Lewis in Hampton and Fayer, *Voices of Freedom*, 206; Stokely Carmichael, with Ekwrieme Michael Thelwell, *Ready for Revolution: The Life and Struggles of Stokley Carmichael (Kwame Ture)* (New York: Scribner, 2003), 318.

76 Forman, *Making of Black Revolutionaries*, 408–9.

77 Marlon Brando in Louie Robinson, "Brando Fights for Civil Rights," *Ebony* 18 (Oct. 1963): 61.

78 Sugrue, *Sweet Land of Liberty*, 284.

79 Daniel Martinez HoSang, "Racial Liberalism and the Rise of the Sunbelt West: The Defeat of Fair Housing on the 1964 California Ballot," in *Sunbelt Rising: The Politics of Space, Place, and Region in the American South and Southwest* D. Dochuck and M. Nickerson (Philadelphia: University of Pennsylvania Press), 191; "Owner Agrees to Integrate Torrance Tract," *Los Angeles Times*, July 13, 1963; "Brando Fights," 65–67; and Malcolm Boyd, "Blind No More," *Pittsburgh Courier,* August 10, 1963, 11.

80 See Sugrue, *Sweet Land of Liberty*, 200–250; and Biondi, *To Stand and Fight*, 118, for other northern cities and states.

81 HoSang, "Racial Liberalism," 190–91.

82 Raymond E. Wolfinger and Fred I. Greenstein, "The Repeal of Fair Housing in California: An Analysis of Referendum Voting," *American Political Science Review* 62, no. 3 (Sept. 1968): 753.

83 Letter from William L. Becker to Gregory Peck, March 2, 1964; form letter for Stars for Freedom, June 1, 1964; and letter from Edmund G. Brown to Gregory Peck, May 29, 1964, F. "Proposition 14," Gregory Peck Papers, Special Collection, Margaret Herrick Library–Academy of Motion Pictures Arts and Sciences, Beverly Hills, California (hereafter referred to as MHL-AMPAS).

84 "Meeting Executive Committee, Californians Against Proposition 14," August 17, 1964, F. "Prop 14," Gregory Peck Papers, Special Collection, MHL-AMPAS.

85 "California: Proposition 14," *Time*, September 25, 1964, 23.

86 HoSang, "Racial Liberalism," 199.

87 Emilie Raymond, *'From My Cold, Dead Hands': Charlton Heston and American Politics* (Lexington: University Press of Kentucky, 2006), 83.

88 Press Release, "Arts Division—Californians Against Proposition 14," n.d. (c. September 1964), F. 15, Box 5, Max Mont Collection, Special Collections and Archives, Oviatt Library, California State University Northridge (hereafter referred to as MM Collection).

89 Army Archerd, "Just for Variety," *Variety*, September 4, 1964.

90 Minutes from First Meeting of the Arts Division Committee, August 8, 1964, F. "Proposition 14," Gregory Peck Papers, Special Collection, MHL-AMPAS.

91 "Meeting Executive Committee," 2; and press release "Hollywood Bowl October 4," n.d. (c. September 1964), F. 15, Box 5, MM Collection.

92 "Liz and Dick to Do Bowl Benefit to Defeat Prop. 14," *Variety*, September 11, 1964, 2; and "Meeting Executive Committee," 2–3.

93 Letter from George Schlaff to Gregory Peck, November 3, 1964, F. "Prop. 14," Gregory Peck Papers, Special Collection, MHL-AMPAS; and Thomas W. Casstevens, *Politics, Housing, and Race Relations: California's Rumford Act and Proposition 14* (Berkeley: Institute of Governmental Studies, University of California, 1967), 66.

94 "An Open Letter," *Variety*, September 18, 1964; and "Is There Time?" *Variety*, October 27, 1964.

95 "Meeting Executive Committee," 4–5.

96 "No on 14" newsletter, August 27, 1964, F. "Proposition 14," Gregory Peck Papers, Special Collection, MHL-AMPAS.

97 Notes for speech for "No on Prop 14"—Thousand Oaks Luncheon, n.d. (c. August 1964); Peck Speech, n.d. (c. August 1964); letter from Mrs. Dick Van Dyke to Gregory Peck, October 17, 1964, F. "Proposition 14," Gregory Peck Papers, Special Collection, MHL-AMPAS; report on operation of NAACP Headquarters, November 12, 1964, F. 21, Box 5, MM Collection.

98 Mark Brilliant, *The Color of America Has Changed: How Racial Diversity Shaped Civil Rights Reform in California, 1941–1978* (Oxford: Oxford University Press, 2012), 194.

99 Ibid., 200–203.

100 HoSang, "Racial Liberalism," 205; and Brilliant, *Color of America*, 208.

101 Robert O. Self, *American Babylon: Race and the Struggle for Postwar Oakland* (Princeton: Princeton University Press, 2003), 265.

102 Press release, "No on 14," September 4, 1964, F. 15, Box 5, MM Collection.

103 Kate Burford, *Burt Lancaster: An American Life* (New York: Alfred A. Knopf, 2000), 235.

104 Harold Heffernan, "Actors in Politics Say; 'I've Had It,'" *Citizen-News*, November 3, 1964, A-7.

105 Dick Gregory in Drew Pearson, "Special Report from Washington," May 4, 1964; and "Washington Merry-Go-Round," May 17, 1964, AUL-SC.

106 Dick Gregory in Drew Pearson, "Special Release," May 19, 1964, AUL-SC.

107 Dick Gregory in Drew Pearson "Washington Merry-Go-Round," May 17, 1964, AUL-SC.

108 Lewis, who was also a founding member, says that ACT "was here and then 'poof!' it was gone." Levy, *Civil War*, 105; "Civil Rights Chiefs Form National Unit," *New York Times*, April 17, 1964, 18; and Lewis interview.

109 Claiborne Carson, ed., *Malcolm X: The FBI File* (New York: Carroll and Graf Publishers, 1991), 38–39.

110 Ossie Davis and Ruby Dee, *With Ossie and Ruby: In This Life Together* (New York: William Morrow and Company, 1998), 307–8; FBI File, Malcolm X, Part 21; and Manning Marable, *Malcolm X: A Life of Reinvention* (New York: Viking, 2011), 342.

111 William Sales, *From Civil Rights to Black Liberation: Malcolm X and the Organi-*

zation of Afro-American Unity (Boston: South End Press, 1994), 106; and James 67X Warden in Marable, *Malcolm*, 378.

112   Sales, *From Civil Rights*, 106.

113   Gregory, *Up from Nigger*, 85.

114   Richardson interview.

115   "Cost of Living in 1960s," accessed, October 15, 2014, http://pix.cs.olemiss .edu/econ/1960s.html.

116   Gregory, *Up from Nigger*, 68; and Drew Pearson, "Washington Merry-Go-Round," November 26, 1964, AUL-SC.

117   Chester Higgins, "Sammy: Santa's Helper in Mississippi Turkey Airlift: 'No Jewish Santa Claus?'" *Jet,* January 7, 1965, 58–62.

118   Drew Pearson, "Washington-Merry-Go-Round," December 2, 1964, AUL-SC.

119   Drew Pearson, "Washington-Merry-Go-Round," December 23, 1964, AUL-SC; and "Gregory's Turkey Act Arrives in Mississippi," *Victoria Advocate*, December 24, 1964.

120   Letter from Dick Gregory to Roy Wilkins, December 3, 1964, F. "Gregory, Dick—General, 1962–65," III: A148, NAACP Papers, MD-LOC.

121   "Will Christmas in Mississippi . . . Be Like Christmas in America," flyer, 1964 Ben-Ami (Rabbi David Z.) Papers, Civil Rights in Mississippi Digital Archives, University of Southern Mississippi Archives.

122   Joanne Gavin, e-mail interview with author, January 13, 2014; and Drew Pearson, "Washington-Merry-Go-Round," December 25, 1964, AUL-SC.

123   Gregory, *Up from Nigger*, 75.

124   Carson, *Malcolm X*, 320.

125   Austin C. Wehrwein, "252 Protesters Held in Chicago," *New York Times*, June 12, 1965, 16.

126   Austin C. Wehrwein, "Dr. King's Drive Ends in Chicago," *New York Times,* July 27, 1965, 18; "Chicago Rights Protest Taken to Mayor's Home," *New York Times*, August 2, 1965, 15; and Ralph, *Northern Protest*, 37.

127   Memo from Gloster B. Current to Messrs. Wilkins, Carter, Morsell, Moon, Mitchell, "Subject: Dick Gregory," April 25, 1963, F. "Gregory, Dick—General, 1962–65," Group III: A148, NAACP Papers, MD-LOC.

128   Drew Pearson, "The Washington Merry-Go-Round," June 16, 1963, AUL-SC.

129   Gregory, *Callous on My Soul*, 104.

NOTES TO CHAPTER 6

       Dick Gregory, *Up from Nigger* (New York: Stein and Day, 1976), 95.

1   Sidney Poitier in David Anderson, "Negro Actors at Hearing Assail Bias in Casting," *New York Times,* October 30, 1962, 37.

2   J. Fred MacDonald, *Blacks and White TV: Afro-Americans in Television since 1948* (Chicago: Nelson-Hall Publishers, 1983), 69.

3   Michael Curtin argues that in response to this pressure, the networks changed their broadcast news programming and invested more in documentaries, but Bodroghkozy shows the spillover effect into network program-

ming with dramatic shows. Michael Curtin, *Redeeming the Wasteland: Television Documentary and Cold War Politics* (New Brunswick, NJ: Rutgers University Press, 1995), 19, 24; and Aniko Bodroghkozy, *Equal Time: Television and the Civil Rights Movement* (Urbana: University of Chicago Press, 2012), 44.

4   *East Side/West Side* enjoyed solid ratings and critical praise, but CBS cancelled the series after only one year, largely due to sponsorship problems.

5   MacDonald, *Blacks and White TV*, 103–5.

6   Diahann Carroll, *The Legs Are the Last to Go* (New York: Amistad, 2008), 25.

7   Harry Belafonte, *My Song: A Memoir* (New York: Knopf, 2011), 177; and Wil Haygood, *In Black and White: The Life of Sammy Davis, Jr.* (New York: Alfred A. Knopf, 2003), 359.

8   Belafonte, *My Song*, 307.

9   Ossie Davis and Ruby Dee, *With Ossie and Ruby: In This Life Together* (New York: William Morrow and Company, 1998), 225, 283–84.

10   Ossie Davis, *Life Lit by Some Large Vision: Selected Speeches and Writings* (New York: Atria Books, 2006), 89.

11   Ossie Davis in Von Hugo Washington, "An Evaluation of the Play 'Purlie Victorious' and Its Impact on the American Theatrical Scene," PhD diss., Wayne State University, 1979, 132–33.

12   Loften Mitchell, *Black Drama: The Story of the American Negro in the Theatre* (New York: Hawthorn Books, 1967), 188–90.

13   Davis, *With Ossie and Ruby*, 291.

14   Manning Marable, *Malcolm X: A Life of Reinvention* (New York: Viking, 2011), 324; and Roy Wilkins, letter to "NAACP Member," October 18, 1961, F. "Davis, Ossie, 1961–65," III: A94, NAACP Papers, Manuscripts Division, Library of Congress (hereafter referred to as MD-LOC).

15   James V. Hatch, ed., and Ted Shine (consultant), *Black Theater, U.S.A.: Forty-Five Plays by Black Americans, 1847–1974* (New York: The Free Press, 1974), 653–54.

16   Davis and Dee, *With Ossie and Ruby*, 313; and "Ruby Dee: A Hit in Two Stage Dramas," *Jet,* July 22, 1965, 61.

17   Carroll, *Legs Are the Last to Go*, 31–33.

18   Sammy Davis in "Perspective 117, Conversation with Sammy Davis, Jr., Pt. 1," September 1, 1965, RG:306:EN-PT.4422, U.S. Information Agency, Voice of America, Sound Recordings, Motion Picture, Sound, and Video Records LICON, Special Media Archives Services Division, College Park, Maryland.

19   "Sammy Davis," *Life Magazine,* November 13, 1964, 85.

20   Ibid., 89, 93.

21   Ruby Dee in Davis and Dee, *With Ossie and Ruby*, 310.

22   Dick Gregory, *Callus on My Soul: A Memoir* (Atlanta: Longstreet Press, 2000), 100–101.

23   Ibid.

24   Marable, *Malcolm X*, 458–59.

25   Russell J. Rickford, *Betty Shabazz* (New York: Sourcebooks, 2003), 262; and

"Malcolm's Widow Aided by Benefit: Goal Is House for Her and Children of Slain Leader," *New York Times*, August 9, 1965.

26 Malcom's image was also aided by the publication of his autobiography later that year, and by the development of the Black Arts movement. Manning Marable, "Rediscovering Malcolm's Life: A Historian's Adventures in Living History," *Souls* 7 (Winter 2005): 21–22.

27 Letter from Betty Garman to Thomas A. Johnson, December 23, 1964, Box 31, F. 1, "Financial Records, Correspondence, 1961–64," James Forman Papers, MD-LOC.

28 "A Note about the Friends of SNCC groups—what do they do?" n.d. (c. 1965), Box 31, F. 7, "Financial Records, Fundraising, 1965," James Forman Papers, MD-LOC.

29 Letter from James Forman to Ruby Dee and Ossie Davis, July 11, 1962, Student Nonviolent Coordinating Committee Papers, reel 6 (hereafter referred to as SNCC Papers); and "Report on Special Gifts Fundraising: August, 1965," SNCC Papers, reel 27.

30 Letter from Casey Hayden to Bill Mahoney, July 17, 1963, SNCC Papers, reel 27.

31 "Special Gifts Fundraising Report," n.d. (c. 1964), SNCC Papers, reel 27.

32 Meeting of September 30, 1964; and "Special Gifts Fundraising Report," SNCC Papers, reel 27.

33 Meeting of October 7, 1964; and "Special Gifts Fundraising Report," SNCC Papers, reel 27.

34 Memo to SNCC staff from Marion Barry, Jr., and the New York Office staff, Box 31, F. 5, "Financial Records, Fundraising, 1964," James Forman Papers, MD-LOC. Letter from Theodore Bikel to Patricia, June 3, 1963; letter from Theodore Bikel to Mrs. Frank Bedman, June 26, 1963; letter from Theodore Bikel to Mahalia Jackson, June 26, 1963; and letter from Alice [Conklin, Bikel's secretary] to Jim [Forman], n.d. (c. 1963); all in SNCC Papers, reel 27.

35 Bob Zellner, telephone interview with the author, February 5, 2014.

36 Theodore Bikel, interview with author, January 13, 2011, Westwood, California.

37 Gloria Richardson, telephone interview with the author, August 26, 2013.

38 Dinky Romilly, telephone interview with the author, August 13, 2013.

39 Memo from Charlotte Carter regarding New York FOS, October 1964, Box 31, F. 5, "Financial Records Fundraising, 1964," James Forman Papers, MD-LOC.

40 "Friends of SNCC, Contributions to Atlanta since October 12, 1964 to December 31, 1964," SNCC Papers, reel 27.

41 Letter from James Forman to Allen Sagner, December 9, 1964, SNCC Papers, reel 27.

42 John Lewis, interview with the author, Washington, DC, September 11, 2013.

43 David Garrow, *Protest at Selma: Martin Luther King, Jr., and the Voting Rights Act of 1965* (New Haven: Yale University Press, 1978), 30.

44 Ibid., 20–21, 31.

45 Bodroghkozy, *Equal Time*, 118.

46   Garrow, *Protest at Selma*, 39.

47   Ibid., 15–25.

48   Lynch, John, "71 Arrested in Selma Alabama Voter Drive," *Chicago Daily Defender*, January 20, 1965, 10.

49   After being clubbed in the head with an ax handle, NBC's Selma correspondent delivered his report the next day from his hospital bed. Garrow, *Protest at Selma*, 43–61; and Bodroghkozy, *Equal Time*, 124.

50   Garrow, *Protest at Selma*, 70–78; and Bodroghkozy, *Equal Time*, 115.

51   Garrow, *Protest at Selma*, 84–111.

52   Ibid., 115–18; and John Lewis, *Walking in the Wind: A Memoir of the Movement* (New York: Simon and Schuster, 1998), 341.

53   Gregory, *Up from Nigger*, 88.

54   John Herbers, "Taunted Sheriff Hits Rights Aide," *New York Times*, February 17, 1965; and John Herbers, "Dr. King Urges Selma Negroes to Wage a More Militant Drive," *New York Times*, February 18, 1965.

55   Lewis, *Walking in the Wind*, 342.

56   Louis Calta, "Civil Rights Show Backed By Mayor," *New York Times*, March 19, 1965, 31; and Louis Calta, "Reply to Selma Stirs Broadway, *New York Times*, March 27, 1965, 14.

57   Belafonte, *My Song*, 301–2.

58   Sammy Davis, Jr., *Why Me? The Sammy Davis, Jr., Story* (New York: Farrar, Straus and Giroux, 1989), 161.

59   Richard D. Leonard, *Call to Selma: Eighteen Days of Witness* (Boston: Skinner House Books, 2002), 90–94.

60   Gregory, *Up from Nigger*, 94–95; Lewis, *Walking in the Wind*, 345; Lewis interview.

61   Charlton Heston, *The Actor's Life: Journals, 1956–1976* (New York: E. P. Dutton, 1978), 221; and "Marked for Montgomery, Stars' Fell on Alabama with Fear and Conviction," *Jet*, April 8, 1965, 58–60.

62   Lewis interview.

63   Shelley Winters, *Shelley: Also Known as Shirley* (New York: William Morrow and Company, 1980), 438.

64   Belafonte, *My Song*, 302–3.

65   Winters, *Shelley*, 439; and Billy Rowe, "Izzy Rowe's Notebook," *Pittsburgh Courier*, April 3, 1965, 17.

66   Taylor Branch, *At Canaan's Edge: America in the King Years, 1965–68* (New York: Simon and Schuster, 2006), 157.

67   Rowe, "Izzy Rowe's Notebook," 17.

68   Winters, *Shelley*, 439.

69   Harris Wofford, *Of Kennedys and Kings: Making Sense of the Sixties* (New York: Farrar, Straus, Giroux, 1980), 195.

70   Renata Adler, "Letter from Selma," *New Yorker*, April 10, 1965, accessed, October 23, 2014, http://www.newyorker.com/magazine/1965/04/10/letter-from-selma.

71 "March on Montgomery," CBS News special report, March 25, 1965, Paley Center for Media, New York City (hereafter referred to as PCM); and Gregory, *Up from Nigger*, 96.

72 Belafonte, *My Song*, 304.

73 "March on Montgomery," CBS.

74 Robert Hohler in Leonard, *Call to Selma*, 139.

75 Fred Friendly, *Due to Circumstances Beyond Our Control* (New York: Random House, 1967), 171.

76 Ben A. Franklin, "Top Entertainers in Alabama Tonight," *New York Times*, March 24, 1965, 33; Roy Reed, "25,000 Go to Alabama's Capitol . . .," *New York Times*, March 26, 1965, 1; Jack Gould, "TV: Conveying the Depths of Feelings," *New York Times*, March 26, 1965, 70; Betty Washington, "Legion on to Capitol in Triumph," *The Chicago Defender*, March 27, 1965, 1.

77 Leonard, *Call to Selma*, 102–3.

78 Charles Fager, *Selma, 1965* (New York: Scribner, 1974) 155; and "Stars at Work," *Jet*, April 8, 1965, 31.

79 Branch, *At Canaan's Edge*, 152.

80 Leonard, *Call to Selma*, 112–16.

81 Garrow, *Protest at Selma*, 117–18.

82 John Molleson, "'Answer to Selma' Benefit Raises Record $150,000," *New York Herald Tribune*, April 5, 1965.

83 "Headliners Star in Uptown Drama," *New York Times*, June 18, 1965, 54.

84 Molleson, "Answer to Selma"; and "Broadway Answers Selma," report, SNCC Papers, reel 27.

85 Branch, *At Canaan's Edge*, 152; and Edith Evans Asbury, "Rights Workers Learn and Help," *New York Times*, August 15, 1965, 72.

86 "Stars Answer Selma with $150,000; First Time for Many," *Jet*, April 22, 1965, 61.

87 Gene Roberts, "Paradox for Negroes," *New York Times*, August 8, 1965, 58.

88 Gregory, *Callus on My Soul*, 110; Gregory, *Up from Nigger*, 113–16; CBS special report on race riot in Watts, August 15, 1965, sound recording: RG 200-MR-2007, Motion Picture, Sound, and Video Records LICON, Special Media Archives Services Division, National Archives, College Park, Maryland.

89 Harry Belafonte, July 19, 1966, U.S. Information Agency, Voice of America, ARC ID: 126883, Motion Picture, Sound, and Video Records LICON, Special Media Archives Services Division, National Archives, College Park, Maryland.

90 Fundraising conference memo and agenda, March 8, 1965; "Minutes-Meeting of April 29, 1965"; and "Artists Committee Sponsoring SNCC Concerts," SNCC Papers, reel 27.

91 Letter from Julie Belafonte to [SNCC supporter], March 18, 1965; letter from Julie Belafonte to [SNCC supporter], n.d. (c. March/April 1965); "Sunday Evening with SNCC" invitation; "Progress Report," March 24, 2965; and April 29, 1965, minutes, SNCC Papers, reel 27. Also, "Dinner at Hilton in March to Aid Civil Rights Unit," *New York Times* (February 24, 1966: 31), 31.

92   Letter from Clifford A. Vaughn to Mike Standard, June 14, 1965, SNCC
      Papers, reel 27.

93   Peter Barthollywood, "Liberals vs. Their Movies," *New York Times*, August 19,
      1965, X9.

94   Fundraising conference memo and agenda, March 8, 1965, SNCC Papers, reel 27.

95   A message from Harry Belafonte: "Sammy Younge, Jr." n.d. (c. Spring 1966);
      "War Refugee," May 1966; and "Fear" June/July 1966, SNCC Papers, reel 27.

96   Herbert H. Haines, "Black Radicalization and Funding of Civil Rights: 1957–
      1970," *Social Problems* 32, no. 1 (Oct. 1984): 36.

97   Letter from Betty Garman to Harold Leventhal, March 1, 1965, SNCC Papers,
      reel 27.

98   Letter from Hilda Wilson to James Forman, March 1, 1965; and letter from
      Hilda Wilson to Reginald Robinson, March 1, 1965, Box 17, F. 10, "SNCC
      Correspondence 1965, March," James Forman Papers, MD-LOC.

99   Memo from Reggie Robinson to James Forman, Betty Garman, and Elizabeth
      Sutherland, March 10, 1965, SNCC Papers, reel 27.

100   Letter from James Garner to Friend, March 21, 1966; letter from James
      Garner to Celebrity Sponsor, n.d., (c. April 1966); letter from Elizabeth
      [Sutherland] to Cathy, March 30, 1966; Celebrity Billiard Tournament flyer,
      May 1966; and letter from Alice Richman to James Forman, May 2, 1966;
      all in SNCC Papers, reel 27.

101   Letter from Thomas J. Brandon to James Forman, March 10, 1965, Box 17,
      F. 10, "SNCC Correspondence 1965, Mar.," James Forman Papers, MD-LOC.

102   Northern Staff Meeting Minutes, n.d. but circa 1965, Box 31, F. 6, "Financial
      Records Fundraising, 1965 Jan.–Dec.," James Forman Papers, MD-LOC.

103   Belafonte, *My Song*, 307.

104   Northern Staff Meeting Minutes.

105   Bob Zellner, e-mail interview with the author, March 29, 2014; and notes
      from Betty [Garman], n.d. (c. 1965), Box 31, F. 8, "Financial Records, Fund-
      raising, 1966–67," n.d., James Forman Papers, MD-LOC.

106   "Minutes Ad Hoc Emergency Personnel Committee, September 2, 1964," Box 35,
      F. 12, "SNCC Meetings 1964, September," James Forman Papers, MD-LOC.

107   "Minutes-Meeting of April 29, 1965," SNCC Papers, reel 27.

108   "Memo from Betty Garman to Friends of SNCC, July 20, 1965," Box 31, F. 2,
      "Financial Records, Correspondence, 1965," James Forman Papers, MD-LOC.

109   "Minutes of Steering Committee Meeting, October 8, 1964," Box 35, F. 14,
      "SNCC Meetings 1964, Oct (1 of 2)"; and Northern Staff Meeting Minutes,
      James Forman Papers, MD-LOC. At this point, a number of SNCC field
      workers had come to appreciate the NAACP's laying the groundwork and
      underground support. Dave Dennis, telephone interview with the author,
      January 29, 2014.

110   Haines, "Black Radicalization," 37; Branch, *At Canaan's Edge*, 372; and Harry
      Belafonte, recorded interview with Vicki Daitch, May 20, 2005, 19, John F.
      Kennedy Library, Oral History (hereafter cited as JFKOH).

111 FBI File, Sammy Davis, Jr., 100-450712 (hereafter referred to as Davis FBI File).

112 Belafonte, *My Song*, 309.

113 "Dr. King, Belafonte Are Swedish Heroes: Rights Drive Gets Widespread Backing," *Chicago Daily Defender*, April 4, 1966, 4; "Europeans Give Generously to Dr. King's Rights Fund," *Chicago Daily Defender*, April 6, 1966, 6; "Dr. King Receives $100,000 Donation," *New York Times*, July 6, 1966, 15; Glenn Douglass, "Sweden Gives King $100,000 for His Work, *Chicago Defender*, July 16, 1966, 4; and Belafonte, JFKOH, 21.

114 Thomas A. Johnson, "Sammy Davis, Jr. Apptn'd to N.A.A.C.P. Post," *New York Times*, April 14, 1966, 24; Theresa Fambro Brooks, "'Sammy' to Host Cocktail Fete for NAACP Life Memberships," *Chicago Daily Defender*, April 27, 1968, 17; and "Yul Brynner Now a Life Member of the NAACP," *Chicago Defender*, September 3, 1966, 14.

115 Martin N. Marger, "Social Movements and Response to Environmental Change: The NAACP, 1960–1973," *Social Problems* 32, no. 1 (Oct. 1984): 23–26.

116 Letter to Sammy Davis, Jr., from Dr. Frederick G. Adams (president, Danbury Branch, NAACP), August 4, 1965, F. "Davis, Sammy, Jr., 1958–65," Group III: A94; letter from Leonard H. Carter (regional director NAACP) to Sammy Davis, Jr., July 29, 1969, F. "Davis, Sammy, Jr.," 1969, IV: 26; and telegram from D'Orsay D. Bryant (Baton Rouge branch president NAACP) to Roy Wilkins, August 14, 1969, F. "Davis, Sammy, Jr., 1969," IV: 26, all in NAACP Papers, MD-LOC.

117 A. S. "Doc" Young, "How Harry Belafonte Patched SCLC, SNCC Strategy Rupture," *Chicago Daily Defender*, May 5, 1965): 4.

118 James Meredith with William Doyle, *A Mission from God: A Memoir and Challenge for America* (New York: Atria Books, 2012), 198.

119 Gregory, *Up from Nigger*, 130.

120 Meredith, *Mission from God*, 204.

121 Gregory, *Up from Nigger*, 133.

122 Branch, *At Canaan's Edge*, 483, 491.

123 Davis FBI File.

124 "Sammy Davis, Jr., Will Head Film Troupe to Mississippi," *New York Times*, June 22, 1966, 37.

125 Gene Roberts, "Meredith Leads the March on Eve of Rally in Jackson," *New York Times*, June 26, 1966, L1.

126 Gregory, *Up from Nigger*, 135.

127 "The March in Mississippi," CBS News special report, June 26, 1966, PCM.

128 Douglass, "Sweden Gives," 4.

129 Meredith, *Mission from God*, 221.

130 Dennis interview and Walker interview.

131 Casey Hayden, telephone interview with the author, July 30, 2013.

132 Lewis interview.

133 Zellner interview and Walker interview.

134 Donald Critchlow and Emilie Raymond, eds., *Hollywood and Politics: A Source-book* (New York: Routledge, 2009), 109.

135 Emilie Raymond, *'From My Cold, Dead Hands': Charlton Heston and American Politics* (Lexington: University Press of Kentucky, 2006), 136, 166–68.

136 Peter Bart, "33-Hour Teach-In Attracts 10,000" *New York Times,* May 23, 1965, 26; and Dick Gregory, "The Pacifica Radio/UC Berkeley Social Activism Sound Recording Project: Anti-Vietnam War Protests in the San Francisco Bay Area & Beyond," originally broadcast on KPFA, 1965, accessed, October 16, 2014, http://www.lib.berkeley.edu/MRC/pacificaviet.html.

137 Max Frankel, "Demonstrators Decorous—3 White House Aides Meet with Leaders: Thousands Join Antiwar March," *New York Times,* November 28, 1965, 1.

138 "Belafonte in Paris Assails Policy of U.S. in Vietnam," *New York Times,* March 25, 1966, 37.

139 Gregory, *Callus on My Soul,* 123.

140 Branch, *At Canaan's Edge,* 642, 648.

141 Gregory, *Callus on My Soul,* 161–65.

142 Aram Goudsouzian, *Sidney Poitier: Man, Actor, Icon* (Chapel Hill: University of North Carolina Press, 2004), 234–35; and "The Bahamas, Amid Pomp and Calypso, Becomes Independent," *New York Times,* July 11, 1974, 2.

NOTES TO CHAPTER 7

Sidney Poitier, *This Life* (New York: Knopf, 1980), 328.

1 Howard Thompson, "Davis Film Draws Slim Attendance," *New York Times,* September 27, 1963, 16.

2 Howard Thompson, "'Gone Are Days' Closes Monday, *New York Times,* October 24, 1963, 37; and Bosley Crowther, "The Negro in Films," *New York Times,* December 6, 1963, 29.

3 Sammy Davis, Jr., in Howard Thompson, "Golden Boy Turns to the Trumpet for Film: Sammy Davis Doing 'Man Called Adam' Between Shows," *New York Times,* November 26, 1965, 44.

4 "Ike Jones Set as 1st Negro Producer of Major Film," *Jet,* September 16, 1965, 58.

5 Ossie Davis in Wil Haygood, *In Black and White: The Life of Sammy Davis, Jr.* (New York: Alfred A. Knopf, 2003), 358.

6 Mark A. Reid, *Redefining Black Film* (Berkeley: University of California Press, 1993), 71–73.

7 Aram Goudsouzian, *Sidney Poitier: Man, Actor, Icon* (Chapel Hill: University of North Carolina Press, 2004), 270.

8 Joan Barthel, "He Doesn't Want to Be Sexless Sidney," *New York Times,* August 6, 1967, 89.

9 Ibid.

10 "Poitier Now Romantic Hero," *Bay State Banner,* July 11, 1968, 7.

11 Vincent Canby, "The Screen: Poitier's Metamorphosis," *New York Times,* July 18, 1968, 26.

12 Murray Schumasch, "NAACP Scores Film Labor Units: Crafts Said to Bar Negroes—Gains for Actors Noted," *New York Times,* June 1, 1964, 33.

13 NAACP petition and resolution, n.d. (circa July 1965), F. "NAACP #1, Association of Motion Pictures and Television Producers (AMPTP)," Special Collection, Margaret Herrick Library–Academy of Motion Pictures Arts and Sciences, Beverly Hills, California (hereafter referred to as MHL-AMPAS).

14 "Report on Progress of Employment Opportunities for Negro Extras," n.d. (c. May 1965); and AMPTP report "on Employment of Negroes," March 1964, F. "NAACP #2 Casting Minority Reports," AMPTP, MHL-AMPAS.

15 "NAACP Weighs Movie Job Suits," *New York Times,* July 9, 1965, 16.

16 "Push Negro Employment in Movie Industry," *Chicago Defender,* April 25, 1966, 15.

17 Walter Burrell, "Negro Job Openings Aid Whites Too," *Chicago Defender,* July 15, 1967, 22.

18 "Negro Employment in Motion Pictures," quarterly reports between 1965 and 1967, F. "NAACP #2 Casting Minority Reports," AMPTP, MHL-AMPAS.

19 Fraser Heston telephone interview with the author, January 21, 2011; and Burrell, "Negro Job Openings," 22.

20 "Conversations '68 with Guest Bill Cosby," August 25, 1968, U.S. Information Agency, Voice of America, Sound Recording: RG 306-EN-XT, 8890, Motion Pictures, Sound, and Video Records LICON, Special Media Archives Sources Division, College Park, Maryland.

21 *The Jack Paar Collection,* May 8, 1964, University of California–Los Angeles Film and Television Archive (hereafter referred to as UCLA-FTA).

22 Donald Bogle, *Prime Time Blues: African Americans on Network Television* (New York: Farrar, Straus and Giroux, 2001), 119–21.

23 Robert Culp on *The O'Reilly Factor,* transcript, November 10, 2007, accessed February 20, 2013, http://www.network54.com/Forum/172251/thread/ 1194727911/1195017480/Here+is+the+transcript!; "Danny Was a Million Laughs, *I Spy,* October 20, 1965; and "Affair in T'Sien Cha," *I Spy,* December 29, 1965.

24 "Conversation '68 with Guest Bill Cosby."

25 J. Fred MacDonald, *Blacks and White TV: Afro-Americans in Television since 1948* (Chicago: Nelson-Hall Publishers, 1983), 107–11; and Bogle, *Prime Time Blues,* 124.

26 Evelyn Cunningham, "Sammy Davis Series Will Help Negroes," *Chicago Daily Defender,* November 8, 1965, 20.

27 MacDonald, *Blacks and White TV,* 113.

28 Kenneth Gouldthrope, "A Big-Star Stomp through Oldtime Harlem," *Life* (1966): 68–78; Karen Beavers, "Lead Man Holler: Harry Belafonte and the Culture Industry" (PhD diss., University of Southern California, 2008), 239–

53; and "The Strollin' Twenties," CBS-TV, February 21, 1966, Paley Center for Media, New York City (hereafter referred to as PCM).

29   Harry Belafonte, *My Song: A Memoir* (New York: Knopf, 2011), 317–18; and Beavers, "Lead Man Holler," 259.

30   Christine Acham, *Revolution Televised: Prime Time and the Struggle for Black Power* (Minneapolis: University of Minnesota Press, 2004), 9–19.

31   Paul Gardner, "Dark Laughter in a Snow White Land," *New York Times,* April 2, 1967, 117.

32   Thomas Sugrue, *Sweet Land of Liberty: The Forgotten Struggle for Civil Rights in the North* (New York: Random House, 2008), 402–10, 425.

33   Mel Watkins, *On the Real Side: Laughing, Lying, and Signifying: The Underground Tradition of African-American Humor that Transformed American Culture, from Slavery to Richard Pryor* (New York: Simon & Schuster, 1994), 64.

34   Pigmeat Markham, with Bill Levinson, *Here Come the Judge!* (New York: Popular Library, 1969), chapter 9 (no page numbers in book).

35   "ABC Stage 67: A Time for Laughter," ABC-TV, April 6, 1967, PCM.

36   Markham, *Here Come the Judge!,* chapter 3.

37   Ibid., chapter 1.

38   Hal Erickson, *From Beautiful Downtown Burbank: A Cultural History of Rowan and Martin's Laugh-In, 1968–1973* (Jefferson, NC: McFarland & Company, 2000), 145.

39   *Rowan and Martin's Laugh-In,* March 25, 1968, UCLA-FTA.

40   *Rowan and Martin's Laugh-In,* March 17, 1969, PCM.

41   Sammy Davis, Jr., on *The Tonight Show,* March 25, 1968, UCLA-FTA.

42   "Belafonte Power," *Newsweek,* February 19, 1968, 101.

43   Gardner, "Dark Laughter," 117; and Sugrue, *Sweet Land of Liberty,* 400. Sugrue says that "only 17 percent of its residents stated they would stay in Harlem if they could find housing options elsewhere."

44   Sammy Davis, Jr., *Why Me? The Sammy Davis, Jr., Story* (New York: Farrar, Straus and Giroux, 1989), 210.

45   Richard Iton, *Solidarity Blues: Race, Culture, and the American Left* (Chapel Hill: University of North Carolina Press, 2000), 219.

46   Betty Washington, "Black, White Together Join in Dr. King's Last March for Rights," *Chicago Defender,* April 10, 1968, 3; and "Martin Luther King, Jr., Funeral," CBS News report, April 19, 1968, PCM.

47   James Gavin, *Stormy Weather: The Life of Lena Horne* (New York: Atria Books, 2009), 362, 388–89.

48   Goudsouzian, *Sidney Poitier,* 291; and Belafonte, *My Song,* 333.

49   Davis FBI File.

50   Faith Berry, "The Anger and Problems, and Sickness of the Poor of the Whole Nation . . .," *New York Times,* January 7, 1968, SM5.

51   Belafonte, *My Song,* 337.

52   Vanessa Murphree, *Selling of Civil Rights: The Student Nonviolent Coordinating Committee and the Use of Public Relations* (New York: Routledge, 2006), 141–42.

53 "Bikel Scores Attack on Jews by S.N.C.C. and Quits Group," *New York Times,* August 17, 1967, 27.

54 Theodore Bikel, *Theo: The Autobiography of Theodore Bikel* (New York: Harper-Collins Publishers, 1994), 259–62.

55 Belafonte, *My Song*, 308.

56 Ward, *Just My Soul*, 310.

57 Sugrue, *Sweet Land*, 314–15; and Ingrid Monson, *Freedom Sounds: Civil Rights Call Out to Jazz and Africa* (Oxford: Oxford University Press, 2007), 226.

58 Dick Gregory, *Up from Nigger* (New York: Stein and Day, 1976), 137; Harry Belafonte, July 19, 1966, U.S. Information Agency, Voice of America, ARC ID: 126883, Motion Picture, Sound, and Video Records LICON, Special Media Archives Services Division, National Archives, College Park, Maryland; and Belafonte, *My Song*, 308.

59 Goudsouzian, *Sidney Poitier*, 321.

60 Henry Hampton and Steve Fayer, *Voices of Freedom: An Oral History of the Civil Rights Movement from the 1950s through the 1980s* (New York: Bantam Books, 1990), 512.

61 Ossie Davis et al., "Police Shooting of Oakland Negro," *New York Times,* May 6, 1968, 46.

62 Morris Kaplan, "Panther Officer Jumps Bail Here," *New York Times,* December 19, 1969, 49.

63 "Slate Panther Defense Confab for March 6–8," *Chicago Daily Defender,* February 3, 1970, 5; "2-Day Parley on Panthers," *Chicago Daily Defender,* March 5, 1970, 2; and "Panther Backers Urge Week to End Genocide," *Chicago Daily Defender,* September 19, 1970, 1.

64 Davis FBI File.

65 Hampton and Fayer, *Voices of Freedom*, 511–12.

66 "Panther Backers Urge Week," 1.

67 Davis, *Why Me?*, 194, 214–16.

68 Ibid.; and Diahann Carroll and Ross Firestone, *Diahann: An Autobiography* (New York: Little Brown & Company, 1986), 151.

69 Lawrence E. Davies, "Black Panthers Denounce Policemen," *New York Times,* April 13, 1968, 12; and Marlon Brando, *Songs My Mother Taught Me* (New York: Random House, 1994), 300–303.

70 David Richards, *Played Out: The Jean Seberg Story* (New York: Random House, 1981), 217; and "Daughter of Aide in Canada on Bail," *New York Times,* October 4, 1969, 35.

71 Richards, *Played Out*, 213–16, 219–21.

72 Jane Fonda, *My Life So Far* (New York: Random House, 2005), 227.

73 "Panthers Give Up Convention Plan," *New York Times,* November 29, 1970, 34; "Black Panther Aide Surrenders Here," *New York Times,* September 20, 1970, 27; John Darnton, "Newton and Seale Reunited Briefly," *New York Times,* August 22, 1970, 11; and "Actress Jane Fonda Vows to Back Panthers," *Chicago Defender,* February 8, 1971, 17.

74 Davis, *With Ossie and Ruby*, 347.

75 Richards, *Played Out*, 237.

76 Mary Hershberger, *Jane Fonda's War: A Political biography of an Antiwar Icon* (New York and London: The New Press, 2005); 51–54 and Richards, *Played Out*, 250–54.

77 "Hoover Holds Panthers' Hatred Causes Clashes with the Police," *New York Times*, May 9, 1970, 21.

78 David Dennis interview, telephone interview with the author, January 29, 2014.

79 Tom Wolfe, *Radical Chic and Mau-Mauing the Flak Catchers* (New York: Noonday Press, 1970), 3–42.

80 "Leonard Bernstein Asserts F.B.I. Used 'Dirty Tricks' Against Him," *New York Times*, October 22, 1980, A20.

81 Richard Iton, *In Search of the Black Fantastic: Politics and Popular Culture in the Post-Civil Rights Era* (Oxford: Oxford University Press, 2008), 87–94.

82 Robin Kelley, *Yo' Mama's Disfunktional! Fighting the Culture Wars in Urban America* (Boston: Beacon Press, 1997), 6.

83 Paul Delaney, "Panthers Exchanging Guns for Ballots: Panthers, in a Policy Change, Trade Guns for Ballots," *New York Times*, August 20, 1972, 1 and 59.

84 Iton, *In Search of the Black Fantastic*, 94.

85 Memo from Herbert L. Porter to John N. Mitchell, "Talking Points for Meeting with Sammy Davis, Jr.," April 13, 1973, F. "Celebrities" (2 of 4), Box 14, Jeb S. Magruder Papers, Richard Nixon Presidential Library and Museum, Yorba Linda, California (hereafter referred to as RNPL); Dean Kotlowski, "Black Power—Nixon Style: The Nixon Administration and Minority Business Enterprise," *Business History Review*, vol. 72, no. 3 (Autumn 1998): 410–12, 431, and 436; Robert J. Brown, "Black Memories of the White House: Nixon," *American Visions* 10 (Feb./Mar. 1995: 44–46), 46.

86 Sammy Davis, Jr., *Why Me? The Sammy Davis, Jr., Story* (New York: Farrar, Straus and Giroux, 1989), 250; and James Conaway, "Sammy Davis Jr. Has Bought the Bus," *New York Times*, October 6, 1972, 117.

87 Memo from Jeffrey Donfeld for the President's File, "President's Meeting with Mr. Sammy Davis, Jr.," July 21, 1971, F. "Celebrities" 3 of 3, Box 9, H. R. Haldeman Donated Papers, Subseries A Working Files, RNPL.

88 Kotlowski, "Black Power," 431, 437.

89 Sammy Davis, Jr, "Why I Went to the Troops," *Ebony* (June 1972): 141–47; Davis in Porter, "Talking Points"; and Sammy Davis, Jr., *Hollywood in a Suitcase* (New York: William Morrow and Company, 1980), 248–51.

90 Letter from Sammy Davis, Jr., to Richard M. Nixon, February 3, 1972, F. "Celebrities" 3 of 3, Box 9, Haldeman Papers, RNPL.

91 Robert E. Weems, Jr., with Lewis Randolph, *Business in Black and White: American Presidents and Black Entrepreneurs in the Twentieth Century* (New York: New York University Press, 2009), 108.

92 Floyd McKissick's all-black town "Soul City" in North Carolina, for example,

received a $14 million federally guaranteed loan. Joshua D. Farrington, "The National Committee for a Two-Party System: A Political Alternative for Black Voters in the 1970s," unpublished paper, presentation at the Policy History Conference, Columbus, OH, June 4, 2014, pgs. 3–4.

93   Manning Marable, *How Capitalism Underdeveloped Black America* (Boston: South End Press, 1983), 176, 181; Manning Marable, *Black Liberation in Conservative America* (Boston: South End Press, 1997), 216–17; Matthew D. Lassiter, *The Silent Majority: Suburban Politics in the Sunbelt South* (Princeton: Princeton University Press, 2006), 251–70; Bruce J. Schulman, *The Seventies: The Great Shift in American Culture, Society, and Politics* (Cambridge, MA: Da Capo Press, 2001), 38–40; Kelley, *Yo' Mama's Disfunktional!*, 89; Joan Hoff, *Nixon Reconsidered* (New York: Basic Books, 1994), 77–114; Hugh Davis Graham, *The Civil Rights Era: Origins and Development of National Policy, 1960–1972* (New York: Oxford University Press, 1990), 322–65; Kotlowski, "Black Power," 420.

94   Memo from Paul Jones to Bart Porter, January 31, 1972, F. "The Black Vote" (1 of 5), Box 12, Jeb S. Magruder Papers, RNPL; and letter from Davis to Nixon.

95   Sean Campbell, *The Sitcoms of Norman Lear* (Jefferson, NC: McFarland and Company, 2007), 3–4.

96   Carroll, *Diahann*, 145–63.

97   MacDonald, *Blacks and White TV*, 156–60.

98   Acham, *Revolution Televised*, 72–77.

99   *"All in the Family*: Sammy's Visit," February 19, 1972, UCLA-FTA.

100 Haygood, *In Black and White*, 421; Matt Birkbeck, *Deconstructing Sammy: Music, Money, Madness, and the Mob* (New York: Amistad, 2008), 15; and Campbell, *Sitcoms of Norman Lear*, 26.

101 Bob Zellner, telephone interview with the author, February 5, 2014.

102 Memo from Herbert L. Porter to H. R. Haldeman, "Celebrities," January 31, 1972, F. "Celebrities" (3 of 4), Box 14; and memo from Jeb S. Magruder to H. R. Haldeman, "Celebrities," March 10, 1972, F. "Celebrities" (1 of 4), Box 14, both in Magruder Papers, RNPL; memo from Raymond Caldiero to Gordon Strachan, "Flip Wilson," July 18, 1972, F. "Celebrities II" (2 of 2), Box 9, Haldeman Papers; and Haygood, *In Black and White*, 428.

103 "List of Celebrities in Hollywood for the President and the Number of Events They Attended," F. "Celebrities for the President—1972" (1 of 2), Box 137, President's Personal File, RMNPL; memo from Raymond Caldiero to Clark MacGregor, "Celebrity/American Music Update," September 12, 1972, F. "Celebrities II" (1 of 2), Box 9, Haldeman Papers, RMNPL; CBS News special, "Campaign '72—Election Year—The," August 21, 1972, Washington: University of Washington, item from Coll. MR: 200-MR-4395d, University of Washington Collection, ca. 1931–c. 1977, Motion Picture, Sound and Video Records LICON, Special Media Archives Services Division, National Archives, College Park, MD.

104 Davis, *Why Me?*, 263.

105 Haygood, *In Black and White*, 429.

106 Farrington, "National Committee," 6–7.

107 Davis, *Why Me?*, 264, 267; and Haygood, *In Black and White*, 440.

108 Jon Lewis, *American Film: A History* (New York: W. W. Norton and Company, 2008), 238.

109 Goudsouzian, *Sidney Poitier*, 286, 320–25; and Hollis Alpert, "SR Goes to the Movies: The Lost Movie," *Saturday Review,* June 28, 1969, 23.

110 Sidney Poitier, interview with Ruby Dee, Sidney Poitier—Unedited Version, Box 1, F. "A Talk about Film with Sidney Poitier," n.d. (c. 1968), Ossie Davis and Ruby Dee Drama Collection, Schomburg Center for Research in Black Culture, Harlem, New York.

111 Goudsouzian, *Sidney Poitier*, 331.

112 "Is It Better to Be Shaft or Uncle Tom? Movies," *New York Times,* August 26, 1973, 117.

113 Ed Guerrero, *Framing Blackness: The African American Image in Film* (Philadelphia: Temple University Press, 1993), 78; and Darius James, *That's Blaxploitation: Roots of the Baadasssss 'Tude (Rated X by an All-Whyte Jury)* (New York: St. Martin's Griffin, 1995), 30–39.

114 George Gent, "Black Films Are In, So Are Profits," *New York Times,* July 8, 1972, 22.

115 Gordon Parks and Julius Griffin, "Black Movie Boom—Good or Bad," *New York Times,* December 17, 1972, D3.

116 "Blacks vs. Shaft" and "Filth vs. Lucre: The Black Community's Tough Choice," *Psychology Today* 7 (Feb. 1974): 99.

117 Scot French, *The Rebellious Slave: Nat Turner in American Memory* (Boston: Houghton Mifflin Company, 2004), 257.

118 Ossie Davis in Nat Henthoff, "Never Sell More of Yourself Than You Can Buy Back," *New York Times,* May 5, 1968, D15.

119 Earl Calloway, "Nat Turner Controversy Settled, Jones Slated for Title Role," *Chicago Daily Defender,* February 15, 1969, 15; and French, *Rebellious Slave*, 265–71.

120 *Cotton Comes to Harlem* (dir. Ossie Davis, 1970); Leonard Courtney Archer, *Black Images in the American Theatre: NAACP Campaigns—Stage, Screen, Radio, and Television* (Brooklyn, NY: Pageant-Poseidon, 1973), 304; and Davis in *Ossie and Ruby*, 335–36.

121 Davis in *With Ossie and Ruby*, 337.

122 Goudsouzian, *Sidney Poitier*, 320; and "Belafonte Plays Angel On and Off the Screen," *Ebony* (Oct. 1969): 76.

123 Davis in *With Ossie and Ruby*, 337, 356.

124 Belafonte, *My Song*, 349–50.

125 "Poitier, Belafonte on 'Soul!'" *Bay State Banner,* March 23, 1972, 14.

126 Poitier, *This Life*, 327; and Ruby Dee in Davis and Dee, *With Ossie and Ruby*, 354–55.

127 Ruby Dee in Goudsouzian, *Sidney Poitier*, 339.

128 Genia Fogelson, *Belafonte* (Los Angeles: Holloway House, 1980), 189–90.

129 Clayton Riley, "'Shaft Can Do Everything—I Can Do Nothing," *New York Times,* August 13, 1972, D9.

130 Poitier, *This Life,* 328.

131 Sharon Scott, "Two Top Black Actors Discuss Their New Movie, Buck and the Preacher," *Chicago Daily Defender,* April 1, 1972, 20.

132 Sidney Poitier in Michael E. Ross, "Sidney Poitier on 40 Years of Change," *New York Times,* February 28, 1989, C18.

NOTES TO EPILOGUE

1   Kirk Jackson, "Anti-Apartheid Protest Grows," *Washington Informer,* December 12, 1984, 1.

2   Clifford D. May, "'We Are the World' Meets a Continent of Misery," *New York Times,* June 26, 1985, A2.

3   David Dennis interview, telephone interview with the author, January 29, 2014.

4   "Ossie Davis Hosts NYC Rally to Save Mumia Abu-Jamal," *New York Beacon,* February 24, 1995, 2; and "Black Panther to Be Executed," *Michigan Citizen,* June 24, 1995, A1. Abu-Jamal was removed from death row in 2012.

5   Jay Z, "Nickels and Dimes," *Magna Carta Holy Grail* (2013).

6   Harry Belafonte in Lana K. Wilson-Combs, "Harry Belafonte Shares His Wisdom," *Sacramento Observer,* January 10, 2013, E2.

7   Julian Bond, e-mail interview with the author, March 10, 2014.

8   John Lewis, interview with the author, Washington, DC, September 11, 2013.

9   Bill Cosby, "Address at the NAACP on the 50th Anniversary of *Brown v. Board of Education,*" American Rhetoric, May 17, 2004, accessed October 17, 2014, http://www.americanrhetoric.com/speeches/billcosbypoundcakespeech.htm.

10   *Barbershop* (MGM 2002), directed by Tim Story.

11   "Image Awards Rekindle 'Barbershop' Controversy," CNN.com, accessed April 28, 2014, http://web.archive.org/web/20060629060508/http://www.cnn.com/2003/SHOWBIZ/TV/03/08/image.awards.ap/.

12   Stacy L. Smith and Marc Choueiti, "Black Characters in Popular Film: Is the Key to Diversifying Cinematic Content Held in the Hand of the Black Director?" Annenberg School for Communication and Journalism, University of Southern California, 2008, accessed October 17, 2014, http://annenberg.usc.edu/Faculty/Communication%20and%20Journalism/~/media/BlackCharacters_KeyFindings.ashx.

13   Viola Davis in Zach Johnson, "Viola Davis: I'll Never Play a Maid Again," *Us Weekly,* February 7, 2013, accessed October 17, 2014, http://www.usmagazine.com/entertainment/news/viola-davis-ill-never-play-a-maid-again-201372.

BIBLIOGRAPHY

ARCHIVAL COLLECTIONS

Ben-Ami (Rabbi David Z.) Papers. Civil Rights in Mississippi Digital Archives. University of Southern Mississippi.

Federal Bureau of Investigation.

John F. Kennedy Presidential Library. Oral Histories. Boston, Massachusetts.

Library of Congress. Manuscript Division. Washington, DC.

Margaret Herrick Library. Core Collection. Academy of Motion Picture Arts and Sciences. Beverly Hills, California.

———. Special Collections. Academy of Motion Picture Arts and Sciences. Beverly Hills, California.

Motion Picture, Sound, and Video Records. National Archives. College Park, Maryland.

Oviatt Library. California State University, Northridge. Special Collections and Archives. Max Mont Collection.

Pacifica Radio Archive. www.pacificaradioarchive.org

Paley Center for Media, New York City.

Richard Nixon Presidential Library and Museum. Yorba Linda, California.

Schomburg Center for Research in Black Culture. Harlem, New York.

Student Nonviolent Coordinating Committee Papers. Microfilm.

University of California–Los Angeles Film and Television Archive.

"Washington Marry-Go-Round." American University Library-Special Collections, Washington DC.

INTERVIEWS

Theodore Bikel
Julian Bond
Gloria Richardson Dandridge
David Dennis
Joanne Gavin

William Hansen
Casey Hayden
Fraser Heston
John Lewis
Constancia "Dinky" Romilly
Rev. Wyatt Tee Walker
Bob Zellner

FILMS

Barbershop. Directed by Tim Story. Santa Monica, California: MGM Entertainment. 2003.

Bright Road. Directed by Gerald Mayer. Burbank, California: Warner Home Video. 2013.

Buck and the Preacher. Directed by Sidney Poitier. Culver City, California: Sony Pictures Home Entertainment. 2000.

Carmen Jones. Directed by Otto Preminger. Beverly Hills, California: Twentieth Century Fox Home Entertainment. 2002.

Cotton Comes to Harlem. Directed by Ossie Davis. Santa Monica, California: MGM Home Entertainment. 2001.

Island in the Sun. Directed by Robert Rossen. Los Angeles: Twentieth Century Fox Home Entertainment. 2005.

King: Go Beyond the Dream to Discover the Man. Directed by Tim Beacham, Tom Keenan, and Shoshana Guy. Distributed by New Video. New York: A & E Television Networks, 2008.

No Way Out. Directed by Joseph L. Mankiewicz. Beverly Hills: Twentieth Century Fox Home Entertainment. 2005.

Ocean's 11. Directed by Lewis Milestone. Burbank, California: Warner Home Video. 2008.

Porgy and Bess. Directed by Otto Preminger. Culver City, California: Columbia Pictures. 1959.

Porgy and Bess: An American Voice. Directed by Nigel Noble. Princeton, NJ: Films for the Humanities and Sciences, 1999.

The Rat Pack's Las Vegas. Directed by Rhys Thomas. West Long Branch, New Jersey: White Star Studio. 2002.

Scandalize My Name: Stories from the Blacklist. Edited by Doug Rossini. Thousand Oaks, CA: Urban Works Entertainment, 1999.

BOOKS AND ARTICLES

"And Nuttin's Plenty for Me." *Commonweal* 70 (Aug. 14, 1959): 424–5.

"Blacks vs. Shaft" and "Filth vs. Lucre: The Black Community's Tough Choice." *Psychology Today* 7 (Feb. 1974): 97–99 and 102.

"Hearing Regarding Communist Infiltration of Minority Groups—Part I and II." *Hearings Before the Committee on Un-American Activities, House of Representatives, Eighty-First Congress, First Session* (Jul. 13, 14, and 18, 1949): 479–83.

"Two Preminger Pictures." *New Republic* 141 (Jul. 13, 1959): 23–23.

Acham, Christine. *Revolution Televised: Prime Time and the Struggle for Black Power.* Minneapolis: University of Minnesota Press, 2004.

Allen, Ivan. *Mayor: Notes on the Sixties.* New York: Simon and Schuster, 1971.

Alpert, Hollis. *The Life and Times of Porgy and Bess: The Story of an American Classic.* New York: Alfred A. Knopf, 1990.

Anderson, Christopher. *Hollywood TV: Studio System in the Fifties.* Austin: University of Texas Press, 1994.

Archer, Leonard Courtney. *Black Images in the American Theatre: NAACP Campaigns— Stage, Screen, Radio, and Television.* Brooklyn, NY: Pageant-Poseidon, 1973.

Arsenault, Nelson. *Freedom Riders: 1961 and the Struggle for Racial Justice.* Oxford: Oxford University Press, 2006.

Bailey, Pearl. *The Raw Pearl.* New York: Harcourt, Brace & World, 1968.

Baldwin, James. "On Catfish Row: *Porgy and Bess* in the Movies." *Commentary* 28 (Sept. 1959): 246–48.

Balio, Tino. *Hollywood in the Age of Television.* Boston: Unwin Hyman, 1990.

Beavers, Karen. "Lead Man Holler: Harry Belafonte and the Culture Industry." PhD diss., University of Southern California, 2008.

Belafonte, Harry. *My Song: A Memoir.* New York: Knopf, 2011.

Benford, Robert D., and Scott A. Hunt. "Dramaturgy and Social Movements: The Social Construction and Communication of Power." *Sociological Inquiry* 62, no. 1 (Feb. 1992): 36–55.

Berg, A. Scott. *Goldwyn: A Biography.* New York: Knopf, 1989.

Bernadi, Daniel, ed. *Classic Hollywood, Classic Whiteness.* Minneapolis: University of Minnesota Press, 2001.

Bikel, Theodore. *Theo: The Autobiography of Theodore Bikel.* Madison: University of Wisconsin Press, 2002.

Birkbeck, Matt. *Deconstructing Sammy: Music, Money, Madness, and the Mob.* New York: Amistad, 2008.

Biondi, Martha. *To Stand and Fight: The Struggle for Civil Rights in Postwar New York City.* Cambridge, MA: Harvard University Press, 2003.

Bodroghkozy, Aniko. *Equal Time: Television and the Civil Rights Movement.* Urbana: University of Chicago Press, 2012.

Bogle, Donald. *Brown Sugar: Eighty Years of America's Black Female Superstars.* New York: Harmony Books, 1980.

———. *Dorothy Dandridge: A Biography.* New York: Amistad, 1997.

———. *Primetime Blues: African Americans on Network Television.* New York: Farrar, Straus and Giroux, 2001.

———. *Toms, Coons, Mulattoes, Mammies, and Bucks: An Interpretive History of Blacks in American Films.* New York: Continuum, 2001.

Boyar, Burt. *Photo by Sammy Davis, Jr.* New York: Regan, 2007.

Bracey, John H., Jr., and August Meier. "The NAACP as a Reform Movement, 1909–1965: 'To Reach the Conscience of America.'" *Journal of Southern History* 59, no. 1 (Feb. 1993): 3–30.

Branch, Taylor. *At Canaan's Edge: America in the King Years, 1965–68*. New York: Simon and Schuster, 2006.

———. *Parting the Waters: America in the King Years, 1954–63*. New York: Simon and Schuster, 1988.

Brando, Marlon. *Songs My Mother Taught Me*. New York: Random House, 1994.

Brilliant, Mark. *The Color of America Has Changed: How Racial Diversity Shaped Civil Rights Reform in California, 1941–1978*. Oxford: Oxford University Press, 2012.

Brown, Robert J. "Black Memories of the White House: Nixon." *American Visions* 10 (Feb./Mar. 1995): 44–46.

Brownell, Kathryn Cramer. *Showbiz Politics: Hollywood in American Political Life*. Chapel Hill: University of North Carolina Press, 2014.

Bullion, John L. *Lyndon B. Johnson and the Transformation of American Politics*. New York: Pearson Longman, 2008.

Burford, Kate. *Burt Lancaster: An American Life*. New York: Alfred A. Knopf, 2000.

Campbell, Sean. *The Sitcoms of Norman Lear*. Jefferson, NC: McFarland and Company, 2007.

Carmichael, Stokley. With Ekwrieme Michael Thelwell. *Ready for Revolution: The Life and Struggles of Stokley Carmichael (Kwame Ture)*. New York: Scribner, 2003.

Carroll, Diahann. *The Legs Are the Last to Go*. New York: Amistad, 2008.

Carroll, Diahann, and Ross Firestone. *Diahann: An Autobiography*. New York: Little Brown & Company, 1986.

Carson, Clayborne. *In Struggle: SNCC and the Black Awakening of the 1960s*. Cambridge, MA: Harvard University Press, 1981.

———, ed. *Malcolm X: The FBI File*. New York: Carroll and Graf Publishers, 1991.

———. *The Papers of Martin Luther King, Jr., Vols. 3–5*. Berkeley: University of California Press, 1992.

———. *The Student Voice, 1960–1965: Periodical of the Student Violent Nonviolent Coordinating Committee*. Westport, CT: Meckler, 1990.

Casstevens. Thomas W. *Politics, Housing, and Race Relations: California's Rumford Act and Proposition 14*. Berkeley: Institute of Governmental Studies, University of California, 1967.

Corwin, Norman. *Trivializing America: The Triumph of Mediocrity*. Secaucus, NJ: Carol Publishing Company, 1986,

Countryman, Matthew. *Up South: Civil Rights and Black Power in Philadelphia*. Philadelphia: University of Pennsylvania Press, 2006.

Cripps, Thomas. *Making Movies Black: The Hollywood Message Movie from World War II to the Civil Rights Era*. New York: Oxford University Press, 1993.

———. *Slow Fade to Black: The Negro in American Film, 1900–1942*. New York: Oxford University Press, 1977.

Cripps, Thomas, and David Culbert. "*The Negro Soldier* (1944): Film Propaganda in Black and White." In *Hollywood as Historian: American Film in a Cultural Context*, edited by Peter C. Rollins, 109–33. Lexington: University Press of Kentucky, 1983.

Critchlow, Donald T. *When Hollywood Was Right*. Cambridge University Press, 2013.

Critchlow, Donald, and Emilie Raymond, eds. *Hollywood and Politics: A Sourcebook*. New York: Routledge, 2009.

Curtin, Michael. *Redeeming the Wasteland: Television Documentary and Cold War Politics*. New Brunswick, NJ: Rutgers University Press, 1995.

Dandridge, Dorothy, and Earl Conrad. *Everything and Nothing: The Dorothy Dandridge Tragedy*. New York: Abelard-Schuman, 1970.

Davis, Ossie. *Life Lit by Some Large Vision: Selected Speeches and Writings*. New York: Atria Books, 2006.

Davis, Ossie, and Ruby Dee. *With Ossie and Ruby: In This Life Together*. New York: William Morrow and Company, 1998.

Davis, Sammy, Jr. *Hollywood in a Suitcase*. New York: William Morrow and Company, 1980.

———. *Why Me? The Sammy Davis, Jr., Story*. New York: Farrar, Straus and Giroux, 1989.

———. *Yes, I Can: The Story of Sammy Davis, Jr.* New York: Farrar, Straus and Giroux, 1965.

deCordova, Richard. *Picture Personalities: The Emergence of the Star System in America*. Urbana: University of Illinois Press, 1990.

Dittmer, John. *Local People: The Struggle for Civil Rights in Mississippi*. Urbana: University of Illinois Press, 1995.

Doody, Colleen. *Detroit's Cold War: The Origins of Postwar Conservatism*. Urbana, Chicago, and Springfield: University of Illinois Press, 2013.

Dudziak, Mary L. "Josephine Baker, Racial Protest, and the Cold War." *Journal of American History* 81, no. 2 (Sept. 1994): 543–80.

Early, Gerald. *This Is Where I Came In: Black America in the 1960s*. Lincoln: University of Nebraska Press, 2003.

Early, Gerald, ed. *The Sammy Davis, Jr., Reader*. New York: Farrar, Straus and Giroux, 2001.

Eastman, Carol. *The Search for Sam Goldwyn*. New York: William Morrow and Company, 1976.

Ely, Melvin Patrick. *The Adventures of Amos 'n' Andy: A Social History of an American Phenomenon*. New York: Free Press, 1991.

Epstein, Daniel Mark. *Nat King Cole*. New York: Farrar, Straus and Giroux, 1999.

Erickson, Hal. *From Beautiful Downtown Burbank: A Cultural History of Rowan and Martin's Laugh-In, 1968–1973*. Jefferson, NC: McFarland & Company, 2000.

Everett, Anna. *Returning the Gaze: A Genealogy of Black Film Criticism, 1909–1949*. Durham, NC: Duke University Press, 2001.

Fager, Charles. *Selma, 1965*. New York: Scribner, 1974.

Fairclough, Adam. *To Redeem the Soul of America: The Southern Christian Leadership Conference and Martin Luther King, Jr.* Athens: University of Georgia Press, 1987.

Falkner, David. *Great Time Coming: The Life of Jackie Robinson, from Baseball to Birmingham*. New York: Touchstone Books, 1995.

Farmer, James. *Lay Bare the Heart: An Autobiography of the Civil Rights Movement*. Fort Worth: Texas Christian University Press, 1998.

Farrington, Joshua D. "The National Committee for a Two-Party System: A Political Alternative for Black Voters in the 1970s." Unpublished paper. Presentation at the Policy History Conference, Columbus, OH, June 4, 2014.

Finch, Minnie. *The NAACP: Its Fight for Justice.* Mituchen, NJ: Scarecrow Press, 1981.

Finley, Randy. "Crossing the White Line: SNCC in Three Delta Towns, 1963–1967." *Arkansas Historical Quarterly* 65, no. 2 (Summer 2006): 116–37.

Flamming, Douglas. *Bound for Freedom: Black Los Angeles in Jim Crow America.* Berkeley: University of California Press, 2005.

Fogelson, Genia. *Belafonte.* Los Angeles: Holloway House, 1980.

Fonda, Jane. *My Life So Far.* New York: Random House, 2005.

Forman, James. *The Making of Black Revolutionaries.* Seattle: University of Washington Press, 1997.

French, Scot. *The Rebellious Slave: Nat Turner in American Memory.* Boston: Houghton Mifflin Company, 2004.

Friendly, Fred. *Due to Circumstances Beyond Our Control.* New York: Random House, 1967.

Gamson, Joshua, *Claims to Fame: Celebrity in Contemporary America.* Berkeley: University of California Press, 1994.

Garrow, David. *Protest at Selma: Martin Luther King, Jr., and the Voting Rights Act of 1965.* New Haven: Yale University Press, 1978.

Gavin, James. *Stormy Weather: The Life of Lena Horne.* New York: Atria Books, 2009.

Gentile, Thomas. *March on Washington: August 28, 1963.* Washington, DC: New Day Publications, 1983.

Goudsouzian, Aram. *Sidney Poitier: Man, Actor, Icon.* Chapel Hill: University of North Carolina Press, 2004.

Graham, Hugh Davis. *The Civil Rights Era: Origins and Development of National Policy, 1960–1972.* New York: Oxford University Press, 1990.

Greenstein, Fred I., and Raymond E. Wolfinger. "The Repeal of Fair Housing in California: An Analysis of Referendum Voting." *American Political Science Review* 62, no 3. (Sept. 1968): 753–69.

Gregory, Dick. *Callus on My Soul: A Memoir.* Atlanta: Longstreet Press, 2000.

———. *Up from Nigger.* New York: Stein and Day, 1976.

Gregory, Dick, with Robert Lipsyte. *Nigger: An Autobiography.* New York: E. P. Dutton and Company, 1964.

Guaralnick, Peter. *Dream Boogie: The Triumph of Sam Cooke.* New York: Little, Brown, 2005.

Guerrero, Ed. *Framing Blackness: The African American Image in Film.* Philadelphia: Temple University Press, 1993.

Haines, Herbert H. "Black Radicalization and Funding of Civil Rights: 1957–1970." *Social Problems* 32, no. 1 (Oct. 1984): 31–43.

Haley, Alex. "*Playboy* Interview: Sammy Davis, Jr." *Playboy* (Dec. 1966): 99–100, 102, 105–20, 124.

Hampton, Henry, and Steve Fayer, eds. *Voices of Freedom: An Oral History of the*

Civil Rights Movement from the 1950s through the 1980s. New York: Bantam Books, 1990.

Hatch, James V., ed., and Ted Shine (consultant). *Black Theater, U.S.A.: Forty-Five Plays by Black Americans, 1847–1974*. New York: The Free Press, 1974.

Hatch, Robert. "Films." *Nation* 189 (Jul. 4, 1959): 19.

Haygood, Wil. *In Black and White: The Life of Sammy Davis, Jr.* New York: Alfred A. Knopf, 2003.

Hershberger, Mary. *Jane Fonda's War: A Political Biography of an Antiwar Icon*. New York: The New Press, 2005.

Heston, Charlton. *The Actor's Life: Journals, 1956–1976*. New York: E. P. Dutton, 1978.

———. *In the Arena: An Autobiography*. New York: Simon and Schuster, 1995.

Heyward, Dubose. *Porgy*. New York: George H. Doran Company, 1925.

Hirsch, Foster. *Otto Preminger: The Man Who Would Be King*. New York: Knopf, 2007.

Hoff, Joan. *Nixon Reconsidered*. New York: Basic Books, 1994.

Horowitz, Joseph. *"On My Way": The Untold Story of Rouben Mamoulian, George Gershwin, and Porgy and Bess*. New York: W. W. Norton and Company, 2013.

HoSang, Daniel Martinez. "Racial Liberalism and the Rise of the Sunbelt West: The Defeat of Fair Housing on the 1964 California Ballot." In *Sunbelt Rising: The Politics of Space, Place, and Region in the American South and Southwest*, edited by D. Dochuck and M. Nickerson, 188–213. Philadelphia: University of Pennsylvania Press, 2011.

———. *Racial Propositions: Ballot Initiatives and the Making of Postwar California*. University of California Press, 2010.

Iton, Richard. *In Search of the Black Fantastic: Politics and Popular Culture in the Post-Civil Rights Era*. Oxford: Oxford University Press, 2008.

———. *Solidarity Blues: Race, Culture, and the American Left*. Chapel Hill: University of North Carolina Press, 2000.

James, Darius. *That's Blaxploitation: Roots of the Baadasssss 'Tude (Rated X by an All-Whyte Jury*. New York: St. Martin's Griffin, 1995.

Johnson, John H. *Succeeding Against the Odds*. New York: Warner Books, 1989.

Kaba, Lansine. "From Colonialism to Autocracy: Guinea under Sekou Toure, 1957–1984." In *Decolonization and African Independence: The Transfers of Power, 1960–1980*, edited by Prosser Gifford and William Roger Louis, 225–44. New Haven: Yale University Press, 1988.

Kelley, Robin. *Yo Mama's Disfunktional! Fighting the Culture Wars in Urban America*. Boston: Beacon Press, 1997.

Kennedy, Robert. *In His Own Words: The Unpublished Recollections of the Kennedy Years*. New York: Bantam Books, 1998.

King, Martin Luther, Jr. *Why We Can't Wait*. New York: Signet Classics, 2000.

Knight, Arthur. "Star Dancers: African-American Constructions of Stardom, 1925–60." In *Classic Hollywood, Classic Whiteness*, edited by Daniel Bernardi, 402–5. Minneapolis and London: University of Minnesota Press, 2001.

Kotlowski, Dean. "Black Power—Nixon Style: The Nixon Administration and Minority Business Enterprise." *Business History Review* 72, no. 3 (Autumn 1998): 409–45.

Kunstler, William. *Deep in My Heart*. New York: Morrow, 1966.

Lassiter, Matthew T. *The Silent Majority: Suburban Politics in the Sunbelt South*. Princeton: Princeton University Press, 2006.

Leonard, Richard. *Call to Selma: Eighteen Days of Witness*. Boston: Skinner House Books, 2002.

Levy, Peter B. *Civil War on Race Street: The Civil Rights Movement in Cambridge, Maryland*. Gainesville: University Press of Florida, 2003.

Lewis, John. *Walking with the Wind: A Memoir of the Movement*. New York: Simon and Schuster, 1998.

Lewis, Jon. *American Film: A History*. New York: W. W. Norton and Company, 2008.

Lord, M. G. *The Accidental Feminist: How Elizabeth Taylor Raised Our Consciousness and We Were Too Distracted by Her Beauty to Notice*. New York: Walker and Company, 2012.

Luper, Clara. *Behold These Walls*. Oklahoma City: Jim Wire, 1979.

Maccann, Richard Dyer. "Independence, with a Vengeance." *Film Quarterly* 15, no. 4 (Summer 1962): 14–21.

MacDonald, J. Fred. *Blacks and White TV: Afro-Americans in Television since 1948*. Chicago: Nelson-Hall Publishers, 1983.

Mack, Dwayne. "Hazel Scott: A Career Curtailed." *Journal of African-American History* 91, no. 2 (Spring 2006): 153–70.

Marable, Manning. *Black Liberation in Conservative America*. Boston: South End Press, 1997.

———. *How Capitalism Underdeveloped Black America*. Boston: South End Press, 1983.

———. *Malcolm X: A Life of Reinvention*. New York: Viking, 2011.

———. "Rediscovering Malcolm's Life: A Historian's Adventures in Living History." *Souls* 7 (Winter 2005): 20–35.

Marger, Martin N. "Social Movements and Response to Environmental Change: The NAACP, 1960–1973." *Social Problems* 32, no. 1 (Oct. 1984): 16–30.

Markham, Pigmeat, with Bill Levinson. *Here Come the Judge!* New York: Popular Library, 1969.

McAdam, Doug. *Freedom Summer*. New York: Oxford University Press, 1988.

Meier, August. *CORE: A Study in the Civil Rights Movement, 1942–1968*. New York: Oxford University Press, 1973.

Meredith, James, with William Doyle. *A Mission from God: A Memoir and Challenge for America*. New York: Atria Books, 2012.

Mitchell, Loften. *Black Drama: The Story of the American Negro in the Theatre*. New York: Hawthorn Books, 1967.

Monson, Ingrid. *Freedom Sounds: Civil Rights Call Out to Jazz and Africa*. Oxford: Oxford University Press, 2007.

Morris, Aldon. *Origins of the Civil Rights Movement: Black Communities Organizing for Change*. New York: Free Press, 1984.

Murphree, Vanessa. *Selling of Civil Rights: The Student Nonviolent Coordinating Committee and the Use of Public Relations*. New York: Routledge, 2006.

Nickel, John. "Disabling African-American Men: Liberalism and Race Message Films." *Cinema Journal* 44, no. 1 (Fall 2004): 25–48.

Noonan, Ellen. *The Strange Career of Porgy and Bess: Race, Culture, and America's Most Famous Opera*. Chapel Hill: University of North Carolina Press, 2012.

Oates, Stephen B. *Let the Trumpet Sound: The Life of Martin Luther King, Jr.* New York: Harper and Row, 1982.

Petkov, Steven, and Leonard Mustazza, eds. *The Frank Sinatra Reader*. New York: Oxford University Press, 1995.

Podair, Jerald. *Bayard Rustin American Dreamer*. Lanham, MD: Rowman & Littlefield Publishers, 2009.

Poitier, Sidney. *The Measure of a Man: A Spiritual Autobiography*. San Francisco: Harper, 2007.

———. *This Life*. New York: Knopf, 1980.

Ponce de Leon, Charles L. *Self Exposure: Human Interest Journalism and the Emergence of Celebrity in America, 1890–1940*. Chapel Hill: University of North Carolina Press, 2002.

Postman, Neil. *Amusing Ourselves to Death*. New York: Penguin, 2005.

Preminger, Otto. *Preminger: An Autobiography*. Garden City, NY: Doubleday, 1977.

Ralph, James R., Jr. *Northern Protest: Martin Luther King, Jr., Chicago, and the Civil Rights Movement*. Cambridge, MA: Harvard University Press, 1993.

Raymond, Emilie. *'From My Cold, Dead Hands': Charlton Heston and American Politics*. Lexington: University Press of Kentucky, 2006.

Reid, Mark A. *Redefining Black Film*. Berkeley: University of California Press, 1993.

Richards, David. *Played Out: The Jean Seberg Story*. New York: Random House, 1981.

Rickford, Russell J. *Betty Shabazz*. New York: Sourcebooks, 2003.

Riffel, Brent. "In the Storm: William Hansen and the Student Nonviolent Coordinating Committee in Arkansas, 1962–1967." *Arkansas Historical Quarterly* 63, no. 4 (Winter 2004): 404–19.

Rippy, Marguerite H., "Commodity, Tragedy, Desire: Female Sexuality and Blackness in the Iconography of Dorothy Dandridge." In *Classic Hollywood, Classic Whiteness*, edited by Daniel Bernadi, 179–201. Minneapolis: University of Minnesota Press, 2001.

Roeder, George H., Jr. *The Censored War: American Visual Experience during World War II*. New Haven: Yale University Press, 1993.

Rojek, Chris. *Celebrity*. London: Reaktion Books, 2001.

———. *Frank Sinatra*. Cambridge, MA: Polity Press, 2004.

Ross, Steven J. *Hollywood Left and Right: How Movie Stars Shaped American Politics*. Oxford: Oxford University Press, 2011.

Sales, William. *From Civil Rights to Black Liberation: Malcolm X and the Organization of Afro-American Unity*. Boston: South End Press, 1994.

Schulman, Bruce. *The Seventies: The Great Shift in American Culture, Society, and Politics*. Cambridge, MA: Da Capo Press, 2001.

Self, Robert O. *American Babylon: Race and the Struggle for Postwar Oakland*. Princeton: Princeton University Press, 2003.

Sellers, Cleveland. *The River of No Return: The Autobiography of a Black Militant and the Life and Death of SNCC*. Jackson: University Press of Mississippi, 1990.

Sinatra, Tina, with Jeff Coplon. *My Father's Daughter: A Memoir*. New York: Simon and Schuster, 2000.

Stoper, Emily. *The Student Nonviolent Coordinating Committee: The Growth of Radicalism in a Civil Rights Organization*. Brooklyn, NY: Carlson Pub., 1989.

Sugrue, Thomas. *Sweet Land of Liberty: The Forgotten Struggle for Civil Rights in the North*. New York: Random House, 2008.

Talese, Gay. "Frank Sinatra Has a Cold." In *Smiling Through the Apocalypse: Esquire's History of the Sixties*, edited by Harold Hayes, 280–310. New York: McCall Publishing Company, 1969.

Ward, Brian. *Just My Soul Responding: Rhythm and Blues, Black Consciousness, and Race Relations*. Berkeley: University of California Press, 1998.

Washington, Von Hugo. "An Evaluation of the Play 'Purlie Victorious' and Its Impact on the American Theatrical Scene." PhD diss., Wayne State University, 1979.

Watkins, Mel. *On the Real Side: Laughing, Lying, and Signifying: The Underground Tradition of African-American Humor that Transformed American Culture, from Slavery to Richard Pryor*. New York: Simon & Schuster, 1994.

Watson, Bruce. *Freedom Summer*. New York: Penguin, 2010.

Watts, Jill. *Hattie McDaniel: Black Ambition, White Hollywood*. New York: Amistad, 2005.

Watts, Steven. *Mr. Playboy: Hugh Hefner and the American Dream*. Hoboken, NJ: Wiley and Sons, 2008.

Weems, Robert E., with Lewis Randolph. *Business in Black and White: American Presidents and Black Entrepreneurs in the Twentieth Century*. New York: New York University Press, 2009.

Weisbrot, Robert. *Freedom Bound: A History of America's Civil Rights Movement*. New York: Norton, 1990.

West, Darrel M., and John Orman. *Celebrity Politics*. Upper Saddle River, NJ: Prentice Hall, 2003.

Winters, Shelley. *Shelley: Also Known as Shirley*. New York: William Morrow and Company, 1980.

Wofford, Harris. *Of Kennedys and Kings: Making Sense of the Sixties*. New York: Farrar, Straus, Giroux, 1980.

Wolfe, Tom. *Radical Chic and Mau-Mauing the Flak Catchers*. New York: Noonday Press, 1970.

Wolff, Daniel J. *You Send Me: The Life and Times of Sam Cooke*. New York: W. Morrow, 1995.

INDEX